KIERKEGAARD AND DEATH

Indiana Series in the Philosophy of Religion

MEROLD WESTPHAL, EDITOR

Kierkegaard and Death

Edited by

PATRICK STOKES *and* ADAM BUBEN

Indiana University Press

BLOOMINGTON AND INDIANAPOLIS

This book is a publication of

Indiana University Press
601 North Morton Street
Bloomington, Indiana 47404-3797 USA
www.iupress.indiana.edu

Telephone orders 800-842-6796
Fax orders 812-855-7931

∞ The paper used in this publication meets the minimum requirements of the American National Standard for Information Sciences—Permanence of Paper for Printed Library Materials, ANSI Z39.48-1992.

Manufactured in the United States of America

1 2 3 4 5 16 15 14 13 12 11

Library of Congress
Cataloging-in-Publication Data

Kierkegaard and death / edited by Patrick Stokes and Adam Buben.
p. cm. — (Indiana series in the philosophy of religion)
Proceedings of a conference held in Dec. 2007 at St. Olaf College, Northfield, Minn.
Includes bibliographical references and index.
ISBN 978-0-253-35685-7 (cloth : alk. paper)
ISBN 978-0-253-22352-4 (pbk. : alk. paper)
ISBN 978-0-253-00534-2 (ebook) 1. Kierkegaard, Søren, 1813–1855—Congresses. 2. Death—Congresses. I. Stokes, Patrick, [date] II. Buben, Adam, [date] III. Title. IV. Series.

B4378.D43K54 2011
128'.5092—dc22 2011015256

Contents

Acknowledgments

The idea for this book emerged over a plate of Chinese pork dumplings in December 2005, just after the Kierkegaard and Asia conference held at the University of Melbourne. Since then the project has been well traveled, with editorial work taking place in Australia, Minnesota, New Mexico, Florida, Guam, Denmark, and England. And along with the frequent flyer miles, we've also accumulated a great many debts of gratitude, which it is our pleasure to acknowledge here.

Work on this project has been made possible by funding from various sources: a Kierkegaard House Foundation Fellowship, a Danish Research Council for the Humanities Postdoctoral Fellowship and a European Commission Marie Curie Fellowship (Stokes), and a University of South Florida Presidential Doctoral Fellowship and a Fulbright Fellowship (Buben). Our thanks to our hosts at St. Olaf College, the Søren Kierkegaard Research Centre, the University of South Florida, the University of Hertfordshire, and the University of Guam.

We owe a particular debt to Gordon Marino and Cynthia Lund and to all the staff and scholars at the Hong Kierkegaard Library at St. Olaf College, Northfield, Minnesota. The library generously hosted a two-day conference on Kierkegaard and Death in early December 2007, which was the source of several papers presented in this volume. We would like to thank the more than forty attendees and presenters at this conference, especially Anthony Rudd, Myron B. Penner, and the late Howard V. Hong, for their comments.

The *International Kierkegaard Commentary* list of abbreviations is used with kind permission of Series Editor Robert L. Perkins and Mercer University Press.

We'd like to offer our thanks to the following people who have provided help and encouragement at various stages of the project: Andrew

Burgess and Janice Schuetz, Niels Jørgen Cappelørn, Jon Stewart, James Giles, Sinead Ladegaard Knox, Robert L. Perkins, Søren Landkildehus, John Lippitt, Rick Anthony Furtak, Dario Gonzalez, Jonathan Weidenbaum, Jack Mulder, Eric Berg, Daniel Leichty, Antony Aumann, and J. Michael Tilley.

Finally, we thank our respective friends and families for their support and encouragement, and especially Jessica Doyle for her help throughout the entire project, and Megan Altman for her invaluable assistance.

Abbreviations

ENGLISH TRANSLATIONS

BA	*The Book on Adler,* trans. Howard V. Hong and Edna H. Hong (Princeton, N.J.: Princeton University Press, 1995)
CA	*The Concept of Anxiety,* trans. Reidar Thomte in collaboration with Albert B. Anderson (Princeton, N.J.: Princeton University Press, 1980)
CD	*Christian Discourses* and *The Crisis and a Crisis in the Life of an Actress,* trans. Howard V. Hong and Edna H. Hong (Princeton, N.J.: Princeton University Press, 1997)
CI	*The Concept of Irony* together with "Notes on Schelling's Berlin Lectures," trans. Howard V. Hong and Edna H. Hong (Princeton, N.J.: Princeton University Press, 1989)
CUP	*Concluding Unscientific Postscript to "Philosophical Fragments,"* 2 vols., trans. Howard V. Hong and Edna H. Hong (Princeton, N.J.: Princeton University Press, 1992)
EO	*Either/Or,* 2 vols., trans. Howard V. Hong and Edna H. Hong (Princeton, N.J.: Princeton University Press, 1987)
EUD	*Eighteen Upbuilding Discourses,* trans. Howard V. Hong and Edna H. Hong (Princeton, N.J.: Princeton University Press, 1990)
FSE	*For Self-Examination* and *Judge for Yourself!,* trans. Howard V. Hong and Edna H. Hong (Princeton, N.J.: Princeton University Press, 1990)

FT	*Fear and Trembling* and *Repetition,* trans. Howard V. Hong and Edna H. Hong (Princeton, N.J.: Princeton University Press, 1983)
JC	*Johannes Climacus, or De omnibus dubitandum est.* See *Philosophical Fragments*
JFY	*Judge for Yourself!* See *For Self-Examination*
JP	*Søren Kierkegaard's Journals and Papers,* ed. and trans. Howard V. Hong and Edna H. Hong, assisted by Gregor Malantschuk (Bloomington: Indiana University Press, 1, 1967; 2, 1970; 3 and 4, 1975; 5–7, 1978)
KJN 1	*Kierkegaard's Journals and Notebooks: Vol. 1, Journals AA–DD,* ed. Niels Jørgen Cappelørn, Alastair Hannay, David Kangas, Bruce H. Kirmmse, George Pattison, Vanessa Rumble, and K. Brian Söderquist (Princeton, N.J.: Princeton University Press, 2007)
PC	*Practice in Christianity,* trans. Howard V. Hong and Edna H. Hong (Princeton, N.J.: Princeton University Press, 1991)
PF	*Philosophical Fragments* and *Johannes Climacus,* trans. Howard V. Hong and Edna H. Hong (Princeton, N.J.: Princeton University Press, 1985)
PV	*The Point of View for My Work as an Author, The Single Individual, On My Work as an Author* and *Armed Neutrality,* trans. Howard V. Hong and Edna H. Hong (Princeton, N.J.: Princeton University Press, 1998)
R	*Repetition.* See *Fear and Trembling.*
SLW	*Stages on Life's Way,* trans. Howard V. Hong and Edna H. Hong (Princeton, N.J.: Princeton University Press, 1988)
SUD	*The Sickness unto Death,* trans. Howard V. Hong and Edna H. Hong (Princeton, N.J.: Princeton University Press, 1980)
TDIO	*Three Discourses on Imagined Occasions,* trans. Howard V. Hong and Edna H. Hong (Princeton, N.J.: Princeton University Press, 1993)
TM	*"The Moment" and Late Writings,* trans. Howard V. Hong and Edna H. Hong (Princeton, N.J.: Princeton University Press, 1998)
UDVS	*Upbuilding Discourses in Various Spirits,* trans. Howard V. Hong and Edna H. Hong (Princeton, N.J.: Princeton University Press, 1993)

WA *Without Authority,* trans. Howard V. Hong and Edna H. Hong (Princeton, N.J.: Princeton University Press, 1997)

WL *Works of Love,* trans. Howard V. Hong and Edna H. Hong (Princeton, N.J.: Princeton University Press, 1995)

DANISH TEXTS

SKS 1 *Af en endnu Levendes Papirer; Om Begrebet Ironi,* ed. Niels Jørgen Cappelørn, Joakim Garff, Johnny Kondrup, and Finn Hauberg Mortensen (Copenhagen: Gads, 1997)

SKS 2 *Enten—Eller. Første del,* ed. Niels Jørgen Cappelørn, Joakim Garff, Johnny Kondrup, and Finn Hauberg Mortensen (Copenhagen: Gads, 1997)

SKS 3 *Enten—Eller. Anden del,* ed. Niels Jørgen Cappelørn, Joakim Garff, Johnny Kondrup, and Finn Hauberg Mortensen (Copenhagen: Gads, 1997)

SKS 4 *Gjentagelsen; Frygt og Bæven; Philosophiske Smuler; Begrebet Angest; Forord,* ed. Niels Jørgen Cappelørn, Joakim Garff, Johnny Kondrup, and Finn Hauberg Mortensen (Copenhagen: Gads, 1997)

SKS 5 *Opbyggelige taler, 1843–44; Tre Taler ved tænkte Leiligheder,* ed. Niels Jørgen Cappelørn, Joakim Garff, Jette Knudsen, Johnny Kondrup, and Finn Hauberg Mortensen (Copenhagen: Gads, 1998)

SKS 6 *Stadier paa Livets Vei,* ed. Niels Jørgen Cappelørn, Joakim Garff, Jette Knudsen, Johnny Kondrup, and Finn Hauberg Mortensen (Copenhagen: Gads, 1999)

SKS 7 *Afsluttende uvidenskabelig Efterskrift,* ed. Niels Jørgen Cappelørn, Joakim Garff, Jette Knudsen, and Johnny Kondrup (Copenhagen: Gads, 2002)

SKS K7 *Kommentarer til SKS 7,* by Tonny Aagaard Olesen (Copenhagen: Gads, 2002)

SKS 8 *En literair Anmeldelse; Opbyggelige Taler i forskjellig Aand,* ed. Niels Jørgen Cappelørn, Joakim Garff, and Johnny Kondrup (Copenhagen: Gads, 2004)

SKS 9 *Kjerlighedens Gjerninger,* ed. Niels Jørgen Cappelørn, Joakim Garff, and Johnny Kondrup (Copenhagen: Gads, 2004)

SKS 10 *Christelige Taler,* ed. Niels Jørgen Cappelørn, Joakim Garff, and Johnny Kondrup (Copenhagen: Gads, 2004)

SKS 11 *Lilien paa Marken og Fuglen under Himlen; Tvende ethisk-religieuse Smaa-Afhandlinger; Sygdommen til Døden; "Ypperstepræsten"—"Tolderen"—"Synderinden,"* ed. Niels Jørgen Cappelørn, Joakim Garff, Anne Mette Hansen, and Johnny Kondrup (Copenhagen: Gads, 2006)

SKS K11 *Kommentarer til SKS 11,* by Niels Jørgen Cappelørn, Joakim Garff, and Tonny Aagaard Olesen (Copenhagen: Gads, 2006)

SKS 12 *Indøvelse i Christendom; En opbyggelig Tale; To Taler ved Altergangen om Fredagen,* ed. Niels Jørgen Cappelørn, Joakim Garff, Anne Mette Hansen, and Johnny Kondrup (Copenhagen: Gads, 2008)

SKS 13 *Dagbladsartikler 1834–48; Om min Forfatter-Virksomhed; Til Selvprøvelse,* ed. Niels Jørgen Cappelørn, Joakim Garff, Johnny Kondrup, Tonny Aagaard Olesen, and Steen Tullberg (Copenhagen: Gads, 2009)

SKS 15 *Sendebrev til Heiberg; Johannes Climacus; Bogen om Adler* (Copenhagen: Gads, forthcoming)

SKS 16 *Synspunktet for min Forfatter-Virksomhed; Den bevæbnede Neutralitet; Dømmer Selv!* (Copenhagen: Gads, forthcoming)

SKS 17 *Journalerne AA · BB · CC · DD,* ed. Niels Jørgen Cappelørn, Joakim Garff, Jette Knudsen, and Johnny Kondrup (Copenhagen: Gads, 2000)

SKS 18 *Journalerne EE · FF · GG · HH · JJ · KK,* ed. Niels Jørgen Cappelørn, Joakim Garff, Jette Knudsen, and Johnny Kondrup (Copenhagen: Gads, 2001)

SKS 20 *Journalerne NB · NB2 · NB3 · NB4 · NB5,* ed. Niels Jørgen Cappelørn, Joakim Garff, Jette Knudsen, and Johnny Kondrup (Copenhagen: Gads, 2003)

SKS 21 *Journalerne NB6 · NB7 · NB8 · NB9 · NB10,* ed. Niels Jørgen Cappelørn, Joakim Garff, Jette Knudsen, and Johnny Kondrup (Copenhagen: Gads, 2003)

SKS 22 *Journalerne NB11 · NB12 · NB13 · NB14,* ed. Niels Jørgen Cappelørn, Joakim Garff, Jette Knudsen, and Johnny Kondrup (Copenhagen: Gads, 2005)

SKS 23 *Journalerne NB15 · NB16 · NB17 · NB18 · NB19 · NB20,* ed. Niels

Jørgen Cappelørn, Joakim Garff, Anne Mette Hansen, and Johnny Kondrup (Copenhagen: Gads, 2007)

SKS 24 *Journalerne NB21 · NB22 · NB23 · NB24 · NB25*, ed. Niels Jørgen Cappelørn, Joakim Garff, Anne Mette Hansen, and Johnny Kondrup (Copenhagen: Gads, 2007)

SKS 25 *Journalerne NB26 · NB27 · NB28 · NB29 · NB30*, ed. Niels Jørgen Cappelørn, Joakim Garff, Anne Mette Hansen, and Johnny Kondrup (Copenhagen: Gads, 2008)

SKS 26 *Journalerne NB31 · NB32 · NB33 · NB34 · NB35 · NB36*, ed. Niels Jørgen Cappelørn, Joakim Garff, Anne Mette Hansen, and Johnny Kondrup (Copenhagen: Gads, 2009)

SKS 27 *Løse papirer 1833–55*, ed. Niels Jørgen Cappelørn, Joakim Garff, Johnny Kondrup, Tonny Aagaard Olesen, and Steen Tullberg (Copenhagen: Gads, 2011)

KIERKEGAARD AND DEATH

Introduction

Patrick Stokes and Adam Buben

On Wednesday, July 29, 1835, two days before the first anniversary of his mother's death, a twenty-two-year-old theology student writes of his experience of standing atop Gilbjerg Hoved, a small cliff just outside the North Zealand coastal town of Gilleleje:

> This has always been one of my favorite spots. Often, as I stood here on a quiet evening, the sea intoning its song with deep but calm solemnity, my eye catching not a single sail on the vast surface, and only the sea framed the sky and the sky the sea, while on the other hand the busy hum of life grew silent and the birds sang their vespers, then the few dear departed ones rose from the grave before me, or rather, it seemed as though they were not dead. I felt so much at ease in their midst, I rested in their embrace, and I felt as though I were outside my body and floated about with them in a higher ether—until the seagull's harsh screech reminded me that I stood alone and it all vanished before my eyes, and with a heavy heart I turned back to mingle with the world's throng—yet without forgetting such blessed moments (KJN 1, 9/SKS 17, 13–14).

Three days later, Kierkegaard would write the famous entry so often cited as presaging and framing his entire authorial project: "What I really need is to be clear about *what I am to do . . .* the thing is to find a truth which is truth *for me,* to find *the idea for which I am willing to live and die*" (KJN 1, 19/SKS 17, 24). But that stunningly prescient entry tends to overshadow another key strand of Kierkegaard's authorship that also begins in Gilleleje that week: his remarkable, lifelong preoccupation with death, dying, and the dead. Just as the "few dear departed ones" hover over that young student as he stands alone on a hill, trying to make sense of the enormity of loss, so the themes of death and mortality haunt Kierkegaard's signed and pseudonymous works, a constant presence appearing in a variety of guises and concerns.

And just as the very name "Kierkegaard" is homonymous with "graveyard" in Danish, so it has become virtually synonymous with death. Biographically, the specter of death is a constant presence for Kierkegaard, who endured the deaths of all but one of his immediate family members. Though the details are unclear, the Kierkegaard family seemed to interpret these deaths as some sort of divine retribution, according to which none of Michael Pedersen Kierkegaard's children would live to be thirty-four (Christ supposedly died at age thirty-three).[1] Only two children—Søren and Peter—surpassed this age, and Søren expresses surprise, almost disbelief, on reaching his thirty-fourth birthday.[2] Yet Kierkegaard *was* fated to die at the relatively young age of forty-two, of mysterious causes that, once again, he interpreted in terms of a religious destiny.[3] The medical examiner who admitted Kierkegaard to Frederik's Hospital in October 1855, Harald Krabbe, noted that the patient held some definite and unsettling views on his condition:

> He considers his illness to be fatal. His death is necessary for the cause upon the furtherance of which he has expended all his intellectual energies, for which alone he has labored, and for which alone he believes he has been intended. Hence the strenuous thinking in conjunction with the frail physique. Were he to go on living, he would have to continue his religious battle, but then people would tire of it. Through his death, on the other hand, his struggle will retain its strength, and, as he believes, its victory.[4]

It seems that Kierkegaard viewed his death as the final act of his "martyrdom" in the service of "true Christianity," the culmination of the idea for which he was "to live and die."[5] The trajectory of the short authorial life running between the haunted week of resolution at Gilleleje and the strange ending at Frederik's Hospital was shaped, defined, and informed by the thought of death. It should therefore come as no surprise that dying, death, and the dead are ever-present themes throughout Kierkegaard's prodigious authorial production.

From the *Symparanekromenoi,* the "Fellowship of the Buried" in the early, pseudonymous *Either/Or* (1843) to the late *For Self-Examination* and *Judge for Yourself!* (1851), which outline the notion of Christian dying to the world, the sheer variety of ways in which death appears throughout

Kierkegaard's writings never loses its capacity to amaze. But precisely this diversity creates headaches for the reader who wants to come to grips with Kierkegaard's thoughts on death—or perhaps come to grips with the thought of death via Kierkegaard. How does one get one's bearing within such polyvocal material? And how, if at all, are these disparate claims about death to be integrated? Perhaps for this reason, the impact Kierkegaard's work on death has had on Western (let alone Eastern)[6] thought has yet to be fully uncovered and reckoned. Nor has Kierkegaard's potential contribution to contemporary debates on the unique metaphysical and ethical problems posed by death been fully assessed. The guiding thought behind the present book is that such a thorough engagement with Kierkegaard's views on death-related issues, across a number of thematic fronts and via a range of approaches, is long overdue. The contributors to this volume engage with the various facets of Kierkegaard's thanatology to provide a comprehensive guide to readers of Kierkegaard and those with an interest in the burgeoning philosophical literature on death. Our path through Kierkegaard's discussions of death will take us through four general stages: the boundaries between life and death, death and the meaning of life, twentieth-century receptions of Kierkegaard's work on death, and the ontological and ethical status of the dead.

The Boundaries of Life and Death

Contemporary philosophical discussions of death tend to distinguish sharply between *death* and the process of *dying,* and restrict themselves primarily to the former. While the border between the states of life and death may be biologically fuzzy, it's nonetheless assumed that some such boundary exists[7] and that whatever is philosophically interesting is to be found on the posthumous side of it.[8] Yet Kierkegaard's use of tropes such as "dying to the world" and "living death" suggests the boundaries may be far more conceptually and phenomenally porous than we might normally assume. Death and life, in Kierkegaard's account of moral and religious existence, can come to intersect and interpenetrate each other in surprising ways.

In the preface to *The Sickness unto Death,* Anti-Climacus states that "in Christian terminology death is indeed the expression for the state of deepest spiritual wretchedness, and yet the cure is simply to die, to die to the world" (*at døe, at afdøe*) (SUD, 6/SKS 11, 118). This quote, in which the language of death is paradoxically applied to certain modes of *life,* encapsulates a distinction between two kinds of living death—two classes of "Kierkegaardian zombies"—that seem to come up in different ways throughout his authorship. On the one hand is the living death of despair, or sinful separation from the divine, in all its manifestations. And on the other hand is the antidote to this doomed state—more death—but still without perishing.

George Connell's "Knights and Knaves of the Living Dead: Kierkegaard's Use of Living Death as a Metaphor for Despair" focuses on the first sort of Kierkegaardian zombie, the self locked in a despairing state of "living death." Connell points to motifs of living death that feature in Kierkegaard's writings from the early ruminations on the tortured immortals Ahasverus (the Wandering Jew of medieval folklore) and the "Unhappiest One" in *Either/Or*.[9] Yet a relatively late use of this trope—in Anti-Climacus's description of despair—has been underdiscussed in the literature. Connell notes a problem that again concerns the question of boundaries: If death is regarded as annihilation, a state with *no* experiential content whatsoever, what phenomenal features of a situation like despair could possibly license us in calling it "living death"? Connell demonstrates the cogency of the "living death" metaphor by fleshing out several respects in which the state of death can indeed impinge upon the phenomenal experience of the living. For the various "knights" that populate what Connell calls Kierkegaard's "aristocracy of spirit," this will come as no surprise: they live their all-too-self-aware despair on a grand, poetic scale. But Anti-Climacus also posits another class of people who are blissfully unconscious of their despair—those Connell refers to as "knaves," who are in despair but experience themselves as thriving. Kierkegaard's claim that such perfectly satisfied lives can nonetheless be regarded as asymptomatic states of living death runs counter to the irony, liberalism, and secularism (as articulated by Rorty, MacIntyre, and Taylor, respectively) that are defining elements of modernity. Kierkegaard's claim that the knave will turn out to be stuck in the living death of despair when seen "in the light of truth" rests on a theological viewpoint inimical to our pluralist, post-Enlightenment context. But as Connell notes, Kierkegaard also has recourse to a three-pronged epistemological approach to defend his claim that even unconscious despair counts as a state of living death.

In "To Die and Yet Not Die: Kierkegaard's Theophany of Death," Simon D. Podmore joins Connell in exploring significant metaphorical uses of the imagery of death in Kierkegaard's work. For instance, invoking ancient views about theophany, Podmore describes the sort of death that is risked in encountering God. The "dangers" of theophany signify an intermediary stage that must come just before full-fledged dying to the self and just after the spiritually dead state of despair. The first step on the path away from this initial despair—or as Podmore puts it, the "living death of estrangement" from the divine—in the direction of a cure involves turning toward God. But such taking notice of the divine in an attempt to relate oneself to it properly is not necessarily a joyous experience. Rather, it is a shocking glimpse of the distance between oneself and God. Before such an infinitely powerful being, one's frail, finite self simply melts away (like the faces of those who looked inside the Ark of the Covenant at the end of *Raiders of the Lost Ark*). Fear of this judgment or loss of self in the face of God can actually lead to an even more profound or "fantastic" sense of despair, in which one might rather attack God than risk annihilation or humiliation. In order to overcome even this sort of despair, and take the final step toward being in the right relationship to God, one must approach with no self at all. Podmore explains that "it is only through undergoing a spiritual self-denial (*Anfægtelse*)—a death of the self that in despair wills to be itself—that the individual can become a self before God. By dying to the self . . . one will be saved from the prospect of dying before God." Fortunately, Christians have a model for guidance along the difficult path to becoming selfless.

So the remedy for the "sickness unto death" of despair is paradoxically dying to the worldly self, swapping one form of Kierkegaardian zombie-existence for another. Adam Buben's "Christian Hate: Death, Dying, and Reason in Pascal and Kierkegaard" considers the Pascalian and Kierkegaardian appropriations of the traditional Christian attitude of *memento mori* and the related (so he will argue) practice of sacrificing, or "dying to," selfish bodily and worldly desires and preoccupations in order to purify the spirit and come closer to God. Perhaps the most difficult and disturbing aspect of such dying to worldliness is the idea that reason itself, and the desire to understand or know, actually stands in the way of a proper relationship with God. Thus it would seem that one must in some sense, or to some degree, kill off one's rational impulses if Christianity is to take hold. As it turns out, Kierkegaard, particularly in later works such as *For-Self Examination,* is far more extreme in his opposition to rationality than Pascal, and Buben suggests the possibility of making use of this difference to draw some conclusions on the hotly contested topic of Kierkegaard's so-called "irrationalism." Because Kierkegaard's description of dying to reason is often so powerful, one should be careful not to portray him as an apologetic Pascalian figure who simply wants "to demonstrate how 'reasonable and happy' one can be in Christianity, and how 'foolish and unhappy' one can be without it."

After these extended discussions of the nuances of "dying to," we must once again foray into the issue of the living death of despair in order to address the ultimate peril, suicide. In his chapter "Suicide and Despair," Marius Timmann Mjaaland explicates not only this danger but also the universality of despair (even the pagan, who is ignorant of these things and in favor of suicide, despairs) and the idea that "a process of committing suicide, or at least trying to do so, is continuously going on within despair." Given that Anti-Climacus defines the self as a particular kind of self-relation, and despair as a failure to relate to oneself properly, despair is always an attempt to be rid of one's self. The really troubling thing about despair is that the less intense it is, the harder it is to recognize and cure. Thus it is necessary, for Anti-Climacus, to "*provoke* the risk" of actual physical suicide in the intensification of despair, so that one might instead seek an escape from the "sickness unto death"—a provocation, as Mjaaland notes, that might strike us as ethically questionable at best!

Mjaaland goes on to compare Anti-Climacus's analysis with the early sociologist Émile Durkheim's work *Le Suicide.* As it turns out, the four-part account of despair seen in the musings of Kierkegaard's pseudonym finds almost perfect parallels in the four types of suicide outlined in Durkheim's study of the phenomenon. The notable difference, however, is that for the latter, "risk is accepted but not enhanced, and crises should be avoided as far as possible." While there is surely much to be learned in looking at their similarities, it is differences like this one that make for the most interesting questions. Mjaaland concludes his chapter by suggesting that the religious, psychological, and social ramifications of Kierkegaard's and Durkheim's respective views on suicide deserve increased attention, and he raises several pertinent concerns based on his comparison.

Death and the Meaning of Life

The topics of death and the meaning and purposefulness of life have always been intertwined. Kierkegaard's discussions of death reflect this close bond, as they regularly emphasize the power of death to impact upon and transfigure the life of the *living.* Consider the following:

> death is the briefest summary of life, or life traced back to its briefest form. This is also why it has always been very important to those who truly think about human life to test again and again, with the help of the brief summary, what they have understood about life. No thinker grasps life as death does (WL, 345/SKS 9, 339).

This passage stresses just how central, transformative, and indispensable an engagement with the thought of this temporally distant and experientially unavailable event is for us in the here-and-now. In fact, in assessing its impact on our lives, one might suggest (as Heidegger seems to) that death becomes more than a mere event; it takes on a "living" role in our experience of life.

The problem of the meaning of death for the living is of course an ancient one. Like death, the figure of Socrates haunts Kierkegaard's entire authorship, and it is no accident that the "wise man of old" who taught that philosophy is preparation for death should exert such an influence on Kierkegaard.[10] Kierkegaard's "Socratic gadfly" Johannes Climacus in particular uses death as an example of a key "existence problem" in highly influential sections of the *Concluding Unscientific Postscript.* Socrates's last utterance was to insist on offering a sacrifice to the medicine god Asclepius in gratitude for the fatal dose of hemlock, and in like manner Climacus offers death—or at least the thought of it—to the reader for therapeutic purposes. In "Thinking Death into Every Moment: The Existence-Problem of Dying in Kierkegaard's *Postscript,*" Paul Muench pays particular attention to the specific type of reader that constitutes the "philosophical patient" the *Postscript* seems to be aimed at: neither the "simple" person who has no interest in philosophy, nor the hardcore Hegelian (who would be unlikely to sit through such sustained abuse!), but the philosophically inclined person who runs the risk of absent-mindedness. In an age dizzy with speculative fervor and eager to encompass world history philosophically, such a reader may wish to "go beyond" the task of understanding with inwardness what it is to exist. The *Postscript,* according to Muench, forces them to slow down and consider how they have been too hasty in assuming they are finished with the task of attending to themselves, and holds out the prospect of showing them "a manner of doing philosophy that is compatible with this task."

"Existence-problems" such as what it is to die may seem too simple to satisfy the philosophically inclined, but if such a person approaches the question in the right mode, they will find such topics sufficient fodder for an entire life. Indeed, they may struggle to understand such problems precisely *because* they come at them reflectively. The aim for such a reader, then, is to become a "simple wise person" (like Socrates)—a very different type of philosopher to the Hegelian speculator, but, on Muench's account, a philosopher nonetheless. Climacus's (Socratic) strategy is to continually put the brakes on his overeager reader by claiming, for instance, that while he knows as much about death as anyone else, he hasn't *understood* it—calling into question whether the reader herself has understood it either. And the ever-present possibility of death makes this matter all the more urgent. The task, according to Climacus, is to think death "into every moment" of life in order to get to grips with the irreducibly first-personal quality *my* death has for me (something lost on the philosophically "absentminded," as exemplified in the comical figure Soldin). What might all this mean? Ultimately, Muench concludes, Climacus doesn't really tell us, at least not clearly—but this is perhaps the whole point. Climacus leads his philosophical patient to a way of thinking about *their* death that makes such thought into an *act* within the broader ethical project of becoming subjective. In teaching his reader self-restraint, and thereby subjective self-attention, Climacus shows them how to evade the dangers of philosophy without having to deny their philosophically inclined natures.

David D. Possen's "Death and Ethics in Kierkegaard's *Postscript*" focuses on Climacus's peculiar reluctance to tell us anything *about* death. Possen calls death one of the "case studies" that Climacus suggests can be utilized to bring about a return to an ancient (i.e., Socratic) way of viewing ethics. But the vagueness of Climacus's discussion of thinking death "into every moment" seems to leave his reader with nothing but "a tantalizing mix of urgency and fog." By considering both what is not said about death and Climacus's general strategy in the other case studies/existence problems (immortality, thanking God, and marriage), however, Possen sets out to solve the "riddle" of death in the *Postscript*.

The problem with modern objective ethics is that it deals with ethical difficulties in an inhuman "once and for all" manner, while the ancient subjective ethics that Socrates espouses is meant to occupy an individual for a lifetime. Because Climacus's case studies, according to Possen, are examples of problems with such a high degree of uncertainty that they simply cannot be resolved during one's lifetime, they are precisely the sorts of issues that encourage the never-ending inwardness that Socrates is looking for. Like this ancient wise man, Climacus believes that life ought to be approached in a perpetual state of "concerned ignorance." This explains why Climacus doesn't attempt to fill out the concept of death: "if thinking death is to ignite and sustain a life that is ethical in the ancient/subjective sense, this must be because the thought of death rouses our unceasing concern in and about our ignorance."

Edward F. Mooney's "The Intimate Agency of Death" further explores some of the ways in which death ramifies through and alters our experience of life—not simply by standing as a distant, terrifying reminder, but as a thought with which we are to become "intimate," something we are to adopt, as Climacus puts it, as our dancing partner. Mooney, like Muench and Possen, strongly identifies Climacus and Socrates and sees both as advocating a mode of philosophy in which the thought of birth and death introduces radical discontinuities into experience that focus our attention on the "contours" of this life. Yet this raises the Epicurean question of how such nonexperienceable events can affect us so profoundly. In response, Mooney invokes our capacity to imaginatively "occupy" points in the past and future, a "transgression of temporal limits" that gives past and future standpoints "agency" over our present. We can be simultaneously in the present and imaginatively beyond it, occupying standpoints after death and before birth that in a direct experiential sense are closed to us. Only through taking such a standpoint outside my life can "posthumous and prenatal spans have an enigmatic, intimate agency" therein, calling us to a sharpened state of moral urgency and alertness.

This is only part of the profound ambiguity of death that Mooney discusses. The different contexts in which the concept of death is operative make the extension of the concepts life and death "anomalous" and fluid. Kierkegaard was "alive" in his brother's moral universe long after his civically recognized death and burial, and in our cultural context he lives still. To look for a "correct" context that would allow us to fix the definitive boundaries of Kierkegaard's life and death (by giving priority to the death certificate for instance) would be to miss crucial dimensions of the concept(s) of death and the way events that appear to occur at temporally specifiable points can bleed into their past and future in significant ways. What Kierkegaard calls "death's decision" can ramify throughout a life long before the cessation of metabolism. Again, the content of that decision and its meaning for my life can be shadowy and ambiguous, but no less real and important for that.

But beyond shadowy and ambiguous, Gordon D. Marino believes that such content might be better described as inhumane, and it is this inhumanity that is the subject of his "A Critical Perspective on Kierkegaard's 'At a Graveside.'" Drawing on both his own experiences of death-related grief and Tolstoy's *The Death of Ivan Ilych,* Marino ponders the aspects of dying that Kierkegaard coldly excludes from his meditation on "the earnest thought of death." While Kierkegaard scoffs at death's more social aspects and the "moods" that these engender, the character Ilych provides a rich first-person account of how he feels toward those around him as he traverses his final days. Although acknowledging the various motivations that may have led to the peculiar nature of Kierkegaard's graveside discourse, Marino suggests that perhaps there are valuable insights to be gleaned from the emotional content connected with leaving loved ones behind and saying good-bye to the only world one has ever known. More attention to the other related issues surrounding death within this discourse might have provided more practical advice on how to be with our fellow humans in general. But the personal and ethical impact of death on life may go even deeper than we have considered thus far.

For Kierkegaard, the importance of death for the living holds even down to the level of how we conceive of and individuate ourselves as agents. In recent years Kierkegaard has been seen as endorsing something like a "narrative" conception of human selfhood, linking him with a diverse range of contemporary thinkers such as Alasdair MacIntyre, Paul Ricoeur, and Charles Taylor.[11] The "Narrative Approach" has, however, recently drawn significant criticism, with one recurring complaint centering on how death fits into the narrative picture. Some narrativists have held that narrative identity *needs* death; a story without an ending is *not* a story, and human lives need deathly finitude in order to be thinkable as unified wholes in the way essential to narrative self-intelligibility.[12] On the other hand, critics have charged that the radical contingency of death poses a particularly difficult problem for narrative theory: how a story *ends* is crucial to the meaning of the entire story, but if the end of my life-narrative (and everything that comes after it) is inaccessible to me, then I might be living out a radically different life-narrative to the one I take myself to be leading.

Building on his extensive work on Kierkegaardian narrative selfhood in his chapter "Life-Narrative and Death as the End of Freedom: Kierkegaard on Anticipatory Resoluteness," John J. Davenport offers an answer to this problem. Distinguishing between four levels of agential unity (starting from the basic unity of apperception), Davenport argues that while human subjects are already fundamentally narratively unified, a greater level of unity is required to avoid conflicts between our fundamental cares. Such conflicts restrict autonomy and can only be avoided via attaining the highest level of unity, a volitional "wholeheartedness" that can only be developed across time. Against John Lippitt, Davenport argues that such freedom from volitional conflicts requires that the subject acknowledge the authority of ethical norms; even the most committed and clear-eyed aesthete cannot, in fact, become "earnest" in this way.

Death features in this picture as a sort of regulative eschatological concept: "at death, our practical identity *is* eternally what it has become, our freedom to change ends and our character is *forever fixed*." For the subject, the urgency of this quest for wholeheartedness is conferred by the thought that there will come a point at which death will preclude further progress. But as noted above, the ever-present possibility of death has been thought by critics to suffuse human life with an element of contingency that forecloses the possibility of understanding our lives in terms of a projective narrative. Davenport's response is threefold. The objection involves an exaggeration, for we often *do* know when we are dying, or at least have less time left, and perhaps experience final moments filled with enormous significance; even those who die suddenly often have achieved a sense of unity in their practical identity such that the meaning of their life *cannot* be altered by sudden death; and by living in awareness of the omnipresent possibility of death we can have a metaphorical *experience* of our death such that it becomes part of our narrative. In this way, as Kierkegaard puts it, "the thought of death gives the earnest person the right momentum" (TDIO, 83/SKS 5, 453). Implicit in this is a faithful hope for an eschatological "eucatastrophe," "the joy of a reprieve beyond all rational hope that is felt as grace" whereby, absurdly, all our ethical striving will be completed.

Kierkegaardian Death in the Twentieth Century

Kierkegaard's thoughts on death play a considerable—and not always easy to assess—role in several key strands of twentieth-century thought. In particular, Martin Heidegger, Emmanuel Levinas, and Jacques Derrida all appropriate or reject key Kierkegaardian themes on the topic of death. For example, perhaps borrowing directly from Kierkegaard (but with only a few cryptic footnotes on related issues as evidence of this borrowing), Heidegger's notion of the "mineness" of death seems clearly indebted to Kierkegaard's notion that the deaths of others cannot help us in our quest to understand ourselves. Reacting to both Kierkegaard and Heidegger, Levinas rejects this dismissal of the death of the Other, while Derrida in turn defends the intuition that one's own death is of primary importance to our ethical understanding of our own existence. This issue of whose death is most significant binds the following three contributions to this volume together, but each in turn also deals with other unique nuances of the twentieth-century reception of Kierkegaard's thought on death.

Charles Guignon's "Heidegger and Kierkegaard on Death: The Existentiell and the Existential" begins with a brief overview of the evidence that suggests Kierkegaard's profound impact on Heidegger's early thought, despite the fact that it remains unclear exactly which texts Heidegger was relying on. The more pressing issue for Guignon is making sense of

Heidegger's critical "compliments" in the few places where he actually mentions Kierkegaard. Specifically, what does it mean when Heidegger accuses Kierkegaard of having only an "existentiell" understanding of various topics? In this accusation, Heidegger is making the perhaps not inaccurate claim that Kierkegaard's evaluation of mankind's ailments is operating under certain "ontic" presuppositions and concerns, particularly those of a Christian. In the case of death in Kierkegaard's "At a Graveside," Guignon argues that while Kierkegaard does not clearly acknowledge any theological perspective, "the distinctively religious intention motivating this discourse becomes apparent when Kierkegaard says that 'the earnest thought of death has taught the living person to permeate the most oppressive dissimilarity . . . with the equality before God.'"

Heidegger, on the other hand, treats death in an "ontological" manner, eschewing all theological, anthropological, and other derivative ontic scientific perspectives when describing the finitude of "Dasein." Nonetheless, Guignon acknowledges several strong parallels with the work of Kierkegaard, if not full-blown examples of direct influence, in *Being and Time.* In particular, there is the reliance upon "everyday" attitudes toward death—including the view of death as some kind of limit—for indicating the proper way to understand death, even though many common views about death are problematic. Perhaps the most important similarity is the idea that ultimately death must not be seen as some kind of event standing before us, but rather as a way of being that, counter Epicurus, we always in some sense "are." As Guignon puts it, "what is of existential interest about death, then, is not the existentiell phenomenon of *passing away* or *demise,* but rather the distinctive way of being human as being mortal." As a way to be, death, according to Heidegger, reveals Dasein both in its "wholeness" and in its potential "authenticity." Even though Kierkegaard's notion of "earnestness" in thinking about death may not be as "primordial" or "ontological" as Heidegger's "authentic being-toward-death," Guignon concludes that Kierkegaard might have reason to be suspicious of the sort of grandiose project that Heidegger is engaged in.

Laura Llevadot's "Kierkegaard, Levinas, Derrida: The Death of the Other" returns to Heidegger, who, as previously mentioned, seems to have appropriated Kierkegaard's alleged aversion to finding significant meaning in the death of the Other. In fact, turning back to Plato's *Phaedo,* Llevadot suggests that philosophy has a long, and perhaps misguided, tradition of prioritizing one's own death. Breaking from this tradition, Levinas claims that ethics is based primarily on the notion of being responsible for the deaths of others and the possibility of "dying for the Other." Thus, while Levinas rejects Heidegger's account of death, he is particularly critical of Kierkegaard's take on Abraham's willingness to suspend ethics and kill his own son. What Levinas seems to miss, according to Llevadot, is "the importance of the death of the Other in Kierkegaard's second ethics, as developed in *Fear and Trembling, The Sickness unto Death,* and *Works of Love.*"

While Kierkegaard is often associated with existentialism (broadly construed), his work also exerts a considerable influence on poststructuralist and deconstructionist thinking as well. Thus a key moment in the twentieth-century reception of Kierkegaard's work on death is Derrida's *The Gift of Death,* part of his late ruminations on ethics and religion. Relying on Derrida's interpretation of what Kierkegaard is up to in *Fear and Trembling,* Llevadot offers a double-pronged critique of the "universal ethics of duties and rights," which she (like Derrida) opposes to Kierkegaard's higher, absolute ethics as presented in *Works of Love.* This second ethics starts out by assuming our failure to live up to the first (we are weak and sinful beings). In Levinasian terms, we let the Other die; even if, in preferential love, we preserve the lives of some, we let others go, and we must accept this guilt and relate ourselves appropriately to the dead Other. In recollecting one who is dead—the one who can do nothing for us—Kierkegaard claims that we can learn to love as we should. As Llevadot puts it, "the duty to love the dead expresses the duty to love unconditionally and without interest," the "concept of love" that is "lodged in the second ethics."

Ian Duckles's "Derrida, Judge William, and Death" offers a more detailed defense of Derrida's (sometimes controversial) reading of *Fear and Trembling.* Derrida challenges one of the fundamental assumptions of post-Kantian ethics: that we are freest or most responsible when we act in accord with universal norms, such that we can justify how we have acted to others. For Derrida, the ethical demand to justify our actions cuts us off from our "singularity," "dissolving" our uniqueness into universal concepts. Norm-based ethical systems thus involve an "irresponsibilization." In this context, Abraham's silence[13] during the *akedah* amounts to his "refus[al] to place moral responsibility for his actions onto impersonal ethical norms" and so shirk responsibility for them. In the Christianized worldview that superseded the Greek, it is *my death,* as an event that only *I* can undergo, that is the *principium individuationis* of the responsible agent: "my mortality and the consequent necessity of my death is what defines and distinguishes me from all others." And thus the denial of *singularity* at the heart of norm-based ethical systems amounts to "a strategy for avoiding a confrontation with one's own mortality."

Duckles argues that when this understanding of the ethical is read back into Judge William's discussions of ethics in *Either/Or* and *Stages on Life's Way,* we can see the contours of Kierkegaard's rejection of the ethical more clearly. For Judge William is well aware that the ethical translates the particularity of the individual into the universal. Indeed, he celebrates this fact: his paradigm instance of ethical action, marriage, takes the singular instance of falling in love and sublates it into the socioethical category of marriage (in Duckles's phrase, "translating the immediacy of love into a public event"). But for William's interlocutor, the young aesthete A, this is a reason to *avoid* the ethical: it hinders genuine autonomy by subsuming the individual in the general and universal. William claims that the ethical takes us beyond the finite and focuses us on the infinite and eternal, and thereby promises the "dissolution of temporality," but this is precisely a denial of the individual singularity in its moral finitude. Hence Judge William's relative silence on the topic of death; the ethical life that he recommends is actually a covert flight from the thought of mortality.

The Dead

Llevadot's discussion of *Works of Love* raises the question of Kierkegaard's controversial claim that we have a duty (at least one) to the dead—to recollect them—even while he insists that dead persons are "no one." The philosophical problem of whether we can have duties to people who no longer exist goes at least as far back as Aristotle, and in modern discussions it has been closely associated with the question of whether death itself is a harm—or whether, as Epicurus claimed, it is a state of annihilation which by definition we cannot experience and thus should regard as "nothing to us."[14] Indeed, both critics of the ethics of *Works of Love,* such as Theodor Adorno, and prominent defenders of the text, such as M. Jamie Ferreira, Louise Carroll Keeley, and Pia Søltoft, have implicitly claimed that Kierkegaard does *not* mean we have actual moral duties to the dead. Rather, the work of love in remembering one who has died is to be understood as a heuristic device or standard against which to judge how we carry out our duties *to the living.* But is this correct? Are our only ethical duties to the living, or can the dead be objects of love and moral obligation as well? Both Jeremy J. Allen and Patrick Stokes explore this question and answer in the affirmative, but on very different grounds.

Allen's "The Soft Weeping of Desire's Loss: Recognition, Phenomenality and the One Who Is Dead in Kierkegaard's *Works of Love*" argues that Kierkegaard's discussion of recollecting the dead is tied in important ways to Hegel's account of mutual recognition in the *Phenomenology of Spirit.* Following Merold Westphal's reading of Hegel, Allen understands the "communitarian" process whereby self-consciousness intersubjectively constitutes itself via mutual recognition as one of agapic love. But recognition of the other requires their phenomenal "presence," and our duty, according to Kierkegaard, is to love the people we *see.* And we don't see the dead, for the dead lack "phenomenality." Genuine phenomenality requires embodiment, which the dead lack (although the existence of embodied humans who have phenomenality but lack the capacity for reciprocation shows that phenomenality is not a *sufficient* condition for reciprocity).

So how, then, can a dead person be a true object of a legitimate duty of remembrance? Allen considers three modes of grief: "wish" (which posits that the dead continue to exist, but disconnects the dead individual from the ground of mutual recognition and ontological interdependence that gave it its identity in the first place), "resignation" (a renunciation of the finite world, which entails renouncing the person we love *before they are dead,* violating our duty to love the people we see), and "faith." Both the wish and resignation approaches ultimately turn out to be strategies for evading the death of the other. Faith, however, fully accepts the loss of the other, but holds out hope of getting the lost one back. Drawing on work by Davenport and Mooney, Allen argues that it's the prospect of an absurd, divinely actuated "awakening" of the deceased that makes sense of our ethical beholdenness to the dead. To love the dead is to remember them in the hope that in some future eschatological scenario we shall encounter them again in their full phenomenality.

Stokes, by contrast, argues that for Kierkegaard, the dead retain their status as moral patients by virtue of our capacity to recollect them with a phenomenal sense of "co-presence" (thus rejecting Allen's claim that the dead lack phenomenality altogether). His chapter "Duties to the Dead? Earnest Imagination and Remembrance" defends the claim that Kierkegaard's injunction to love the dead is indeed a direct duty *to* the dead, rather than an indirect duty to the *living*—which connects the penultimate chapter of *Works of Love* to the ongoing question of whether the dead can be harmed or benefited. Both "At a Graveside" and *Works of Love* seem to endorse the Epicurean claim that the dead are nonexistent. But in the later work, Kierkegaard echoes another Epicurean, Lucretius,[15] in drawing a parallel between the dead and the as-yet unborn: neither are capable of reciprocating love, yet both, according to Kierkegaard, are nonetheless genuine and nonfungible objects of loving duty. Stokes explains how this is possible by appealing to "At a Graveside's" claim that we can become phenomenally *co-present* with our death, via an "earnest" self-reflexive mode of contemplation. In "At a Graveside" this property of co-presence allows me to envisage my own "dead self" in such a way that "I see what I imaginatively contemplate as conferring normative obligation directly upon *me.*"

Applying this thought to *Works of Love* yields the claim that recollecting the dead allows the dead to appear to us as enjoining us *morally.* Our grief at the loss of another discloses to us what has been lost from the world—but if this insight into the uniqueness and preciousness of the deceased is to be preserved, the psychological state of grief must be transfigured into the morally enjoined practice of remembrance, which lets the dead continue to exist as distinctive others. Thus, in a curiously circular fashion, the dead persist as "neighbors" (and thus put us in the Levinasian "infinite debt") because in discharging our duty to remember them, we *give* them the very phenomenality that makes them objects of duty. They remain objects of love even though they cannot impress themselves upon the living or engage with us in any kind of reciprocal or communicative relationship.[16]

So much for how the dead might appear *to the living;* what about the dead themselves? As a Lutheran author with a concern for orthodoxy, Kierkegaard could be expected to endorse the Christian doctrine of personal immortality—which was among the most ferociously contested topics of the immediate post-Hegelian context in which Kierkegaard was educated.[17] And such doctrines seem to demand some sort of posthumous survival more robust than the dead simply persisting in the loving recollection of the living (let alone the Hegelian sublation of the individual consciousness into the world-spirit). Yet one searches Kierkegaard's work in vain for any account of what the afterlife might be *like.* Kierkegaard avoids such explicit discussions of "life after death," and for stridently articulated reasons: he views the question of *whether* there is such a thing as posthumous survival, and what form it might take, as a distraction from the ethical task conferred upon us *by* the thought of the afterlife. Like Heidegger, Kierkegaard takes it that the question death presents to us existentially is a thoroughly "this-worldly" one, concerned with how we comport ourselves *now* to the fact of our own finitude.

Yet Kierkegaard's choice for his epitaph, the final lines from Brorson's hymn "Hallelujah! I Have Found My Jesus," is curious for its vision of the afterlife as the setting for a sort of Christianized version of Aristotelian eternal contemplation: "Then I may rest / In bowers of roses / And unceasingly, unceasingly / Speak with my Jesus."[18] And Kierkegaard, as Tamara Monet

Marks demonstrates in our final chapter, "Kierkegaard's Understanding of the Afterlife," took the orthodox Christian account of the afterlife, with its insistence on personal immortality, judgment, and resurrection, very seriously indeed. Turning once more to the "wise man of old," Marks provides a thorough account of the twists and turns that Kierkegaard's authorship takes with respect to Socrates on the topic of belief in the afterlife. Beyond the famous portrayal of Socrates as an "exemplary figure" in the discussion of the subjective appropriation of the afterlife in *Postscript* (which Possen discusses), Marks points out that the appraisal of Socrates's views is less complimentary in Kierkegaard's dissertation *The Concept of Irony*. Furthermore, in the early upbuilding discourses, Socratic irony seems an inappropriate way to approach the issue of the afterlife; hence, Socrates is absent from the discussion. By the time Kierkegaard gets to the late *Christian Discourses,* where he most clearly espouses his belief in something like a traditional Christian afterlife, Marks argues "that Socrates cannot help Christians concerned with their eternal salvation." The problem is that while the Socrates of the *Postscript* is a paragon of the virtue of subjectivity, the explicitly Christian notion of the afterlife also depends heavily on objective, specific, historically revealed content. Providing content like "Jesus Christ was raised from the dead and so shall I be" is obviously not something that the Socratic view of immortality is capable of. For the Christian believer, the afterlife presents itself as an unavoidable certainty, one that, *contra* the prevailing attitudes of the post-Hegelian philosophical environment, cannot be separated from the question of personal judgment. Hence, from the Christian perspective, the "question" of immortality ceases to be a question at all: "Fear it, it is only all too certain; do not doubt whether you are immortal—tremble, because you are immortal" (CD, 203/SKS 10, 212).

We reach, then, a "dead end" in which we are confronted, as so often in Kierkegaard, with a stark choice between faith and offense. Yet this is not the last word on Kierkegaard and the subject of death—far from it. We hope that, taken together, the chapters assembled here provide a comprehensive jumping-off point for future exploration of Kierkegaard's thought on this important subject. After all, he reminds us that there is often no telling when our dealings with death will be concluded, and in the meantime, there is much that can be learned at the feet of this great educator—*if* we are willing to be taught. Kierkegaard asserts that "death is the schoolmaster of earnestness, but in turn its earnest instruction is recognized precisely by its leaving to the single individual the task of searching himself so it can then teach him earnestness as it can be learned only by the person himself" (TDIO, 75–76/SKS 5, 446). And yet, beyond the lessons that he sees in death, there remains something about death itself that always seems to call for more work. It is an enigma, a never-ending source of wonder to inquire about. Just before Kierkegaard concludes his graveside discourse, he tells the reader, "here again earnestness is: that we should not be overhasty in acquiring an opinion with regard to death.... Therefore, the discourse will refrain from any explanation. Just as death is the last of all, so this will be the last thing said about it: It is inexplicable" (TDIO, 100/SKS 5, 468).

NOTES

1. Joakim Garff, *Søren Kierkegaard: A Biography,* trans. Bruce H. Kirmmse (Princeton, N.J.: Princeton University Press, 2005), pp. 136–37.

2. Garff, *Søren Kierkegaard,* p. 505.

3. There is still no consensus as to the exact nature of Kierkegaard's final illness; Guillain-Barré Syndrome, Geschwind Syndrome, Scheuermann's Disease, and Pott's Disease have all recently been advanced as candidates. See Ib Søgaard, "What Does the Doctor Really Know? Kierkegaard's Admission to Frederik's Hospital and His Death There in 1855," trans. Bruce Kirmmse, in *Kierkegaard Studies Yearbook 2007,* ed. Niels Jørgen Capperlørn, Herman Deuser, and K. Brian Söderquist, pp. 381–400 (Berlin: de Gruyter, 2007); and Joseph Brown, "The Health Matter Briefly Revisited: Epilepsy, 'Hunchback,' and That Tiny Word (Tubercl?)," *Søren Kierkegaard Newsletter* 49 (August 2005): pp. 13–17.

4. Garff, *Søren Kierkegaard,* pp. 782–83.

5. Martyrdom becomes a recurrent and significant theme in Kierkegaard's journals and published writings in the late 1840s; see Garff, *Søren Kierkegaard,* pp. 625–36. For recent discussions of Kierkegaard's own "martyrdom" in the context of his essay "Does a Human Being Have the Right to Let Himself Be Put to Death for the Truth?" see Lee C. Barrett, "Kierkegaard on the Problem of Witnessing while Yet Being a Sinner" and Andrew J. Burgess, "Kierkegaard, Moravian Missions, and Martyrdom," both in *International Kierkegaard Commentary: Without Authority,* ed. Robert L. Perkins, pp. 147–75 and 177–201, respectively (Macon, Ga.: Mercer, 2007).

6. On Kierkegaard's philosophical impact in Japan, see Finn Hauberg Mortensen, *Kierkegaard: Made in Japan* (Odense: Odense University Press, 1996); and James Giles, ed., *Kierkegaard and Japanese Thought* (Hampshire: Palgrave, 2008). On the specific topic of death in that context, see Adam Buben, "Living With Death: Kierkegaard and the Samurai," in Giles, *Kierkegaard and Japanese Thought,* pp. 141–58; and "Background for a Comparison: Kierkegaard and the Samurai," in *Kierkegaard and Religious Pluralism,* ed. Andrew Burgess, pp. 16–30 (Eugene, Ore.: Wipf and Stock, 2007). For an example of discussion relating Kierkegaard to other Eastern philosophical traditions, see Karen L. Carr, "Sin,

Spontaneity, Nature, and God: Comparative Reflections on Kierkegaard and Zhuangzi," in *Kierkegaard and Religious Pluralism,* ed. Andrew Burgess, pp. 1–15 (Eugene, Ore.: Wipf and Stock, 2007); and Karen L. Carr and Phillip J. Ivanhoe, *The Sense of Anti-Rationalism: The Religious Thought of Zhuangzi and Kierkegaard* (New York and London: Seven Bridges, 2000).

7. For a recent discussion of this boundary (and many other issues in the philosophy of death) see Christopher Belshaw, *Annihilation* (Stocksfield: Acumen, 2008).

8. See for example John Martin Fischer's "Introduction: Death, Metaphysics, and Morality," in the seminal collection *The Metaphysics of Death,* ed. John Martin Fischer, esp. pp. 3–8 (Stanford, Calif.: Stanford University Press, 1993).

9. See George Connell, "Four Funerals: The Experience of Time By the Side of the Grave," in *International Kierkegaard Commentary: Prefaces/Writing Sampler and Three Discourses on Imagined Occasions,* ed. Robert L. Perkins, pp. 419–38 (Macon, Ga.: Mercer University Press, 2006).

10. "[T]he one aim of those who practice philosophy in the proper manner is to practice for dying and death"; *Phaedo,* 64a, in Plato, *Five Dialogues,* trans. G. M. A. Grube and John M. Cooper (Indianapolis, Ind.: Hackett, 2002). On the role of Socrates in Kierkegaard's thinking, see Jacob Howland, *Kierkegaard and Socrates: A Study in Philosophy and Faith* (Cambridge: Cambridge University Press, 2006); and Edward F. Mooney, *On Søren Kierkegaard: Dialogue, Polemics, Lost Intimacy, and Time* (Surrey: Ashgate, 2007).

11. This is among the topics of the seminal collection edited by John J. Davenport and Anthony Rudd, *Kierkegaard After MacIntyre: Essays on Freedom, Narrative, and Virtue* (Chicago: Open Court, 2001).

12. E.g., Jeff Malpas, "Death and the Unity of a Life," in *Death and Philosophy,* ed. Jeff Malpas and Robert C. Solomon, pp. 120–34 (London: Routledge, 1998).

13. Daniel W. Conway has recently argued that Kierkegaard overdraws (in instructive ways) the silence of the *akedah* narrative, for the Abraham presented in Genesis actually says far more than Johannes *de silentio* presents him as saying; see his "Abraham's Final Word," in *Ethics, Love, and Faith in Kierkegaard,* ed. Edward F. Mooney, pp. 175–95 (Bloomington: Indiana University Press, 2008).

14. Epicurus, "Letter to Menoeceus," in *The Philosophy of Epicurus,* trans. and ed. George K. Strodach (Evanston, Ill.: Northwestern University Press, 1963), p. 180.

15. Titus Lucretius Carus, *The Way Things Are,* trans. Rolfe Humphries (Bloomington: Indiana University Press, 1968), pp. 110, 114.

16. Interestingly, in the last half-decade of Kierkegaard's life, the dead suddenly *did* appear to communicate with the living, as the "table-turning" craze of the 1850s swept up such eminent Copenhageners as Hans Lassen Martensen and Johan Ludvig Heiberg. See Thomas Overskou, *Om Mit Liv og Min Tid 1819–1878,* edited with a postscript by Robert Neiindam (Copenhagen: Nyt Nordisk Forlag Arnold Busck, 1962), pp. 194–97; and Patrick Stokes, "The Science of the Dead:

Proto-Spiritualism in Kierkegaard's Copenhagen," in *Kierkegaard and the 19th Century Crisis of Culture* (*Acta Kierkegaardiana Vol. 4*), ed. Roman Kralik, Abrahim H. Khan, Peter Sajda, Jamie Turnbull, and Andrew J. Burgess, pp. 132–49 (Šal̆a, Slovakia: Kierkegaard Society of Slovakia/Kierkegaard Circle, University of Toronto, 2009).

17. On the post-Hegelian debate on personal immortality, see István Czakó, "Becoming Immortal: The Historical Context of Kierkegaard's Concept of Immortality," in *Kierkegaard and Christianity (Acta Kierkegaardiana Vol. 3)*, ed. Roman Králik, Abrahim H. Khan, Peter Šajda, Jamie Turnbull, and Andrew J. Burgess, pp. 58–71 (Šal̆a, Slovakia: Kierkegaard Society of Slovakia/Kierkegaard Circle, University of Toronto, 2008); Jon Stewart, *A History of Hegelianism in Golden Age Denmark Tome I: The Heiberg Period: 1824–1836* (Copenhagen: C. A. Reitzel, 2007), pp. 37–53, 222–27, 542; and Tamara Monet Marks, "Kierkegaard's 'New Argument' for Immortality," *Journal of Religious Ethics* 38, no. 1 (January 2010): pp. 143–86.

18. Alastair Hannay, *Kierkegaard: A Biography* (Cambridge: Cambridge University Press, 2001), p. 418.

1.

Knights and Knaves of the Living Dead: Kierkegaard's Use of Living Death as a Metaphor for Despair

George Connell

> Despair is the sickness unto death, this tormenting contradiction, this sickness of the self, perpetually to be dying, to die and yet not to die, to die death. For to die signifies that all is over, but to die death means to experience dying, and if this is experienced for one single moment, one thereby experiences it forever.
>
> —KIERKEGAARD, *THE SICKNESS UNTO DEATH*

> For some time now the impression has been growing on me that everyone is dead.
>
> It happens when I speak to people. In the middle of a sentence it will come over me: yes, beyond a doubt, this is death. There is little to do but groan and make an excuse and slip away as quickly as one can. At such times it seems that the conversation is spoken by automatons who have no choice in what they say. I hear myself or someone else saying things like: "In my opinion the Russian people are a great people, but—" or "Yes, what you say about the hypocrisy of the North is unquestionably true. However—" and I think to myself: this is death.
>
> —WALKER PERCY, *THE MOVIEGOER*

Among the endlessly repeated motifs of the horror genre, none more reliably evokes a shudder than the idea of the undead, of humans doomed to wander between life and death. This response has a variety of deep psychological sources. Our anxiety in the face of our own mortality plays a part, as does a physiological revulsion to decaying bodies. Further, the sense of the living dead as ontologically other evokes in us a sense of numinous dread. Following Mary Douglas, the way such beings transgress the boundary separating life and death renders them both dangerous and impure.[1]

Given the resonances such imagery evokes, it is significant that Kierkegaard's pseudonym, Anti-Climacus, frames his discussion of despair in *The Sickness unto Death* in terms of living death. This, however, has not figured large in scholarly discussions of the book. This scholarly silence is perhaps largely explained by the way Anti-Climacus makes little explicit use of death as a metaphor for despair after the opening sections of the book. There is also, no doubt, a tendency for literal-minded philosophers to dismiss talk of living death as either "mere metaphor" or bald contradiction. Still, the despair-death identification is central in the "Preface," "Introduction," and "Part One, A" of *The Sickness unto Death.* What sense, then, can we make of the idea that despair is a sort of living death? What agendas lead Anti-Climacus to evoke this imagery in his analysis of despair? Since Anti-Climacus is a different sort of pseudonym from all others in the authorship, addressing these questions stirs up major questions concerning Kierkegaard's overall project and how we should place it in the context of contemporary thought and culture.[2] Specifically, Kierkegaard's analysis of despair as living death highlights his ambiguous relation to contemporary consciousness. One aspect of his analysis, his account of conscious despair as living death, is profoundly resonant with contemporary ideas and fears. But alongside the Kierkegaard who surprises readers by his preternatural contemporaneity stands another, antimodern Kierkegaard. This other Kierkegaard is nowhere more evident than in his analyses of unconscious despair. I will argue that his idea of unconscious despair as living death sets Kierkegaard in sharp opposition to irony as described by Richard Rorty, liberalism as described by Alasdair MacIntyre, and secularism as described by Charles Taylor. Since irony, liberalism, and secularism are defining features of the contemporary scene, this second aspect of his analysis of despair as living death starkly highlights the antimodern Kierkegaard. Having shown the countercultural spirit of Kierkegaard's analysis of unconscious despair, I conclude by examining the basis of his judgment: from what vantage point, in terms of what evidence, and by what authority does he pronounce the apparently contented lives of ordinary people to be forms of living death?

Living Death: A Plausible Notion?

Before we can appreciate the simultaneous timeliness and untimeliness of Kierkegaard's analyses of despair, it is crucial to establish the coherence of the idea of living death in the first place. On its face, the notion of living death seems contradictory. There are, however, a variety of ways in which we can make good sense of it. First, the notion of despair as living death has the deepest possible roots in Kierkegaard's development as a thinker. One of his first significant intellectual undertakings was an analysis of the "three great ideas," Don Juan, Faust, and Ahasverus, who represent to the Middle Ages three forms of existence outside of faith: sensuality, doubt, and despair. Ironically, Ahasverus, who represents despair, is doomed to a living death precisely by being condemned to a deathless life.

Kierkegaard's investigations of the three great ideas eventually bear fruit in the first volume of *Either/Or.* There, the linkage of despair and living death is emphatic, both in the name of A's morbid confraternity, the *Symparanekromenoi* (the society of the already dead), and especially in A's essay, "The Unhappiest One." There, A identifies the winner of a contest for that dubious title specifically as the one who cannot die, the one whose grave is empty not because he rose from the dead, but because his curse denies him the peace of death.[3] Additionally, one can see Johannes the Seducer as a vampire who must repeatedly parasitize the immediate desire of his female victims to sustain his own jaded interest in life. Clearly, Kierkegaard's analysis in *The Sickness unto Death* of despair as living death needs to be read against the backdrop of his early explorations of that theme.

Showing that the notion of despair as living death is deeply rooted in Kierkegaard's thought does not suffice to render it plausible. We need to unpack this metaphor to discern its phenomenological basis, its experiential "cash value." If we try to take it literally, we run into several problems. First, to speak of a form of life that is simultaneously death seems to violate the principle of noncontradiction. Further, despair typically designates a form of suffering, while death designates the cessation of awareness. Kierkegaard points a way beyond these dead ends when he writes, "For to die signifies that all is over, but to die death means to experience dying" (SUD, 18/SKS 11, 133). In this passage, Kierkegaard distinguishes between the idea of death as the end of all experience and dying as the experience of the movement from life to death. But if dying is what he means when he speaks of living death, then doesn't his preference for paradoxical metaphors simply muddy the waters? Wouldn't it be better to keep the terms "death" and "dying" clearly distinct from each other? By sharply demarcating the two terms, one implies that dying is a process that leads to a result that is entirely separate from the process itself. Epicurus is, no doubt, the thinker who most starkly draws out the consequences of this sharp demarcation when he argues that as long as I am, death isn't, and as soon as death is, I no longer am.[4] Since death and I can never be co-present, it need not concern me. Against this Epicurean thinking, Kierkegaard invokes the idea of dying as living death to say that death is not sharply demarcated from life, that it can encroach upon life so that it becomes experientially present.[5]

While Kierkegaard himself describes this blurring of lines between life and death, a brief look at Leo Tolstoy's *The Death of Ivan Ilyich* serves to show the variety of forms such encroachment takes.[6]

a. *Death as failure of the body*: At the most basic level, death is the breakdown and failure of the body to carry out the physiological processes of life. During the dying process, that breakdown and failure are often vividly present to the one dying, resulting in a fundamentally altered experience of one's embodiment. Tolstoy captures this powerfully in a scene late in Ivan's illness by juxtaposing the ways Ivan and his daughter experience their bodies. Ivan's body is weak and wasting, already showing the pallor of death. Each new pain and each lost capacity carries with it a message of his imminent death. In contrast, his daughter lives her body exultantly as the locus of her youthful flourishing: "His daughter came in all decked out in a gown that left much of her young flesh exposed; she was making a show of that very flesh which, for him, was the cause of so much agony. Strong, healthy, obviously in love, she was impatient with illness, suffering, and death, which interfered with her happiness."[7]

b. *Death as impotence and dependency:* The failure of the dying body is closely associated with a more general impotence associated with death. To be dead is to lose one's capacity to effect one's will in the world. Even when one leaves a last will and testament, disposing of one's assets and imposing one's intent on the living, one depends radically on others to see that those wishes are carried out. Ivan experiences this impotence and dependency already in his illness. Tolstoy sensitively portrays Ivan's dependency on Gerasim, a peasant boy assigned to care for him. While Ivan does move from embarrassment and resentment at such dependency to gratitude and a sense of connection, Tolstoy shows that the impotence and dependency of death already pervade the consciousness of the dying Ivan.

c. *Death as isolation:* One of the most terrifying features of death for both the dying and for their surviving loved ones is the thought of severed ties and resulting isolation. While Ivan does establish a connection with Gerasim, Tolstoy portrays him as increasingly isolated from his wife, children, friends, and co-workers as his illness progresses. Clearly, the loneliness of the grave is already experienced in the isolation of the sickbed.

Tolstoy writes, "During the last days of the isolation in which he lived, lying on the sofa with his face to the wall, isolation in the midst of a populous city among numerous friends and relatives, [he experienced] an isolation that could not have been greater anywhere, either in the depths of the sea or the bowels of the earth."[8]

d. *Death as closing the future:* Tolstoy presents Ivan as an ambitious social climber, always looking for the main chance to advance in the bureaucracy and associated social world that are the limits of his imagination. As such, he is constantly projecting ahead of himself, living vicariously in an anticipated (and idealized) future. Just as death slams the door on the future, the dying Ivan experiences this closure already in his illness as the anticipation of death displaces all other hopes and plans for the future.

e. *Death as emptying the present:* Death doesn't just close the future; it obliterates the present. Before Ivan's illness, he delighted in losing himself in the present moment of inconsequential amusements such as card games, but the ill Ivan loses this ability. The proximity of his death, the nearing moment when he will have no present moment, prevents him from fully living in the present moments he still has left. The resulting vacuity of the actual present gives rise to boredom and restlessness, just as his incessant pain makes the present an ordeal to escape rather than a precious fleeting moment to savor.

f. *Death as re-evaluating the past:* Because we understand human lives in terms of their narrative unity, there is something necessarily provisional about all evaluations of lives that are still running their courses.[9] Solon captures this provisional quality in his famous dictum that we should judge no one happy prior to his or her death. Death, however, reduces this indeterminacy in two ways: first, it fixes the set of events and experiences with which the interpreter must potentially deal, and second, the manner of the end of a life retroactively influences the significance and meaning of earlier moments of life.[10] Typically, as mourners gather at a funeral, they endeavor to fit together their memories of the deceased life into a coherent sense of who the deceased fundamentally was. Once again, this feature of death is already very much part of the dying process. Tolstoy writes, "[D]uring the last days of that terrible isolation, Ivan Ilyich lived only with memories of the past. One after another images of his past came to mind. His recollections always began with what was closest in time and shifted back to what was most remote, to his childhood and lingered there."[11] Ivan's death struggle increasingly becomes a struggle to reassess his life in a manner radically different from the complacent self-image of his adult

> years. He cries out in "moral agony" the question, "What if my entire life, my entire conscious life, simply was *not the real thing?*"[12] Only when he manages to accept a radical renarration of his life, one that holds up as true even in the harsh light of imminent death, does Ivan find peace.

These six parallels between death and dying suffice to show that the metaphor of living death has a solid experiential basis. Death is not just a result that ensues upon the completion of the dying process; it encroaches upon life, making itself manifest in a variety of ways. While Tolstoy's classic literary exploration of dying establishes the bona fides of the notion of living death, Kierkegaard uses the notion as a way to characterize despair. How apt is this use?

Despair as Living Death

While much of *The Sickness unto Death* shows a passion for taxonomy that seems more like Linnaeus than Kierkegaard, "Part One, A: Despair Is the Sickness unto Death" speaks of despair in an encompassing way. Before viewing it from multiple perspectives and in its multiple forms, Anti-Climacus says that all despair is a sickness of the spirit, a failure of the self to relate properly to itself and to the power that created it. It is overwhelmingly in this brief opening section of the book that Anti-Climacus identifies despair as living death. The penultimate paragraph of this section reads:

> Such is the nature of despair, this sickness of the self, this sickness unto death. The despairing person is mortally ill. In a completely different sense than is the case with any illness, this sickness has attacked the most vital organs, and yet he cannot die. Death is not the end of the sickness, but death is incessantly the end. To be saved from this sickness by death is an impossibility, because the sickness and its torment—and the death—are precisely this inability to die (SUD, 21/SKS 11, 136).

By following this encompassing diagnosis of the universal human malady with differentiated and even counterposed analyses of specific forms of despair, Anti-Climacus unavoidably opens himself to the possibility that the living death metaphor will seem more apt when applied to some forms of despair than others. Of Anti-Climacus's differentiations, none is more significant than his contrast between conscious despair ("The Despair that is Conscious of Being Despair") and unconscious despair ("The Despair that is Ignorant of Being Despair"). Conscious despair involves felt psychological pain and some level of cognitive awareness of one's condition. Unconscious despair, in contrast, is either oblivious to its pathology, mistakenly regarding itself as thriving, or it radically misconstrues its felt suffering so as not properly to recognize it as despair. Throughout his authorship, Kierkegaard consistently admires great passion and penetrating awareness while expressing contempt for meager lives of dull contentment and dim awareness, so it is no surprise that in *The Sickness unto Death* he presents conscious despair rather grandly, in the forms of romantic figures, whose greatness shines through even in their misery. In contrast, he writes contemptuously of unconscious despair, calling into question whether such persons fully qualify as human. Since Kierkegaard uses the term "knight" as a generic category for various sorts of aristocracy of spirit (knights of infinite resignation and knights of faith), my title reference to "knights of the living dead" (apologies to George Romero) is to those who suffer conscious despair. I allude to Kierkegaard's contemptuous attitude toward those whose despair is unconscious by labeling them knaves.

Implicit in this juxtaposition of knights and knaves, of conscious and unconscious despairers, is the challenge of coming to terms with Kierkegaard's notion of despair as living death. For contemporary readers, it is plausible and even compelling to describe anguished sufferers as enduring a living death. But Anti-Climacus's description of people living contented but spiritually inadequate lives as the living dead shocks contemporary sensibilities. In what follows, I will focus on the sharply contrasting plausibilities of the two different ways of using the metaphor of living death.

The Contemporary Plausibility of Conscious Despair as Living Death

Despite the apparent contradiction involved in the idea of living death, this notion fascinates us in ways that bespeak a certain resonance: it taps into fears that are psychologically real and imaginatively plausible. The specific form of these fears varies historically and culturally. Kierkegaard's discussions of living death are rooted in fears of a postmortem outer darkness, of a continued conscious existence as a self in a state of unalterable separation from God. Kierkegaard's imaginative handle on the idea of living death is clearly traditional, rooted in a European religious imagination that was already giving way to a secularized imagination in Kierkegaard's own day. Edgar Allan Poe, a rough contemporary of Kierkegaard, reflects this secularization in his dark imaginings of living death when he plays on powerful nineteenth-century fears of being buried alive. Though we still get a shiver from supernaturalist renditions of the notion of living death and are still horrified by Poe's claustrophobic nightmares, as citizens of the developed world our own deep-seated fears of living death concentrate on the prospect of high-tech medical interventions keeping us alive in a radically diminished state. Two recent films, Alejandro Amenábar's "The Sea Inside" (2004) and Julian Schnable's "The Diving Bell and the Butterfly" (2007), both based on actual cases, are powerful and sensitive explorations of contemporary fears of living death.

In both films, healthy and thriving men are abruptly rendered almost entirely paralyzed by unforeseen events, a diving accident resulting in spinal injury in "The Sea Inside," and a stroke in "The Diving Bell and the Butterfly." Without modern medical interventions, both men would have quickly died, but both experience their medically prolonged lives as living deaths. Ramon Sampedro's campaign to die is the focus of "The Sea Inside," and one of Jean-Dominique Bauby's first messages when he establishes communications by blinking his eyelid is to ask to die.

Why this shared sense that life as a paralytic is worse than death? Part of the answer is their exuberant love of their prior active, creative, connected, and (by very different standards) successful lives. The contrast between their current diminished lives and their prior flourishing lives follows closely the six parallels between death and dying identified above: (1) they experience their bodies as inert, unresponsive matter; (2) they are radically impotent and dependent; (3) their paralysis isolates them from others; (4) they lose a sense of the future as an open horizon as it becomes clear that their paralysis is permanent; (5) their ability to savor the present, while not wholly extinguished, is dramatically reduced; and (6) both replay events in their pasts, renarrating them in ways deeply influenced by their current conditions.

These films warrant special attention for several reasons. First, they render the problematic notion of living death horrifically plausible by making it imaginatively gripping. Second, they point to the equivocality of the word "life." Philosophers have often fixated on the idea that life and death are logical opposites. To be alive is for the requisite complement of physiological processes (heartbeat, neurological activity, digestion) to continue; to be dead is for them to cease. To speak of living death is thus to utter a contradiction. These films bring home that mere prolongation of minimal physiological processes is a mockery of what we really have in mind when we speak of life: the repertory of characteristically human activities. Once we appreciate these two senses, we can construe living death as prolongation of the first, biological sense of life when the possibility of the second, Aristotelian sense of characteristic activities disappears. Third, and most importantly for this chapter, the films show us living death as an excruciatingly self-aware phenomenon. The dramatic impact of the films derives from the overwhelming sense of loss and frustration felt by Ramon Sampedro and Jean-Dominique Bauby. In both cases, this sense is intensified by the abrupt and unexpected transition from flourishing life to total incapacity. More typically, incapacitating illnesses and normal aging steal capabilities away gradually, so that awareness of loss is attenuated. Often, the very processes that remove capabilities also diminish awareness of the losses. In the two films, we encounter worst-case scenarios of radical loss of physical capability combined with undiminished awareness, resulting in maximal anguish. It is precisely this mismatch of able mind and impotent body that makes the label "living death" so apt: only an oxymoron can capture the paradoxical juxtaposition of full ability in one dimension of life and complete disability in another.

These two films have strong but problematic resonances with Kierkegaard. Just as the undiminished awareness of Ramon Sampedro and Jean-Dominique Bauby is key to their status as paradigms of living death, so Kierkegaard ties degree of awareness to depth of despair:

> The ever increasing intensity of despair depends upon the degree of consciousness or is proportionate to its increase: the greater the degree of consciousness, the more intensive the despair. This is everywhere apparent, most clearly in despair at its maximum and minimum. The devil's despair is the most intensive despair, for the devil is sheer spirit and hence unqualified consciousness and transparency; there is no obscurity in the devil that could serve as a mitigating excuse. Therefore his despair is the most absolute defiance. This is despair at its maximum (SUD, 42/SKS 11, 157).

While there is a shared focus on conscious despair as living death in the two films and Kierkegaard, significant differences quickly emerge on closer inspection. First, Kierkegaard and the two films construe consciousness in sharply different ways. For Kierkegaard, the relevant consciousness is theological: one's awareness of oneself as defying God. In the two films, the relevant consciousness is of lost capacity and connection. (When a paraplegic priest tries to persuade Ramon Sampedro to construe his situation in theological terms, he brusquely dismisses the priest.) Further, in my reading of the films, I have argued for a notion of living death that is essentially for-itself, that necessarily involves a moment of subjectivity that is by its nature self-aware. In contrast, Kierkegaard wavers between similarly treating awareness as an essential feature of despair and seeing it simply as an intensifying factor. The above passage continues:

> Despair at its minimum is a state that—yes, one could humanly be tempted almost to say that in a kind of innocence it does not know that it is despair. There is the least despair when this kind of unconsciousness is greatest; it is almost a dialectical issue whether it is justifiable to call such a state despair (SUD, 42/SKS 11, 157).

We can discern in Kierkegaard's ambivalence two conflicting impulses. As a dialectician and a phenomenologist, he grasps the close connections between despair and consciousness. He writes that despair is the most terrifying of dangers because it is a sickness of the self and the self is unavoidably and eternally an awareness of itself.[13] Further, he draws on his own experience of unrelenting self-awareness in depicting the restless despair of reflective aesthetes. These reflective aesthetes are his knights of living death, patterned after Faust and Ahasverus, grand in their self-awareness, their suffering, their dignity, and their style. But as an observer of the human condition, Kierkegaard sees himself surrounded by people living pathetic, banal lives. His distaste for such lives leads him to see them as forms of despair. But many of these people seem quite content with their lives. Out of a complex mixture of aristocratic contempt and Christian compassion, Kierkegaard dismisses the self-consciousness of these knaves of the living dead as deeply false, writing, "That this condition [unconscious despair] is nevertheless despair and is properly designated as such manifests what in the best sense of the word may be called the obstinacy of the truth" (SUD, 42/SKS 11, 157). It is this second impulse that raises difficult conceptual issues and sets Kierkegaard deeply at odds with major currents of the contemporary cultural scene.

Unconscious Despair as Living Death: A Contemporary Stumbling Block

As contemporary readers struggle to make sense of Kierkegaard's analysis of despair in *The Sickness unto Death,* they almost inevitably turn to the familiar contemporary concept, depression, to get their bearings. While this assimilation seems to work well for some of the specific forms of despair described by Kierkegaard, it spectacularly fails in the case of his discussion of unconscious despair. Andrew Solomon offers a useful statement of our current understanding of what it is to be depressed:

> The only way to find out whether you're depressed is to listen to and watch yourself, to feel your feelings and think about them. If you feel bad without reason most of the time, you're depressed. If you feel bad most of the time with reason, you're also depressed, though changing the reasons may be a better way forward than leaving circumstance alone and attacking the depression. If the depression is disabling to you, then it's major. If it's only mildly distracting, it's not major.[14]

Solomon pokes fun at the authoritative *Diagnostic and Statistical Manual, 4th Edition* (DSM-IV) for listing nine characteristic symptoms of depression and classifying anyone with five or more symptoms as depressed while anyone with four or fewer not, but both Solomon and DSM-IV make depression a function of two main factors: psychological pain and impaired function.

In contrast, Kierkegaard describes unconscious despair as perfectly consistent with a robust sense of psychological well-being and exemplary performance in all one's social roles:

> Just by losing himself in this way, such a man [one in finitude's despair] has gained an increasing capacity for going along superbly in business and social life, indeed, for making a great success in the world. Here there is no delay, no difficulty with his self and its infinitizing; he is as smooth as a rolling stone, as *courant* [passable] as a circulating coin. He is so far from being regarded as a person in despair that he is just what a human being is supposed to be. As is natural, the world generally has no understanding of what is truly appalling. The despair that not only does not cause one any inconvenience in life but makes life cozy and comfortable is in no way, of course, regarded as despair (SUD, 34/SKS 11, 149–50).

It is amusing to consider the response of a psychologist or psychiatrist to a client who reports enjoying life, functioning well as spouse, parent, employee, and citizen, but who nonetheless claims to be in despair. Surely the client would meet blank incomprehension followed by speedy dismissal.

Similarly, many philosophers will find the idea of unconscious despair incoherent. Despair is psychological pain and pain is necessarily felt, so the idea of unconscious despair appears manifestly incoherent. Merold Westphal nicely captures this view:

> The "customary" or "common" view assumes . . . that I am the criterion of my own spiritual health. Despair is a psychic state just like the raw feelings that have become so prominent in recent philosophy of mind. For such states the difference between appearance and reality is inoperative. I cannot feel that I have a pain or an itch and then discover that I didn't have one after all. If it felt like it hurt, it hurt (even if I can find no adequate physical cause of the pain). My own reports about these matters are either incorrigible, or, if not, the closest approximation to incorrigibility about empirical fact one could hope for.[15]

Just as, on this view, the experience of pain is incorrigible, so is one's non-experience of pain, including psychological pain. If I don't experience myself as in despair, then I'm not.

Westphal, of course, states this view in order to discredit it. His essay "Kierkegaard's Psychology and Unconscious Despair" explains and defends Kierkegaard's problematic notion so effectively that I will briefly summarize what I take to be key points of his analysis. To explain Kierkegaard's refusal to identify mind or spirit with "the surface of consciousness that is the domain of raw feelings,"[16] Westphal places him in reference to three major figures from the history of philosophy: Aristotle, Descartes, and Hegel. Given that people can and do have erroneous conceptions of human virtue, Aristotle's notion of happiness as a life of virtuous activity implies that people may misjudge their own conditions. For example, a hedonist's self-satisfaction over a life rich in sensual indulgence is, on Aristotle's view, erroneous. Similarly, Kierkegaard believes many people have fundamentally distorted views of what their genuine good is and so are ill-placed to judge their own spiritual health.

There is nonetheless a Cartesian dimension to Kierkegaard's psychology: at a fundamental level the self is its awareness of itself. Kierkegaard defines the self as a relation that relates itself to itself and this relation is, at least initially, an awareness of self. Where Descartes sees this self-awareness as immediate, Kierkegaard joins Hegel in seeing it as mediated by the other: the self comes to know itself by seeing itself mirrored in the eyes of the other. But who is the relevant other whose view confers identity on one? For Hegel, it is the human other, both the particular others of our immediate circle and the more generalized other of the social world. But for Kierkegaard, God is the crucial other, the mirror whose view of one reflects one truthfully. Since people can all too easily forget this divine other, focusing entirely on achieving a favorable image in the mirror of the social realm, it is entirely coherent and dreadfully common for them to have radically distorted understandings of their own well-being. They can, in short, be in despair and not know it.

I take Westphal to have succeeded thoroughly in defending the conceptual coherence of unconscious despair, but I believe he needs to qualify his claim that that analysis establishes Kierkegaard as a "true contemporary."[17] I grant Westphal's point that "readers in an era overflowing with theories of false consciousness, Marxian, psychoanalytic, hermeneutical and structuralist"[18] will recognize Kierkegaard's suspicion of the subject's sense of itself as part of a more general anti-Cartesian tendency.[19] As Charles Taylor puts it, a broadly Freudian sense of the self as opaque to itself represents "the surrounding context of understanding" that is "very deeply entrenched" and "intuitively understandable to almost everyone."[20]

But, as Taylor sees it, this contemporary "sense that there are as yet unsaid depths in us" is qualitatively different from the sense of depth characteristic of the premodern era. Taylor writes, "Under the old cosmos notions, particularly the 'Platonic' cosmos defined by Ideas, the nature of [a] thing was in a sense not within it, but belonged to the structure of the cosmos."[21] A self within such an order has depth (= is not transparently available to itself) because "the discovery of what I really am requires that I come to grasp this nature by studying the orders of human social life and the cosmos."[22] In contrast, Taylor sees the post-Cartesian self's depth as a function of its "dark genesis": its sense of its identity as rooted in the abysses of evolutionary time, in the contingencies of personal history, and in the too, too solid flesh of its material embodiment.[23]

Taylor is uncharacteristically terse in sketching out this fascinating contrast between two contrasting versions of the self's depth, but what he says is full of significance for this inquiry. In Taylor's terms, Kierkegaard's analysis of unconscious despair is rooted in a sense of cosmos rather than of universe. In *The Sickness unto Death,* Kierkegaard does not sound the self's depths by plumbing its "dark genesis" but by understanding the structures of its relations to itself, to its surrounding reality, and to God. In declaring that ultimately despair is sin, that it designates a misrelationship between the self and the transcendent source of its being, that it represents a failure by the self to fulfill its ontologically grounded destiny, and thus constitutes a living death, Kierkegaard connects himself to the "cosmic outlook" Taylor associates with premodernity.

To highlight the antimodern dimensions of Kierkegaard's analysis of unconscious despair, I will briefly set that analysis over against key aspects of modernity discussed by Richard Rorty, Alasdair MacIntyre, and Charles Taylor: irony, liberalism, and secularity. In many ways, Kierkegaard lines up nicely with all three of these modernist trends, and all three thinkers have used Kierkegaard as a case study in their articulations of the modern condition. When, however, we view Kierkegaard's account of unconscious despair alongside these three salient features of modernity, the untimeliness of that account is striking.

Rorty on Irony

For Rorty, as for Kierkegaard, irony designates not just a literary trope, but more fundamentally, an existential stance. In Rorty's case, it involves self-consciousness about our radical contingency, especially the contingency of our ways of describing the world.

> I shall define an "ironist" as someone who fulfills three conditions: (1) She has radical and continuing doubts about the final vocabulary she currently uses, because she has been impressed by other vocabularies, vocabularies taken as final by people or books she has encountered; (2) she realizes that argument phrased in her present vocabulary can neither underwrite nor dissolve these doubts; (3) insofar as she philosophizes about her situation, she does not think that her vocabulary is closer to reality than others, that it is in touch with a power not herself.[24]

Over against the ironist stands the theologian or metaphysician, who "believes there is an order beyond time and change which both determines the point of human existence and establishes a hierarchy of responsibilities."[25]

However ubiquitous irony is in Kierkegaard's authorship, his judgments concerning unconscious despair in *The Sickness unto Death* are unmistakably "theological" and "metaphysical" in Rorty's senses of the words. He writes, "[I]f a man is presumably happy, . . . although considered *in the light of truth* he is unhappy, he is usually far from wanting to be wrenched out of his error" (SUD, 43/SKS 11, 158, my italics). Note the contrast is not between the way a Christian would judge the man's life and the way he himself sees it; the contrast is between false self-understanding and the hard reality revealed by "the light of truth."

A Rortean ironist cannot but be offended at Kierkegaard's insistence on the ultimacy of the Christian standard of evaluating what is real life and what is self-deluded living death.

MacIntyre on Liberalism

Given Kierkegaard's final assault on official Christianity, one would naturally expect him to be broadly sympathetic to liberal political arrangements. Alasdair MacIntyre describes such a political order in *After Virtue* as "any society where government does not express or represent the moral community of the citizens, but is instead a set of institutional arrangements for imposing a bureaucratized unity on a society which lacks genuine moral consensus."[26] Obviously, Kierkegaard nowhere speaks in favor of "imposing a bureaucratized unity," but this minimalist state does seem implicit in Kierkegaard's push for individual responsibility in ethical and religious matters. But as MacIntyre shows in his later *Whose Justice? Which Rationality?*, an irony at the heart of the liberal political order makes it no neutral arbiter but rather a substantive tradition with its own overriding values and corresponding aversions. Unsurprisingly, the liberal social and political order takes its own perpetuation as an ultimate good and educates a citizenry of "liberal individuals" to this end. These liberal individuals move easily in a world where "it appears normal that a variety of goods should be pursued, each appropriate to its own sphere, with no overall good supplying any overall unity to life."[27] Not only are goods plural, they also vary from person to person: "For in the liberal public realm individuals understand each other and themselves as each possessing his or her own ordered schedule of preferences."[28] These preferences are the determinants of the pluriform, shifting, and individualized goods of the population.

For such a liberal individual, Kierkegaard's judgment of many apparently satisfactory lives as living death is offensive and paradoxical. First, it represents an inappropriate imposition of one person's "schedule of preferences" on others; second, its insistence on a single overriding good (in Kierkegaard's case, right relation to God) is profoundly out of step with liberalism's tendency to "diversify" its existential investments. MacIntyre quotes John Rawls: "Human good is heterogeneous because the aims of the self are heterogeneous. Although to subordinate all our aims to one end does not strictly speaking violate principles of rational choice . . . it still strikes us as irrational or more likely mad. The self is disfigured."[29] Apart from his conception of right relation to God as the single, ultimate human telos, Kierkegaard's analysis of unconscious despair as a living death makes no sense. Clearly, that analysis is out of step with the liberal social and political order described by MacIntyre.

Taylor on Secularism

Charles Taylor's monumental *A Secular Age* locates the distinguishing feature of modernity in the radically changed situation of religious belief from premodern times. Taylor's narration of the West's spiritual itinerary from 1500 to the present identifies three distinct senses of secularization: (1) disentangling religion from the institutions of political power, (2) "the falling off of religious belief and practice," and (3) a transition from "a society in which it was virtually impossible not to believe in God, to one in which faith, even for the staunchest believer, is one human possibility among others."[30] Given his final attack on official Lutheranism and his persistent emphasis on personal choice in matters ethical and religious, the first and third seem not just compatible with Kierkegaard but thoroughly laudable from his point of view. At the most heated moments of his battle with the state church, Kierkegaard even called for secularism in the second sense, labeling participation in public worship a mockery of God.

Despite these genuine sympathies with dimensions of secularization, Kierkegaard's analysis of unconscious despair runs directly counter to major currents in secularization as described by Taylor. As Taylor sees it, secularization did not and could not take the form of a direct transition from belief to disbelief but proceeded via the intermediary of Deism. In the wake of the devastating religious wars of the seventeenth century, European intellectuals turned for relief to a religion of reason. This attenuated version of religious belief largely drops its transcendent aspirations, reducing God's will for humankind to purely immanent thriving.[31]

Whereas traditional Christianity (like the other great postaxial religions) held in tension the goals of worldly flourishing and of attaining a higher good beyond such immanent well-being, Deism gives rise to what Taylor labels "the modern moral order" through its purely immanent conception of the human good. And once this order is in place, traditional religious admonitions to reach higher are met not just with incomprehension but outright hostility.[32]

Kierkegaard's analysis of despair is utterly at odds with such a purely immanent conception of the human good, and, unsurprisingly, his analysis has drawn just the sort of wrath described by Taylor. In the introduction to *The Sickness unto Death,* Kierkegaard speaks almost dismissively of "earthly and temporal suffering: need, illness, misery, hardship, adversities, torments, mental sufferings, cares, grief" (SUD, 8/SKS 11, 124) as minor matters compared to the ultimate danger, despair (i.e., failure to achieve the transcendent good of right relation to God). Later, he uses an architectural metaphor to deride those whose lives are consumed with temporal goods, likening them to people who inhabit a grand multistory house but who "prefer to live in the basement" (SUD, 43/SKS 11, 158), i.e., the realm of the sensate. Once again, it is evident that Kierkegaard's analysis of despair places him athwart main currents of modernity.

Knavery as Living Death

By setting Kierkegaard over against Rorty, MacIntyre, and Taylor, I seek to highlight the startling character of his diagnosis of despair: the knaves, who may think they are doing fine, as well as the knights, who suffer grandly, are the living dead. While we readily accept "living death" as a way to describe self-conscious impotence, isolation, and hopelessness, Kierkegaard applies that epithet to the hosts of us who muddle through from day to day, playing our social roles, taking little satisfactions, and evading disturbing thoughts of death, responsibility, and all things ultimate.

This judgment about the knaves is phenomenologically ambiguous. On the one hand, it carries clear phenomenological import; the lived experience of the knaves is qualitatively other than a real experience of life. On the other hand, this judgment discounts the knaves' sense of themselves. Their lives are judged to be a sort of death even though they would vigorously protest such a description.

Kierkegaard's judgments about knights and knaves parallel the distinction between lucid dreaming and ordinary dreaming. Dreaming is (presumably) a deficient state of consciousness as compared to waking awareness, just as despair is a deficient spiritual condition. Like the lucid dreamer, Kierkegaard's knights recognize their condition as deficient, but Kierkegaard's knaves are as captivated by their living death as dreamers are by their dreams. To invoke another philosophically resonant metaphor, they are dwellers in Plato's cave who don't have a clue about a world beyond the cave.

By setting Kierkegaard against Rorty, MacIntyre, and Taylor, I've highlighted the ways such a judgment about the knaves presumes a privileged vantage point, postulates a single ultimate good, and identifies that good as transcendent. While the judgment that the knights are in despair appeals directly to their own anguished senses of themselves, the judgment about the knaves challenges and even dismisses their self-experience. Clearly this judgment regarding the knaves raises epistemological questions of a completely different order than those raised by Kierkegaard's parallel judgment of his knights.

"In the light of truth": The Epistemological Basis of Kierkegaard's Analysis of Despair

From what vantage point, in terms of what evidence, and with what authority does Kierkegaard pronounce the apparently contented lives of ordinary people to be forms of living death? What is the "light of truth" he cites as revealing a truth at odds with these people's subjective sense of themselves? While Kierkegaard never takes this issue on directly in *The Sickness unto Death,* the text suggests at least three main ways of answering this challenge: (1) an appeal to expertise, (2) an appeal to repressed dimensions of lived experience of those in despair, and (3) retrospective judgment.

Appeal to Expertise

From the first paragraph of the preface to *The Sickness unto Death,* Kierkegaard invokes medical metaphors to orient his discussion, saying that Christian accounts of despair must always bear "a resemblance to the way a physician speaks at a bedside" (SUD, 5/SKS 11, 117). In the first instance, this metaphor serves to emphasize that the discourse is practically concerned and the stakes are profound, so that the typical disinterested stance of academic discourse is inappropriate. But inherent in the metaphor of the physician at the bedside is the additional notion of the expert attending to the nonexpert. Kierkegaard uses the superior epistemological perspective of the physician as compared to the patient to undermine our sense that we are competent judges of our own spiritual health (SUD, 23/SKS 11, 139).

Merold Westphal emphasizes this motif of expert perspective in his analysis of Kierkegaard on unconscious despair:

> Just as we take it for granted in the physical realm that a person with a serious problem of high blood pressure or cancer may at a given time feel perfectly comfortable and well, so Kierkegaard wants to claim that in the realm of the spirit the patient's report that all is well stands open to correction by the physician whose knowledge makes for a more reliable judgment.[33]

Appeal to Repressed Dimensions of Experience

While Kierkegaard says that unconscious despair is "the most common in the world" (SUD, 45/SKS 11, 160) and describes that despair as potentially "cozy and comfortable" (SUD, 34/SKS 11, 150), a number of passages in *The Sickness unto Death* indicate that despair, even unconscious despair, always manifests itself somehow in the conscious life of the one in despair. One of the most important ways in which unconscious, repressed despair shows up is in the form of anxiety:

> Just as a physician might say that there very likely is not one single living human being who is completely healthy, so anyone who really knows mankind might say that there is not one single living human being who does not despair a little, who does not secretly harbor an unrest, an inner strife, a disharmony, an anxiety about an unknown something or a something he does not even dare to know, an anxiety about some possibility in existence or an anxiety about himself, so that, just as the physician speaks of going around with an illness in the body, he walks around with a sickness, carries around a sickness of the spirit that signals its presence at rare intervals in and through an anxiety he cannot explain (SUD, 22/SKS 11, 138).

In saying that despair always "signals its presence," even if only episodically and indirectly, Kierkegaard identifies an epistemological basis for his assertion that "in the light of truth" apparently contented lives can be seen as despair, as living death.

Appeal to Retrospective Judgment

In cases where empirical evidence is ambiguous and claims to expertise are disputed, parties to a disagreement often appeal to an imagined future judgment of the case that will settle it decisively. The words "You'll be sorry!" that are often thrown out in the heat of argument invoke a future state of the self against whom one is arguing who will have come to share one's judgment on the matter. Similarly, martyrs for progressive causes often appeal to the judgment of history for their vindication.

Kierkegaard makes a strikingly eschatological appeal to retrospective judgment in support of his analysis of unconscious despair:

> And to me an even more horrible expression of this most terrible sickness and misery is that it is hidden—not only that the person suffering from it may wish to hide it and may succeed, not only that it can so live in a man that no one, no one detects it, no, but that it can be so hidden in a man that he himself is not aware of it! And when the hourglass has run out, the hourglass of temporality, when the noise of secular life has grown

> silent and its restless and ineffectual activism has come to an end, when everything around you is still, as it is in eternity, then . . . eternity asks you and every individual in these millions and millions about only one thing: whether you have lived in despair or not (SUD, 27/SKS 11, 143).

Here, Kierkegaard imagines eternity as a doubly privileged vantage point. First, it is free of the distractions of temporal existence. Second, by personifying eternity as a questioner, Kierkegaard renders the reader starkly aware of his or her "being-for-another," here before an ideal other whose penetrating gaze lays us bare, banishing all self-deception.

A Hybrid Approach

Having reviewed three distinct epistemological bases for Kierkegaard's claim that "in the light of truth" apparent contentment can be seen to be unconscious despair, I venture that none by itself is compelling. Socrates long ago taught us to be wary of so-called experts; if personal experience were a clear signal of despair, Kierkegaard would not have any need for the category of unconscious despair; the bare possibility of a radically different assessment of my present condition at some future moment can hardly override the evidence of how my condition seems to me now.

Though subject to challenge when considered alone, these three epistemological themes make a much more compelling case when combined. One version of such a combination occurs in a psychotherapeutic situation. The analysand, guided by an expert, the analyst, reflects on present and past experience to achieve enlightened self-understanding. Read in this way, *The Sickness unto Death* creates a vicarious therapeutic situation for his readers. The pseudonym, Anti-Climacus, represents himself as an expert as he discusses the forms and sources of despair. Insofar as his anthropological theory and taxonomic discussions of despair allow readers greater insight into their own murky struggles toward selfhood, his self-presentation as expert will win acceptance.

The Freudian echoes of this way of combining the three approaches seems strikingly modernist and much more in keeping with a "dark genesis" sense of the self's depths. Truer to Kierkegaard's actual project is the metaphor of a spiritual guide or confessor. (This is evident in the subtitle of *The Sickness unto Death: A Christian Psychological Exposition for Upbuilding and Awakening.*) Here, the authority of the spiritual physician is not simply a function of the analysand's felt satisfaction over insight achieved. That authority is also, even primarily, a function of the revealed truth about the cosmic order in whose name the confessor speaks. The dialectical interplay between insight and authority is at the heart of much of Kierkegaard's authorship, so it is not surprising to find it implicit in his analysis of despair as living death.

Conclusion

In this chapter, I've shown that a central element in Kierkegaard's analysis of despair is his use of the metaphor of living death. While that metaphor has strong resonance and wins easy acceptance in the case of conscious despair, his use of it in the case of unconscious despair runs counter to a number of main currents of modernity and cannot but offend and perplex many contemporary readers. Given that Kierkegaard's aim is to jolt readers into radical reappraisals of their own spiritual condition, it makes perfect sense that he would employ jarring metaphors in his project. Whether we are ultimately convinced that this metaphor is apt or not, our reaction to it serves as an occasion for the sort of self-examination Kierkegaard attempted to provoke throughout his authorship.

NOTES

The first epigraph is from SUD, 18/SKS 11, 133.

The second epigraph is from Walker Percy, *The Moviegoer* (New York: Vintage, 1998), pp. 99–100.

1. Mary Douglas, *Purity and Danger* (New York: Routledge, 1991).

2. After initially planning to publish *The Sickness unto Death* under his own name, Kierkegaard attributed the book to Anti-Climacus in recognition of his personal failure to meet the ideal demands laid out there. Rather than using pseudonymity to back away from the bold claims of the text, Kierkegaard uses it to underline how seriously he takes the diagnosis of the human condition offered by Anti-Climacus: "The difference from the earlier pseudonyms is simply but essentially this, that I do not retract the whole thing humorously but identify myself as one who is striving" (SUD, xx/SKS 22, 151).

3. I discuss "The Unhappiest One" in "Four Funerals: The Experience of Time by the Side of the Grave," in *International Kierkegaard Commentary: Prefaces and Writing Sampler and Three Discourses on Imagined Occasions,* ed. Robert L. Perkins, pp. 425–31 (Macon, Ga.: Mercer University Press, 2006).

4. Diogenes Laertius, *Diogenes Laertius, Lives of Eminent Philosophers,* trans. R. D. Hicks (Cambridge, Mass.: Harvard University Press, 1979–80), vol. II, p. 650.

5. Patrick Stokes carefully works out the exact nature of Kierkegaard's disagreement with Epicurus in "The Power of Death: Retroactivity, Narrative, and

Interest," in *International Kierkegaard Commentary: Prefaces and Writing Sampler and Three Discourses on Imagined Occasions,* ed. Robert L. Perkins, pp. 387–417 (Macon, Ga.: Mercer University Press, 2006).

6. Stokes also uses Tolstoy's novel to shine light on Kierkegaard's understanding of death and dying. Stokes, "The Power of Death," p. 412.

7. Leo Tolstoy, *The Death of Ivan Ilyich,* trans. Lynn Solotaroff (New York: Bantam, 1981), p. 114.

8. Tolstoy, *The Death of Ivan Ilyich,* p. 122.

9. The relevance of narrative unity to Kierkegaard's thought is the topic of a series of exchanges between Anthony Rudd, John Davenport, and John Lippitt. In their introduction to *Kierkegaard After MacIntyre: Essays on Freedom, Narrative and Virtue* (Chicago: Open Court, 2001), John Davenport and Anthony Rudd describe MacIntyre's understanding of human life in narrative terms as "particularly Kierkegaardian." John Lippitt critiques that linkage in "Telling Tales: Johannes Climacus and 'Narrative Unity,'" in *Kierkegaard Studies Yearbook 2005,* ed. Niels Jørgen Cappelørn and Herman Deuser, pp. 71–89 (Berlin: de Gruyter, 2005); and "Getting the Story Straight: Kierkegaard, MacIntyre and Some Problems with Narrative," *Inquiry* 50, no. 1 (Feb. 2007): pp. 34–69. Rudd has responded with "Kierkegaard, MacIntyre and Narrative Unity—Reply to Lippitt," *Inquiry* 50, no. 5 (Oct. 2007): pp. 541–49; "Reason in Ethics Revisited: *Either/Or,* 'Criterionless Choice' and Narrative Unity," in *Kierkegaard Studies Yearbook 2008,* ed. Niels Jørgen Cappelørn and Herman Deuser, pp. 179–99 (Berlin: de Gruyter, 2008); and "In Defence of Narrative," *European Journal of Philosophy* 17, no. 1 (Jan. 2009): pp. 60–75. See also John J. Davenport's contribution to this volume, "Life-Narrative and Death as the End of Freedom: Kierkegaard on Anticipatory Resoluteness."

10. For a sustained discussion of this theme, see Stokes, "The Power of Death."

11. Tolstoy, *The Death of Ivan Ilyich,* p. 122.

12. Tolstoy, *The Death of Ivan Ilyich,* p. 126.

13. "The person in despair cannot die; 'no more than the dagger can slaughter thoughts' can despair consume the eternal, the self at the root of despair, whose worm does not die and whose fire is not quenched" (SUD, 18/SKS 11, 134).

14. Andrew Solomon, *The Noonday Demon: An Atlas of Depression* (New York: Scribner, 2001), pp. 19–20.

15. Merold Westphal, "Kierkegaard's Psychology and Unconscious Despair," in *International Kierkegaard Commentary: The Sickness unto Death,* ed. Robert L. Perkins, p. 50 (Macon, Ga.: Mercer University Press, 1897).

16. Westphal, "Kierkegaard's Psychology and Unconscious Despair," p. 51.

17. Westphal, "Kierkegaard's Psychology and Unconscious Despair," p. 51.

18. Westphal, "Kierkegaard's Psychology and Unconscious Despair," p. 51.

19. See Merold Westphal, *Suspicion and Faith: The Religious Uses of Modern Atheism* (New York: Fordham University Press, 1999).

20. Charles Taylor, *A Secular Age* (Cambridge, Mass.: Harvard University Press, 2007), p. 348.

21. Taylor, *A Secular Age*, p. 348.

22. Taylor, *A Secular Age*, p. 348.

23. Taylor, *A Secular Age*, p. 349. Taylor offers a parallel analysis, also quite brief, in *The Sources of the Self* (Cambridge, Mass.: Harvard University Press, 1989), pp. 189–90.

24. Richard Rorty, *Contingency, Irony, and Solidarity* (Cambridge: Cambridge University Press, 1989), p. 73.

25. Taylor, *Sources of the Self*, p. xv.

26. Alasdair MacIntyre, *After Virtue: A Study in Moral Theory*, 2nd ed. (Notre Dame, Ind.: University of Notre Dame Press, 1984), p. 254.

27. Alasdair MacIntyre, *Whose Justice? Which Rationality?* (Notre Dame, Ind.: University of Notre Dame Press, 1989), p. 336.

28. MacIntyre, *Whose Justice? Which Rationality?*, p. 338.

29. John Rawls, *A Theory of Justice*, 4th ed. (Cambridge, Mass.: Harvard University Press, 2001), p. 486.

30. Taylor, *A Secular Age*, pp. 1–3.

31. Taylor, *A Secular Age*, p. 242.

32. Taylor, *A Secular Age*, p. 262.

33. Westphal, "Kierkegaard's Psychology and Unconscious Despair," p. 50.

2.

To Die and Yet Not Die: Kierkegaard's Theophany of Death

Simon D. Podmore

Introduction: Knowing Death and Knowing Thyself

> *Periissem, nisi periissem* [I would have perished, had I not perished] still is and will be my life motto. This is why I have been able to endure what long since would have killed someone else who was not dead.[1]
>
> —KIERKEGAARD, *SØREN KIERKEGAARD'S JOURNALS AND PAPERS*

Confessing in this journal entry from 1848 that, without dying willingly, death would have prevailed over him, Kierkegaard discloses how a life of suffering has prevented death from laying its claim to one who was already dead. Kierkegaard's appropriation of the Latin aphorism further expresses an integral spiritual dialectic at the heart of Lutheran Christian subjectivity, that is, the power of a metaphorical or symbolic death to deliver the soul from the prospect of its actual eternal death. Or, more existentially, the voluntary death to oneself by which the self is delivered from its own living spiritual death: an undead condition of the self—articulated by Kierkegaard through the rubric of despair—that anticipates or forebodes its final, absolute death at the conclusion of a life unconscious, or defiant, of the recognition that it exists inexorably *before God.*

Kierkegaard's life motto can thus be read as evoking the themes of this present chapter in two important respects. First, the notion that it is via a metaphorical submission to "death" that the self will transcend the reach of absolute death. Secondly, that "dying to" is a *process,* which causes the self to be negated, to vanish, to become as nothing *before God.* And it is precisely by this "disappearing"—or by coming to what *The Sickness unto*

Death calls a self-resting "transparently [*gjennemsigtigt*—'see-through'] in the power that established it" (SUD, 14/SKS 11, 130)—that the self will not be "annihilated" before God, even though the thought of existing before God is fraught by the anxious prospect of the biblical injunction that to see God is to die (Exod. 33:20).

At the dialectical axis of the self's relation to death, therefore, resides a characteristically ambivalent *anxiety,* a relation that Vigilius Haufniensis informs us is always "sympathetic and antipathetic," an ambivalent serpentine dance of fascination and revulsion (CA, 103/SKS 4, 405). In this sense, death constitutes a *mysterium tremendum et fascinans,* a mystery to be both feared and desired. Death is the secret "unknown" that simultaneously holds the key to self-knowledge, and also to the self's own destruction. Furthermore, it is precisely the God-given *eternity* of the soul—described by Anti-Climacus in terms of "eternity's claim upon" the self (SUD, 21/SKS 11, 137)—which grounds the self's meditations upon the paradoxical meaning and mystery of its own "death." In other words, it is from the purportedly divine ground (*grund*) of being that the soul contemplates the abyss (*Afgrund*) of its nonbeing.

Such a theological vision of death—a vision that potentially mystifies the boundaries between immortality and mortality, being and nonbeing, annihilation and salvation—is contaminated by an anxiety from whose numinous clutches more materialistic philosophy has sought to emancipate the human subject. "Why should I fear death?" as the Hellenistic philosopher Epicurus (c. 341–271 BCE) famously reflected. "If I am, death is not. If death is, I am not. Why should I fear that which cannot exist when I do?"[2] Stemming from an organic belief in the mortality and materiality of the soul, Epicurus thus asserts what in subsequently Kierkegaardian terms one might call an epistemological "infinite qualitative difference" between death and life. Death cannot coexist alongside the mortal soul, thus there is no need to contemplate the anxious prospect of experiencing death, or annihilation—let alone the scrupulous anxiety of judgment, damnation, or salvation. If there is an ineffable abyss of unknowing between life and death, then any contemplation of death is destined to fail to yield any greater knowledge of the soul.

Such Epicurean reflections upon death are clearly distinguished from the Christian vision of death as a gateway to knowledge of God and the true immortal self. Death as unknowable annihilation, or nothingness, is in sharp ostensible contrast to the biblical notion that fear of death (which, according to Hegel, is signified by the Absolute Lord or Master) is the beginning of all wisdom (Prov. 1:7; 9:10; Psalm 111:10).[3] Insofar as

Kierkegaard's vision of the self can be described as a modern inheritor of the Christian belief in the immortality or eternity of the soul, his writings relate a consequent rhetorical blurring of any absolute distinction (or difference) between life and death—particularly where the struggle for subjectivity is described. The contemplation of death in all its poetic, spiritual, and visceral forms thereby becomes a mysterious and fecund wellspring of hidden self-knowledge and knowledge of the divine. And yet, as Kierkegaard's rhetoric of the self before God recognizes only too well, such a conviction concerning the eternity of the soul also implicitly opens the way for the most dreadful spiritual and existential possibilities of a *living death:* despair, the melancholy fear of damnation, and the most dreadful living death of all (a living death that foreshadows the eternal death of the soul), the spiritual trial (*Anfægtelse*) of God-forsakenness.

Confirming this realization, it quickly becomes clear that when one immerses oneself in Kierkegaard's writings one is confronted by a relation between self and God that finds its most arresting descriptions in terms of a sickness unto death, a desire to behold a God whose face (*panim*—presence) brings the fear of annihilation and an inescapable "death struggle" (JP, 4:438/SKS 26, 238), a mortal conflict in which the individual strives paradoxically "to be over 70,000 fathoms and yet be joyful" (SLW, 477/SKS 6, 439). This anxious ambivalence between fear and desire, life and death, conveys a dialectical tension repeatedly evoked throughout the imagery of Kierkegaard's vision of selfhood. In order to "know thyself" according to one of Kierkegaard's earliest injunctions, for instance, one must become willing to undergo what Johannes Climacus succinctly calls "the autopsy of faith" (PF, 70/SKS 4, 270). By faith's dissection of one's most interior spaces, the self becomes able to see itself (Greek: *autos*—self; *optos*—seen) and therefore to begin to know itself through an initial anatomy of its own disintegration. Of course, it is only postmortem that an autopsy is performed, and so it is that one must die to oneself in the autopsy of faith. And yet this is no meager undertaking. "It is well known that men are afraid to see themselves physically, that superstition thought that to see oneself was an omen of death" Kierkegaard explains, "And so it is spiritually: to see yourself is to die, to die to all illusions and all hypocrisy—it takes great courage to dare look at yourself—something which can only take place in the mirror of the Word" (JP, 4:40/SKS 24, 425).

It is via such dialectical junctures that the positive is revealed in the negative—that life is revealed in death and death in life. For example, it is, according to Anti-Climacus's diagnosis, the very recognition of primal despair, "the sickness unto death," that actually reveals to the individual the eternal life of the self, the initial presentiment of an inner hellfire that burns but does not devour the soul. Therefore, it could be discerned that it is not so much the fear of death as the material annihilation of the body, or the inevitable decay of being to nonbeing, that is central to Kierkegaard's vision of self-knowledge. Rather it is the self's reconciliation to the unrealizable prospect of its own metaphorical living death that is primary to knowing the self—specifically the self as it is known *before God.* It is to this emerging recognition that attention now turns. By coming to terms with this existential reality, therefore, the ground will be laid for the notion that while Kierkegaardian selfhood is initially fraught with the melancholy and despair of a metaphorical living death, it is ultimately the self as it is known "before God" that promises deliverance from the abyss of the fear of death and judgment[4] via the infinite qualitative difference of divine forgiveness. However, before contemplating the prospect of this theophany of death (the second sphere) and the subsequent death to self (the third sphere) that the divine mirror requires of the individual, one must first anatomize the primal sickness unto death of the human condition, the first sphere of the living death of despair.

First Sphere: "Not Buried, Yet Dead": The Living Death of Despair

In 1836 a lyrically precocious young Kierkegaard formulated the dramatically all-embracing diagnosis that "[t]he present age is the age of despair, the age of the wandering Jew (many reforming Jews)" (JP, 1:343/SKS 27, 207). According to Kierkegaard's assessment, it is the melancholic iconography of the Semitic exile, Ahasverus, the Wandering Jew—a memorial figure of God-forsakenness, alienation, nihilism, and estrangement—that typifies the modern consciousness. This melancholy archetype can be traced from the Adamic banishment, via the homelessness of Cain, to the medieval legends and Romantic literary myths of the Jew who spurned Christ and was cursed to wander the earth, a fugitive from redemption, until judgment day. But more than being a thread of alienation woven through the tapestry of human history, the Wandering Jew, as George Pattison summarizes, "symbolizes for Kierkegaard the despair of the present age, a despair rooted in its separation from its substantial ground of religion and manifesting itself in both political reform movements and philosophical nihilism."[5] One might therefore say that the Wandering Jew of Kierkegaard's nineteenth century is the illegitimate son of a modern humanism whose tragedy can be traced to his severance from the lifegiving light of soteriological hope. His despair is thus, in Kierkegaardian terms, an eternal sickness unto death, without alleviation and without relation to a lifegiving creator, a half-life endured within the lacuna of a vanishing Absolute. "The Wandering Jew," as Kierkegaard therefore muses, "seems to have his prototype in the fig tree Christ commanded to wither away [Matt. 21:19]" (SKS 19, 95). The Wandering Jew is therefore taken to be an icon of God-forsaken existence, seeking an elusive redemption in the soul-withering twilight between life and death.

For Kierkegaard, this Romantic motif of the Wandering Jew, by conveying the "undead" and perennially abyssal elements of the human condition, provides an apposite and evocatively hubristic image for the living death of the modern melancholy self. What is more, the Wandering Jew's melancholic motif of abject immortality is further reminiscent of an expressly Romantic meditation from Kierkegaard's young aesthete A: namely *Either/Or*'s reflection upon the pitiable plight of "The Unhappiest One."[6] The phrase itself consciously recalls Hegel's numerous considerations of the "Unhappy Consciousness," but in Kierkegaard's poetic reflection the title refers directly to the mysterious adornment on a gravestone in England. A, in this address, considers the meaning of the legend in light of the apparently ironic supposition that the tomb itself is mysteriously empty. Could this absence mean that there is no such person as the Unhappiest One? Or is this tombstone essentially a monument to a secret and melancholy truth? "Then why the tomb was empty could be explained," he conjectures, "namely, to indicate that the unhappiest one was the one who could not die, could not slip down into a grave" (EO, 1:220/SKS 2, 214). As such, the Unhappiest One is one who is consigned to wander perpetually in his longing to rest in the grave that awaits and yet remains continually elusive to him.

This despair is later conceptually paralleled by Anti-Climacus's survey in *The Sickness unto Death* that "the torment of this despair is precisely this inability to die . . . to be sick unto death is to be unable to die" (SUD, 18/SKS 11, 133). And so Kierkegaard returns us stylistically to the despair of the present age, the despair of the age of the Wandering Jew, the withering fig tree: "the sickness unto death, this tormenting contradiction, this sickness of the self, perpetually to be dying, to die and yet not die, to die death" (SUD, 18/SKS 11, 134).

Yet A's discourse is also a commentary on Hegel's Unhappy Consciousness:

> In all of Hegel's systematic works there is one section that discusses the unhappy consciousness. One always comes to the reading of such

> investigations with an inner uneasiness and palpitation of the heart, with a fear that one will learn too much or too little. . . . Ah, happy is the one who has nothing more to do with the subject than to write a paragraph about it; even happier the one who can write the next. The unhappy one is the person who in one way or another has his ideal, the substance of his life, the plenitude of his consciousness, his essential nature, outside himself. The unhappy one is the person who is always absent from himself, never present to himself (EO, 1:222/SKS 2, 215–16).

This reference further reinforces the latent connection between the living death of despair and the anxiety over the loss or death of God to which the Wandering Jew had also alluded. Hegel had explicitly identified the relation between loss of "self" and loss of "God" in terms of the alienation expressed by the Unhappy Consciousness. The Unhappy Consciousness, as it experiences "the conscious loss of itself and the alienation of its knowledge about itself," expresses its anguish in the "hard saying that 'God is dead.'"[7] In this lament over the death of God, the Unhappy Consciousness implicitly testifies to a loss of hope in the triumph of life over death—a despair before the horrifyingly visceral vision of the crucified God at Golgotha as well as over the more symptomatically modern *horror vacui* of the absence of God—and consequently a potential despair over salvation, which Anti-Climacus shall render in more explicit terms in *The Sickness unto Death.* This is the expression of an "infinite grief" existing historically as "the feeling that 'God Himself is dead,' upon which the religion of more recent times rests; the same feeling that Pascal expressed in, so to speak, empirical form: 'Nature is such that it *signifies* everywhere a *lost* God both within and outside man.'"[8]

The melancholy of the undead self thereby finds itself intractably bound, consciously or unconsciously, to death, specifically the death, loss, or absence of God. Within Kierkegaard's writings, however, the mood of melancholy (*melancholi/Tungsind*) also encapsulates the sense of secular vanity and boredom incurred by an existence drained of existential and spiritual meaning. Such *ennui* is expressed once again by the melancholic A, for whom the abyss of boredom once again takes on the elegiac complexion of a living death: "My soul is like the Dead Sea, over which no bird is able to fly; when it has come midway, it sinks down, exhausted, to death and destruction" (EO, 1:37/SKS 2, 46). A's rhetoric of existence as a living death expresses in agonizingly poeticized form the melancholy known to the modern aesthete.[9] However, as his dialectical counterpart Judge William strives to elicit, such a lyrically self-indulgent melancholy fails to fully realize the abyssal depths of despair—a state that is later diagnosed by Anti-Climacus as a sickness unto death, a profound misrelation between self and *God.* Nonetheless, while perhaps evading the more radically "eternal obligations" of the self before God, the Unhappy Consciousness, the Unhappiest One, and the Wandering Jew mutually express the self's interminable and ultimately unrealizable longing for death as the means of emancipating itself from the melancholy dis-ease of despair. All are implicitly allied to Anti-Climacus's insistence that despair is expressed as an inner hellfire that, by virtue of its inability to devour the self, indirectly attests to the irrevocable eternity of the self. The root of existence as a living death is actually discovered in the depths of despair, a diagnosis that also points toward its cure in the form of "dying-to" this existence of despair.[10] Every human being, according to Anti-Climacus, is mutually allied under "the sickness unto death" (despair) and in consequent, if unconscious, need of salvation from this universal disease of isolated selfhood. In this regard, Anti-Climacus scrutinizes the phenomenon of despair, in its conscious and unconscious forms, and discerns within it something reminiscent of the Socratic proof, via intractable inner suffering, of the universal immortality of the soul:

> Socrates [Plato, *Republic,* X, 609d] demonstrated the immortality of the soul from the fact that sickness of the soul (sin) does not consume it as sickness of the body consumes the body. Thus, the eternal in a person can be demonstrated by the fact that despair cannot consume his self. . . . If there were nothing eternal in a man, he could not despair at all; if despair could consume his self, then there would be no despair at all (SUD, 20–21/SKS 11, 136).

Hence, a "cold fire" of despair ignites within the nascent self and, by its "impotent self-consuming," implicitly affirms the indestructible but anguished presence of the eternal within (SUD, 18/SKS 11, 134). The torturous living death of the self's inability to be itself and the impossibility of knowing itself paradoxically assert the inviolable and primal reality of the unrealized self. Yet as long as this "self" is not yet known as a self *before God,* its inward reality is felt as the living death of despair. Again, the fact that the self is at once sick unto death and yet unable to will its own death testifies to the tormenting yet indelible stigmata of eternity upon the self. At its hidden wellspring, the dark heart of despair is revealed as a will toward death, a desire to achieve suicide as a means of escaping the interminable living death that is the sickness unto death of despair (SUD, 20/

SKS 11, 136). But even if one wishes to evade despair by refusing to become conscious of it, refusing to become conscious of the self, then eternity will reveal one's despair to oneself and "nail him to himself" so that he cannot escape himself or his despair (SUD, 21/SKS 11, 136).

The self that is crucified to itself by despair is indeed an apposite and evocative image for the obligation of eternity. Eternity thus enforces the anguished consciousness of an unrealizable living death upon the self. The self thus bears the hidden wounds of eternity's stigmata: the wounds of death in one living. This despair is eternity's dreadful obligation upon the self, but it is also the birth-pain of the metamorphosis of spirit [*ånd*]. As such, despair is the wound of a double-edged sword, both a gift and an obligation: "Eternity is obliged to do this, because to have a self, to be a self, is the greatest concession, an infinite concession, given to man, but it is also eternity's claim upon him" (SUD, 21/SKS 11, 137). And it is this obligation of eternity, this metamorphosis of spirit, that hopes to drive the self out from the reclusive shadows of melancholy's living death and into the illuminating and salvific light of living transparently *before God.*

Second Sphere: The Theophany of Death

This realization does not, however, bring an end to the prospect of death. By standing before God, the self does not merely escape the shadow of death through simply recognizing the heterogeneous power of eternity over itself. Indeed, the *tremendum* of eternity's claim upon the self may induce an even deeper abyss of anxiety and despair before God. The recognition that there is a Wholly Other God before whose numinous gaze one is accountable may in fact cause the self to feel, even more acutely than melancholy's lifeless existence, the living death of its separation from the eternal, the abyssal depth and breadth of the "infinite qualitative difference" between self and God. One may easily become, as Kierkegaard describes in a student sermon in 1842, "crushed by the thought that you were a nothing and your soul lost in infinite space" (JP, 4:50–51/SKS 27, 251). To such a lost soul, it may appear that in some way God has become nothing but the abyss itself—the infinitely forbidding difference between humanity and divinity, the holy abyss that overwhelms the eye with dizziness. Indeed, the potential for such anxiety over God-forsakenness (the ultimate spiritual living death, "the last spiritual trial [*Anfægtelse*]" [JP, 4:423/SKS 25, 151]) resides latently within each individual soul: "Deep within every human being there still lives the anxiety over the possibility of being alone in the world, forgotten by God, overlooked among the millions and millions in this enormous household" (JP, 1:40/SKS 20, 230).

At this point, the rise in the consciousness of the eternal thus entails an emerging reciprocal awareness that "God and man are two qualities separated by an infinite qualitative difference [*uendelig Qualitets-Forskjel*]" (SUD, 126/SKS 11, 237). As such, the shadow of death emerges once more in this infinite difference as the individual comes to the ominous realization that "[a]s sinner, man is separated from God by the most chasmic qualitative abyss [*Qvalitetens meest svælgende Dyb*]" (SUD, 122/SKS 11, 233). Here, as the consciousness of sin asserts itself within the self before God, the abyss (*Afgrund*) between the human and the divine yawns wide open, revealing a vertiginous mass of darkness into which one fears to fall, in which one loses the ground (*grund*) on which the self endeavors to stand before God. The prospect of death emerges from the very heart of darkness, which divides humanity and God. Hence, for the anxious gaze of the sinner, "the conception of God's holiness [*Guds Hellighed*]" weighs "more heavily than the sleep of death." The sinner becomes "like one dying," unable to gaze upon the God in whom one sought salvation, choosing instead to close one's eyes and contemplate the inner darkness of death (WA, 130/SKS 11, 266). Perhaps then all that remains is to succumb to despair, to plunge into the hedonistic abyss of sin, and embrace the vanity of life and death: "Let us eat and drink, because tomorrow we shall die" (1 Cor. 15:32). And yet, as Kierkegaard discerns, "[t]his very remark echoes with the anxiety about the next day, the day of annihilation, the anxiety that insanely is supposed to signify joy although it is a shriek from the abyss [*Afgrunden*]" (CD, 77/SKS 10, 86). It seems that even the hedonistic flight from the abyss of human-divine *alterity* and into the intoxicating abyss of sinfulness is not immune from the anxiety of death. Authentic existence before God must therefore be derived from a courageous engagement with the abyss itself. "Just as the shipwrecked person who saved himself by means of a plank and now, tossed by the waves and hovering over the abyss [*Afgrunden*] between life and death, strains his eyes for land, so indeed should a person be concerned about his salvation" (CD, 220/SKS 10, 228).

And yet the question Kierkegaard refuses to shrink from is: How can one gaze toward the promised land of salvation, while "hovering over the abyss, between life and death," if "the conception of God's holiness" weighs "more heavily than the sleep of death"? In other words, how can one gaze upon a God whom none may see and live? Here, in more explicitly optical terms, is the anxious theophany of death that appears at the same time to both promise life and threaten death to the self: "[N]o wonder then that the Jews assumed that the sight of God was death and the pagans that the God-relationship was the harbinger of madness" (CUP, 1:484/SKS 7, 439).[11] Likewise, Judge William also comments that "the person who saw God must die. [But] This was only a figurative expression, it is literal and true that one loses one's mind in the same way as the lover does when he sees the beloved and, which he also does, sees God" (SLW, 122/SKS 6, 115–16). Kierkegaard here draws upon a traditionally Christian meditation upon death rooted in the biblical notion that none may see the face of God and live. Such a prospective theophany of death is itself a potential source of further melancholy and a proliferation of the notion that all existence is defined by an inescapable tension between life and death.

Such a melancholy meditation is already realized within Augustine's implicitly Neoplatonic appropriation of this biblical idiom. Augustine earlier expresses the restless and melancholic desire for God with a similar evocation of the paradoxical longing for life in the midst of death: "Hide not Thy face from me. Even if I die, let me see Thy face lest I die."[12] This maxim returns us to the ambivalent tension between life and death invoked by Kierkegaard's own "life motto": *periissem, nisi periissem.* The absence of the face of the Divine Beloved means an arid living death; the theophany of the Divine Face promises life at the paradoxical cost of annihilation. This death-melancholy, as Johannes Climacus pertinently observes, can also be discerned from the perspective of the divine: "There was a people who had a good understanding of the divine; this people believed that to see the god was death.—Who grasps the contradiction of this sorrow: not to disclose itself is the death of love; to disclose itself is the death of the beloved" (PF, 30/SKS 4, 236).

Returning to the more familiar human perspective, existing as a self before God therefore seems to capture the individual once again in a living death—stranded between the melancholy absence of God and the self-annihilating prospect of a theophany of death. The conception of God thus appears to promise desolation over salvation. Before the conception of God, the self therefore feels closer to death than life, imprisoned more than liberated, as Johannes Climacus describes:

> But the bird in the cage, the fish on the beach, the invalid on his sickbed, and the prisoner in the narrowest prison cell are not as captive as the person who is captive in his conception of God, because, just as God is, the captivating conception is everywhere present and at every moment (CUP, 1:484/SKS 7, 438–39).

This harrowing element within Kierkegaard's depictions of existing before God is further enforced in the words of Johannes's "higher" namesake Anti-Climacus:

> To exist before God may seem unendurable to a man because he cannot come back to himself, become himself. Such a fantasized religious person would say (to characterize him by means of some lines): "That a sparrow can live is comprehensible; it does not know that it exists before God. But to know that one exists before God, and then not instantly go mad or sink into nothingness" (SUD, 32/SKS 11, 148).

Such a "fantastic" (*Phantastiske*) vision of the *mysterium horrendum* evoked by the prospect of existing before God may inevitably elicit despair's deicidal retaliation toward a theophany of death. In this sense, atheism emerges within the self in despair as a defiant or demonic response to the divine gaze of death. "To see God is to die"; or else, as is well illustrated by Nietzsche's infamous inversion, "The god who saw everything, *even man*—this god had to die!" In Nietzsche's mythology the "death of God" is itself initiated by an ostensibly Lutheran sense of the guilt-inducing voyeuristic gaze of God. It is the "Ugliest Man" who murdered "God" because he could neither bear the intrusion of "God's" witness to his shame, nor could he shake his resentment of "God's" pity for him:

> But he *had to* die: he saw with eyes that saw everything; he saw man's depths and ultimate grounds, all his concealed disgrace and ugliness. His pity knew no shame: he crawled into my dirtiest nooks. This most curious, overobtrusive, overpitying one had to die. He always saw me: on such a witness I wanted to have revenge or not live myself. The god who saw everything, *even man*—this god had to die! Man cannot bear it that such a witness live.[13]

Here it may be revealing to further illustrate this act of deicide in terms of Hegel's account of the dialectical struggle for self-consciousness between the self and the other. To see God is to die; "each seeks the death of the other."[14] Indeed Emmanuel Levinas remarks, "In [Kierkegaardian] belief, existence is always trying to secure recognition for itself, just like consciousness in Hegel. It struggles for this recognition by seeking forgiveness and salvation."[15] But in the despair of defiant unbelief, as well as belief, consciousness seeks recognition for itself—albeit in the struggle to free itself from the gaze of a God who declares that consciousness must recognize itself through the eyes of a Wholly Other. Perhaps such an analogous struggle for a consciousness emancipated from the gaze of the LORD could also be read in Hegel, as has been suggested.[16]

According to Hegel's dialectic of "Independence and Dependence of Self-Consciousness: Lordship and Bondage," a self-consciousness confronted by another self-consciousness strives to overcome what it perceives as the threat of "this otherness of itself."[17] But this perceived threat is reciprocal. A shared mutuality of self-consciousness threatens to disrupt the sovereign subjectivity of each "being-for-self." And so, aptly, the conflict begins with a gaze: "They *recognize* themselves as *mutually recognizing* one another."[18] Hegel thus describes a struggle based upon a recognition of the reciprocity of the other, based on an antagonistic and recognized mutuality between the gaze of the self and the gaze of the other, and not on what Jacques Derrida identifies as "this abyssal dissymmetry"[19] between the gaze of the *mysterium tremendum* (the Wholly Other) and one's own. The threat of annihilation is mutual and is not founded upon the ontological oppression of the individual by the absolute: "they prove themselves and each other through a life-and-death struggle."[20]

Yet it is through this struggle that the bondsman "has experienced the fear of death, the absolute Lord."[21] Hegel apparently evokes the God of the Old Testament at the point when he declares that "fear of the lord is indeed the beginning of wisdom."[22] But Kierkegaard asserts an infinite qualitative difference between the divine and the human, and therefore between God and the "thought of God." Kierkegaard was emphatic that "one cannot kill God; on the other hand, as is said, one certainly can kill the thought of Him . . . becoming oneself the master instead of the bondservant" (CD, 66–67/SKS 10, 75). The dreadful theophany of Anti-Climacus's "fantasized religious person" itself derives from a "fantastic" (*Phantastiske*) conception of what it means to exist before God. For this "fantasized" individual, existing before God seems ontologically unendurable: madness or annihilation present themselves as the only resolutions for the tension between infinite and finite. But, crucially for Anti-Climacus, this self has become "fantastic" and therefore "leads a fantasized existence in abstract infinitizing or in abstract isolation, continually lacking its self, from which it moves further and further away" (SUD, 32/SKS 11, 148). It is through the "fantasy" of the imagination (*Phantasi*) that infinitizing can lose itself in the potentially delusional realm of the "fantastic." The danger is that "in fantasy this infinitizing can so sweep a man off his feet that his state is simply an intoxication" (SUD, 32/SKS 11, 148).

Likewise the despair of Nietzsche's Ugliest Man—a despair that descends into pathological deicide—results from a conception of God as, in Michel Haar's apposite description, "the dysfunctional projection of a persecution complex and a delirium of self-accusation. 'God' is only the hypostasis of a delirious bad conscience, magnified by the metaphysical dimension into a constant presence."[23] One cannot kill God, as Kierkegaard claims, "only the thought of God." In this sense, through despair one becomes only the assassin of the idol of one's own neurotic imagination. The death of God signifies the death of an element of the self in sublimated form. Furthermore, by discerning the self's implicit though frequently unrecognized dependence upon God, Kierkegaard warns that "[t]o slay God is the most dreadful suicide [*Selvmord*]" (CD, 67/SKS 10, 75). The fantastic theophany of death must therefore be supplanted by the divine promise of forgiveness as an expression of the self's deliverance, not only from the fear of death or annihilation before the Holy, but also from the melancholy dis-ease of a living death in separation from God (sin). The self's authentic self-becoming before God is ultimately characterized by a decisive deliverance of the self from the melancholy estrangement of the Unhappy Consciousness, the Unhappiest One, the despair of the Wandering Jew, and the prospective theophany of death. The remaining question is therefore how the self can exist before the God in whom there is salvation from the living death of estrangement without also succumbing to the "fantastic" despair by which to see God is to die. The resolution—described here as a third sphere in which the first and second spheres are dialectically reconciled—is once more found in death: namely, the death to self (spiritual trial—*Anfægtelse*) through which the gift of forgiveness and life may be realized.

Third Sphere: 'Spirit is to will to die'

It remains difficult to escape the sense in which, despite this postulation of deliverance from the sickness unto death, the God-relationship continues to appear for Kierkegaard as inescapable "suffering, anguish, a death struggle" (JP, 4:438/SKS 26, 238). Kierkegaard thus persists in describing the pathos of the God-relationship via the metaphors of death and dying: "there is a life and death battle between God and man; God hates man just as man hates God" (JP, 4:432/SKS 26, 22). Here Kierkegaard is expressing the inherent primal hostility that exists between God and "spiritless" humanity in contrast to that which most radically endangers the thought of God, namely modernity's obviation of the radical tensions required by the God-relationship. In doing so, Kierkegaard is polemically intent upon rehabilitating the sense of the death struggle, which he discerns as a radical implication of the infinite qualitative difference between humanity and divinity. It is only through undergoing a spiritual self-denial (*Anfægtelse*)—a death of the self that in despair wills to be itself—that the individual can become a self before God. By dying to the self (*mors mystica*) one will be saved from the prospect of dying before God (God-forsakenness). Kierkegaard thus claims that, contrary to prevailing bourgeois sensibilities, "God is indeed a human being's most appalling enemy, your mortal enemy, he wants you to die, die unto the world; he hates specifically that in which you naturally have your life, to which you cling with all your zest for life" (TM, 177/SKS 13, 227).[24]

To die unto the world and unto the "worldly" self, which in despair wills to be itself without God, thus involves a willingness to undergo the radical and mortally precarious metamorphosis of spirit (*ånd*).[25] But what is spirit? "Spirit is restlessness," as Kierkegaard describes it, and "Christianity is the most profound restlessness of existence—so it is in the New Testament" (JP, 4:255/SKS 27, 650). However, the mere recognition of spirit's restless longing does not equate to the fulfillment of a longing for the eternal that may appear to remain continually and frustratingly defied. Spirit is the inner longing for God; but it must strive in the inner and outer worlds of "spiritlessness" (*åndløsheden*). This restless agitation does not resolve itself in a fluent transmutation of the individual into spirit, since spirit struggles in an inner world divided against itself. "Flesh and blood or the sensate—and spirit are opposites. . . . From what do flesh and blood shrink from most of all? From dying. Consequently spirit is to will to die, to die to the world" (JP, 4:250/SKS 26, 156). As flesh and blood resist their transubstantiation, so spirit's restlessness is further manifest through mortal conflict between the individual and the divine, a conflict evocative of Jacob's struggle with the divine stranger at Beth'el (Gen. 32). For Kierkegaard, to become spirit thus incurs the grave danger of finding oneself out of one's element in spiritlessness: "Every creature feels best in its own element, can really live only there. The fish cannot live in the air, the bird cannot live in the water—and for spirit to have to live in an environment devoid of spirit means to die, agonizingly to die slowly so that death is a blessed relief" (TM, 78/SKS 13, 124). Again the notion of living death revives in relation to the metamorphosis of spirit. And here the source of this living death of despair is identified as the suffocation of spirit in a world of spiritlessness. Once again recalling the Socratic demonstration of the immortality of the soul, the undead suffering of despair is indicative of the presence and obligation of the eternal, in this instance the strife of spirit. Thus the presence of the eternal in an individual is further indicated by one's willingness to freely enter into the dark tomb of one's inner death and resurrection: "Just as one knows that an insect wants to become a butterfly when it begins to spin a cocoon" (JP, 4:432/SKS 26, 35).

Just as the sickness unto death has been described as an inner hellfire, which cannot devour the self, so Kierkegaard declares, "Spirit is fire. From this comes the frequent expression: As gold is purified in fire, in the same way the Christian is purified" (JP, 4:251/SKS 26, 211). Yet a mortal danger remains in the apparent prospect that not everyone who enters into this combustible tension between humanity and God will emerge transformed by the metamorphosis of spirit. "Spirit is fire," but there is, Kierkegaard warns, always a danger in casting oneself to the flames: "not all are burned out to spirit, a few are burned out to ashes—that is, they do not become spirit in the fire" (JP, 4:251/SKS 26, 211). And so the prospect of death remains central to the narrative of the self's journey to become itself before God. In this sense, Kierkegaard even ventures so far as to compare following Christ with not only living as if dead, but with the tortuous practice of vivisection "in which animals are 'kept alive in a state of death'" (SKS 27, 671).

The "essential expression" of this God-relationship is thus the struggle of "spiritual trial" (*Anfægtelse: fægte*—"fight"), an expression of the tension between spirit and spiritlessness signified by the infinite qualitative difference between humanity and God. The self's individual struggle with *Anfægtelse* thus itself evidently occupies a precarious position between life and death inversely reminiscent of the strife of spirit. As Johannes Climacus articulates in *Concluding Unscientific Postscript,* "captive in the absolute conception of God" the individual in *Anfægtelse* is captured like the bird imprisoned in a cage or like the fish stranded on the shore, "lying on the ground outside its element, so, too, the religious individual is captive, because absoluteness is not directly the element of a finite existence" (CUP, 1:483/SKS 7, 438). In other words, just as spirit languishes out of its environment in the world of spiritlessness, so the self before the absolute conception of God suffers from venturing out beyond its usual element.

In order to further express this forbidding incongruity, Johannes Climacus also describes *Anfægtelse* as "a nemesis [*Anfægtelsen er Nemesis*] upon the intense moments in the absolute relation" (CUP, 1:459/SKS 7, 417). *Anfægtelse* thus expresses the deadly opposition of the absolute against the individual, specifically the tension implicit in the sinful individual's fledgling attempt to relate to something Wholly Other. It is the strenuously high price for asserting the heterogeneous God-relationship; it is the suffering of desire, which must nonetheless refuse to succumb to the abandonment of the relationship itself. It may appear that God has abandoned the self, that salvation is *impossible,* but really the spiritual trial is to ensure that one does not abandon God, that one places faith in the triumph of divine *possibility* over human *impossibility.* Confronted with such abyssal incongruity, it may appear that death itself is preferable to this mortal struggle: "But a person is not to give in; he is to fight against it, thank God that God has *commanded* that one *ought* to pray to him, for otherwise it is hardly possible to force one's way through the spiritual trial [*Anfægtelse*]." Instead of succumbing to the living death of despair over sin, therefore, the believer is to deny oneself and place faith in the divine gift of forgiveness. The believer "is to remember that God is love, the God of patience and consolation, and that God is not one who adopts vain titles but is completely different from anything I am able to comprehend of what he says himself to be" (JP, 2:404/SKS 21, 105).

In order to endure such spiritual trial and die to self, Kierkegaard exhorts, one must ultimately seek to declare "Before you, O God, I am nothing; do with me as you will, let me suffer all this which almost drives me to madness; you are still the one to whom wisdom and understanding belong, the loving Father. . . . If this agony collides with a passionate self-centered willfulness which cannot become nothing before God, it must end with the sufferer losing his mind" (JP, 4:259/SKS 21, 114). In struggling against the temptation to believe that one has been forsaken by God and delivered over to eternal death, the individual in spiritual trial (*Anfægtelse*) is encouraged to look, above all, to the struggle of Christ (echoing Luther's affirmation of the *angefochtene christus*) in order to recognize what it truly means to die to self-will, to declare, as Christ did at Gethsemane, "not my will but thy will." Through faith in Christ, there is not only consolation but salvation by which such thoughts can be mastered (JP, 4:258/SKS 21, 113). The self before God therefore responds to the call of Christ to "come unto me" given to those "whose residence has been assigned among the grave," that is, according to Anti-Climacus, to the one who is "not buried, yet dead . . . belonging neither to life nor to death . . . you, too, come here, here is rest, and here is life" (PC, 18/SKS 12, 28).

Conclusion: "God desires to have Is"

> There is a beautiful expression which the common man uses about dying: that God or our Lord "brightens" for him. Accordingly, at the very time everything becomes darkest—for what is as dark as the grave—God "brightens" (JP, 1:335/SKS 18, 221–22).

This movement of faith in the face of despair evokes the true theophany of the self before God, a theophany of death to self, of forgiveness and acceptance, which finally delivers the self from the abyssal despair of the melancholy theophany of death. This (characteristically Lutheran) transition from the prospect of annihilation before God to grace through Christ is analogously expressed by Johannes Climacus's allegory of the king who takes on a lower guise in order to enter into a relationship with the lowly maiden. In order to mitigate the apparently fatal consequences of a theophany for the human soul (and the divine grief over being unable to express the fullness of love), a human-divine love-relationship is only possible via a gracious divine descent to the lowliness of the maiden. In this allegory, the incognito of "the god" thereby becomes a divine concession of the lover to the beloved, "for he did not want his own glorification but the girl's" (PF, 29/SKS 4, 236). Despite the inherent primal fear of ontological extinction, despite the fact that one *imagines* that one will sink into nothingness before God, one is decisively *not* annihilated but reconciled through a gracious act of divine love, which makes room for the *life* of the self. In other (avowedly imperfect and human) words, divine love becomes the moderation of divine omnipotence, as Kierkegaard himself expresses elsewhere:

> It is said that God's omnipotence crushes a human being. But it is not so; no man is so much that God needs omnipotence to crush him, because for omnipotence he is nothing. It is God's love that even in the last moment manifests his love by making him to be something for it (CD, 128/SKS 10, 139).

As such, omnipotence, intriguingly and apparently contradictorily, actually ensures human life and freedom, rather than bringing the absolute death that the individual has come to fear. Human independence is the gift of divine omnipotence—just as the self is the gift and obligation of the eternal. Rightly considered, divine omnipotence does not necessitate the harrowing dependence of the human being, since, as Kierkegaard reflects in his journals:

> [I]t also must contain the unique qualification of being able to withdraw itself again in a manifestation of omnipotence in such a way that precisely for this reason that which has been originated through omnipotence can be independent. . . . Only omnipotence can withdraw itself at the same time it gives itself away, and this relationship is the very independence of

> the receiver. God's omnipotence is therefore his goodness. For goodness means to give oneself away completely, but in such a way that by omnipotently taking oneself back one makes the recipient independent. . . . It is incomprehensible that omnipotence is not only able to create the most impressive of all things—the whole visible world—but is able to create the most fragile of all things—a being independent of that very omnipotence (JP, 2:62/SKS 20, 57–58).

Despite the fear of annihilation, the fear of the sinful self's damnation and absolute death before God, divine omnipotence does not crush a person, but instead withdraws through the concessive gift of independence in the freedom and life of the forgiven self before God. Hence, returning to Anti-Climacus's words, "to have a self, to be a self, is the greatest concession, an infinite concession, given to a man, because it is also eternity's claim upon him" (SUD, 21/SKS 11, 137). And yet this concession is also an obligation, and freedom thereby inevitably becomes anxious. But the concession of divine omnipotence expresses God's desire for the individual to become something (life) rather than a mere nothing (death), to become potent as a self (spirit)—as a subject freely capable of relation—since "[t]o be *spirit* is to be *I*. God desires to have *Is*, for God desires to be loved" (JP, 4:248/SKS 26, 111). Understood from this perspective, the infinite qualitative difference—which previously appeared as nothing but death, an irremediably abyssal and vertiginous depth—actually creates the life-affirming space in which the self becomes itself, not in isolation, but in the independence which freely relates back to God as an individual:

> According to Christian doctrine man is not to merge in God through a pantheistic fading away or in the divine ocean through the blotting out of all individual characteristics [itself a kind of death], but in an intensified consciousness "a person must render account for every careless word he has uttered" [Matt. 12:36], and even though grace blots out sin, the union with God still takes place in the personality clarified through the whole process (JP, 4:36/SKS 17, 259).

The prospect of post-mortem judgment, then, actually intensifies, rather than destroys, the self in which "the union with God" takes place. What is more, this prospect of judgment testifies to the inexorable reality that one cannot hide from God, cannot escape God's hand in the end, even in death. Indeed, the fact that God does not annihilate the one who comes into God's holy presence actually preserves one in the inescapable fear and trembling of freedom and anxiety. As Kierkegaard admonishes, there is finally no escape in the living death of despair since "[p]recisely because you are immortal, you will not be able to escape God, will not be able to mislay yourself in a grave and behave as if nothing has happened; and the criterion by which you will be judged is that you are immortal" (CD, 207/SKS 10, 215).

The death, resurrection, and life of selfhood are, from beginning to end, determined by the inescapable and often harrowingly inexorable veracity of the immortality of the soul. And yet it is in the light of the eternal that the self must recontemplate the meaning of the shadow of death in life. The self's authentic self-becoming "before God" is ultimately characterized by a decisive deliverance of the self from the fatalism of despair and the theophany of death. And yet it is a deliverance from death before God, which finds new life in the act of dying to one's (sinful or despairing) self. It is, therefore, through the harrowing yet "upbuilding" struggle with *Anfægtelse,* implicit in becoming a self before God, that one may begin to see how the dreadful theophany of death becomes supplanted by the divine promise of forgiveness and reconciliation as the self's deliverance, not only from the fear of death or annihilation before the Holy, but also from the melancholy dis-ease of a living death.

NOTES

1. JP, 6:9/SKS 20, 391. Kierkegaard's adoption of this motto probably derives from J. G. Hamann's letter to Johann Gotthelf Linder, May 2, 1764—though the original Latin aphorism most likely dates from the Middle Ages. See additionally JP, 5:237/SKS 18, 183. Frater Taciturnus also employs this as the motto for "Guilty?/ Not Guilty?" (SLW, 194/SKS 6, 182).

2. Cf. Epicurus, "Letter to Menoeceus," in *The Philosophy of Epicurus,* trans. and ed. George K. Strodach (Evanston, Ill.: Northwestern University Press, 1963), p. 180. Kierkegaard notes in his journals that: "Scriver [Christian Scriver, *Seelen-Schatz* (Leipzig: 1715)] says that it is good to have business with death—the advantage is ours ('to die is gain')." Cf. "This is a more splendid way of tricking death than that of Epicurus: Death cannot get hold of me, because when I am, death is not, and when death is, I am not" (See JP, 1:338/SKS 24, 238).

3. G. W. F. Hegel, *Phenomenology of Spirit,* trans. A. V. Miller (Oxford: Oxford University Press, 1977), B, IV, 195, pp. 117–18.

4. "Christianity took away the fear of death and replaced it with the fear of judgment; this is a sharpening but is a step forward as well" (JP, 1:338/SKS 26, 107).

5. George Pattison, *Kierkegaard, Religion and the Nineteenth-Century Crisis of Culture* (Cambridge: Cambridge University Press, 2002), p. 76. See also the outline in Pattison's "'Cosmopolitan Faces:' The Presence of the Wandering Jew

in *From the Papers of One Still Living,*" in *International Kierkegaard Commentary: Early Polemical Writings,* ed. Robert L. Perkins, pp. 109–30 (Macon, Ga.: Mercer University Press, 1999).

6. "In *Either/Or* this figure [the Wandering Jew] is presented as the unhappiest of all persons because he could not die; consequently he is doomed to endless wandering about the earth in search of a grave of rest and peace" (Sylvia Walsh, "Patterns For Living Poetically," in *Søren Kierkegaard: Critical Assessments of Leading Philosophers Vol. 1.,* ed. Daniel W. Conway, p. 288 [London: Routledge, 2002]). See also George Connell's chapter in this volume.

7. Hegel, *Phenomenology of Spirit,* VII, 752, pp. 454–55.

8. G. W. F. Hegel, *Faith and Knowledge,* trans. Walter Cerf and H. S. Harris (Albany: State University of New York Press, 1977), p. 190. In this sense, the Unhappiest One—whose "mournful grave" resides "in the unhappy West"—provides an ironic parallel to the death of Christ, "a man of sorrows acquainted with grief" (Isa. 53), whose "sacred sepulcher" lies "in the happy East" (EO, 1:220/ SKS 2, 213–14). See also John E. Hare, "The Unhappiest One and the Structure of Kierkegaard's *Either/Or,*" in *International Kierkegaard Commentary: Either/Or I,* ed. Robert L. Perkins, pp. 102–4 (Macon, Ga.: Mercer University Press, 1995). See also David J. Kangas, *Kierkegaard's Instant: On Beginnings* (Bloomington: Indiana University Press, 2007), pp. 47–56.

9. Hence, according to John E. Hare, the Unhappiest One "is thus the prototype of the aesthetic life, brought to its greatest pitch of self-awareness" ("The Unhappiest One and the Structure of Kierkegaard's *Either/Or,*" p. 96).

10. "[T]he 'cure' and 'dying-to' of which Kierkegaard [in *The Sickness unto Death*] speaks can be seen in terms of the *mors mystica* [mystical death; contrasted with *mors corporis* (death of the body) and *mors animae* (death of the soul)]. Although they are never made into an explicit theme, they serve from the beginning as navigational markers guiding the course of the text" [Michael Theunissen, "The Upbuilding in the Thought of Death. Traditional Elements, Innovative Ideas, and Unexhausted Possibilities in Kierkegaard's Discourse 'At a Graveside,'" in *International Kierkegaard Commentary: Prefaces/Writing Sampler and Three Discourses on Imagined Occasions,* ed. Robert L. Perkins, p. 344 (Macon, Ga.: Mercer University Press, 2006)].

11. In reference to the pagan notion of divine madness, see *Phaedrus* 244a–245b.

12. Augustine, *Confessions,* trans. Albert C. Outter (Nashville, Tenn.: Thomas Nelson, Inc., 1999), Book I, p. 5.

13. Friedrich Nietzsche, "Thus Spoke Zarathustra: Fourth Part," in Walter Kaufmann, ed., *The Portable Nietzsche* (London: Penguin, 1976), pp. 378–79.

14. Hegel, *Phenomenology of Spirit,* B, IV, 187, p. 113.

15. Emmanuel Levinas, "Existence and Ethics," in *Kierkegaard: A Critical Reader,* ed. Jonathan Reé and Jane Chamberlain, p. 30 (Oxford: Basil Blackwell, 1998).

16. Jean Hyppolite, for example, has commented that "God is the master and man is the slave. A form of alienation that reduces man to an existential nothingness results in a humiliation of man which, as Feuerbach noted, might have serious moral consequences" (*Studies on Marx and Hegel,* ed. and trans. John O'Neill [New York: Harper and Row, 1973], p. 133).

17. Hegel, *Phenomenology of Spirit,* B, IV, 180, p. 111.

18. Hegel, *Phenomenology of Spirit,* B, IV, 184, p. 112.

19. Jacques Derrida, *The Gift of Death,* trans. David Wills (Chicago: University of Chicago Press, 1996), p. 28.

20. Hegel, *Phenomenology of Spirit,* B, IV, 187, pp. 113–14.

21. Hegel, *Phenomenology of Spirit,* B, IV, 194, p. 117.

22. Hegel, *Phenomenology of Spirit,* B, IV, 195, pp. 117–18 (Prov. 1:7; 9:10; Psalm 111:10).

23. Michel Haar, "Nietzsche and the Metamorphosis of the Divine," in *Post-Secular Philosophy,* ed. Philip Blond, p. 162 (London and New York: Routledge, 1998).

24. "'To die to' means to regard everything as one will see it at the moment of death and consequently to bring death as close as possible" (JP, 1:337/SKS 23, 438).

25. See also Adam Buben's chapter in this volume.

3.

Christian Hate: Death, Dying, and Reason in Pascal and Kierkegaard

Adam Buben

> Whoever comes to me and does not hate father and mother, wife and children, brothers and sisters, yes, and even life itself, cannot be my disciple. —JESUS OF NAZARETH (LUKE 14:26)

> We proclaim Christ crucified, [an offense] to Jews and foolishness to Gentiles. —PAUL (1 COR. 1:23)

Should Søren Kierkegaard be listed among Christian apologists such as Anselm, Thomas Aquinas, or even Blaise Pascal? Focusing on his connections to Pascal, twentieth-century scholars Denzil G. M. Patrick and José Raimundo Maia Neto claim that Kierkegaard is, in fact, engaged in the same sort of project.[1] Kierkegaard himself seems to lend support to these claims when he states, "I have never broken with Christianity . . . from the time it was possible to speak of the application of my powers, I had firmly resolved to employ everything to defend it, or in any case to present it in its true form" (PV, 80/SKS 16, forthcoming). Even without the lens of the comparison with Pascal, passages like this one have led to some confusion about Kierkegaard's views on rationality in the service of faith.[2] But I believe that his defense as "true description" is not the sort of defense that an apologist of Pascal's stripe is engaged in. Simply put, Kierkegaard, unlike Pascal, is not interested in helping Christianity appear more reasonable or seem more palatable.

What makes Pascal, rather than others with this sort of tendency toward rational appeals, ideal for the sake of this comparison, though, is that he is so similar in other ways to Kierkegaard. Against this backdrop of similarity, the relevant divergence between them will be particularly conspicuous. Perhaps the most remarkable congruence concerns the use of the thought of death in the service of Christian dying to the world; and it is the exploration of the "dying to" connection that will ultimately suggest a parting of the ways that finds Pascal firmly entrenched in a tradition of thinkers who use reason to talk people into Christianity and Kierkegaard outside of such a tradition. It is hoped that the nuance that distinguishes between these two might prove helpful, on some future occasion, in resolving the long-standing debate within Kierkegaard Studies concerning faith and reason.[3]

Death of Christ, Death of Christian

Sylvia Walsh touches on a Christian's dying to the world when she speaks of "a qualitative change from one's old way of life to a new way of life, from the natural life to spiritual life, from life oriented in and toward the finite to a life concerned absolutely for the eternal."[4] This dying of the pre-Christian self and the subsequent rebirth as a follower of Christ, which this death makes possible, is a recurring theme throughout the New Testament. Jesus often warns his disciples that a life of worldly concerns is not conducive to the proper care of the soul (e.g. Matt. 16:24–26). Because a worldly life is inhospitable to a striving Christian, such a life must end before Christianity can take root (2 Cor. 4:10–12, 5:14–19). But how exactly is one to understand death as the precondition for Christian life? Fortunately for the aspiring Christian, Christ's own life provides a model for finding life in death.

Just as Christ is said to have died on the cross to overcome the sin of the world but later rose from the dead, one who would be a follower of Christ must also die to the sin of the world in order to live free from its tyranny (1 Peter 2:24). There are two senses in which this analogy might hold true for the Christian. First, there is a sense in which one must physically die in order to be reborn in a heavenly afterlife, free from the sinful world. Second, there is a sense in which one must figuratively die to the sinful desires and preoccupations that come from being in the world in order to become ready for Christ-like living. Romans 6:6–8 states that "we know that our old self was crucified with him so that the body of sin might be destroyed . . . if we have died with Christ, we believe that we will also live with him." While this passage might support both senses, it is the latter, figurative sense of dying to the world that plays an important role in the work of both Pascal and Kierkegaard. Given the explicitly Christian concerns they have in common, it might come as no surprise that they each emphasize this understanding of the dying discussed throughout the New Testament. What is particularly interesting, however, is that they both recommend the same sort of meditation on personal physical death in order to aid aspiring Christians in their figurative dying to the world.[5]

Pascal

At the risk of painting an overly simplistic picture of Pascal's historical context, it seems necessary to say a few words regarding some prevalent issues of his day. Having lived his short life in France during the mid-seventeenth century, Pascal finds himself in the middle of a world profoundly influenced by both philosophical skepticism and the religious thought of the Jesuits. In the skeptical context of thinkers like Michel de Montaigne, Pierre Charron, and René Descartes,[6] Pascal comes to wonder about the legitimacy and limits of skepticism and reason in general in the service of Christian belief. Similarly, faced with the domination of the church by the Jesuits, the Jansenist-leaning Pascal comes to wonder about what he sees as the Jesuits' rationalistic attempt to "combine God and the world"[7] in such a way that the true nature of Christianity is lost. It is at least partially with these issues in mind that Pascal's *Pensées* turns to the thought of death in order to focus attention clearly on the state of humankind in the world and the essence of Christianity.

For Pascal, physical death is significant as the deadline by which an individual must make a decision concerning belief in the immortality of the soul, or else risk unpleasant consequences. He states that "eternity exists, and death, which must begin it and which threatens them every hour, must in a short time inevitably put them under the horrible necessity of being annihilated or unhappy eternally" (*Pensées* [hereafter "P"], 221). Given the obvious importance of making what Pascal would see as the "right" decision about the eternal (P, 217), there are a few things about the deadline that ought to be kept in mind. The first of these can be seen in the passage quoted above—death can come at any moment without warning. But the indeterminate side of the death coin cannot be separated from the other, much less ambiguous side. Regarding life in the world, Pascal claims that "it is certain we will not exist in it for long and uncertain if we will exist in it for one hour" (P, 51). Further, death is something that an individual faces alone, and so one must not think that anyone else can help them once the deadline has been reached. There are some aspects of one's existence that are necessarily private and solitary and one would do well to act accordingly (P, 50). These three basic points should be sufficient to understand the connection between thinking about death and dying to the world according to Pascal.

When one focuses on death, and what comes after it, in the way Pascal describes, one experiences a sense of urgency and individual responsibility in life that one might not experience otherwise. Each person has a limited but indeterminate amount of time to set his or her affairs in order, most importantly those pertaining to what happens after death, since life concerns are far more temporary. For one who genuinely comes to appreciate this precarious situation, it is evident, according to Pascal, that one must alter one's life in various ways, neglecting matters that do not pertain to one's decision about the eternal. Consider the following appeal:

> let us . . . judge those who live without thinking of the ultimate end of life, who let themselves be guided by their inclinations and their pleasures without reflection and without concern, as if they could annihilate eternity by turning their thought away from it, and think only of making themselves happy for the moment (P, 221).

This passage suggests that by turning to thoughts of death and what comes after it, one might be led to avoid temporal or worldly ideas and passions. That is, seen in the light of one's impending postmortem situation, daily concerns about traffic, salary, and romantic prospects seem fairly insignificant and maybe even worth letting go of altogether. Pascal's letting go or excising of worldliness is precisely what is meant when the New Testament speaks of dying to the sinful world and all the pride and bodily desires that go with it (P, 47). Among other things, Jesus and Paul suggest giving up wealth, personal possessions, sex, marriage, and even loved ones (e.g. Matt. 4:18–22, 19:24; Luke 14:26; 1 Cor. 6:12–7:9).

But thinking of death as Pascal recommends only begins to expose the full implications of dying to the world. Such dying is ultimately a disregarding, or *hatred* (P, 81) of the worldly self, which includes one's selfishness, self-confidence, self-reliance etc., and this dying is necessary in order for an individual to be open to receiving Christ through grace. Pascal declares that "true conversion consists in self-annihilation before that universal Being whom we have so often irritated . . . there is an insurmountable opposition between God and us, and . . . without a mediator there can be no communion with him" (P, 107). There are many different ways in which one can understand how "having" a self might prevent having a relationship with God, but perhaps the most important impediment, according to Pascal, is the self-confidence and self-reliance that are manifested in the use of reason.

For the sake of existing in the world, it seems that there is nothing more valuable to a human being than reason. Besides the mathematic-like security that reason provides rationalists such as Descartes on purely speculative matters,[8] more often than not reason also serves people well in everyday dealings with the world; and it has therefore received an apparently well-deserved vote of confidence. But as Pascal explains, there is an opposition between God and the world, worldly reason included. The opposition between God and reason is quite apparent when one considers the numerous difficulties of Christian doctrine, whether it is the virgin birth, the divinity of a man named Jesus, or Pascal's personal favorite: original sin.[9] The purpose of recognizing such opposition is, according to Pascal, to acknowledge that reason can only go so far and that dying to the world includes, in some sense, dying to reason. Pascal holds that we cannot know ourselves in God "through the proud exertions of our reason, but through its simple submission" (P, 37). Although these ideas will be developed in greater detail below, perhaps it will aid in understanding them now to recall here exactly whom Pascal has in mind when he limits reason in Christianity in this way. No matter how much the Jesuits might protest that all of their worldly activities are done in the service of Christ, Pascal believes that they intentionally leave behind the (early) Christian ideal of dying to worldliness that he cherishes in order to combat the encroaching world of modern science and reason on its own terms.[10] Pascal's focus on this dying illuminates not only his chief concern about the Jesuits, but also a most interesting point of connection to the thought of Kierkegaard.

Kierkegaard

While Kierkegaard could not have become aware of the full scope of Pascal's work until relatively late in life (JP, 3:419/SKS 24, 98), he was an avid reader of Pascal and books about him.[11] There is also strong evidence that Kierkegaard was for the most part fond of Pascal, both the man and his writings. In fact, Pascal turns up quite frequently in Kierkegaard's notebooks, especially in the later years, and many times Pascal's name is followed by kind words of support for the life and ideas of the Frenchman. For example, Kierkegaard states that "there is much truth and pertinence in what Pascal says, that later Christianity with the help of some sacraments excuses itself from loving God" (JP, 1:222/SKS 25, 256). Although Pascal comes up only once in Kierkegaard's published writings (SLW, 460/SKS 6, 424), it is clear from notebook entries like these that Kierkegaard feels a kinship with him, particularly concerning Pascal's struggle with the Jesuits and his own struggle against the Danish Lutheran church of his day (JP, 3:421–22/SKS 24, 115–16).[12] They both see in their opponents a diluting of the true nature of Christianity, and they both want to depict this nature as accurately as possible in order to prevent people from believing that simply going through the motions is sufficient for a proper relationship with Christ.[13] Setting aside other parallels between these two thinkers for now,[14] it will be most enlightening to see how thinking death and dying to the world serve this prevention in Kierkegaard as compared to Pascal.

In the short discourse "At a Graveside" from 1845, Kierkegaard proclaims that "the thought of death gives the earnest person the right momentum in life and the right goal toward which he directs his momentum" (TDIO, 83/SKS 5, 453). But this gift might seem like a tall order for a simple thought to fill. Fortunately, like Pascal, Kierkegaard suggests several aspects of this thought that are particularly illuminating and helpful for realizing the proper momentum and goal. To begin with, he posits the necessity of focusing primarily on one's own death. Death may be "the human condition," but it is only a trivial contemplation of death unless "you are thinking it as your lot" (TDIO, 73, 75/SKS 5, 444, 446). Kierkegaard, continuing to follow in Pascal's footsteps (although perhaps not yet realizing this), also highlights the importance of keeping both the certainty and the uncertainty of death in mind.[15] He asserts that "death is indefinable—the only certainty, and the only thing about which nothing is certain" (TDIO, 91/SKS 5, 460). In other words, while one's death will surely come, there is no way of knowing when it will happen or what, if anything, might happen afterward. Taken together, these few aspects of the earnest thought of death play a powerful role in helping one die to the world in a Kierkegaardian sense.

Because these particular aspects of thinking about death teach me that I will surely die, and at possibly any moment, Kierkegaard emphasizes the same sense of urgency that Pascal feels. Kierkegaard states that "death itself produces a scarcity of time . . . for the dying" (TDIO, 84/SKS 5, 453). Given this scarcity, Kierkegaard believes that one ought to avoid becoming too wrapped up in "vain pursuits," or what he calls "accidental" (or "incidental") matters (TDIO, 75, 96/SKS 5, 446, 464). These sorts of matters are those that demand completion, noticeable in the external world, and a certain amount of time to complete them, time which no one can guarantee. Rather, Kierkegaard believes that one ought to behave in accordance with one's uncertain temporal situation and choose to focus on matters that do not have a temporal requirement. But what sorts of matters do not demand time? Since time-dependent concerns are about what one accomplishes in the external world, Kierkegaard seems to hold that non-time-dependent concerns are about how, internally, one does whatever one is doing. He explains,

> with incidental work, which is in the external, it is essential that the work be finished. But the essential work is not defined essentially by time and the external, insofar as death is the interruption. Earnestness, therefore, becomes . . . the choosing of work that does not depend on whether one is granted a lifetime to complete it well or only a brief time to have begun it well (TDIO, 96/SKS 5, 464).

By leading one toward concerns about how one is doing whatever it is that one is doing, it could be said that Kierkegaard's thought of death in "At a Graveside" helps one die to the vain "what" concerns of the world in which one lives.[16]

But it is in the 1851 *For Self-Examination* (and the *Christian Discourses* of 1848) that Kierkegaard, perhaps by this point feeling the influence of Pascal's thoughts on Christian existential death and rebirth (JP, 3:419–20/SKS 24, 98–99), provides a more robust and distinctively Christian account of what dying to the world means. Here he claims that "in a certain sense . . . love of God is hatred toward the world" (FSE, 85/SKS 13, 105). While thinking about death can point toward a Christian dying to the world, it would not be accurate to suggest that Kierkegaard believes that such thinking is capable, on its own, of bringing about a full-fledged Christian dying to the world. An individual's dying to the world, in this sense, can only happen by the grace of God.[17] Kierkegaard states that "the life-giving Spirit is the very one who slays you; the first thing the life-giving Spirit says is that you must enter into death, that you must die to . . . in order that you may not take Christianity in vain" (FSE, 76–77/SKS 13, 98). It is only by dying to the world, with the help of God, that one can avoid making Christianity into a "what" concern. That is, in dying to the world one leaves behind selfish concerns about what one has done in the world to make oneself Christian, in order to leave oneself open for the further grace that is necessary for new life in Christ (FSE, 76–77, 81/SKS 13, 97–99, 102).

The selfishness that Kierkegaard speaks of is not the greedy, childish inability to share that might immediately come to mind when one hears this word, but rather the same sort of dependence on oneself that Pascal condemns. Kierkegaard explains,

> the apostles were indeed dead, dead to every merely earthly hope, to every human confidence in their own powers or in human assistance. Therefore, death first; you must first die to every merely earthly hope, to every merely human confidence; you must die to your selfishness, or to the world, because it is only through your selfishness that the world has power over you; if you are dead to your selfishness, you are also dead to the world (FSE, 77/SKS 13, 99).

What is most interesting about this passage is that dying to the world and to selfishness involves dying to human powers, assistance, and confidence. Among the human capacities Kierkegaard believes an individual must abandon for the sake of becoming a Christian is reason. He exclaims that "the way is narrow—it is . . . impassable, blocked, impossible, insane [*afsindig*]! . . . To walk this way is immediately, at the beginning, akin to dying! . . . along this way sagacity [*Klogskab*] and common sense [*Forstand*] never walk—'that would indeed be madness [*Galskab*]'" (FSE, 61–62/SKS 13, 84). The life of a Christian is madness, and thus against reason, because just as Christ entered into the backward situation of willingly dying in order to live, individuals must also willingly die to the world in order to be born as Christians (FSE, 60–61/SKS 13, 83–84). But even though reason seems to be a problem for the aspiring Christian on Kierkegaard's view, is his notion of dying to reason exactly what Pascal has in mind?

Faith and Reason

There is obviously a great deal of agreement between Pascal and Kierkegaard on the use of the thought of death for the sake of Christian dying to the world. Besides the similarities concerning the certainty and uncertainty of death and the urgency that arises as a result of focusing on these qualities of death, there is also a connection with regard to the issue of losing oneself. Pascal and Kierkegaard are almost certainly in agreement on this issue so far as it concerns dying to one's sinful worldly desires, passions, and projects, which stand in the way of proper Christian commitment. They also appear to be mostly on the same page regarding a rejection of one's pride and self-reliance for the sake of becoming Christian. Even in the case of the rejection of reason, there is much that Pascal and Kierkegaard have in common. But while the former advocates a mere *suspension or humbling* of reason when dealing with the faith-based acceptance of Christian matters (P, 31), the latter recommends a more extreme approach, and this approach marks the most crucial difference between these two thinkers.

Pascal is able merely to suspend reason in certain cases because he posits the existence of another faculty—the heart (*le cœur*)—by which humans can gain something like knowledge. The heart is roughly faith, a nonrational capacity by which principles, in this case Christian principles, can be felt and lived out. Just after introducing his famous wager[18] Pascal asserts that "it is the heart that experiences God, and not reason. Here, then, is faith: God felt by the heart, not by reason. The heart has its reasons, which reason does not know" (P, 215–16).[19] Even though the heart is capable of things that reason is not, Pascal does not believe that the heart ought to be left to its own devices. Reason still has a place in the service of Christianity according to Pascal, and thus reason and faith must work together within the aspiring Christian: "if we submit everything to reason, our religion will have nothing mysterious and supernatural. If we offend the principles of reason, our religion will be absurd and ridiculous" (P, 53).[20] It is because Christianity must, in some sense, be compatible with reason (or at least be able to offer "reasons" in its defense from the perspective of faith) that Pascal emphasizes the importance of at least some minimal amount of "verifiable" evidence in the form of miracles.[21] He claims that "we would not have sinned in not believing in Jesus Christ, lacking miracles" (P, 54). It is precisely this sort of claim that Kierkegaard would *not* make.

Faith (as more of a lived experience than an epistemic capacity) is of course central for Kierkegaard as well, but he does not believe that it coexists and works with reason to guide an individual toward Christianity. He explains that "faith is against understanding [*Forstand*]; faith is on the other side of death. And when you died or died to yourself, to the world, then you also died to all immediacy in yourself, also to your understanding" (FSE, 82/SKS 13, 103). Because faith is opposed to reason for Kierkegaard, he is more willing than Pascal to embrace Christianity as essentially absurd and offensive (see, for example, FSE, 82–83/SKS 13, 103–4). Thus Kierkegaard is not nearly as interested as Pascal in finding reasons, such as miracles, for help in becoming and remaining a Christian. Kierkegaard claims,

> some . . . sought to refute doubt with reasons [*Grunde*]. . . . they tried to demonstrate the truth of Christianity with reasons . . . these reasons fostered doubt and doubt became the stronger. The demonstration of Christianity really lies in *imitation*. This was taken away. Then the need for "reasons" was felt, but these reasons, or that there are reasons, are already

> a kind of doubt . . . thus doubt arose and lived on reasons. . . . the more reasons one advances, the more one nourishes doubt and the stronger it becomes . . . offering doubt reasons in order to kill it is just like offering the tasty food it likes best of all to a hungry monster one wishes to eliminate. No, one must not offer reasons to doubt—at least not if one's intention is to kill it—but one must do as Luther did, order it to shut its mouth, and to that end keep quiet and offer no reasons (FSE, 68/SKS 13, 90).[22]

This passage is likely not directed at Pascal personally, as he does not really seem interested in definitively *proving* Christianity by pointing out miracles, or by any other means. Nonetheless, Pascal *does* multiply reasons in defense of Christianity—providing evidence meant to make belief more compelling—in a way that Kierkegaard, according to this passage, does not endorse (P, 49–50). The ultimate difference between Pascal and Kierkegaard is, therefore, that while the former has a notion of Christian dying to the world that involves setting reason aside only at the proper moments, the latter's notion of Christian dying to the world demands silence and a corresponding total renunciation of reason, at least so far as one's Christianity is concerned.[23]

This difference between Pascal and Kierkegaard on the subject of dying to reason is manifested most clearly in their respective goals as authors. Pascal's primary aim is to produce *An Apology for the Christian Religion,* which was the original title for the ideas that are now known as Pascal's *Pensées* (P, xi). An apology of this sort, as evidenced by some of Pascal's own claims, is meant to demonstrate how "reasonable and happy" one can be in Christianity, and how "foolish and unhappy" one can be without it (P, 51). Kierkegaard, on the other hand, never portrays the Christian and the unbeliever in such a way. Rather, his fundamental goal is to describe what a life in Christ is really like—it is absurd, offensive, painful, difficult, and dangerous—when removed from the relative comfort of the degenerate life in Christendom. As if the dying to one's former self is not miserable enough, unlike physical death, which ends things, dying to self is just the beginning of one's physical sufferings (FSE, 79/SKS 13, 100–1). These sufferings of a Christian, dead to the world in a sense, but still physically living in it, might include ridicule, persecution, or even martyrdom (FSE, 84–85/SKS 13, 104–5).[24] This sort of life hardly sounds reasonable or happy.[25] In fact, it would seem much more reasonable to choose any life but this one.

Thus, while I find significant parallels between Pascal and Kierkegaard, insofar as Pascal's work attempts to make Christianity more attractive to believers and unbelievers alike, Kierkegaard's attempt to preserve the possibility of offense for everyone is importantly opposed. Such opposition is clearly expressed in this 1850 notebook entry:

> if I had to find a beautiful expression for the Mynsterian approach and one which would please him, I would quote a passage from Pascal's *Pensees,* where he speaks of how one should approach those who repudiate religion or are ill-disposed toward it: "One should begin with proofs, showing that religion does not quarrel with reason; next, show that it is venerable and try to inspire respect for it; then make it pleasant and appealing (ingratiate it) and awaken the desire in them for it to be true, something one shall then drive home with irrefutable proofs; but it mainly depends on making it pleasant and appealing in their eyes" (JP, 3:423–24/SKS 24, 119).

Given Kierkegaard's well-known distaste for the "Mynsterian approach," associating Pascal's use of reason with the bishop's is certainly no compliment. Kierkegaard recognizes that Pascal is mostly trying to engender longing for the truth of Christianity, and not simply trying to demonstrate its truth; but as I have argued, Kierkegaard rejects the former strategy just as he constantly belittles the latter. If I am right that the nature of his relationship to something like the former strategy has been a source of controversy within the realm of Kierkegaard interpretation, then perhaps the contrast with Pascal's views on dying to reason could prove useful in clearing things up.[26]

Final Remarks

Perhaps the most difficult and controversial question related to dying to the world concerns the extent to which reason must be sacrificed in order to be a proper Christian. While most Christian thinkers speak of the pitfalls of worldliness, and therefore of some degree of dying to the world, it is this issue of dying to reason that really exposes whether one is merely wary of the world or interested in the possibility of a thoroughgoing eschewal of it. To be dead to reason is really to lose one's last shreds of comfort and security in worldly existence; it is a switching off of life support in the hopes that God will sustain one's being in some form or another. Kierkegaard has shown that he is focused, at least in his description of Christianity, on precisely this extreme sort of dying to the world, but it would seem that Pascal is not ready to deny all worldly comfort to the Christian. In a note from 1854 on a different but perhaps not entirely unrelated topic, Kierkegaard actually questions whether Pascal might be attempting to "coddle" himself instead of facing up to the fact that proper Christian dying to the world could lead to "martyrdom, a bloody martyrdom" (JP, 2:367–68/SKS 25, 482). But whether or not Kierkegaard is right in suggesting that Pascal is holding onto a little selfish prudence specifically to avoid the most dangerous of worldly predicaments, Pascal has certainly not given up on every last glimmer of self-reliant hope that threatens genuine faith according to Kierkegaard.[27]

NOTES

The first epigraph comes from *The New Oxford Annotated Bible,* 3rd ed., ed. Michael D. Coogan (Oxford: Oxford University Press, 2001). In the second epigraph, I have altered the text to correspond to the version that Kierkegaard so often quotes.

1. See Denzil G. M. Patrick, *Pascal and Kierkegaard,* vol. 2 (London: Lutterworth, 1947), p. 302; and José Raimundo Maia Neto, *The Christianization of Pyrrhonism: Scepticism and Faith in Blaise Pascal, Søren Kierkegaard, and Lev Shestov* (Ann Arbor, Mich.: University Microfilms International, 1992), p. 15.

2. Karen L. Carr provides an excellent account of the Kierkegaardian landscape, dividing interpretations of Kierkegaard's position with respect to reason and faith into three camps: irrationalist, rationalist, and supra-rationalist. Taking the first two as more clearly untenable, Carr then opposes the supra-rationalist reading to her view of Kierkegaard as antirationalist. See "The Offense of Reason and the Passion of Faith: Kierkegaard and Anti-Rationalism," *Faith and Philosophy* 13, no. 2 (April 1996): pp. 236–51.

3. Interestingly, even though Alasdair MacIntyre, one of the key figures at the center of the disagreement, goes out of his way to identify Pascal as an important precursor to Kierkegaard's understanding of the relationship between Christianity and reason (Alasdair MacIntyre, *After Virtue* [Notre Dame, Ind.: University of Notre Dame Press, 1981], pp. 39, 52), many of the other authors involved in this debate seem to overlook the potential value of the sort of comparison I am drawing in this chapter. For illustration of my point, notice that Pascal's name is missing from the index to *Kierkegaard After MacIntyre,* edited by John J. Davenport and Anthony Rudd (Chicago: Open Court, 2001).

4. Sylvia Walsh, *Living Christianly: Kierkegaard's Dialectic of Christian Existence* (University Park: The Pennsylvania State University Press, 2005), p. 81.

5. This similarity is perhaps easily explained by the close proximity of Stoicism (and Neoplatonism) during Christianity's formative years in the Roman Empire, and the resulting attitude of *memento mori* that has been an important aspect of Christian thought throughout Christian history. However, it is by no means the case that every Christian writer emphasizes personal physical death in the same way that Pascal and Kierkegaard do. For example, while Martin Luther

has many similar things to say about dying to the world, he approaches the issue of physical passing away in a manner that might conflict somewhat with the claims of Pascal and Kierkegaard (Martin Luther, "A Sermon on Preparing to Die," in *Luther's Works,* vol. 42, ed. Martin O. Dietrich, trans. Martin H. Bertram [Philadelphia: Fortress Press, 1969]).

6. For excellent accounts of the differences between Pascal and his precursors/contemporaries concerning skepticism, see Maia Neto, *Christianization of Pyrrhonism*; and Richard H. Popkin, *The History of Scepticism from Erasmus to Spinoza* (Berkeley: University of California Press, 1979). The relationship between Pascal and these other figures on the topic of death and dying is also an interesting one, worth exploring elsewhere. Compare his claims with those found in Michel de Montaigne, *The Complete Essays of Montaigne,* trans. Donald Frame (Stanford, Calif.: Stanford University Press, 1958), pp. 56–68; and Peter (Pierre) Charron, *Of Wisdom,* trans. Samson Leonard (New York: De Capo Press, 1971 [before 1612; reprint]), p. 242. Notice also the similarity between Charron's discussion of death and Descartes's project in the *Meditations.*

7. Blaise Pascal, *Pensées,* trans. and ed. Roger Ariew (Indianapolis, Ind.: Hackett Publishing Company, 2005), p. 311 (hereafter "P").

8. A primary complaint of Pascal's (and perhaps the main reason for viewing Pascal as some kind of "proto-existentialist") about rationalists like Descartes (and empiricists for that matter) is that they tend to exclude other important aspects of the human experience; they "delve too deeply in the sciences" (P, 148). I am grateful to Pat Stokes for helping me to become clear on this point.

9. Many Christian thinkers, most notably Augustine, claim that the opposition between God and human reason is the result of humankind's "original" corrupted state (Augustine, *On Free Choice of the Will,* trans. Thomas Williams [Indianapolis, Ind.: Hackett Publishing Co., 1993], pp. 106–8).

10. This Jesuit issue obviously deserves more attention than I can give it here. For a more thorough description of the Jesuit *raison d'être,* see Malachi Martin, *The Jesuits* (New York: Linden Press/Simon and Schuster, 1987), especially pp. 168, 176–81.

11. Kierkegaard owned three different German editions of a still incomplete *Pensées* when he died (H. P. Rohde, ed., *Auktionsprotokol over Søren Kierkegaards Bogsamling* [Copenhagen: Det Kongelige Bibliotek, 1967], pp. 48–49). For more on what Pascal and works about Pascal Kierkegaard had access to, see for example, JP, 3:421/SKS 24, 113, 115; August Neander, *Über die geschichtliche Bedeutung der Pensées Pascal's für die Religionsphilosophie insbesondere* (Ein zur Feier des Geburtstages Seiner Majestät des Königs in der öffentlichen Sitzung der Akademie am 16. Oktober 1846 gehaltener Vortrag, 2. opl., Berlin 1847 [1846]); Blaise Pascal, *Gedanken Paskals, mit Anmerkungen und Gedanken von J.F.K.,* trans. J. F. Kleuker (Bremmen: Johann Heinrich Cramer, 1777); and Blaise Pascal, *Gedanken über die religion und einige andern Gegenstände,* vols. 1 and 2, trans. Karl Adolf Blech (Berlin: Wilhelm Besser, 1840).

12. See also Patrick, *Pascal and Kierkegaard,* vol. 2, p. 316.

13. Maia Neto, *Christianization of Pyrrhonism,* p. 164. Given the Augustinianism of the Jansenists, I think it is no accident that Pascal and Kierkegaard, who happens to be highly influenced by a certain Augustinian monk—Luther—both take issue with a religious status quo that seems to have forgotten Augustine's lessons about the nature and importance of a faithful relationship with God.

14. One could point out, for example, their long battles with physical ailments, their bachelorhood, and the persecution or mockery they endured for expressing their religious views. See also E. L. Allen, "Pascal and Kierkegaard," *London Quarterly Review* (1937); and Maia Neto, *Christianization of Pyrrhonism,* pp. 163–64, among others.

15. Among other interesting parallels to consider, see their views on the fear of death (e.g. P, 177; TDIO, 88/SKS 5, 457).

16. Kierkegaard also states that the thought of death helps one "to renounce worldly comparison" (TDIO, 91/SKS 5, 459) with others. I deal with this and other issues from "At a Graveside" in greater detail in my "Living with Death: Kierkegaard and the Samurai," in *Kierkegaard and Japanese Thought,* ed. James Giles, pp. 141–58 (Houndmills, Hampshire: Palgrave Macmillan, 2008). Also see Charles Guignon's chapter in this volume.

17. Because it is not clear that Pascal holds a similar view, one subtle yet significant difference between Pascal and Kierkegaard could be that while grace is only necessary for Christian rebirth according to the former, it is also necessary for the death that must precede the rebirth according to the latter. This difference might be a manifestation of the still to be discussed general disagreement between them concerning the value of reason in Christianity.

18. Although it is unclear whether Kierkegaard was aware of the wager (it is among those parts of *Pensées* that became available only later in his lifetime), one might speculate as to how he would view it. Even though the wager is not intended to produce faith, it is meant to demonstrate why someone would, or maybe should, *want* to be faithful. Since Kierkegaard often seems uninterested in convincing people of the benefits of Christianity (after all, he is writing for an audience that has taken these benefits for granted), I believe he would be opposed to the wager. Additional support for this belief can be found in Tamara Monet Marks's discussion of the *Concept of Irony* (especially CI, 68/SKS 1, 126) in this volume. I discuss this matter in greater detail in "The Existential Compromise in the History of the Philosophy of Death" (PhD diss., University of South Florida, 2011), p. 117.

19. I take this last, and seemingly paradoxical, statement about unreasonable reasons to mean a couple of things: first, that something might seem ridiculous to an outsider, but make perfect sense to those "in the know," and second, that some course of action or belief might seem like a very bad idea (perhaps in the sense that a desirable outcome is unlikely—see the wager) and yet it is still possible to explain why someone might proceed along this course. With this statement,

Pascal is sneaking reason back into Christianity in order to aid faith after excluding it temporarily in order to form faith.

20. Pascal does acknowledge that Christianity is, in a sense, foolish, but this foolishness is obviously not entirely incompatible with reason (P, 90, 212).

21. He also spends a great deal of time discussing the importance of fulfilled prophecy as evidence in favor of the truth of Christianity (P, 96–102, 239–61).

22. While Pascal might rule "Reason" out of Christian faithfulness temporarily but allow it back in later in the form of reasons, Kierkegaard can now be seen to rule out both Reason (*Forstand*) and reasons (*Grunde*) in the service of faith. Perhaps some will suggest both that Kierkegaard is making a distinction between *Forstand*, which is commonly translated as "understanding" (although "reason," the dictionary tells us, or "common sense," as we see in the Hong translation above, would not be inappropriate), and *Fornuft*, which is translated as "reason" or "rationality" more strictly, and that he opposes only the former but not the latter to faith. After all, *Fornuft* never shows up in *For Self-Examination*, at least not in noun form, while *Forstand* is ever-present throughout Kierkegaard's works. In response to such suggestions, it must be pointed out that Kierkegaard seems to use these words almost interchangeably in places, just as they can be used in English. See for example, Kierkegaard's statement that "no glance is so sharp-sighted as faith's, and yet faith is, humanly speaking, blind; for reason [*Fornuft*], understanding [*Forstand*], is, humanly speaking, that seeing, but faith is against understanding [*Forstand*]" (SKS 11, 268). On Kierkegaard's use of these terms and the difficulties of translating them, see JP, 3:903–8; and Andrew J. Burgess, "*Forstand* in the Swenson-Lowrie Correspondence and in the 'Metaphysical Caprice,'" in *International Kierkegaard Commentary: Philosophical Fragments and Johannes Climacus*, ed. Robert L. Perkins, pp. 109–28 (Macon, Ga.: Mercer University Press, 1994).

23. One possible explanation of this key difference is that while Pascal is still reacting to a largely Catholic world, Kierkegaard is at least a theological generation and hundreds of miles removed from such a world. At the risk of oversimplifying the situation (and ignoring other relevant historical developments), Luther's legacy of opposition to reason has already done much of the heavy lifting when it comes to cleansing Kierkegaard's religious understanding of the rationality that was present in the Catholic church, via the scholastics and Jesuits, in the sixteenth and seventeenth centuries. Of course, Pascal was aware of Lutheranism, but it is unlikely that its sort of extreme mistrust of reason could have been as well-ingrained in Pascal in seventeenth-century France as it was in Kierkegaard, despite their Augustinian connections and other similarities between their situations.

24. For more on the dangers of dying to the world and to the self, see Simon Podmore's chapter in this volume.

25. Of course, Johannes Climacus points out that it is precisely this kind of worldly suffering that is indicative of one's eternal happiness or salvation (*evige Salighed*), but beyond this experience of suffering, an individual existing in the

world does not necessarily have any experience of such happiness (CUP, 1:452/SKS 7, 411). Given that Pascal and Kierkegaard (in *For Self-Examination*) both seem to be describing the life of a Christian in the world (and as worldly beings, what else could they describe?), it seems appropriate to focus on the absurdity and misery when talking about Kierkegaard's position. Again, I thank Pat Stokes for helping me to clarify this issue.

26. Although I cannot take this issue up in greater detail here, I would associate Pascal's position with the supra-rationalist view that Carr describes as advocating a "happy marriage" of faith and reason once reason learns its subordinate role. I would also, given Kierkegaard's divergence from Pascal, grant her claim that Kierkegaard is not a supra-rationalist but an antirationalist (he holds that whether or not reason *can* be appealed to, for the sake of genuine faith it *must not* be appealed to). See Carr, "Offense of Reason," pp. 245–49.

27. For assistance in developing the ideas presented in this chapter, I thank Roger Ariew, Charles Guignon, Sinead Ladegaard Knox, Gordon Marino, James Sellmann, and Patrick Stokes. I am also grateful to the Howard V. and Edna H. Hong Kierkegaard Library, and the attendees (among them, Søren Landkildehus) of both the "Kierkegaard and Death" conference at St. Olaf College in December of 2007, and the conference titled "Blaise Pascal, His Times and Influence: 350 Years after the *Provincial Letters*" at the University of South Florida in October of 2007.

4 ·

Suicide and Despair

Marius Timmann Mjaaland

There is but one truly serious philosophical problem, and that is suicide.
—ALBERT CAMUS, *THE MYTH OF SISYPHUS*

The Sickness unto Death. Already the title indicates a deep affliction with the problem of suicide, although the book is presented as a treatise on the modern self in despair. Suicide is not mentioned until a later stage of the analysis, when Kierkegaard suddenly breaks into a short discussion of how suicide influences despair. Then he admits, albeit in brackets, that this is what the *entire* investigation is about—in a "more profound" sense. The question of suicide thus seems unavoidable for any reading of *The Sickness unto Death,* but its significance has, so far, hardly been acknowledged or properly analyzed. In remedying this lack, I see here a chance to approach the entire problem of self and despair once more, from different angles including sociological, cultural, and psychological, as well as theological and philosophical.

From a theoretical perspective, the problem of suicide raises basic questions concerning religion and the very meaning of existence. It thereby affects the individual on a personal level and is frequently an issue for psychology, philosophy, and literature. However, it is also a sociological and cultural problem, as shown by Émile Durkheim in his famous study *Le suicide* (1897). In *The Sickness unto Death,* published by Kierkegaard in 1849 under the pseudonym Anti-Climacus, the individual and the sociological aspects seem to be closely intertwined.[1] Suicide is, after all, a troubling symptom of cultural, spiritual, and psychological sickness, a sickness *unto* death in the most literal sense.

Self, Spirit, Suicide

According to the initial definition offered in *Sickness*, "A human being is spirit" (SUD, 13/SKS 11, 129). Spirit is then further defined as the self, and the self is in turn defined as a self-reflexive relationship, a "relation's relating itself to itself." A person who does not relate to him- or herself is not yet a self. He or she is thus "spiritless," i.e., unconscious of being a self in the sense of spirit. Such ignorance of being a self, Kierkegaard claims, is the most common form of despair (SUD, 45/SKS 11, 161). Despair proper does, however, presuppose a certain consciousness of being a self and thus consciously relating to oneself. The basic structure of *conscious* despair is double or twofold: in despair not willing to be oneself, and in despair willing to be oneself. This double origin of the sickness unto death makes it necessary to analyze it dialectically.[2]

Kierkegaard's definition of spirit deliberately relates to the Christian tradition. Hence he points out that his criteria for what despair is, and for defining someone as being in despair, cannot be given by aesthetic standards or by so-called pagan standards, such as nation, state, or culture (SUD, 46/SKS 11, 161). He insists on the Christian definition of despair as the only valid definition—although it is applied universally, regardless of religious commitment. The definition appears to be what we would now call "inclusivistic." Hence even the pagan, the atheist, or anyone else who would presumably be ignorant of being in despair falls under this definition.[3] Ignorance is no excuse. And the principal difference between the spirit and the spiritless, Kierkegaard claims, becomes visible in their differing judgments on *suicide*:

> That is why the pagan (to cite this as an example, although it touches this whole investigation in a much more profound way) judged suicide with such singular irresponsibility, yes, praised suicide, which for spirit is the most crucial sin, escaping from existence in this way, mutinying against God. The pagan lacked the spirit's definition of a self, and therefore it judged *sui*cide [*S e l v mord: self*-murder] in that way; and the same pagan who judged suicide in that way passed severe moral judgment on stealing, unchastity, etc. He lacked the point of view for suicide, he lacked the God-relationship and the self; in purely pagan thinking, suicide is the indifferent [*det Indifferente*], something entirely up to the pleasure of each individual, since it is no one else's business (SUD, 46/SKS 11, 161; trans. modified).

As soon as suicide is mentioned as an example, Kierkegaard admits that the whole inquiry is in fact deeply concerned with the problem. It touches upon the issues of (i) self, (ii) spirit, and (iii) despair in the most profound ways. I see the problem as being relevant to all three levels of the discourse and will discuss all three in sequence.

The problem of *self* is already built into the Danish term *Selvmord,* as it is in the Latin *sui-cidium.* Moreover, the self faces both the existential problem of death and the moral and juridical problem of murder. Secondly, we have the question of spirit (*pneuma*), as a perspective on human beings which differs distinctly from the soul (*psychē*) and the body (*sōma*). "Spirit" is also related to a particular use of language, a point that adds to the difficulties of the analysis.[4] And thirdly, we have the problem of despair, of a self that is sick in a cultural, psychological, and religious sense and thus is analyzed psychologically and dialectically. Kierkegaard's approach is explicitly *not* therapeutic; he analyzes the sickness and not its cure.[5] I think there are methodological reasons for this, connected to the independence of the reader (*indirække Meddelelse*), as well as reasons connected to his substantive criticism of church, society, and contemporary Hegelian philosophy and theology. But that does not, of course, prevent a therapeutic relevance of his theory in relation to a dialectical therapy for despair, for depression, or even for suicidality.[6]

The Suicidal Structure of Self-Consciousness

Let me take the problem of self and its entanglement with the moral problem of suicide as a point of departure. Ethically, Kierkegaard condemns suicide as murder, just as Abraham, under an ethical perspective, is accused of intentional murder in *Fear and Trembling.*[7] From a religious perspective, however, suicide means the opposite of Abraham's sacrifice: whereas Abraham was *obedient* to God, Kierkegaard argues, in the passage quoted above, that the person committing suicide is *mutinying* against God. The pagan who praises suicide, as the Stoics and Seneca did,[8] is thus accused of *indifference* (Danish *Indifferents*), i.e., failing to regard the earnest thought of death as being important at all.[9]

I have previously argued that the problem of death in *Sickness* first raises the question of self.[10] Behind the question of temporal life and death there is the terrifying notion of eternal death. Within this horizon, suicide ultimately becomes the example *par excellence* of a despairing self; detached from any spiritual authority, suicide is in fact an indifferent act. But death's "retroactive power" in life[11] shows why Kierkegaard thinks suicide is not defendable; if death is *indifferent,* it implies that life is indifferent, and thus devalued. Suicide corresponds to both basic forms of despair: *not* willing to be oneself, hence "escaping from existence," but also despairingly *willing* to be oneself in refusal of any higher authority, whether divine, moral, or human.

The self as defined by Kierkegaard is basically a *relational* self, implying relations to others, to God, and to oneself. All three relations include responsibilities. Suicide would imply neglecting all these responsibilities as far as Kierkegaard understands them: becoming oneself, being there for the other, and accepting God's superiority as the power that *established* the self. Hence it is seen as unacceptable and judged as the "most serious sin"; both in religious and ethical respects, Kierkegaard rejects and condemns suicide.

There must be another sense in which suicide touches upon the investigation in the most *profound* way, namely, by killing oneself in a *spiritual* sense, and by the suicidal individual's hubris in not accepting any other authority. Precisely this double tendency, i.e., the double structure of despair, is rejected and condemned, but it is nevertheless identified as the most typical human attitude toward oneself and toward others. As previously mentioned, despair is profoundly *suicidal* in these two respects: (1) Despairingly not willing to be oneself, hence seeking to "rid himself of [*blive af med*] the relation to himself," without being able to; and (2) in despair willing to be oneself, hence being incessantly occupied with oneself to the exclusion of otherness. Kierkegaard calls the latter "inclosing reserve," and this tendency is deeply rooted in despair—as it is in his understanding of suicide as "mutinying against God." In this particular double sense, Kierkegaard has already *inscribed* suicide into his description of despair, viz. by accusing the despairing individual of giving himself death (French: *se donner la mort*),[12] by *bringing* the sickness unto death *upon* himself:

> Every actual moment of despair is traceable to possibility; every moment he is in despair he *is bringing* it upon himself. . . . The reason for this is that to despair is a qualification of spirit and relates to the eternal in man. . . . He cannot throw it away once and for all, nothing is more impossible . . . he must have thrown it or is throwing it away—but it comes again, that is, every moment he is in despair he is bringing his despair upon himself. . . . A person cannot rid himself of [*blive af med*] the relation to himself any more than he can rid himself of his self, which, after all, is one and the same thing, since the self is the relation to oneself (SUD, 17/SKS 11, 133).

The last sentence indicates that a process of committing suicide, or at least trying to do so, is continuously going on within despair; it is not only a feeling of melancholy, as in *Either-Or.* It is not the psychological abyss of anxiety, into which the single individual is drawn in the most ambiguous way.[13] Despair is an effort aimed at getting rid of oneself while not being able to get rid of oneself. That is the contradiction in which the despairing person lives, and despair is thus a continuous suffering under the contradictions of suicide, in despair willing *and* not willing to be oneself.

Hence, suicide, which in a moral sense is strictly prohibited, is applied as the despairing subject's overall perspective on the question of self. In *The Concept of Anxiety,* the pseudonym Vigilius Haufniensis writes that the physician at the insane asylum who thinks himself free of madness is probably more foolish than the people inside the hospital.[14] Similarly, although most people do not kill themselves in the literal sense, Kierkegaard identifies the same self-destructive tendency in all people—and the person who thinks himself free of this tendency would be even more foolish than that physician. Every despairing person would have to begin inside the asylum, so to speak, as indicated in the editor's first draft of a postscript to the book: "This book seems to be written by a physician; I, the editor, am not the physician, I am one of the sick" (SUD, 162/SKS 22, 365).

Discovering this suicidal tendency of the self will *eo ipso* lead deeper into conscious despair; hence it dramatically increases the danger of actually *committing* suicide. This discovery introduces an intensification of despair, which is self-destructive but also clarifying:

> As pointed out earlier, the level of consciousness intensifies the despair. To the extent that a person has the truer conception of despair, if he still remains in despair, and to the extent that he is more clearly conscious of being in despair—to that extent the despair is more intensive. The person who, with a realization that suicide is despair and to that extent with a true conception of the nature of despair, commits suicide is more intensively in despair than one who commits suicide without a clear idea that suicide is despair; conversely, the less true his conception of despair, the less intensive his despair. On the other hand, a person who with a clearer consciousness of himself (self-consciousness) commits suicide is more intensively in despair than one whose soul, by comparison, is in confusion and darkness (SUD, 48–49/SKS 11, 163–64).

Suicide does, in fact, become the paradigmatic example of how despair influences self-consciousness and may lead to the most tragic end. Self-consciousness in Kierkegaard (as opposed to Hegel) is not conceived as a speculative dialectic of more and more knowledge and conceptual insight into the nature of the Idea. It is, conversely, conceived as deeper insight into the nature of despair and the extent to which one is oneself in despair. But this increasing consciousness also provokes an intensified despair, through a "dialectical interplay between knowing and willing" (SUD, 48/SKS 11, 163). On the other hand, this insight into oneself and the self-destructive process of despair is necessary to overcome the sickness, i.e., to have any hope of being cured.

Diagnosis and Analysis of the Spirit

What is spirit? That is the point where the entire discussion begins. In a principal reflection upon what a human being is and should be—what is the *truth* of human existence? The discussion includes philosophical, anthropological, religious, cultural, and historical aspects.[15]

In *The Sickness unto Death*, Kierkegaard presents his theory of the spirit in the form of a diagnosis, the diagnosis of a very common cultural sickness of his time. The diagnosis is given in the most dramatic terms, as a hidden cancer, consumption (i.e., tuberculosis), or even *self*-consumption, which, due to its hiddenness, remains unacknowledged but all the more dangerous (SUD, 18/SKS 11, 134). The hiddenness of despair requires an indirect communication (*indirækte Meddelelse*), which makes the reader aware of the sickness through self-reflection and self-view (*autopsy* in different senses of that word).[16] Kierkegaard thus develops a comprehensive dialectical theory of despair, in continuous dialogue with the reader, since "just as the level of consciousness of what despair is can vary exceedingly, so also can the level of consciousness of one's own state that it is despair" (SUD, 48/SKS 11, 162). The strategy is to demask and expose the complex dia-lectics of the sickness unto death, in order to set the dia-gnosis.

Due to modernity turning apostate, however, the cultural and religious conflict between pagan and Christian represents a particular twist of the problem, again exemplified by their conflicting judgments of suicide:

> The point that suicide is basically a crime against God completely escapes the pagan. Therefore, it cannot be said that the suicide is despair, for such a remark would be a thoughtless hysteron-proteron; but it may be said that such a judging of suicide by the pagan was despair.
>
> Yet there is and remains a difference, and it is a qualitative difference, between paganism in the stricter sense and paganism in Christendom, the

> distinction that Vigilius Haufniensis pointed out with respect to anxiety: namely, that paganism does indeed lack spirit but that it still is qualified in the direction of spirit, whereas paganism in Christendom lacks spirit in a departure from spirit or in a falling away and therefore is spiritlessness in the strictest sense (SUD, 46–47/SKS 11, 161–62).

Three distinctions are introduced here that influence the analysis of suicide. First, Kierkegaard distinguishes between *suicide* as such, which cannot yet, *de facto*, be qualified as despair (hence a "hysteron-proteron," which "thoughtlessly" presupposes the condition that is introduced by the Christian understanding of spirit), and the *judgment of suicide*, which, *de jure*, is. Despair proper presupposes a certain consciousness of the self, which Kierkegaard cannot expect to find in the pagan, neither in antiquity nor in modernity. But *judging* suicide as an expression of indifference implies the opposite of what Kierkegaard sees as the Christian point of view; hence it is qualified as despair. The judgment falls back on the pagan, so that whether the despairing person is a believer or not, the judgment of suicide as indifference (and hence the entire question of self and self-murder as indifferent) is essentially seen as a crime against God.

Second, there is a historical question involved, in which the direction *toward* or *away from* Christendom plays a role (later in the book, the very term "Christendom" [*Christenhed*] becomes the technical term for a Christian cult and culture which has fallen away from Christ). Lacking spirit when qualified *in the direction of* spirit is implicitly marked with hope. Pagan thinking *within* a Christian culture is seen as a far more threatening problem; pagan ignorance in the name of Christian spirit (cf. Kierkegaard's opinion on Hegel and Hegelianism as well as the contemporary Danish state church) confuses the very possibility of recognizing oneself as spirit and of recognizing suicide as despair.

Third, as a consequence of this "falling away" from Christendom, the once powerful language, the *Word of God*, has become domesticated and impotent, worn-out and almost worthless.[17] He accuses (Hegelian) philosophy and theology of having distorted the language of spirit into "counterfeit money."[18] There are no longer any *pure* and proper concepts available. There is no true language that could identify the problem, i.e., *no separate language of the spirit* that could give an appropriate diagnosis of the problem and prepare the ground for a cure. Therefore, his diagnosis begins with a phenomenological description of different *forms* of despair.

The short passages on suicide in *The Sickness unto Death* play a double role in this analysis: (a) to indicate what despair is, namely a continuous suicide in the spiritual sense of the word, and (b) to identify the reader as a person in despair, by provoking the intensification of the despairing self-consciousness in a dialectic of will and knowledge.

Judging the spiritual perspective as superior to the mental and bodily perspective may, however, become quite problematic in the particular case of suicide. When Kierkegaard suggests that *committing* suicide might be the result of higher consciousness and a clearer insight, this seems like a meager comfort to the bereaved standing at a graveside (cf. SUD, 48/ SKS 11, 163). Moreover, he moves into an ethical minefield when he seems eager to emphasize and even *provoke* the risk involved. The exposure of hidden despair might trigger the crisis that leads to suicide—or, alternatively lead *through* that crisis to the prospective cure of suicidality. Is such a crisis desirable in the first place? And at any cost? Émile Durkheim advocates the exact opposite opinion based on statistical studies of suicide rates: they tend to rise dramatically in times of crisis. That is a clear indication of people becoming less happy and more desperate. The acute problem is that in cases of deep entanglement in despair and suicidal thoughts, even the strictest ethical prohibition of suicide is of little help, if any.[19] And when the deed is done, it is too late.

The Dialectical Forms of Despair

At this point I will return to the definition of despair (iii). As indicated, Kierkegaard adopts a double strategy in order to analyze and expose the structure of despair. He thus presents two different models for his diagnosis: (a) a typology of despair based on the conceptual opposites finitude/ infinitude and possibility/necessity (Chapter C.A.) and (b) a dialectical analysis of its development based on the distinction between despairingly willing and despairingly not willing to be oneself (Chapter C.B.). The passages on suicide are situated at the transition from (a) to (b); hence they are relevant to both, and in particular to the connection between them.

The definition of the self as synthesis in A.A. is taken as a point of departure. Accordingly, Kierkegaard claims that all kinds of human despair may be analyzed according to the following scheme:

(i) Infinitude's despair (lack of finitude)
(ii) Finitude's despair (lack of infinitude)
(iii) Possibility's despair (lack of necessity)
(iv) Necessity's despair (lack of possibility)

He gives a brief description of all four types, not in the form of an exhaustive diagnosis but rather as a character drawing. Paul Ricoeur describes the typology as follows: "The reader's astonishment, unease, admiration, and irritation depend on this incessant oscillation between the most pointed imagery experimentation and the most artificial conceptual dialectic."[20]

Let me just give a summary here of the four types, which I have elsewhere[21] examined in detail. Infinitude's despair, due to lack of finitude, is described as a kind of liberation from society, where the individual sees himself as dissociated from social bonds like family or religion. Kierkegaard describes how the feeling, knowledge, and will of the despairing person become fantastic and thus his self is gradually *volatilized.*[22] Finitude's despair is the opposite, i.e., a person who forgets himself in his immediate social circumstances and the duties of an ordinary life—he becomes what Kierkegaard calls a "copy" or a "mass man."[23]

The two other types are also connected to the distinction between the need for limits and the unlimited. Possibility's despair is described as the refusal to accept the necessary limits of life: "Thus possibility seems greater and greater to the self; more and more it becomes possible because nothing becomes actual. Eventually everything seems possible, but this is exactly the point at which the abyss swallows up the self" (SUD, 36/SKS 11, 151). Necessity's despair, on the other hand, is described as the total lack of possibilities; thus the despairing person experiences a closed universe (as in determinism or fatalism) and sees no real possibility of acting *otherwise.* Everything has thus become *necessary*—or *trivial* (SUD, 40/SKS 11, 155).

All in all, the four types are organized in two sets of opposites, which Kierkegaard describes as dialectical opposites, although in a Socratic rather than Hegelian style of dialectic (there is no *third* concept uniting the two). In the first two, we find the individualistic form of despair (losing oneself in infinity) versus the social or altruistic form, where one loses oneself in the immediate social relations (finitude). Kierkegaard thereby establishes the individual-social opposition as a basic condition for analyzing the self. In the two latter forms, focus shifts toward the definition of *limits* or basic categories for one's life; in the third form, possibility loses its basis in reality and the self dissolves in anomy, whereas in the fourth form, the *nomos* of necessity takes control over one's life and one ends up in fatalism, determinism, or simply the mediocre life of Philistine expectations and probabilities (the so-called *quantum satis*).

Only a short look at Durkheim's work on suicide will suffice to show that he operates with a similar distinction in his analysis of four different types of suicide: egoistic vs. altruistic, and anomic vs. fatalistic (*Suicide* [hereafter "S"], vii, 239). This observation is interesting as such, but for a further analysis I will have to return to Durkheim in the next section.

In connection with the fourth type of despair, Kierkegaard describes a person who is driven to the edge of existence, who despairs over the lack of any further possibilities, which might have saved him from the worst thinkable destiny:

> Imagine that someone with a capacity to imagine terrifying nightmares has pictured himself some horror or other that is absolutely unbearable. Then it happens to him, this very horror happens to him. Humanly speaking, his collapse is altogether certain—and in despair his soul's despair fights to be permitted to despair, to attain, if you please, the composure to despair, to obtain the total personality's consent to despair and be in despair; . . . At this point, then, salvation is, humanly speaking, utterly impossible; but for God everything is possible! This is the battle of *faith*, battling, madly, if you will, for possibility, because possibility is the only salvation (SUD, 38/SKS 11, 154; trans. modified).

The collapse thus described is in fact a breakthrough in Kierkegaard's dialectics of despair. When the despairing person is brought to the edge of existence, all his categories are shaken, and if he survives the crisis, he has learned to live with a basic insecurity—which he takes as an opportunity to hope, even counter to reason, by "madly" fighting for possibility.

According to Kierkegaard, even the determinist and the fatalist will have a God, but their God is necessity. Similarly, the other types of despair presumably have their own gods in society, in fantasy, in fortune, in grief, or in oneself. At this particular point, however, Kierkegaard introduces what he thinks must be the decisive definition of God: "God is this, that everything is possible, or that everything is possible, is God" (SUD, 40/SKS 11, 156; trans. modified).

This is the ultimate point where the dialectics of despair collapses, where the self breaks down in despair. The self thus re-established is a dependent self, which will remain dependent on the other, on God as ultimate possibility. As we have seen, though, the notion of God is not reconstructed by mere chance; what seems to take place is a decentering of the self where God becomes the bearing ground—God is conceived as radical possibility, even in the most desperate situation, e.g., when thoughts of suicide occur.

Suicide and Anomy

Kierkegaard's four types of despair show some striking similarities with the four paradigmatic types of suicide in Durkheim's classic study of suicide from 1897. Still, their views on society, anthropology, and religion are very different (S, 105–239). As Kierkegaard observes, there is a "falling away" from the Christian definition of spirit (into what he calls "Christendom," void of Christianity) during the Hegelian aftermath, which is most clearly expressed during the classical period of criticism of religion by Feuerbach, Marx, Nietzsche, and Freud. And suicide seems to be an issue on which these philosophers diverge.

In *Also sprach Zarathustra* (1883–85), Nietzsche hails suicide, or the "free decision" of taking one's life, as a "noble" expression of superiority and freedom.[24] His proclamation also echoes thoughts from the Stoics, but there is at the same time a polemical sting against the *slave morality* of Christianity, which Nietzsche accuses of nihilism. This is but one example of the various opinions on this question among the intellectuals of the period, and the judgment on suicide shows a parting of the ways in relation to other key issues. Whereas Kierkegaard and Nietzsche remain focused on the single individual and argue, respectively, that religion or atheism plays a significant role, Durkheim appeals to statistics and observes the problem of suicide sociologically. From that point of view, the doctrines of religion and moral judgment become less important. Still, Durkheim, like Kierkegaard, analyzes suicide according to a scheme of four different types, and just as in Kierkegaard's typology, they are organized in two couples, which are then elaborated in detail:[25]

(i) Egoistic suicide
(ii) Altruistic suicide
(iii) Anomic suicide
(iv) Fatalistic suicide

As in Kierkegaard, the first two forms are concerned with the individual versus society. Even though their basic perspectives differ considerably, Durkheim's analysis of egoistic suicide shows some striking similarities with Kierkegaard's definition of infinitude's despair. Durkheim describes a person who starts doubting his faith and no longer feels like "a real participant in the faith to which he belongs, and from which he is freeing himself; the more the family and community become foreign to the individual, so much the more does he become a mystery to himself" (S, 171). This mysterious explanation of who and why and "to what purpose" corresponds with the abstract sentimentality and the fantastic religiosity that, according to Kierkegaard, is a symptom of infinitude's despair. The existential aspects of Durkheim's theory become even more distinct when he explains why excessive individualism is *itself* one of the "suicidogenic causes":

> Egoism is not merely a contributing factor in it; it is its generating cause. In this case the bond attaching man to life relaxes because that attaching him to society is itself slack. The incidents of private life which seem the direct inspiration of suicide and are considered its determining causes are in reality only incidental causes. The individual yields to the slightest shock of circumstance because the state of society has made him a ready prey to suicide (S, 173).

There are also some striking connections between finitude's despair and the second type of suicide, described by Durkheim as altruistic, which is supposed to be the result of social integration that is too strong (S, 175). Durkheim's description focuses on honor and shame, as seen in religiousness (e.g., martyrdom), financial life (e.g., bankruptcy), and times of war (often called "heroic suicide") (S, 198). Altruistic suicides may be perceived as obligatory or optional, but common to all of them is that the individual "must be almost completely absorbed in the group and the latter, accordingly, [is] very highly integrated" (S, 179). Like Kierkegaard's second type of despair, the result is a *lack* of individuation, which according to Durkheim is just as dangerous as excessive or egoistic individuation.

Kierkegaard's third and fourth types of despair are connected to possibility and necessity. The whole dialectic between possibility's and necessity's despair seems to correspond to Durkheim's *anomic* suicide. Anomic suicide differs from egoistic and altruistic suicide "in its dependence, not on the way in which individuals are attached to society, but on how it regulates them" (S, 219). The perspective is now turned the other way around; it is not a question of how the individual relates to society but to what extent the basic categories of social life, including religion, marriage, ethics, politics, etc., are able to regulate social *and* individual life in a way that makes it sensible and meaningful. For some reason, the analysis of necessity is almost absent here. Although Durkheim mentions fatalistic suicide in a footnote "for completeness' sake," he does not undertake a separate analysis of the phenomenon.[26] This is probably due to Durkheim's general assessment of how European societies develop in the late nineteenth century: they are out of equilibrium and rapidly changing. His description of anomy does, however, include what Kierkegaard describes as possibility's despair and necessity's despair. Durkheim's category is broader; it covers both perspectives and the dialectical relationship between them.

Perhaps the most interesting part of *Le Suicide* when we read it today is what Durkheim writes about a period of economic crisis: "It is a well-known fact that economic crises have an aggravating effect on the suicidal tendency" (S, 201). During the years 1873–74 a financial crisis in Vienna is reported to have caused an acute rise in the number of suicides, up 70 percent for the first three months of 1874. Similar tendencies were reported in Frankfurt (Main) and Paris during the following years. Durkheim does not accept the common explanation that this was a reaction caused by "life . . . becoming more difficult" due to increasing poverty (S, 203). If that was the reason, statistics of voluntary deaths should have decreased in good times. But that is not the case. The reason for this increase, according to Durkheim, is the *instability* of the society, the *anomic* period where positions shift and values change rapidly, where some people earn a lot of money while others become bankrupt. *Both* are equally apt to commit suicide.

Hence, the word "crisis" as such has no positive value in Durkheim's vocabulary:

> If therefore industrial or financial crises increase suicides, this is not because they cause poverty, since crises of prosperity have the same result; it is because they are crises, that is, disturbances of the collective order. Every disturbance of equilibrium, even though it achieves greater comfort and a heightening of general vitality, is an impulse to voluntary death (S, 206–7).

Durkheim reflects further on this peculiar fact by comparing humans with animals. The animal has established equilibrium as soon as it has filled the "void" of needs, e.g., food and rest; it has (allegedly) no capacity to reflect beyond its immediate needs, "and the balance is automatic" (S, 207). With humans, Durkheim thinks, everything is different, because most of our needs are *not* dependent on our bodies, but on unpredictable factors like "free combinations of the will," social hierarchies, and unstable feelings, where "our capacity for feeling is in itself an insatiable and bottomless abyss" (S, 208).

Throughout these passages, Durkheim elaborates his general anthropology, his view of religion, and his general estimation of society. He develops a comprehensive theory of society based on the perspective of suicide. It is an odd but brilliant idea, which made him one of the founding fathers of sociology. However, this theory relies heavily on strong presuppositions concerning society, religion, and anthropology. Human beings are, according to this idea, political beings with strong social needs, and society has the function of regulating these needs and stabilizing human existence—and so has God, or the symbol "God." Risk is accepted but not enhanced, and crises should be avoided as far as possible. Himself an agnostic, Durkheim still worries about the fading influence of religion as well as the lack of power exercised by the superior state. According to the theory that Durkheim further elaborates in *The Elementary Forms of Religious Life,* these are, in fact, two sides of the same coin. He understands religion as a *fact* of society, a collective representation, where God consequently becomes an *apotheosis* of society, i.e., society celebrating itself and sanctioning its own institutions.[27]

Questions without Response

The similarities between Kierkegaard and Durkheim are in fact rather astonishing since there is no evidence that Durkheim ever read Kierkegaard. The comparative analysis reveals a social concern in Kierkegaard and a profoundly existential concern in Durkheim, whereas their opposed perspectives may contribute to a more comprehensive and critical theory of suicide, if arguments from both authors are taken together. Still, the dissimilarities prove to be even more interesting and clarifying. Durkheim and Kierkegaard have very different views on society, religion, and the importance of establishing an individual self grounded in *the other.* Kierkegaard criticizes what Durkheim advocates and *vice versa.*

Durkheim's series of statistical observations lay a firm foundation for analyzing tendencies in society, and the existential nerve of the text makes the analysis rather intriguing. When it comes to religion, however, the same statistical approach is applied in a way that reduces its existential relevance and contributes to an overall secular point of view. He argues for a stable society, which regulates people's lives in a reasonable way, regardless of their religious convictions or lack thereof—a society where religion plays a secondary role. From a historical point of view it is not difficult to see how Durkheim's work could be used to support secularism, e.g., the French law of *laïcité,* finally sanctioned in 1905.

In Kierkegaard, the role of religion in society also becomes an issue, but mainly as a target of severe criticism. He accuses his contemporary Danish society of reducing and leveling the importance of Christianity into a social institution called "Christendom."[28] In this social institution the most crucial Christian categories like sin, reconciliation, and spirit lose their founding and liberating sense. They dissolve into a general anthropology, psychology, and "wisdom of life." Moreover, it is this self-contained equilibrium of society that almost drives him insane, and gives him reason to consider whether one should rather let oneself be put to death for the sake of truth.[29]

The *conflict* as defined by Kierkegaard is, in short, about whether basic Christian categories may be *explained* in terms of philosophical anthropology, psychology, or sociology without reducing them to (almost) nonsense. Or, when compared to Durkheim, can the categories of religion be translated into *functions* of religious life, which regulate the relationship between individuals and society in time and space?[30]

The polemical tenor of Kierkegaard's argument is fundamentally opposed to such efforts. *The Sickness unto Death* may be called a diagnostic inquiry; the author elaborates a comprehensive conceptuality for the diagnosis of despair. Still, it points to the limits of therapy, as understood in the modern, secular sense. And exactly here, at the limit between pagan and Christian, between secular and religious, between a self-sufficient self and a self dependent on others, suicide comes to play a decisive role. But why suicide?

The problem of suicide has a tendency to radicalize opposites and give them a sense of urgency: Is there an ultimate meaning to human existence or is everything absurd after all? Is there a governing principle for life, or is God finally "dead"? At this edge of existence, the abstract theoretical subjects become topical: religion versus atheism, society versus the individual, and death versus life. Every instance of suicide tends to disrupt the discourse and trace life (and all the questions of life) "back to its briefest form" (WL, 345/SKS 9, 339).

To a certain extent Kierkegaard anticipates the basic conditions for modern psychology and psychoanalysis; the first step in the direction of a cure for despair is to identify and recognize it as an illness. Secondly, the analysis conceptualizes the problem and makes different categories available in order to define its *causes*. Thirdly, the ultimate goal is to become cured of the sickness, although the book does not identify the way to reach that goal (hence it does not qualify as therapeutic). It indicates some obstacles on the way, though. The despairing person will have to pass through an unavoidable crisis that occurs as soon as one becomes conscious of being in despair and able to analyze it critically. In a short "formula" he indicates the state in which despair is completely rooted out: being conscious of itself, the self would rest transparently in sobriety and faith (cf. SUD, 14, 131/SKS 11, 130, 242).

However, the concept of faith also plays a critical and polemical role here. Kierkegaard claims that there are basically two alternatives for human existence: *either* despair as a continuous suicide, ultimately leading to a living death, *or* the faith in God as an excess of possibility—"that everything is possible, is God." Compared to this decisive distinction between despair and faith, even suffering and death become to him "like a jest" (SUD, 8/SKS 11, 124). The only way out of the self-destructive circle of despair goes through an individualization, where the single individual dissociates from society in order to become transparent and conscious of itself, grounding itself in God as the *absolute* other of unconditional *absolution.*

Although *The Sickness unto Death* polemicizes against any tendency to reduce theological concepts to social categories (e.g., "Christendom"), the author is very conscious of the importance of fellow human beings in breaking up the isolation of a despairing self:

> If this inclosing reserve is maintained completely, *omnibus numeris absoluta* . . . then his greatest danger is suicide. Most men, of course, have no intimation of what such a person of inclosing reserve can endure; if they knew, they would be amazed. The danger, then, for the completely inclosed person is suicide. But if he opens up to one single person, he probably will become so relaxed, or so let down, that suicide will not result from inclosing reserve. Such a person of inclosing reserve with one confidant is moderated by one whole tone in comparison with one who is fully inclosed. Presumably he will avoid suicide (SUD, 66/SKS 11, 180).

In this passage at the end of "Part One" Kierkegaard proves that he believes in the value of dialogue to open up the closed universe of the despairing person. If communication with others is accepted, he believes that even the *inclosing reserve* of despair will be outstripped by the option of an unconditional confidence (SUD, 70–73/SKS 11, 184–86). He clearly believes in the power of communication, like any therapist. But his theory of communication also implies a basic critique of therapy. The theory of *indirect* communication is antitherapeutic in that it places God in the center of communication—thus the interlocutors are both playing minor roles in order to develop a dependent and decentered self. His *positive* notion of freedom is similar to what Habermas has labeled a dependent and *communicative freedom,* based on the excess of possibility, which *makes possible* a decentered and flexible self, in interaction with others.[31]

This goal is not incompatible with Durkheim's main point: that every human being is dependent on the surrounding society in order to discover a meaning in life, in order to carry the burdens of existence and avoid committing suicide. Still, Durkheim asks critical questions that go far beyond Kierkegaard's scope. His book on suicide therefore provides good opportunities to question some of the premises of Kierkegaard's treatise on despair. Where Kierkegaard emphasizes God first, Durkheim points to society as the basis for religious ideas, including the idea of God. And, without sentimentality, he shows that no religion has been able to prevent suicides—not even Christianity, even though both Catholics and Protestants traditionally have strictly condemned it (S, 124–25). Moreover, Durkheim's analysis leaves the reader with other questions that he does not answer explicitly. Is the incessant focus on questions of life and death in Christianity likely to increase the number of suicides? Could the existential nerve of this religion in itself be a suicidogenic factor? Or are the increasing numbers of voluntary deaths a result of its dissolution and the disorientation following from it? Might secularism perhaps be seen as the continuation of Christian society, although void of its social legitimacy, void of its power to frame and regulate human life in a meaningful way? Is that the reason suicide rates steadily increased in Europe throughout the nineteenth century?

When seen from an individual point of view, however, Kierkegaard does, ultimately, present the most sophisticated and challenging problems. What is it to be oneself? Has humanity grown sick and self-sufficient during the period of Enlightenment and modernity? Are humans still able to understand their weakness and unveil the dark matter of their own self-knowledge? Could they possibly make it back to the quest for selfhood through sustained reflection on individuality and sociality, on possibility and necessity?

And then there are the questions directed to the single individual. Are you still able to become sub-ject, subject to a higher authority? Are you able to discover freedom within limits? Would you take the risk of believing in a possibility beyond the limits you know? Or is it that risk that would lead you toward the abyss of enigmatic feelings? Is it the insight into your despair that, in the end, makes you resign your resistance and concede defeat to the deep structure of suicidality inscribed into your conscious and unconscious self?

The problem of suicide seems to raise more questions than it answers. And that is, after all, the reason it breaks open the unease and the disquietude once more; whether it is a suicide bomber in Gaza or a relative who silently, and often depressed, drops out the backdoor of existence, every instance of suicide raises some basic questions concerning the truth and sense of human life. Lives without a conclusion. Questions without response.

NOTES

The epigraph is from Albert Camus, "The Myth of Sisyphus," trans. Justin O'Brien, reprinted in *Ethics*, ed. Steven M. Cahn and Peter Markie, p. 397 (Oxford: Oxford University Press, 2009).

1. For various reasons I will refer to Kierkegaard as the author of *The Sickness unto Death*, as well as other texts in Kierkegaard's writings. I have discussed the problem of pseudonymity elsewhere, but I do not emphasize that aspect of Kierkegaard's philosophy in the present article—although it could have been discussed as an *example* of despair, of trying to escape from existence by adopting another name and poetizing oneself, which touches upon suicide in the "most profound" way. Cf. Marius Timmann Mjaaland, *Autopsia: Self, Death and God after Kierkegaard and Derrida* (Berlin/New York: de Gruyter, 2008), pp. 272–77.

2. Contra Michael Theunissen, *Der Begriff Verzweiflung: Korrekturen an Kierkegaard* (Frankfurt: Suhrkamp, 1993), pp. 16–21. Cf. the detailed argument in Marius Mjaaland, "X. Alterität und Textur in Kierkegaards *Krankheit zum Tode*," *Neue Zeitschrift für Systematische Theologie und Religionsphilosophie* 1 (2005): pp. 58–80.

3. This is a point that has provoked harsh criticism from Michael Theunissen in *Der Begriff Verzweiflung*, p. 29, followed by a vigorous discussion in Niels Jørgen Cappelørn and Herman Deuser, eds., *Kierkegaard Studies Yearbook 1996* (Berlin/New York: de Gruyter, 1996); and Niels Jørgen Cappelørn et al., eds., *Kierkegaard Studies Yearbook 1997* (Berlin/New York: de Gruyter, 1997). I do in fact agree with Theunissen here, even though his argument does not take notice of the important differences in historical context, due to secularization.

4. The particular meaning of *spiritual* language, as transferred or metaphorical meaning, is discussed by Kierkegaard in *Works of Love* (WL, 209–10/SKS 9, 212–13).

5. "[O]nce and for all may I point out that in the whole book, as the title indeed declares, despair is interpreted as a sickness, not as a cure" (SUD, 6/SKS 11, 118).

6. Cf. SUD, 6/SKS 11, 118. More on the constructive therapeutic approach in other works by Kierkegaard in the contributions to this volume by Buben and Podmore.

7. Cf. FT, 30/SKS 4, 126.

8. Kierkegaard refers to the Stoic philosophers and the Roman stoicists, whom he knew from Tennemann's history of philosophy. Cf. SKS K11, 200–1.

9. Cf. Kierkegaard's critique of Epicurus in TDIO, 75–76/SKS 5, 445. For more on this question see Patrick Stokes, "The Power of Death: Retroactivity, Narrative, and Interest," pp. 407–8, and Marius Mjaaland, "The Autopsy of One Still Living," pp. 379–82, both in *International Kierkegaard Commentary: Prefaces/Writing*

Sampler and Three Discourses on Imagined Occasions, ed. Robert L. Perkins (Macon, Ga.: Mercer University Press, 2006).

10. In the introduction, Kierkegaard gives a particular twist to the problem of self and death; see Mjaaland, *Autopsia*, pp. 151–55.

11. Cf. the definition of death's retroactive power in life in *Three Discourses on Imagined Occasions:* TDIO, 97/SKS 5, 465.

12. Cf. Jacques Derrida, *The Gift of Death*, trans. David Wills (Chicago: Chicago University Press, 1995), p. 31.

13. Cf. CA, 42–43/SKS 4, 348–49.

14. Cf. CA, 54/SKS 4, 359.

15. Cf. Mjaaland, "Alterität und Textur in Kierkegaards *Krankheit zum Tode*," p. 62.

16. Cf. Mjaaland, *Autopsia*, pp. 131–33; 293.

17. Cf. Mjaaland, *Autopsia*, pp. 288–90; 317–18.

18. Cf. the discussions of concepts, language, values, and religion in Derrida, *The Gift of Death*, pp. 109–15.

19. According to Durkheim there is at least no effect at the sociological level of a strict warning against suicide. Émile Durkheim, *Suicide: A Study in Sociology*, trans. John A. Spaulding and George Simpson (London: Routledge, 2002), pp. 124–25 (hereafter "S").

20. Paul Ricoeur, "Two Encounters with Kierkegaard," in *Kierkegaard's Truth: Disclosure of the Self*, ed. Joseph H. Smith, p. 322 (New Haven, Conn.: Yale University Press, 1981).

21. Cf. e.g., Mjaaland, *Autopsia*, pp. 212–30.

22. "The fantastic is generally that which leads a person out into the infinite in such a way that it only leads him away from himself and thereby prevents him from coming back to himself" (SUD, 31/SKS 11, 147).

23. "Surrounded by hordes of men, absorbed in all sorts of secular matters, more and more shrewd about the ways of the world—such a person forgets himself . . . finds it too hazardous to be himself and far easier and safer to be like the others, to become a copy, a number, a mass man" (SUD, 33–34/SKS 11, 149).

24. Friedrich Nietzsche, *Thus Spake Zarathustra: A Book for All and None*, trans. Thomas Common (New York: Gordon Press, 1974), p. 39: "My death, praise I unto you, the voluntary death, which cometh unto me because I want it. And when shall I want it?—He that hath a goal and an heir, wanteth death at the right time for the goal and the heir."

25. I first described this parallel in a short article written for the Norwegian journal of suicidology. Marius Mjaaland, "I dødens hule selv," *Suicidologi* 3 (2007): pp. 3–7.

26. "The above considerations show that there is a type of suicide [that is] the opposite of anomic suicide, just as egoistic and altruistic suicide are opposites. It is the suicide deriving from excessive regulation, that of persons with futures

pitilessly blocked and passions violently choked by oppressive discipline. . . . we might call it *fatalistic suicide*" (S, 239n).

27. Émile Durkheim, *The Elementary Forms of Religious Life*, trans. Karen E. Fields (New York: The Free Press, 1995), p. 421.

28. See SUD, 115/SKS 11, 223.

29. Cf. the little treatise called "Does a Human Being Have the Right to Let Himself Be Put to Death for the Truth?" in WA, 51–89/SKS 11, 57–93.

30. Cf. Durkheim, *The Elementary Forms of Religious Life*, pp. 9–11.

31. Jürgen Habermas, "Communicative Freedom and Negative Theology," in *Kierkegaard in Post/Modernity*, ed. Martin J. Matuštík and Merold Westphal, pp. 190–92 (Bloomington and Indianapolis: Indiana University Press, 1995).

5.

Thinking Death into Every Moment: The Existence-Problem of Dying in Kierkegaard's *Postscript*

Paul Muench

Doing philosophy may be hazardous to your health, resulting in a condition of "absentmindedness" or distraction in which you forget yourself.[1] In such a case, philosophy becomes an activity that positively interferes with the age-old Socratic task of attending to and caring for the self, and may even have the opposite effect of making people "incompetent to act" (CUP, 1:135/SKS 7, 126). If you are the type of person who is drawn to philosophy and perhaps insufficiently aware of its hazards, then what could be more valuable than a book that seeks to alert you to these dangers, and in the process even exhibits for you a manner of doing philosophy that is perfectly compatible with attending to yourself? In my view, Kierkegaard's *Concluding Unscientific Postscript* is just such a book. It is a work of philosophy that has both diagnostic and therapeutic aims, drawing its readers' attention to a condition they may have, or to which they may be prone, while also harking back to Socrates and to a "simpler philosophy" that is "presented by an existing individual for existing individuals" and according to which wisdom falls within the domain of ethics and concerns above all the question of how to live (CUP, 1:121/SKS 7, 116; cf. CUP, 1:309/SKS 7, 282).

My focus here will be on a portion of the therapeutic treatment being offered in the *Postscript*. In particular, I shall examine the book's main discussion of death (CUP, 1:165–70/SKS 7, 153–58).[2] My paper has two parts. In the first part, I characterize the book's narrator and the type of philosophical reader that is being addressed, while also describing in more general terms the alternative conception of philosophy that is being offered. Against the backdrop of a Hegelian manner of doing philosophy that allegedly marginalizes the task of attending to oneself, I argue that a key aspect of the treatment being offered consists in getting readers of the *Postscript* to appreciate the need to "restrain oneself" or hold oneself back (*at holde igjen paa sig selv*) (CUP, 1:165/SKS 7, 153). In the second part, I examine the discussion of death in detail, explicating what the existence-problem of dying is and how this relates to the seemingly paradoxical claim that to think about death one must think it "into every moment" of one's life (CUP, 1:167/SKS 7, 155). I contend that a key aim of the discussion of death is to alert readers of the *Postscript* to the possibility that their understanding of death may be incomplete and rest on a tendency to conceive of death in terms that do not include a cognizance of themselves as particular human beings. I offer an account of what thinking death into every moment might involve, tying this to the task of attending to oneself and to the exercise of self-restraint. If the Socratic dynamic of the *Postscript* is successful, then readers will become aware of the dangers of neglecting themselves while also being introduced to a healthy manner of doing philosophy that is compatible with the task of attending to themselves.

Philosophical Patient and Socratic Doctor

The *Postscript* is narrated by a fictional character, Johannes Climacus, who is one of Kierkegaard's best-known pseudonyms. I have argued elsewhere that Climacus is best conceived as a Socratic figure.[3] In response to a tendency his readers may have to neglect themselves and to be in a hurry to "go further" or to "go beyond" the task of attending to themselves (which they may even imagine they have "finished"), Climacus tries to slow things down, to linger a bit, to be, as he puts it, a "loafer" or idler who has plenty of time to think about matters that may seem to his readers to be too trivial or insignificant to satisfy their philosophical appetites.[4] By means of his loafing, Climacus seemingly aims at two things: (1) to get his readers to reflect further about the task of attending to themselves and what can make this difficult, and (2) to introduce them to a manner of doing philosophy that is compatible with this task.

In the chapter in the *Postscript* in which he considers death, Climacus's overall discussion concerns what he takes to be a tendency in his day for people to neglect ethics, neglecting in particular what he calls the task of "becoming subjective" or becoming a proper subject or self. Climacus suggests that what may explain this neglect is people's having fallen under the influence of a Hegelian concern with world history, leading them, on his view, to attach less importance to being an individual person (see, e.g., CUP, 1:355/SKS 7, 324; CUP, 1:16/SKS 7, 25). While attending to world history may shed light on the development of human culture and the human race as a whole, Climacus maintains that this requires a philosophical outlook that is fundamentally directed at the past and what is finished or complete. By his lights, such an outlook does not provide individuals with resources for trying to understand themselves in the midst of their unfolding, unfinished lives or help them to determine future actions:

> [A] Hegelian cannot possibly understand himself with the aid of his philosophy; he can understand only what is past, is finished, but a person who is still living is not dead and gone (CUP, 1:307/SKS 7, 280).

Climacus maintains that the real danger of repeatedly and habitually adopting the world-historical perspective is that this can lead to a condition of absentmindedness in individuals and in their losing track of themselves as ethical agents.

In response to this tendency to neglect ethics and the self, Climacus Socratically presents himself as someone who can't help "attending a little" to himself. While everyone else may have the time and the ability to devote themselves to world history, he maintains that he simply is not up to the task:

> Whereas all the nice people are promptly all set to attend to the future of world history, I am obliged many a time to sit at home and mourn over myself. Although my father is dead and I no longer attend school, although I have not been turned into the public authorities for correction, I have nevertheless seen the necessity of attending a little to myself [*at passe lidt paa mig selv*], even though I would undeniably prefer to go to Frederiksberg and deal with world history (CUP, 1:161/SKS 7, 149–50; trans. modified).[5]

By playing the part of a loafing Socratic figure who is not in a hurry to move on to world history, Climacus thereby casts himself as someone who often has occasion by regularly attending to himself to notice tasks that he alleges are "sufficient for a whole human life." While he admits that he feels the need to "grapple alone" with himself and his poor ethical condition, he does add that there is one person who provides a kind of moral support for his solitary endeavors: "The only one who consoles me is Socrates" (CUP, 1:161/SKS 7, 150).

Mourning over oneself and attending "a little" to oneself are clearly things that Climacus thinks his readers may not be in the habit of doing. One of his ultimate goals in fact seems to be to try to convince them that the task of attending to themselves is actually of greater significance (and difficulty) than they may imagine. Furthermore, given their intellectual inclinations, it also appears to be Climacus's aim to try to convince his readers not only that such a task by its very nature requires a lifelong commitment, but that in the process of carrying it out, "existence-problems" will arise that can also satisfy his readers' intellectual appetites—without, however, leading to the condition of self-forgetfulness and absentmindedness that he alleges results from engaging in modern, Hegelian-style speculative philosophy.[6] As part of his discussion of death, Climacus identifies "dying" (*det at døe*) as a paradigmatic example of an existence-problem; other examples that he considers include "praying," "being immortal," "thanking God," "marrying," and above all the problem of how an eternal happiness can be built on a historical knowledge, that is, the problem of becoming a Christian (see CUP, 1:352/SKS 7, 322). Existence-problems pertain to ethical and religious matters, and Climacus readily admits that for the person who is in the habit of thinking about the narratives of world history these problems may appear, comparatively speaking, insignificant or overly "simple" in nature (CUP, 1:160/SKS 7, 148). Climacus's aim is to impress upon his readers how these seemingly simple problems become much more difficult once they are conceived of in relation to an individual's own life. Since existence-problems concern ethics and religion, part of what makes them difficult stems from their being inherently practical and action-guiding, consisting of "not only a knowing" but "also a *doing* that is related to a knowing" (CUP, 1:160/SKS 7, 149; italics mine). As Climacus sees it, existence-problems are such that, if they are approached in the right way, then they should occupy and concern an individual at every moment for the whole of life and should, accordingly, provide the thinker with topics to think through that will also be engaging for the whole of life. In the case of thinking about death and dying in particular, Climacus argues that the individual should think death "into every moment" of her or his life (CUP, 1:167/SKS 7, 155). What he means by this claim, however, is far from obvious. Surely he is not suggesting that moment by moment one must have running through one's head the thought, "I am going to die" or something of the kind. That would be to advocate a task that is not only difficult but seemingly impossible. We will examine the nature of this claim in greater detail in the second part of this chapter.

If we are to appreciate fully Climacus's discussion of death and what thinking it into every moment might involve, we need to be clear about the intended audience of the *Postscript*. We need, that is, to establish who exactly the philosophical patient is supposed to be. Let's start by considering who Climacus is *not* addressing. In a footnote at the end of his discussion of death, Climacus underscores that his reflections about death and dying are not meant for everyone:

> Although it has been said frequently, I wish to repeat it again here: What is developed here by no means pertains to the simple [*de Eenfoldige*], whom the god will preserve in their lovable simplicity (although they sense the pressure of life in another way), the simplicity that feels no great need for any other kind of understanding, or, insofar as it is felt, . . . finds comfort in the thought that life's happiness does not consist in being a person of knowledge (CUP, 1:170/SKS 7, 158; trans. modified).

What is key here is the idea that some people may feel "no great need" to seek a deeper understanding of matters that arise in their lives. We might characterize the simple person as someone who has few or no philosophical inclinations, someone who is not naturally driven by the problems of life toward thinking and reflection since she or he "sense[s] the pressure of life in another way." In a later discussion of the existence-problem of what it is to marry, Climacus expands further on the sort of person he has in mind:

> [E]veryone who simply and honestly can say that he feels no need for this understanding—he is indeed without blame. Woe to the person who disturbs him . . . woe to the person who risks trying to pull the dangers and horrors of intellectual warfare down upon his blessed security in the enclosure of marriage (CUP, 1:181/SKS 7, 167).

On this view, the simple person doesn't feel a "need" for a deeper understanding and her or his happiness is not thought to depend on obtaining such an understanding. If there are such persons, philosophy not only doesn't occupy them but could actually wind up being a source of unhappiness, where the "blessed security" of the simple might be disrupted by the "intellectual warfare" that sometimes characterizes philosophy.[7]

Yet even though Climacus does not mean to engage simple persons with his writings, he does appeal to what he claims they may more straightforwardly know and understand in order to engage his more philosophically inclined readers. This is part of his strategy of trying to slow his readers down, of trying to get them to dwell a bit more on themselves and the difficulties associated with how to live. He invites his readers to agree that before the wise take up the difficulties of thinking about the world-historical, they should first make sure that they "understand the same thing that the simple person understands," though he imagines that his readers may also be inclined to agree with the following: "But of course this is so easy for the wise person to understand (why else is he called wise?) that understanding it is merely a matter of a moment, and at the very same moment he is in full swing with the world-historical" (CUP, 1:159–60/SKS 7, 148). Climacus does not himself endorse this view of the wise. His aim seems to be to get his readers to discover that there is more to what the simple person understands ("the simple") than they may imagine, and that therefore those who are truly wise will not be those who believe they can dispose of these matters in no time, but rather those who appreciate that the simple can be wholly engaging regardless of one's intellectual makeup. For despite what his readers may be inclined to think, it is Climacus's view that these simple matters actually present peculiar difficulties for the wise:

> Is it not precisely the simple that is most difficult for the wise person to understand? The simple person understands the simple directly, but when the wise person is to understand it, it becomes infinitely difficult (CUP, 1:160/SKS 7, 148; trans. modified).

After first drawing a contrast between the simple and the wise (the latter of which many of his readers may assume themselves to be or aspire to be), Climacus introduces a second sense of what he means by "simple," suggesting that it is the simple more than anything that the wise find difficult to understand. While it is not immediately obvious why the simple should be especially difficult for the wise, this claim should serve to check his readers a bit, if only to make them puzzle over the meaning of these words.

In this context, Climacus holds out for his readers the prospect of a relationship to the simple that rests on a certain "equality" between those who have philosophical inclinations and those who do not (see especially CUP, 1:227–28/SKS 7, 207–8). He maintains that what underwrites this equality is the idea that what they understand is the same, even while the manner in which they understand this is different:

> The wise person relates himself to the simple in this way. When he enthusiastically honors this as the highest, it honors him in turn, for it is as if it became something else through him, although it still remains the same. The more the wise person thinks about the simple (that there can be any

> question of a longer preoccupation with it already shows that it is not so easy after all), the more difficult it becomes for him. Yet he feels gripped by a deep humanness that reconciles him with all of life: that the difference between the wise person and the simplest person is this little evanescent difference *that the simple person knows the essential* and the wise person little by little *comes to know* that he knows it or *comes to know* that he does not know it, but what they know is the same. Little by little—and then also the wise person's life comes to an end—so when was there time for the world-historical interest? (CUP, 1:160/SKS 7, 149).

Climacus's suggestion seems to be that both the simple and the wise can lead lives that are related to the same thing, to what he is calling the simple. While he claims that the simple will know the simple in effect nonreflectively, the wise will always be in the process of reflectively discovering what they know (or don't know) about the very same thing. It is this difference that creates conceptual space for Climacus's alternative conception of the ideal philosopher, someone who does not set herself or himself apart from the ordinary person in terms of content, but who nevertheless leads a more reflective, intellectual life. In this way, "the simple" represents part of his concept of the proper philosopher. Sometimes he calls this individual the "subjective thinker," but elsewhere he uses the term "simple wise person" (the latter, incidentally, being a term that both he and Kierkegaard use to designate Socrates).[8]

This distinction between the simple person and the subjective thinker/simple wise person might seem to suggest that Climacus's intended audience is the committed Hegelian philosopher. There are reasons, however, for thinking that this is not his true target. The speculative philosopher is the frequent butt of numerous jokes in the *Postscript* and is often ridiculed by Climacus. While part of his endeavor is to warn against doing philosophy in this way, it is not obvious that the manner in which he writes about the Hegelian is a very effective way of engaging the Hegelian herself or himself. Would such a person really put up with this sort of treatment over the course of several hundred pages? A better candidate, it seems, is someone who is drawn to philosophy but who has not yet developed a settled philosophical outlook. Such a person remains vulnerable to the condition of absentmindedness but is not yet so set in her or his ways that there is little hope of acquiring a deeper impression of the task of attending to oneself. In the footnote we discussed earlier, where Climacus denies that he is addressing the simple, he says a bit more about his intended audience: "On the other hand, [what has been developed here about death] does pertain to the person who considers himself to have the ability and the opportunity for deeper inquiry" (CUP, 1:170/SKS 7, 158). I think Climacus's reader therefore is best conceived of as someone who seeks "deeper inquiry," but also as someone who can still be convinced that the task of becoming an existing human being is the highest task and that philosophy need not be incompatible with this task. At one point in his discussion, Climacus describes himself as such a person, someone who feels the "need" for a "deeper understanding," one of those who is "not altogether simple" since he does "feel a need to understand" but who, in comparison to the speculative philosopher, may appear "limited" in that he feels "particularly the need to understand the simple." He says that it is in these terms that he has "tried to understand [himself]" and in the process he also arguably serves as an example for his philosophically inclined readers (CUP, 1:180/SKS 7, 166; CUP, 1:182/SKS 7, 168).

Climacus thus holds out to his readers an alternative to becoming a speculative philosopher. As he examines a number of different existence-problems and tries to motivate the alternative conception of philosophy that he claims is exhibited by the subjective thinker/simple wise person, he also specifies further what he thinks the speculative philosopher lacks, and so, by implication, what he thinks his readers need to cultivate. Since the existence-problem of dying is supposed to make thinking about death more difficult, getting clearer about this lack will bear directly on how the thinking person ought to approach death and what it is to think death into every moment of one's life. To return to the image of the speculative philosopher as one who too readily and too quickly imagines that she or he has finished with the task of attending to herself or himself (whereas Climacus, recall, is a loafer who has plenty of time), what such an individual needs above all, according to Climacus, is *self-restraint.* He claims that "since the temptation is to finish too quickly," the individual's "task is to exercise restraint" over herself or himself (CUP, 1:165/SKS 7, 153). That is, individuals need to keep themselves from prematurely ceasing to attend to themselves, from acting on any inclination to conceive of the task of attending to themselves as something they could have finished, where the faster one can do this the more quickly one can turn to world history. Speed is not an admirable quality here. By way of illustration, Climacus compares the quickness of the speculative philosopher to someone who does not make proper use of her or his time:

> Suppose a person is given the task of entertaining himself for one day and by noon is already finished with the entertainment—then his speed would

> indeed be of no merit. So it is also when life is the task. To be finished with life before life is finished with one is not to finish the task at all (CUP, 1:164/SKS 7, 152; cf. CUP, 1:405–6/SKS 7, 369).

One way for Climacus to help his readers to appreciate that the speed of the speculative philosopher is not necessarily something to be emulated is by the way he himself slows things down and takes his time. In the process, this may get his readers to rethink what it is to attend to themselves and to consider what role philosophy may play in such a task.

With respect to his own abilities and capacities, Climacus notes that while he would describe himself as "one of those who have power," he admits that his power "is not that of a ruler or a conqueror" but is limited to an ability "to exercise restraint" (CUP, 1:164/SKS 7, 153; trans. modified). Moreover, he also admits that the scope of this power is "not extensive" since he has "power only over [himself]" and "not even that if [he does] not exercise restraint [over himself] every moment" (CUP, 1:165/SKS 7, 153). In this way Climacus's loafing behavior takes on a new significance. If the speculative philosopher is one who has no patience for attending to herself or himself and imagines that she or he has finished this lifelong task "by noon," then Climacus's ability to slow things down, to rethink topics and approach them from new angles, and basically to "keep on as long as need be" is, above all, a mark of his power of self-restraint (CUP, 1:181/SKS 7, 167). This is something that readers can learn to observe in Climacus's own behavior while also learning to detect the lack of self-restraint that is exhibited in some of the examples he sketches for them of how the speculative philosopher falls into self-forgetfulness. But if his readers are truly to acquire the ability to observe the presence or absence of self-restraint in others then they must learn to restrain themselves. Climacus notes, for example, that the ability to determine whether a person is lying is gained through the practice of restraining and attending to oneself. He cites the example of someone who "speaks of death" and who claims "he has been thinking it and has thought, for example, its uncertainty." To detect whether he is lying or not, one need only "let him talk":

> Just pay attention to the reduplicated presence of the stated thought in every word, in every parenthetical clause, in the digression, in the unguarded moment of simile and comparison . . . —provided that one [also] scrupulously attends to oneself. For the ability to attend in this way [to others] is gained by restraining oneself (CUP, 1:170/SKS 7, 157; trans. modified; cf. CUP, 1:255/SKS 7, 232; CUP, 1:354/SKS 7, 323).

Here reading well and living well are both tied to cultivating the power of self-restraint; through self-restraint comes the ability to attend to oneself. By taking his time and exhibiting his ability to restrain himself (to "keep on as long as need be"), Climacus does not indulge his readers' desire to finish quickly but instead provides them with further opportunities for paying greater attention to themselves. In the process, he also tries to get his readers to appreciate "how the simplest problem is changed by restraint [*Paaholdenhed*] into the most difficult" (CUP, 1:165/SKS 7, 153; trans. modified). If they come to see how restraining or holding themselves back can change the character of these problems, making them more gripping and engaging, then they may be able to wean themselves of their impatient desire to "go further," redirecting their philosophical impulses toward these seemingly simple matters. To get clearer on this, let's turn now to the existence-problem of dying and consider further how self-restraint constitutes part of the treatment being offered by Climacus.

The Existence-Problem of Dying

Climacus begins his discussion of the existence-problem of dying by claiming to know about this topic "what people generally (*i Almindelighed*) know" (CUP, 1:165/SKS 7, 153; trans. modified). He says he knows some of the things that can cause death ("if I swallow a dose of sulfuric acid I will die, likewise by drowning myself, by breathing in coal fumes while sleeping, etc."); he knows there are different attitudes about suicide ("Napoleon always carried poison with him," "Shakespeare's Juliet took it," the Stoics think suicide is courageous, others think it cowardly); he knows death sometimes appears comic, other times tragic ("one can die from such a ludicrous trifle that even the most solemn person cannot help laughing at death"; there is "pathos" when "the tragic hero dies in the fifth act" but not "when an alehouse keeper dies"); he knows the different moods with which poets interpret death; and he knows what the clergy usually say about death (including the "stock themes dealt with at funerals") (CUP, 1:165–66/SKS 7, 153; trans. modified). Between knowing what can cause death, how death can appear to us, and how we often respond to it, Climacus invites his readers to find his knowledge to be pretty comprehensive. If this is so, then for those who find the problem of dying simple in nature and so not worth spending much time on, that will be the end of it. There will be nothing more to bother themselves over with respect to this topic. In mock agreement, Climacus remarks, "If there is no other hindrance to moving on to world history, then I am ready" (CUP, 1:166/SKS 7, 153–54).

Climacus makes clear, however, that he actually thinks that he is far from being ready to move on to world history. In contrast to any comfort that his readers may take in their belief that what they know about death is adequate, he says that even though he knows as much as the next person he still doesn't consider death to be something that he has understood:

> [D]espite this almost extraordinary knowledge or proficiency of knowledge, I can by no means consider death as something that I have understood. So before I move on to world history, . . . it seems to me that I had better think about this, lest existence mock me for having become so erudite that I had forgotten to understand what sometime will happen to me and will happen to every human being—sometime, but what am I saying? Suppose death were so devious as to come tomorrow! (CUP, 1:166/SKS 7, 154; trans. modified).

This passage deals a double blow to his readers' conviction that their knowledge of death is adequate. First, readers are told by Climacus that despite his possessing the same knowledge that they may have been relying on, he does not consider death to be something he has understood, suggesting that their own understanding may also be incomplete or somehow less certain than they may imagine. If this knowledge isn't adequate for Climacus then perhaps it isn't for them either. Furthermore, Climacus raises the prospect that if we aren't careful we might even "forget" to obtain an understanding of something that pertains to each and every one of us, as though we might live through life in an absentminded haze without ever truly becoming aware of what it is to be a human being. While pausing over this possibility (call it the possibility of absentmindedness), readers are then met with a second shock, which is the reminder that death has as one of its characteristic features the property of being temporally uncertain. Death could come tomorrow, or even at this very moment, and if Climacus can't affirm that he has understood death despite all that he proclaims to know about it, even as his own death could happen suddenly and without warning, then addressing this problem can suddenly seem much more pressing and urgent. Readers are now faced with trying to grasp why death isn't something that Climacus, despite his knowledge, is prepared to affirm that he has understood, and with wondering what else a person must possess to be in such a position, all the while remaining aware of how death can come suddenly and unannounced.

Climacus devotes much of his discussion to considering the temporal uncertainty of death. He maintains that trying to come to terms with just this one aspect of death will present his readers with greater difficulties than they may be accustomed to: "Just this uncertainty, if it is to be understood and held fast by an existing person and consequently be thought into everything precisely because it is uncertainty, . . . gives rise to unbelievable difficulties" (CUP, 1:166/SKS 7, 154; trans. modified). The idea that a proper understanding of the uncertainty of death might somehow involve thinking this uncertainty "into everything," while not immediately clear, holds out the prospect of a task of understanding of a different order, something that is ongoing and perhaps never-ending, one of those "tasks that are sufficient for a whole human life" that Climacus says he has a tendency to "catch sight of" and that might provide his readers with a new kind of challenge (CUP, 1:161/SKS 7, 149).[9] Perhaps to heighten the idea of such a challenge, Climacus presents his readers with a few cases where people only think they are thinking the uncertainty of death without actually doing so. In the first case, he cites the example of someone giving a speech who "believes that he thinks the uncertainty of death and yet forgets to think this uncertainty into what he is saying" (CUP, 1:166/SKS 7, 154; trans. modified). To add insult to injury, the subject of the speech just so happens to be the uncertainty of death and how in the face of this one should seek "a purpose for the whole of life." Climacus maintains that the speaker in question has "essentially forgotten" the uncertainty of death since he has not connected the topic of his speech to the very uncertainty at issue (CUP, 1:166/SKS 7, 154). In Climacus's terms, properly to connect them would require that the life-purpose being championed by the speaker be "made dialectical in relation to the uncertainty of death" (CUP, 1:166/SKS 7, 154). Since the speaker presents himself as an authority on the uncertainty of death while himself forgetting to "think the uncertainty into what he is saying about uncertainty," this may seem to be an especially egregious instance of forgetfulness. It's also worth keeping in mind, however, Climacus's earlier claim that truly to understand and grasp this uncertainty would require that it "be thought into everything." This means more generally that the speaker would be at fault whatever the particular subject matter of his speech, since what he forgets to do above all is to think the uncertainty of death into something or other; the task is to think it into everything.[10]

While Climacus's readers may be struck by the comical nature of the speaker's situation without necessarily finding any basis for thinking that this criticism should be directed at themselves, the second set of examples seems more on target. In this case, Climacus denies that thinking the uncertainty of death is a topic that one can meaningfully claim to have done once and for all, or that one can adequately address by merely thinking it on occasion:

> To think this uncertainty once and for all, or once a year at matins on New Year's morning, is nonsense, of course, and is not to think it at all. If the one who thinks it in this way explains world history, what he says about world history can perhaps be splendid, but what he says about death is stupid (CUP, 1:166/SKS 7, 154; trans. modified).

These two scenarios may come closer to making direct contact with Climacus's readers. Insofar as they have the conviction that death is something they have understood, they may fall into the former category, imagining that they have successfully finished with the task of thinking through its uncertainty. Alternatively, they may be in the habit of thinking about death and its uncertainty now and again, perhaps on those occasions when the transience of life is most salient. Climacus's unsettling claim here is that under neither scenario has a person thought the uncertainty of death "at all." Akin to the speaker who has forgotten to think the uncertainty of death while giving a speech on this very topic, those who imagine that they can successfully think the uncertainty of death once and for all or only on occasion are also thereby marked as individuals who have "essentially forgotten" the uncertainty of death. As Climacus represents things, none of them is successfully thinking death even as they all may imagine that they are.

To this point in his discussion, we might characterize Climacus's aim as a kind of Socratic motivation of the idea that the existence-problem of dying is more pressing than his readers may previously have appreciated. First he presents himself, in good Socratic fashion, as someone who lacks an understanding of a topic that his readers may imagine themselves to understand adequately. Presenting himself in this way has the potential to disarm his readers and thereby to create an environment in which they are willing to be more forthcoming (including with themselves) about what their views and convictions actually are. By raising the prospect of this topic's being more difficult to understand than his readers may have thought, and by highlighting some of the ways a person can fail to think well about these matters, Climacus provides his readers with the opportunity to reflect further about how things stand with themselves. Questions may naturally arise (such as, "What would thinking well about this matter look like?") that may serve to heighten their curiosity, and perhaps even make them feel a bit disoriented, as they come to consider how their own grasp of death may or may not differ from what Climacus has claimed is inadequate.

Even if these considerations do give his readers pause, Climacus still needs to say more about what is underwriting his claim about not understanding death. What more is there besides the everyday knowledge that he claims to possess? Why isn't this general knowledge about death adequate? Climacus's main thought seems to be that when it comes to understanding death, there is something above and beyond this general knowledge, something that pertains to what dying is for a given individual that we might call inherently first-personal in nature: what my dying is for me, what your dying is for you, etc. Using himself as an example, Climacus maintains that there is an aspect of death that is quite particular in nature for a given person:

> [F]or me, *my* dying is by no means something in general; [perhaps] for others my dying is some such thing. Nor am *I* for myself some such thing in general; perhaps for others I am some such thing in general (CUP, 1:167/ SKS 7, 155; trans. modified).

By considering the possibility that either his dying or he himself might be "some such thing in general" for other people, Climacus makes clear that he is not denying that part of what dying is can be straightforwardly characterized in general terms and so also understood in general. His claim is that with respect to oneself, grasping what can be grasped in general about death will not suffice for truly coming to grips with the existence-problem of dying. An individual's own dying, on Climacus's view, does not have an "in general" quality for that person; instead, he seems to think that each person's own dying has a particular character that accordingly requires a non-general, first-personal understanding. In my own case, for example, what is crucial is that the dying in question is mine, and that the person in question who will die is me. It's this fact that Climacus suggests we aren't adequately struck by and that points up the limits of our understanding of death.

As he characterizes this personal dimension of understanding death, concerning a given person's relationship to her or his own dying, Climacus also draws his readers' attention to what might explain why their own deaths may not have fully registered with them. He thinks that those who think, for example, that the uncertainty of death can be understood in general (and so be quickly disposed of thereby) may have lost track of themselves and of what it is to be mortal:

> If death is always uncertain and I am mortal, then . . . this uncertainty cannot possibly be understood in general unless I am also such a human being in general. But this I am not. That is something only absentminded people are, for example, Soldin, the bookseller (CUP, 1:167/SKS 7, 154; trans. modified).

This passage seeks to make a point through a kind of playful contradictoriness. The idea of an individual person's being "a human being in general" is clearly meant to sound strange or paradoxical.[11] Call it a riddle. Question: How can someone be a human being in general? Answer: By being absentminded! Similarly, in the case of Soldin, when Climacus reports that "when he [Soldin] was going to get up in the morning, he was not aware [or did not know (*vidste han ikke af*)] that he was dead," we are surely meant to laugh at the extent of his absentmindedness, as it continues to accompany him even after he has died (CUP, 1:167/SKS 7, 155). The warning for Climacus's readers is that one can become alienated from oneself in this way, distracted or absent from oneself, so that being mortal and all that this involves simply does not register. In such a case, one's understanding of oneself, if it can be called an understanding at all, is in effect as if one conceived of oneself as a nonparticular, "some such thing in general" human being. But this hardly amounts to being human at all, and, according to Climacus, what is "most embarrassing of all" about being on "such bad terms with oneself" is when one remains "ignorant of this condition" (CUP, 1:167/SKS 7, 155; trans. modified). This ignorance is precisely what Climacus is Socratically targeting in his readers. They may imagine that they have an adequate understanding of what death is, and yet there is the real danger that they only relate to themselves in the most general terms and, even worse, that they remain ignorant that they relate to themselves in this way.

This is not to say that Climacus is arguing that there is nothing that we can understand in general. Presumably there are some things (e.g., mathematics) that we can understand in general even though none of us is ever a human being in general. Climacus's point seems to be just that there are other things that, as they pertain to human beings, can only be fully grasped if they are tied more closely to the fact that individual human beings, mortal by nature, are clearly such that they are not human beings "in general" but particular human beings who will one day die, and that coming to appreciate this about ourselves is something each one of us must do individually.[12] We might say that it is Climacus's aim to get his readers to reflect further on what being a particular human being amounts to and why, in the case of the problem of dying, paying attention to oneself qua a particular human being can make this seemingly simple problem become more difficult, becoming something that by Climacus's lights must be thought into every moment of one's life.

This contrast between being a human being "in general," which Climacus ties to absentmindedness and distraction (where one is not attending to what one is), and being a particular human being can be fruitfully compared to a distinction he draws between "being a so-called subject of sorts" and "being a [proper] subject or becoming one and being what one is by having become that," the latter being something that he champions as "a very praiseworthy task, a *quantum satis* [sufficient amount] for a human life" (CUP, 1:131/SKS 7, 123; CUP, 1:163/SKS 7, 151). While Climacus allows that there may be a sense in which one begins as a subject of sorts or as a human being in general, he also claims that "if the task is to become subjective [i.e., to become a proper subject], then every subject becomes *for himself* exactly the opposite of some such thing in general" (CUP, 1:167/SKS 7, 155). In the case of the problem of dying in particular, Climacus (speaking in the first person) maintains that as this task of becoming a subject is carried out, "the uncertainty [of death] becomes more and more dialectically penetrating in relation to my personality" (CUP, 1:167/SKS 7, 154). What this means with respect to thinking death in a correct manner is as follows: "It becomes more and more important for me to think it [death] into every moment of my life, because, since its uncertainty is at every moment, this uncertainty is vanquished only by my vanquishing it every moment" (CUP, 1:167/SKS 7, 154–55). While thinking death into every moment of one's life is apparently meant to be a description of what successfully thinking death would involve, it still remains unclear what Climacus means by this. As I noted above, it seems implausible to take him to mean that literally, moment by moment, one must have the occurrent thought "I am going to die" or something similar. As Merold Westphal puts it, "[u]nder this impossible, morbid . . . scenario, whenever offered a penny for my thoughts, I could answer, 'I am thinking about my death.'"[13] Even if we reject, however, the idea that thinking death into every moment means actively having a thought of this sort moment by moment, it is still not easy to say what, exactly, Climacus does mean. This is complicated further by the fact that in the latter half of his discussion of death he actually raises several possible features of death that he suggests a reflective person might spend time thinking through. And while these seem to be straightforward cases of a kind of thinking about death that the philosophically inclined might do, none of what he describes is an obvious candidate for exemplifying what it is to think death into every moment.

So what's going on here exactly? Having drawn a contrast between those who think only occasionally about death and dying, if that, and those who think death into every moment, Climacus has surely, at a minimum, provided his readers with adequate material for bringing them to a halt, at least temporarily. In checking their impulse to move on to world history, he may get them to question whether they themselves have paid adequate attention to themselves and, in this case, to the fact that they are mortal and that they each will die one day. But given their own philosophical inclinations, they will also presumably want to obtain a better understanding of what is at issue here. Even if they grant that Climacus has provided a number of cases where people have not succeeded in thinking death, they will surely also expect Climacus to deliver on what would count as success. Has he done so? Yes and no. After he motivates the problem and indicates how he thinks some people fall short in their engagement with the problem of dying, he then openly imagines a dialogue between himself and someone drawn to world history:

> The exalted devotee of world history can nevertheless not deny me an answer to the question of what it is to die, and the moment he answers, the dialectic begins. Let him give whatever reason he wishes for not dwelling further on such thoughts; it will not help, because the reason will in turn be made dialectical in order to see essentially what it is. Then I would have to ask whether it is at all possible to have an idea of death, whether death can be anticipated and *anticipando* [by being anticipated] be experienced in an idea, or whether it is only when it actually is (CUP, 1:167–68/SKS 7, 155; trans. modified).

After posing this question, Climacus then sketches several possible lines of thought a person might take as she or he thinks this through. If a person denies that we can have an idea of death, this is not the end of the matter since a "negative answer, a no, must be defined dialectically just as fully as a positive answer." Climacus maintains that the "thinking person" will want to have it made "dialectically clear that the answer must be no," and suggests that in the process "this dialectical clarification" will end up relating this "no" to "other existence-problems," leaving the thinker with yet more to think through (CUP, 1:168/SKS 7, 156; trans. modified). This is fine as far as it goes, but these sorts of considerations, things that a thinking person could reflect on, do not seem to be candidates for the still elusive activity of thinking death into every moment. One possibility is that they aren't meant to be. The issues raised in the imagined dialogue between Climacus and the speculative thinker are highly abstract matters that presumably would not much concern the simple person but that certainly could provide the philosophically inclined person with material to exercise her or his philosophical nature. Yet I take it that the fact of one's death is something that both the simple and the philosophically inclined should be struck by and need to engage moment by moment simply in virtue of being human and taking part in the task of becoming subjective, though it may be that we will want to characterize the manner of this engagement differently in the two cases. That is, while the simple may nonreflectively remain aware of death (sensing it "in another way"), it may only be the philosophically inclined who can properly be characterized as *thinking* death into every moment (CUP, 1:170/SKS 7, 158).

Climacus does provide a partial answer to what thinking death into every moment might be when considering what follows if a person answers "yes" to the question of whether or not we can have an idea of death. He points to further lines of thought to be pursued here as well, noting, for example, that there would be a need to think further about what death is given that it's the sort of thing of which we can obtain an idea, including "what it is for the living person, how the idea of it must change a person's whole life, if he, in order to think its uncertainty, must think it every moment in order thereby to prepare himself for it" (CUP, 1:168/SKS 7, 156). Similarly, there would be a need to think further about what "preparation" for death actually is since there's a difference between one's idea of what is to come and death's actually coming. As Climacus sketches these additional topics of thought, he also offers a clue concerning what thinking death into every moment might at least involve: "[F]or the subject it is an *act* to think his death" (CUP, 1:169/SKS 7, 156; italics mine). This recalls a passage I quoted earlier, where Climacus maintains that because existence-problems pertain to ethical and religious matters, they will be inherently practical and action-guiding, consisting of "not only a knowing" but "also a *doing* that is related to a knowing" (CUP, 1:160/SKS 7, 149; italics mine). To help unpack this idea, Climacus contrasts the one who acts by thinking his death with the absentminded person (such as Soldin the bookseller or the speculative philosopher), someone whose condition might be characterized as that of being a human being "in general." In this latter sort of case, Climacus denies that any attempts to think death in general terms (and by such an absentminded person) will constitute an act: "[I]t is merely a some such thing in general, and basically it is not easy to say what a some such thing is" (CUP, 1:169/SKS 7, 156). According to Climacus, then, with respect to the ethical task of becoming subjective or a subject, thinking death becomes an act because "the development of subjectivity consists precisely in this, that [the individual], acting, works through himself in his thinking about his own existence, consequently that he actually thinks what is thought by actualizing it" (CUP, 1:169/SKS 7, 156). More particularly, Climacus draws out this point as follows: "[The individual] does not think for a moment: 'Now you must attend every moment'—but . . . he attends every moment" (CUP, 1:169/SKS 7, 156–57; trans. modified). In thinking death into every moment, one should therefore be constantly attending to oneself and one's mortal nature so that one's mortality remains forever before one's eyes.

But what exactly is the nature of this attending to or watching of oneself? If it isn't thinking the sorts of things that only the philosophically inclined have the capacity and the desire to think, what else could it be? I am not sure that Climacus provides a satisfactory answer to this question, or if he does, I haven't yet developed a full account of his view. That will have to wait for another occasion. I want to conclude, however, by indicating one way in which Climacus's view might be understood, with the caveat that further work needs to be done to flesh this out. To begin with, it may be worth recalling Climacus's claim that what the philosophically inclined (such as himself) gain as a reward for doing the kind of thinking that they do is that "foolish little difference between the simple person's and the wise person's knowledge of the simple thing—that the simple person knows it, and the wise person knows that he knows it or knows that he does not know it" (CUP, 1:181/SKS 7, 167). While the thinking person may have a more reflective relationship to the simple, in either case the manner in which one lives ought to involve a cognizance of oneself and, in the case of death and dying, of one's mortal nature. One possibility is that Climacus is trying to characterize a kind of mindfulness or a mode of living and acting that consists in attending to oneself every moment, where the very act of attending will give one's life a certain character and shape. At the very end of his discussion of death, he suggests that this outlook or stance with respect to death is constituted by relating dying to "the subject's *whole* life," just as earlier he had drawn attention to how the idea of death "must change a person's whole life" if she or he is to think death into every moment (CUP, 1:170/SKS 7, 157; CUP, 1:168/SKS 7, 156; italics mine). This involves proceeding in such a way that one does not fall into distraction or absentmindedness and, as we've seen, Climacus holds that to avoid this condition the subject requires self-restraint. It may be that what it is to give one's life the requisite wholeness at issue just is to lead a life of self-restraint; for, as Climacus maintains, "the ability to attend in this way [to oneself] is gained by restraining oneself" (CUP, 1:170/SKS 7, 157). This is something that both the simple and the more reflective can do. The question will still remain, however, in what respect, if any, this activity of attending to the self should be called thinking. Whatever we ultimately decide, in the most general terms we need to be able to characterize this activity so that we can make sense of its being done nonreflectively as well as reflectively, since both the simple and the simple wise will attend to themselves as they carry out the task of becoming a self, and since, in the case of the existence-problem of dying, for both the simple and the simple wise the fact of their own respective deaths will remain a salient, ever-present feature of how they experience themselves and the lives they lead. If Climacus's readers allow his therapeutic remarks to work on them and to help them to check the impulse to go further, then they might avoid some of the dangers of doing philosophy—without, however, needing to deny their own philosophical natures. Through self-restraint, they will be able to think about death even as they continue to think it into every moment of their lives.[14]

NOTES

1. See, e.g., CUP, 1:145–46/SKS 7, 135–36; CUP, 1:159/SKS 7, 148.

2. See also CUP, 1:82–89/SKS 7, 82–88. While scholars have taken great interest in Kierkegaard's views on death, this portion of the *Postscript* has not received much attention. For helpful exceptions, see Ralph Henry Johnson, *The Concept of Existence in the "Concluding Unscientific Postscript"* (The Hague, Netherlands: Martinus Nijhoff, 1972), pp. 80–86; Merold Westphal, *Becoming a Self* (West Lafayette, Ind.: Purdue University Press, 1996), pp. 109–11.

3. See "The Socratic Method of Kierkegaard's Pseudonym Johannes Climacus," in *Kierkegaard and the Word(s),* ed. Poul Houe and Gordon Marino, pp. 139–50 (Copenhagen: Reitzel, 2003); "Understanding Kierkegaard's Johannes Climacus in the *Postscript,*" in *Kierkegaard Studies Yearbook 2007,* ed. Niels Jørgen Cappelørn, Hermann Deuser, and K. Brian Söderquist, pp. 424–40 (Berlin: de Gruyter, 2007).

4. On the urge to "go further" or to imagine oneself "finished" with tasks that properly speaking ought to occupy a person for an entire lifetime, see, e.g., CUP, 1:606/SKS 7, 550; CUP, 1:466/SKS 7, 423; CUP, 1:276/SKS 7, 251. On Climacus's characterization of himself as a "loafer," see PF, 5/SKS 4, 215; CUP, 1:185/SKS 7, 171 (cf. CUP, 1:83/SKS 7, 82). See also Muench, "Understanding Kierkegaard's Johannes Climacus in the *Postscript,*" pp. 429–31.

5. Climacus employs the verb phrase "at passe paa" a number of times in his discussion of death. This can mean "pay attention to," "watch out for," "take care of," and "look after." In the imperative form, "Pas på!" means "Watch out!" or "Look out!"

6. See, e.g., CUP, 1:168/SKS 7, 156; CUP, 1:304/SKS 7, 276–77; CUP, 1:349–52/SKS 7, 320–22; CUP, 1:386/SKS 7, 351; CUP, 1:556/SKS 7, 505.

7. Thanks to Niels Jørgen Cappelørn and Bruce Kirmmse for pressing me to define more precisely how Climacus conceives of the simple person.

8. Climacus equates the two terms at CUP, 1:353/SKS 7, 323. On the term "subjective thinker," see CUP, 1:72–93/SKS 7, 73–92; CUP, 1:349–60/SKS 7, 320–28. On the term "simple wise person," see CUP, 1:227–28/SKS 7, 207–8. Earlier, Climacus refers to the simple wise person as "the wise person." See CUP, 1:159–60/SKS 7, 148–49; CUP, 1:181–82/SKS 7, 167–68. Climacus refers to Socrates as "that simple wise person" at PF, 19/SKS 4, 228.

9. Throughout his discussion of death, Climacus uses the formulation "thinking death" or "thinking the uncertainty of death" as opposed to thinking "about" either of these. This usage may be one way of trying to mark for his readers a manner of engaging with death that is distinct from how death is typically approached by the absentminded and distracted.

10. Thanks to Patrick Stokes for helping me to get clear on this point.

11. Thanks to K. Brian Söderquist for helping me to appreciate this.

12. It is this particularity, "the purely personal life," that Kierkegaard maintains does not have a place within the systematic treatises of Hegel and his followers. See CI, 166/SKS 1, 215.

13. Westphal, *Becoming a Self,* p. 110.

14. Thanks to the Søren Kierkegaard Research Center and the Department of Philosophy at the University of Copenhagen for providing me with two opportunities to present earlier versions of this chapter, and to both audiences for their helpful questions and comments. Thanks also to David Berger, Adam Buben, Niels Jørgen Cappelørn, Bridget Clarke, Róbert Haraldsson, Ulrich Knappe, Poul Lübcke, David Possen, Richard Purkarthofer, K. Brian Söderquist, Jon Stewart, and Patrick Stokes for their helpful feedback and stimulating conversations.

6.

Death and Ethics in Kierkegaard's *Postscript*

David D. Possen

Modern Ethics, Ancient Ethics, and Death

One of the aims of Kierkegaard's *Concluding Unscientific Postscript* is to recover an "ancient" model of ethics—"the subjective ethics," or "the so-called subjective ethical" (CUP, 1:144–47/SKS 7, 134–36)—and defend it against the "objective" approach that has become the norm "in modern parlance" (CUP, 1:133/SKS 7, 124–25; trans. modified). Johannes Climacus, the *Postscript*'s pseudonymous author, expresses the difference between ancient/subjective ethics and modern/objective ethics as follows. *Modern* ethics, he quips, answers the question fundamental to all ethical inquiry—the question "What am I to do?" (CUP, 1:133/SKS 7, 125)—with "the modern slogan . . . 'What the age demands!'" (CUP, 1:144/SKS 7, 135; trans. modified).[1] Since this answer points me to a fact about the "age" rather than a fact about me, it implies that if I wish to discover my ethical calling, I ought to "strip away . . . my subjectivity" and become as "objective" an "observer" of "world history" as I can (CUP, 1:131–33/SKS 7, 123–25). In Climacus's opinion, however, to overlook one's *self* in this way is to do precisely the opposite of what true ethics requires, namely, attending closely and continuously to one's own nature. Accordingly, Climacus denounces modern/objective ethics as "the demoralizing ethics," a pseudo-ethic that hinders genuine ethical activity (CUP, 1:144/SKS 7, 135).

Ancient ethics, by contrast, begins by presuming that we do not know, and cannot discover directly, what it is that God or the age in truth demands of us.[2] Ancient ethics therefore directs us to "renounce" speculation about such things (CUP, 1:143/SKS 7, 133), much as Socrates famously eschewed talk of Gorgons and Pegasuses in order to concentrate on himself.[3] Climacus calls this approach "the true ethical conception of the ethical," which is "sober and fasting" by nature (CUP, 1:143/SKS 7, 133). If I wish to discover my own ethical calling, ancient/subjective ethics directs me to *look inward,* as Socrates did, to come to know myself (CUP, 1:141–42/SKS 7, 132). But in order to fulfill that Delphic assignment, I must first *become* myself: I must gain a "self" to know.

Climacus terms the latter process *becoming subjective.*[4] And in the course of expounding and defending his ancient/subjective ethics, he presents several case studies of how becoming subjective takes place, which he calls "examples of thinking oriented to becoming subjective" (CUP, 1:129/SKS 7, 121). One such case study famously concerns the thought of *death.* Here Climacus declares that becoming subjective requires us to "think death" continuously, to "think it into every moment" of our lives, and to bring the meaning of death "into relation to [my] whole life" (CUP, 1:167–70/SKS 7, 154–57). Unfortunately for the would-be practitioner of this art, however, Climacus goes on to reveal precious little about what the content of this thinking should be (apart from the fact that death's temporal "uncertainty" [CUP, 1:166/SKS 7, 154] is part of it). In fact, Climacus leaves open the question of whether it is possible to form an idea of death at all (CUP, 1:168/SKS 7, 155), and he closes by confessing that he is "very far indeed from having comprehended death" himself (CUP, 1:170/SKS 7, 157–58).

This yields a tantalizing mix of urgency and fog. Climacus leaves his readers to wonder what he is driving at in exhorting us to "think death" (especially since he disclaims comprehension of death himself!), not to mention what his exhortations hope to teach us about the larger process of "becoming subjective," or about ancient/subjective ethics in general. The result is a provocative interpretive riddle, which a number of commentators have sought to pry open with the aid of close reading.[5]

In this chapter, I too will address this riddle. But I will employ a different approach. Rather than seek to supply, or deduce, what Climacus himself left undefined, I will take Climacus's lack of specifics as itself my object of interest. And I will argue that Climacus's vagueness about "thinking death" is no weak link in his argumentation. On the contrary, it is his strong point. For as I will show, Climacus's failure to offer details about death both reflects and serves his broader rhetorical goal—his defense of the ancient/subjective ethics against its modern/objective rival—in that it both instantiates and befits, superbly so, the *Socratic character* of the ethics that he works to promote.

Climacus's Case Studies: The Big Picture

I have mentioned that Climacus's examination of death has its place in a series of case studies of becoming subjective. To begin our analysis, let us consider the general significance of these case studies to the overall polemic of which they are a part: namely, Climacus's attack on modern/objective ethics in the name of its ancient/subjective predecessor.

One of Climacus's favorite complaints about modern/objective ethics is that it makes it appear as though a human being could discover and discharge his ethical obligations once and for all, and then advance blithely to higher concerns—e.g., to world-historical speculation (CUP, 1:161/SKS 7, 149). Ancient/subjective ethics, by contrast, teaches that what is required for the discovery of one's ethical task—"becoming subjective"—is itself "the *highest* task assigned to a human being" (CUP, 1:129/SKS 7, 121; my italics). Becoming subjective is, moreover, "the task of life"; it lasts "as long as life lasts, that is, the task of living" (CUP, 1:163/SKS 7, 152). This means that becoming subjective is a task with which we are never finished, not even provisionally. We cannot simply complete it and move on to other things.[6]

This claim has important consequences for Climacus's rhetoric. For if becoming subjective is not a task that can be discharged once and for all, then it would be misleading to define it in a way that smacks of deeds to be accomplished or conditions to be met. Rather, becoming subjective is at every moment a *live process,* germane to and compulsory in every life situation. Becoming subjective is thus best illustrated not by a fixed set of instructions, but with an adaptable model that can be applied to many life situations, or, better still, with a *family of paradigms* that cover a wide range of lives. This last strategy, as I see it, is the one Climacus adopts. He does so by offering us a series of case studies of becoming subjective, drawn from a variety of walks of life (CUP, 1:165–81/SKS 7, 153–67). We will now take a rapid tour of these case studies, with an eye not so much to the details of each as to the *life-pattern* that they collectively and gradually disclose.

Climacus's first formal example[7] of becoming subjective is the discussion of death with which we began. The thrust of this discussion, we have mentioned, is that becoming subjective requires that I transform my life by continually facing the thought of my death. Climacus tells us little about what it means to face this thought, except that it involves letting my death's "uncertainty"—the insidious truth that death could come to me at any time, even tomorrow, even right now!—become "more and more dialectically penetrating in relation to my personality" (CUP, 1:167/SKS 7, 154). Beyond this, Climacus tells us little. As we noted previously, he refuses to take a stand on whether death can be thought at all, and he confesses that he himself is far from having comprehended death. For the moment, let us leave these mysteries as they are. Our concern is not to explain them in isolation, but to discern the *pattern* that underlies Climacus's case studies as a group.

Climacus's second case study concerns how to live with the possibility of immortality. The trouble with immortality is its "indefiniteness" in our lives, the fact that we can never be certain of our own immortality, or of its character (e.g., whether we are saved or damned), as long as we are still engaged in becoming subjective, i.e., in living.[8] This is so, Climacus explains, because in order for our immortality to be a "definite" fact for us, it would have to be definite for us "at every moment" (CUP, 1:176/SKS 7, 163); but this is impossible for "existing" human beings, for whom every moment is a fresh opportunity to wonder whether we really are immortal, whether in our lives so far we have earned (or forfeited) an immortal happiness, or whether we are gaining or losing our immortality *right now* (CUP, 1:174–76/SKS 7, 161–63). If we wish to calm such worries, we may certainly commit ourselves to believing that we are immortal, but there is nothing to stop us from wavering in that commitment at a later time. Indeed, the person who "uses his life to become subjective" faces a constant struggle with the "indefiniteness" of immortality (CUP, 1:176/SKS 7, 163). He is "content" with this struggle, for he knows that it is potentially the most important task with which he can occupy himself; it "can easily be sufficient for a person's lifetime, since it is to be sufficient for an eternity" (CUP, 1:177/SKS 7, 163).

With this we can pick up the pace, for the pattern underlying Climacus's examples has already begun to emerge. His third case study concerns the duty to "thank God for the good that he gives me" (CUP, 1:177/SKS 7, 163). The trouble with this duty is that it is both endless and—for a mortal's "poor finite understanding" (CUP, 1:178/SKS 7, 164)—full of snares. As Climacus explains, to thank God only for the good that I recognize as such would be to fail to take account of the fact that God knows far better than I do what is truly good for me, and what I ought truly to be thankful for.[9] I can never know whether or not I have appropriately discharged my duty to thank God, and so "thanking God, this simple matter . . . assigns me one of the most strenuous tasks, one that will be sufficient for my entire life" (CUP, 1:179/SKS 7, 165).

Climacus's final and briefest case study concerns the validity of marriage. Here the trouble lies not in maintaining the marital union, but in the union's legitimacy in the first place. "The question arises whether paganism is not still haunting marriage," that is, whether the institution of marriage is indeed the spiritual "blessing" and "perfection of existence" that the officiating clergy like to call it, or whether it is, instead, an abrogation of the most fundamental principles of "the religious" (CUP, 1:180/ SKS 7, 166). The goal of this example, evidently, is to commend a life that grapples continually with the uncertainty of the status of marriage—i.e., with the possibility that conjugal life might in fact be *sinful*.

Here Climacus stops. "Examples I have aplenty," he declares. "I can keep on as long as need be; I have enough for a lifetime" (CUP, 1:181–82/ SKS 7, 167). The point of this boast is that there is a *pattern* common to Climacus's examples—a pattern that is applicable both at every point in human life and to human life as a whole—that can be used to generate example after example. This pattern has the following structure. There are certain matters that concern us unceasingly, but about which we are, in part, profoundly uncertain; we encounter them not as settled facts but as *issues* about which we are at once ignorant and concerned.[10] Here are four examples, drawn from the case studies that we have just sketched. (1) It is certain enough that I will die, but I cannot foresee when death will come to me, or what it will mean; (2) I recognize that, though I may hold my afterlife in my hands, I can neither perceive nor foretell what my afterlife has in store; (3) I acknowledge that I do not know how I can possibly repay my debt to God; and (4) I wonder—and worry—whether what is called marital bliss might at the end of the day be *sin*.

In each example, becoming subjective requires that I come to terms with my *concerned ignorance* about the issue at hand. Now, before I proceed any further, I would like to make clear that concerned ignorance should by no means be equated with utter ignorance.[11] Quite the contrary! My concerned ignorance presupposes precisely that I know *enough* about an issue to know that I am ignorant of it, and to become concerned about that fact. This means, for example, that I must know enough about the issue to be able to name it meaningfully, much as (to borrow an example from Kierkegaard's *The Concept of Irony*) Socrates could name the ethical and theological concepts that he could not adequately define.[12] In the case of my death, it is my familiarity with death and my certainty that I will someday die that rouses me to concern about my ignorance of my death's precise time and meaning.[13]

To come to terms with our concerned ignorance about an issue, what is needed is not that we issue declarations about it, but that we *transform our lives* by continually acting on our concern about the relevant issue, despite and in the face of our ignorance. For example, I might pay heed to my concerned ignorance about my death by trying to prepare for it at every moment. I might express my concerned ignorance about my immortal soul's existence or fate by striving to care for it constantly. I might give voice to my concerned ignorance about how to thank God by thanking him continually but "shamefacedly" (CUP, 1:179/SKS 7, 165). Last, I might respond to my concerned ignorance about the religious validity of my marriage by laboring tirelessly to ensure that "the spirit within me" is not "obscured" by the "erotic" side of my marital bond (CUP, 1:180/SKS 7, 166).[14]

With this pattern in view, we can shed new light on the features of Climacus's discussion of death that at first struck us as mysterious, i.e., that Climacus fails to specify what death means and that he confesses openly that he has not comprehended its meaning himself. What we can now see is that these need not be signs of esotericism or obfuscation. Rather, a simpler explanation has emerged. They may simply be marks of an effort by Climacus to write about death in a manner that befits his own *concerned ignorance* about it.

Climacus's Underlying Paradigm: Socrates

To see why the above suggestion might be not only plausible but likely, let us step back once more from the details of Climacus's discussion of death and return to the common theme that unites his case studies. In the foregoing, we saw that all four of Climacus's "examples" of becoming subjective are marked by a distinctive shared life-pattern: that of a life lived in continual confrontation with one's own concerned ignorance. Now, if we are widely read in Kierkegaard's authorship, then this life-pattern ought to strike us as familiar. For it is nothing other than the life-pattern emblematized by that *Socrates* whom Kierkegaard and his pseudonyms regularly praise as a paradigm figure: namely, the Socrates of Plato's *Apology*, who devotes his life to acknowledging his own ignorance and disclosing that of others.[15]

It should come as no surprise, therefore, that when in his next chapter Climacus offers a final and definitive vignette about becoming subjective—a fifth and last case study, as it were—this crowning example turns out to be Socrates. Climacus writes:

> Let us consider Socrates. . . . He poses the question . . . if there is an immortality. . . . He stakes his whole life on this "if"; he dares to die, and with the passion of the infinite he has so ordered his whole life that it might be acceptable—*if* there is an immortality. Is there any better demonstration for the immortality of the soul? . . . The "fragment" of uncertainty helped Socrates, because he himself helped with the passion of infinity (CUP, 1:201–2/SKS 7, 184–85).

This passage links the life of Socrates to the first two of Climacus's case studies, on death and immortality. And it makes clear that, at least with respect to those two issues, Socrates's life conforms impeccably to Climacus's standards of (ancient/subjective) ethics. For Socrates knows that he is as ignorant as everyone else about what death brings, and about his own personal fate in the hereafter;[16] but he nonetheless embraces the *possibility* of immortality as a lifelong ethical challenge. In other words, Socrates strives to live in a manner that would be accounted blameless in an afterworld of perfect judgment. In so doing, he prepares himself continuously for the moment of his death,[17] as well as for his death's aftermath, whatever that may be.

With this example in view, Climacus asks archly, "Is there any better demonstration for the immortality of the soul?" The humor in this line is that we have *no* proofs, let alone good or better proofs, of the immortality of the soul, and the life of Socrates certainly cannot help us find such proof.[18] We are all—all of us, including Socrates—profoundly ignorant about our immortality. Yet all the same, it is precisely *Socrates* who teaches us, by his example, what it would mean to be an immortal soul clothed in a mortal coil.

How, then, does Socrates model a life transformed by immortality? On Climacus's account, Socrates does so by working unceasingly to enact and live up to a posited Truth—the immortality of his soul—of which he acknowledges both his ignorance and his concern. In this vein, Climacus writes, "The *Socratic ignorance* was . . . the expression, firmly maintained with all the passion of inwardness, of the relation of the eternal truth to an existing person" (CUP, 1:202/SKS 7, 185; emphasis added). It is precisely in continually acknowledging his ignorance about the eternal Truth, and in continually expressing his concern about it ("the passion of ignorance") that Socrates brings his life into contact ("relation") with it, allows his life to be structured by it—and does so as well as any finite mortal ("existing person") can.

When we read the above in conjunction with Climacus's earlier case studies of becoming subjective, it should become clear to us why, within the *Postscript*, Socrates is identified repeatedly as an *ethicist* (e.g. CUP, 1:247/SKS 7, 155; CUP, 1:503/SKS 7, 456). Namely, Socrates's continual activity of acknowledging his concerned ignorance is precisely what is required for a human being to become subjective, to fulfill the task that ancient/subjective ethics assigns him. Accordingly, if we too seek to become subjective, to be "ethical" in the ancient/subjective sense, then we too must cultivate the Socratic model of letting our concerned ignorance structure our lives. We too must emulate Socrates, the ancient/subjective ethicist *par excellence,* in taking up our own highest ethical task—our "task of life."

Conclusion: Death as an Object of Concerned Ignorance

What all of this suggests, in my view, is that we ought to *expect* the specter of Socrates to haunt the four case studies that precede Climacus's explicit appeal to the Socratic paradigm of concerned ignorance. For example, in his discussion of "thinking death," Climacus's vagueness about the character of death, his confession that he has not comprehended it, his failure even to take a stand on whether death is knowable or not—just the very features of his discussion that are likely to frustrate the reader most—make good sense precisely as anticipatory efforts by Climacus to follow Socrates's ethical example, not only in confessing ignorance himself but also in prompting his hearers (here: readers) to do the same. Even the one facet of death that Climacus does discuss in detail, death's temporal "uncertainty," is itself an artifact and reminder of what he and we do *not* know about death. That too is a confession of concerned ignorance. As Paul Muench has argued, Climacus is in many ways a distinctively Socratic author, with a distinctively Socratic modus operandi.[19] This modus is firmly on display, I submit, in Climacus's excursus on death.

And there is more. Climacus's confessions of concerned ignorance not only manifest his embrace of the particular ethical model offered by *Socrates,* they also befit and reinforce the general logic of Climacus's ancient/subjective ethics. For if the activity of thinking death is genuinely to be an "example" of becoming subjective, then that activity must be a "life-task." It must continually answer, but never exhaust, ethics' fundamental question, "What am I to do?"[20]

This means that thinking death cannot be something that I may accomplish and advance beyond (say, by establishing the objective "facts" about death, and then moving on to other concerns). As Jeremy Walker rightly notes, what Climacus calls *thinking* death can mean *knowing* death only in a "Pickwickian sense," that is, knowing death "only in the sense that [we] raise about [it] a certain sort of self-reflective question."[21] If thinking death is to ignite and sustain a life that is ethical in the ancient/subjective sense, this must be because the thought of death rouses our unceasing concern in and about our ignorance. Death does this, Climacus explains, with its "uncertainty," much as immortality does with its "indefiniteness," and much as the obligation to thank God does with its ambiguity, which makes it a duty with which we can never have done. That is to say, it is as an *object of our concerned ignorance* that the thought of death serves us as an ethical lodestar.

I conclude that the elements in Climacus's discussion of death that may well strike the reader as cagey or hollow—his failure to specify the content of the thought of death; his repeated confessions of ignorance about death—are in fact essential to that discussion's thrust. For it is precisely by means of those Socratic admissions that Climacus practices the ancient/subjective ethics that he preaches. With his vagueness about death, Climacus prompts us to consider what we do or do not know about it ourselves. And he thereby urges us, by both his words and his example, to make our ignorance the object of our enduring ethical concern.[22]

NOTES

1. In "What the age demands!" (*Hvad det er Tiden fordrer*), Climacus mocks the famous words by which Johan Ludvig Heiberg (1791–1860), perhaps the most prominent public intellectual in Kierkegaard's day, had summoned Denmark's intelligentsia to Hegelian speculation in his 1833 manifesto *On the Significance of Philosophy to the Present Age:* "the demands of the age [*Tidens Fordringer*] assert themselves more and more" (Heiberg, *On the Significance of Philosophy to the Present Age and Other Texts,* trans. Jon Stewart [Copenhagen: C. A. Reitzel, 2005], p. 118). In large measure, Climacus's portrait of modern/objective ethics may be regarded as a satire on the efforts of Denmark's Hegelians, chiefly Heiberg and the theologian Hans Lassen Martensen (1808–1884), to promote the activity of world-historical speculation. In addition, as Jon Stewart has shown, Climacus's satire extends to the popular theologian Nicolai Frederik Severin Grundtvig (1783–1872), who, though not a Hegelian, was also much occupied with world history. On this see Jon Stewart, *Kierkegaard's Relations to Hegel Reconsidered* (Cambridge: Cambridge University Press, 2003), pp. 499–502.

2. For his own part—and intriguingly so, given his refusal to call himself a Christian (CUP, 1:617/SKS 7, 560)—Climacus offers what appears to be a dogmatic basis for this presumption. He asserts that while there may well exist a divine plan that specifies my personal ethical task (a *Weltgeschichte* that is also my *Weltgericht*), no "finite spirit can in truth see" what such a plan contains (CUP, 1:141/SKS 7, 132). This is so, he explains, because God possesses, while humanity lacks, "the medium that is the commensurability of the outer and the inner" (CUP, 1:141/SKS 7, 131). It is worth considering whether Climacus would attribute this same conviction about the difference between God's capabilities of vision and ours—a conviction so reminiscent of Paul's theology, or of that of the chastened Job—to *Socrates,* who (as we will shortly see) is Climacus's paradigmatic exemplar of ancient/subjective ethical life.

3. Plato, *Phaedrus,* 229c–230a.

4. "The way is to become subjective, that is, truly to become a subject" (CUP, 1:131/SKS 7, 123).

5. See Paul Muench, "Thinking Death into Every Moment: The Existence-Problem of Dying in Kierkegaard's *Postscript*," in this volume; Merold Westphal, *Becoming a Self: A Reading of Kierkegaard's "Concluding Unscientific Postscript"* (West Lafayette, Ind.: Purdue University Press, 1996), pp. 109–11; Jeremy Walker, *Kierkegaard: The Descent into God* (Kingston, Ont.: McGill-Queen's University Press, 1985), pp. 27–28; and Ralph Henry Johnson, *The Concept of Existence in Kierkegaard's "Concluding Unscientific Postscript"* (The Hague: Martinus Nijhoff, 1972), pp. 74–86.

6. This is because, Climacus contends, becoming subjective is not simply a task that is to be undertaken *in* time, but is a task for which "time itself is the task." And when "life [itself] is the task," Climacus explains, "to be finished with life before life is finished with one is not to finish the task at all" (CUP, 1:164/SKS 7, 152).

7. Climacus's discussion of death is the first to be set off in italics as a distinct "example" (CUP, 1:165/SKS 7, 153). Shortly beforehand, however, Climacus offers a brief discussion of "praying" [*Bønnen*] as an "example from the religious sphere" (CUP, 1:162/SKS 7, 150).

8. "He asks whether it is now definite that he is immortal, what kind of definiteness this immortality has, whether this definiteness . . . is not indeed indefiniteness . . . because the issue has not even been grasped . . . [whether] its definiteness can be possessed by the existing person only in indefiniteness" (CUP, 1:176–77/SKS 7, 162–63). My parenthetical note above about salvation and damnation reflects my sense that Climacus is here alluding—gingerly, very gingerly—to Christianity's stern proclamation, which Kierkegaard will voice explicitly in *Christian Discourses*, that "immortality is judgment," indeed, "the eternal separation between the righteous and the unrighteous" (CD, 205/SKS 10, 214). I ground my surmise in a provocative comment that Climacus makes much later in the *Postscript* to the effect that he has so far deliberately confined his talk of the afterlife to its "positive" side, an "eternal happiness," "in order not to cause unrest by prompting any thought about an eternal *un*happiness" (CUP, 1:369/SKS 7, 336; my emphasis).

9. See discussion at CUP, 1:178/SKS 7, 164.

10. For a related interpretation, see Walker, *Kierkegaard: The Descent into God*, p. 28. I discuss the relevant passage below.

11. I would like to thank Patrick Stokes for pressing me to expand on this point.

12. Although Socrates "was ignorant of the ground of all being, the eternal, the divine," he was nonetheless "conscious of it" in a sense, because he could name it; and yet "he was not conscious of it, inasmuch as the only thing he could say about it was that he did not know anything about it" (CI, 169/SKS 1, 217).

13. On Climacus's familiarity with death, see CUP, 1:165–66/SKS 7, 153–54.

While the relation between death's "uncertainty" and its "certainty" remains implicit in the *Postscript,* it is discussed openly in Kierkegaard's 1845 discourse "At a Graveside": "The certainty is that the axe lies at the root of the tree. Even if you do not notice that death is passing over your grave and that the axe is in motion, the uncertainty is still there at every moment, the uncertainty when the blow falls—and the tree" (TDIO, 93/SKS 5, 462).

14. The details of Climacus's view on marriage are difficult to discern. He *might* be hinting that the most genuinely ethical response to the problem of marriage and sin is in fact to avoid marriage altogether, as Kierkegaard himself chose to do. I cannot pursue this point further here, but I nonetheless thank Adam Buben for raising it, in correspondence, in a thought-provoking way.

15. Cf. CI, 36–37/SKS 1, 98; CA, 3/SKS 4, 310, etc. On the *Apology* as the Platonic dialogue that offers us our closest glimpse of "the actual Socrates," see CI, 80/SKS 1, 138.

16. Plato, *Apology,* 29a–b.

17. In "At a Graveside," however, Kierkegaard seems to suggest that Socrates's appeal to the unknown character of death may manage to *overcome* the thought of death, but does not succeed in letting it thoroughly alter and enrich one's life: "He meets with [death] in his thoughts, he renders it powerless in indeterminability, and this is his victory over death—but death does not come to penetrate his life and transform it" (TDIO, 98/SKS 5, 465). It is not clear what bearing this passage has on the above citation from the *Postscript.*

18. For an explicit polemic against the very idea of seeking proof of immortality, see CD, 213/SKS 10, 221.

19. See especially Paul Muench, "Kierkegaard's Socratic Task" (PhD diss., University of Pittsburgh, 2006).

20. As Ralph Henry Johnson notes, Climacus uses this argument as further ammunition against modern/objective ethics. His reasoning runs as follows. Thinking death, as an inexhaustible life-task, leaves no time over for the study of world history; indeed, it condemns such study, implicitly, as something not "worth beginning" in the first place (CUP, 1:166/SKS 7, 154). Cf. Johnson, *The Concept of Existence,* pp. 83–84.

21. Walker, *Kierkegaard: The Descent into God,* p. 28.

22. I would like to express sincere thanks to Adam Buben, Peter Brickey LeQuire, and Patrick Stokes for their comments on an earlier draft, and to Paul Muench, Richard Purkarthofer, and K. Brian Söderquist for many fruitful discussions of the interpretive puzzles here at issue.

7.

The Intimate Agency of Death

Edward F. Mooney

Dancing With Death

Midway through his fluid meditations in *Moby Dick,* Melville presents us with a particularly hair-raising incident. A fourteenth-century British commander has conquered a French town and demands his fair tribute in victory. He asks for six citizens to step forward to be hanged. The mayor and five others advance with halters around their necks. This fright snaps us alert—not just to cruelty, but to our mortality. And within a page, Melville assures us that a philosopher, sitting by the fire contemplating death, can be as aware, afraid, and deeply cognizant of death as anyone mounting a gallows. We all live, as he puts it, with halters around our necks.[1] He has us aware of our own halters by delivering us to the terror of others—not unlike Kierkegaard's giving us the terror of Abraham, knife drawn, to incite our own worries about faith and the terrible divine.

These intrusions of death can snap us awake the way imminent danger can, but we would hope to learn more than naked fear. Such fear can be overcome, and with courage, it should be; but an awareness of death is more than fear, and it should *not* be overcome. For Kierkegaard, it can be a sustaining and continuously transforming spring of life. For Melville, it can impress us with the melancholy tragedy of life, even amidst life's joys and celebrations, and, perhaps, it can inspire us with heroism.

If we credit the testimony of his last days, for Socrates death is nothing to fear. It brings out a moral heroism, and need not obtrude, as with Melville, as a terrifying nightmare one must master. In *Phaedo* we are taught that the philosopher "practices" death, or takes up with it philosophically; living-toward-death is of a piece with good thinking. One does not *battle* death so much as *move fluidly* with it in dialogue. Kierkegaard may seem close to Socrates here. For him, awareness of death can be a wellspring of good life; it can "accelerate life." But if Socratic meditation on death seems like a *preparation for death,* Kierkegaard's meditations seem like an *intensification* of life. And far from a nightmare or terror, Kierkegaard and Climacus figure death as an amorous partner.

Kierkegaard rejects the possibility that death teaches only fear and trembling, or only *through* fear and trembling. It does not paralyze, or serve as a counterweight to vivid life. The fluid, light steps of life are a dance with death. In the passages we'll cite, death is not a traumatic event so much as a transfiguring, intimate, mobile partner. Neither for the tragic Melville, depicting death in its gritty terror, nor for the pagan Socrates, depicting death with serenity, is death seen as a portal to an afterlife. Nor, for the would-be Christian Kierkegaard, is death covered over by a vision of an afterlife.[2] Death adds luster to *this* life. In his discourse "At a Graveside," Kierkegaard is unambiguously emphatic: "Then [at death] all is over!" (TDIO, 71/SKS 5, 442). Death is a teacher and mentor, a disturber of selves and minister to souls, in *this* life. Death obtrudes in a revelatory restructuring of the attentive soul.[3]

Transformation is often figured as a flash of light, or as the transforming jolt of thunder. True, the thunderclap of death may instill fear and startle one into awareness of one's finitude. It may firm one's resolution to take up the serious, and lose not an instant! Its visceral intrusion can clear out the trivial. "[T]he thought of death . . . accelerate[s] the living," as Kierkegaard puts it (TDIO, 83/SKS 5, 453); "earnestness [or seriousness] grasps the present this very day" (TDIO, 83/SKS 5, 453). But however instructive the thunderclap may be as a figure, in his dialectical works, and even in his discourses, Kierkegaard favors another, surprisingly gentle, image.[4] Climacus takes his writing in *Philosophical Crumbs* as "a *dance with the thought of death.*"[5] In a later discourse, Kierkegaard evokes a man's graveside grieving, and remarks that "death invites him also to the dance" (TDIO, 87/SKS 5, 456). In *Concluding Unscientific Postscript* Climacus figures Socrates as performing a "solo dance" before the divine.[6] If we credit the *Phaedo,* Socrates should be thinking accompanied by and rehearsing the thought of death. Perhaps the moral earnestness death brings in her train is a matter of lightness and grace, not puritanical fear, hard labor, and struggle.

As Plato has it, philosophy is a preparation or rehearsal for death (*Phaedo,* 64a). Although it's seldom the focus of dialectical exchange, Plato must think that wrestling with it is a kind of ground project for the philosopher. If not directly, nevertheless through one's reflective practice, a person on the path to wisdom is never far from coming to terms with its idea and reality. Joining images from *Postscript* and *Philosophical Crumbs,* we get a dialectical Socrates thinking in a rehearsal for death that, as Climacus says, is a *dance* with the thought of death.[7] This secures the intuition that Socrates is more than a thinking-talking head. He will enact a flowing, embodied artistry that somehow is the expressive equivalent of dialectic and an expressive outpouring of a life-in-the-presence-of-death.

In *Postscript,* in at least one instance, Climacus gives us Socrates without speech or interrogation and moving in solitude. His dance, as Climacus has it, is "solo," not a dialogue in the public square. It does not involve public speech partly because it is a conversation with oneself (and one's death) before only the divine, and also because identity is established, it seems, not only in speech but nonconversationally in comportment. In *Phaedo, Crito,* and *Apology* it is Socrates's calm composure and steady posture (as much as any words he utters) that convince us—or many of us—of the wisdom of both his convictions and his way of life. If philosophy is a way of life not only expressed in words but also in comportment and posture, it can be dance. There one's thinking is unspoken in the double sense of not being part of a conversation (with others or with oneself) and of being expressed in comportment, in the way one moves—as in the artistry of Thoreau's thinking-in-walking.[8] Here we have the artistry of Socrates dancing silently under a watchful, appreciative eye.

At one point Climacus says that the subjective thinker must think of death "every moment."[9] Because this thought is "solo," the dance and thought will not be apparent to others and is not expressed in dialogue (though perhaps evident to a sharp observer in the philosopher's comportment). Does the ever-presentness of the thought of death mean that death is an obsessive and explicit focus that always floods one's awareness? That would ruin life and rule out the obvious, that Socrates is aware of so much that is *not* explicitly death: his interlocutors, his path toward a dinner party, his enjoyment of good wine. Socrates is not melancholic but lively.

If secretly one has the thought of death "every moment," how salient is it? Well, I might have any number of thoughts that *stand at the ready* every *moment* without constantly being my *explicit* focus of attention or action. That I love my child, or will be loyal to my friend, might be thoughts "at the ready" every moment—even as I attend fixedly and wholeheartedly on avoiding a traffic jam or fixing a bump in a line of poetry. I close my letter to a distant friend, "You will always be close to my heart!" *Always*! Climacus speaks of the necessary ever-presentness of such essential thoughts to rule out a kind of spiritual cheating. Having the passing thought once a year that I will die, or that I love my child, does not count as truly taking up with the thought of my death, or of my love. Death or love is far from a compelling, subjective center of my existence if it occurs only for a moment on the anniversary of my father's death, or on a birthday, having been reminded by my calendar. Having the thought of death or love with requisite salience and intensity, at the ready *every moment,* is not *dwelling* on death. Thinking death is an *acceleration of life,* Kierkegaard says. "*Death in earnest gives life force as nothing else does*" (TDIO, 83/SKS 5, 453; my emphasis).

Intimations of Birth and Death

In *'Poor Paris!' Kierkegaard's Critique of the Spectacular City,* George Pattison reflects on the unfolding of life from an enigmatic beginning to an enigmatic finale.[10] What links my sense of death and birth is loss and bereavement. I mourn and yearn for continuities lost at the limits of life itself. In birth, I lose continuity "with the life that bore my life," as if birth were the breaking of a primal bond, and in death, I lose continuity with the self that is mine, as if death were the breaking of a primal bond (we are, as Melville avers, born haltered). Here is Pattison:

> The primal loss of continuity with the life that bore my life and the final loss of self in death mark out boundaries that are reinforced by the repeated experience of the births and deaths of others. Both this retrospective primal loss and prospective final loss are implicated in every important life-decision that I make, because they fundamentally condition my sense of life and my sense of myself as belonging or not belonging to it.[11]

What is the basis in my experience for this sense of bereavement and loss? The actual events of my birth and death can't be the source, because the event of my birth begins *before* I have the capacity for experience, and the event of my death ends *after* I have the capacity for experience.[12] Retrospectively I *imagine* a moment before birth or prospectively, a moment after death, and thus delineate, in imagination, a start to the event of birth and an end to the event of death. And I no doubt extrapolate from experience of births and deaths of others, encountered directly or through literature or conversation or the media. Thus experiencing the event of another's birth or death gives me a model for imagining my own. Imagination may give experience of what I cannot have experienced directly, but is it the whole story?[13]

My sense of my having entered life before memory and of having to leave it without memory of that event reminds me that access to events experienced or remembered is not the only way I get a sense of my life. It's not only *events* that affect me deeply. A sense of promise or failure, of impending doom or celebration, can suffuse my life, and these moods are neither events nor sets of events. The blow of life's loss can be experienced as the *looming* or *screaming* or *whispering* of something yet to come. A dark *aura* can jolt me awake, or invite me to dance. A melancholy aura drifting in as a distant wind can intimate a time before I was born, a virgin time, as it were, to cherish as loss. Such looming, ahead or behind, is palpable to the senses. Overarching moods afford access to deep futures and deep pasts, beyond the experience of events. I express them, and find them expressed, in posture, tone of voice, quickness or languor of stride, specifics of diction or countenance, in the look of a face. Moods afford entry to the tonality of deep temporality, a tonality conveyed in poetry and art and liturgy. Such posthumous and prenatal spans have an enigmatic, intimate agency in my life.

To consider my own past and future as carrying earnest, transformative import requires that they are compelling, through mood or imagination, *to me.*[14] A detached, patrician overview of a field that contains me will yield nothing of subjective, existential import. Perhaps not everyone can say to herself, "my *own* death or birth is inflected by loss, and I'm gripped by it." My death and birth might not matter to *me.*[15] If this indifference were not feigned, Kierkegaard would not argue abstractly about meaning but rather intervene with words that might *shake* such a person *out* of indifference. Indifference can be selective; she might not care for her own life but care intensely about her children, say. Conversely, she might be indifferent to the births and deaths of others, but intensely responsive to her own traumas before and ahead. Pervasive indifference to others would subtract from the *moral* gravity she accords her life. The earnestness Kierkegaard sees death bringing into view is not just a self-centered will to survive. Awareness of my own mortality (or natality) may be only loosely connected with moral care for others, and moral care for others be only loosely connected with care for my own mortality (or natality).

Transgressing Boundaries

If my sense of my *own* death can shadow all my actions and inactions, as Pattison and Kierkegaard declare, infusing them with moral seriousness, this reveals something profound yet commonplace about human subjectivity. This capacity to have something outside the limit of my life have transformative agency on what lies within those limits brings to the fore our capacity to occupy two temporal and spatial standpoints simultaneously. I need to think of myself as separate from myself—for instance, as separate from the life that bore me and *was* once mine, and separate from the night that will claim me and *will* be mine. And this means I apparently transgress my temporal limits. Of course we can *wish* or *long* to live in another century, in the wholeness of an Eden behind. But in thinking the agency of death I speak from a position that *enacts a transgression* of temporal limits. Let me give two examples.

A condition of Job's being able to curse the day he was born is his capacity to imaginatively project himself to a time before he was born, and (quite enigmatically) speak and think and imagine from that emptiness. From that prenatal position he resolves that he doesn't want to pass through birth and over into life. Likewise, if Silenus or Ecclesiastes suggest it might be better never to have been born, they ask us to consider from the midst of life what it would be like to consider from a time before birth whether being born is worth the effort. So are we standing in the midst of life or before our birth as we deliberate? Clearly, we are both times, both places, at once. Similarly, a condition of Achilles's being able to rue the day he will die is his capacity to imaginatively project himself to a time after death. He can attain a posthumous position from which, enigmatically, he can speak and think and imagine ruefully, lamenting what he has lost. From that position, he resolves fiercely that he does not want *ever* to pass through the portal of death, to pass out of life. He knows from the other side, as it were, that the other side is ruefully deficient.

A double standpoint is not so obviously at work in assessing the immediate grittiness of death, as with Melville, nor in assessing Socrates's noble, serene indifference to death.[16] Kierkegaard highlights death as bringing an awareness of temporality that can instill moral urgency. But as we've seen, that means we occupy a double standpoint. I am here amidst fellows and calendar time, and yet also, in thought, out of calendar time. I dance elsewhere with the otherness that is death. This sounds obscure, but the idea can be clarified by considering more familiar occasions of our being both *temporally and spatially* here and elsewhere. Consider our capacity to "step into another's shoes." The earnestness that retrospectively befalls me as I think of death is like the earnestness that befalls me when I step into the shoes of another.

Layered Space, Anomalous Time

It's a commonplace that to become morally aware we must learn to see and feel things the way another person sees or feels them, to "step into their shoes," as we say. Now perhaps that's just a metaphor, but I don't think so. I may not slip into your house and slip into your shoes, picking the loafers that fit. Nevertheless, there's nothing "*merely* metaphorical" in my saying that I step into your shoes when I try to adopt your perspective, to empathize with it, to see things from your standpoint.[17] Let's say that moral maturity requires being able to step into another's shoes. How is this relevant to understanding death? Well, if I try to see my life backward from the shadow that is death, it's like stepping into the shoes of death and looking back toward the world—my world—from that shadowed position. I am taking in a span of life from outside that span of life, yet I am, as viewer and viewed, both inside and outside my life. This parallels being in my shoes as I transport myself spatially to slip into your shoes, while still being back in my own. From the position of death, I dance with my life, and from the position of my life I dance with my death, and either way, my dance transgresses temporal and spatial limits, as if I slip into the shoes of death even as I stay in my own.

Most of Pattison's *'Poor Paris!'* deals with Kierkegaard's spatial locations, in and around Copenhagen. The city is a place of spectacle, the place to see and be seen. Even the large family home on Nytorv was there to be seen and admired, looking down on the market square it ruled. And perhaps its interior had spaces for minor spectacles—a drawing room in which to be seen and to see, strict protocol governing who was to be seen and heard by whom and when and about what. But the more obvious sites of spectacles were the bustling streets, the woods and parks newly designed for carriage rides and for viewing the king on his daily row on the lake, visible to all and sundry. There were the churches Kierkegaard entered for worship, or the university with the buzz or drone of lectures. Although these spaces were separate, they were also conjoined and layered. Amidst the drone of university lectures, Kierkegaard, like any student, might be more or less asleep to that space—yet quite alive in that moment to the space of carriage rides in verdant parkland, vivid in his mind's eye. Or amidst the sobriety of worshipers in Vor Frue Kirke, he might be swept into a lively room some blocks away filled with conversation, and with the presence of a pert and pretty girl he fancied.

Considering the way spaces can be conjoined or layered in a 'multiple exposure' helps us grasp the strange business of seeing our life from beyond the grave, from the standpoint of death, even dancing with death. When spaces are layered, rather than merely laid side by side, an ambiguity of spatial location can sink in. If Kierkegaard dreams of a carriage ride in the midst of a lecture, *where*, exactly, is he? His classroom professor might speak either way: "You're *here* (in class), Søren—don't be *there*!" Or equally, "you're *there* (in the carriage), Søren—come back *here*!" This testifies to our spatially and temporally anomalous existence. Søren is on a carriage ride and equally in class, flirting in living rooms and equally in church.

Times of Death

Anomalous results in science beg to be explained, and explained away, by new paradigms or laws. Life and death are not anomalous in *that* way. Life and death do not fall under any uncontested "normative" or "law-like" background against which their shifting shapes can be charted. Am I saying that it's as hard to locate Søren, in church (or not) or in class (or not), as it is to find a "nomos" or overarching pattern to locate life or death? If the background for fixing "death" is the field of coroners or county clerks, death will be located more or less definitively in clock or calendar time. "Life ceased at 12:01 AM!" But if the background in play is the work of cultural critics, then another meaning of "time of death" will become pertinent. Kierkegaard may be dead for the coroner yet for the critic be alive in *my* generation, well past the coroner's declaration. Then the coroner's announcement of death lies strangely idle. One's estimate of Kierkegaard's cultural life may be also unfixed: Will he be alive fifty years from now? *How* alive or moribund? Kierkegaard may be still in his youth. The grid operative for cultural critics can undermine the grid operative for county clerks, and vice versa. The meaning of "*the* time of Kierkegaard's death" radically shifts; that's what makes death anomalous.

We can superimpose a third temporal grid for locating "time of death," increasing the play of anomaly. Beyond the backdrop of cultural history and the practices of county clerks is the arena of family dynamics. Kierkegaard's death then seems to leap over his burial to invade the life of his older brother, becoming a toxin that brought on *Peter's* death. And Peter seems to have died years before his clerk-registered burial.[18] Peter Kierkegaard, the august and powerful church dignitary, died biologically decades after Søren's biological death. Yet Peter became ever more convinced that he had failed his younger brother, and he declined under a burden of guilt, finally resigning his claim to legal competency and delivering himself to the state as its ward. Søren's biological death was the start of his impressive postburial cultural life. The younger brother's biological death was the onset of Peter's spiritual death, which was complete long before his biological heart stopped.

To call death anomalous is to register an ever-expanding set of possible meanings to "death," each presupposing a background making its occurrence dateable, but none particularly congruent with others. To fix a time of death we might check a coroner's report, a critic's evocation, a family drama.[19] There is no "mother of all contexts," no "map of all maps." We are, in some mysterious sense, flying without maps when we ask—as if there were a general, all-purpose answer—*when did death occur, what is death*? From that elevated, irreal but irresistible vantage, death becomes amorphous, anomalous. Luckily we soon enough descend to schooled second nature and inherited intuition to get around without collisions, without exhaustive intelligibility.[20] *When* death shows up will depend on who, locally, is keeping time, and on the time zone we are presumed to inhabit. A family watching their child succumb to a prolonged illness may well sense an elongated time in which death hovers—or not—while the coroner takes quick note of its arrival and departs. Kierkegaard has death as an extended dialectical dance, and Socrates has it as coextensive with philosophy. For many of us, death may show up momentarily in "gritty" accounts of war and murder, in reading a novel, in a medical lab report, or less momentarily in the death of a relative. And then there is the strange presence of death paradoxically in the smile of a child.

Leakages of Time

Kierkegaard lived a number of generative life-segments (or phases) during his forty-odd Copenhagen years, phases that were layered and endlessly extending. Figuring out a narrative of what holds them together brings out, from a different angle, the complexity of pinning down how that narrative unfolds. The point is not to determine how his life "really" unfolded biographically, but to see how aspects of a life are focused by agencies from a different phase than the aspect in question. Looking back at a phase of his life from the region of death can, as we've seen, *accelerate* life. That's one way to find his life focused by agency outside it that nevertheless invades it. Kierkegaard is not alone in finding himself writing from "outside of life," as it were, from a posthumous position. Stanley Cavell, living relatively hale and hearty these days (2010), speaks of his autobiography as a piece of *posthumous* writing.[21] Kierkegaard suggests a subtitle, "A *Posthumous* Work of a Solitary Human Being" (WA, 51/SKS 11, 57; my emphasis). His writing rooted him beyond the time of his living, as he saw it, and a century and a half later, we too find him alive, rooting him in a posthumous life. His presence hovers over numerous conversations and library carrels day in, day out, any recent decade. Clerks and tombstones tell only a bit of the story.

The time of Kierkegaard's childhood (an early phase of life) has a "postchildhood" resonance. Just so, the evening of his life has a postburial, posthumous resonance. His childhood is marked by his exposure to other children, to those who laughed, for instance, at the length of his trousers—an exposure that caused interior hurt. That early hurt might resonate in "postchildhood," translated into a new register, as Kierkegaard turned the tables through the verve and bite of his writing: he would expose the uneven spiritual trousers of others. His early hurt was thus transfigured. It leaked forward into midlife and then was transfigured through the agency of seeing it retrospectively.

Does maturity lie in being able to leave childhood hurt and odd-looking trousers behind, not letting their toxin leak into midlife? Does maturity lie in leaving death to the dead, not letting its toxin leak into the bloom of life? We *want* childhood hurts not to leak forward—however much the child and its wounds ride on past childhood. Similarly, we *want* to stop thoughts of postburial time leaking backward. Excessive concern with childhood hurt or future annihilation can lead to morbid self-preoccupation, self-pity, or a sense of victimization. But deficient attention to early afflictions or inescapable mortality can lead to recklessness, self-aggrandizement, or overweening pride.

Thinking of the overlap and leakage permeating successive phases of life—childhood hurt reaching forward, then being transfigured midlife, for instance—we might ponder a second incident where turmoil from early adulthood works forward, somewhat underground, to provide the impetus for transfiguration later in life. Breaking his engagement exposed Kierkegaard to ridicule and opprobrium.[22] It began as a more or less dateable occurrence and continued through a powerful afterlife. It's not implausible to find it translated into new keys and transformed through his writing. The backward-facing agency of his writing takes up the toxic forward-flowing waves of opprobrium in ways not unlike the agency of his writing taking up the demands and decisions flowing backward from impending death. His writing transfigures the breakup, making it sufferable, perhaps turning the tables. He exposes *others* to the sort of ridicule he had suffered by exposing the shabby unevenness of bourgeois Copenhagen life.

Dancing in Amorphous Time

It may become blurred whether Kierkegaard is in church or elsewhere while in church, and it may become blurred whether as he writes he occupies the time of his earlier hurt, or has left that time behind. He can be alive in two *spaces* at once, and be alive in two *times* at once. If human time is amorphous, there is no ready answer to how the agency of hurt begins or ends, or how far it invades the future. There is no ready answer to how the agency of future emptiness invades the present or induces seriousness or earnestness that "accelerates life." Kierkegaard says that a passion is like a river whose source and endpoint we will never know (CUP, 1:237/SKS 7, 216; trans. modified).[23] Now if we are cartographers in a blimp, we can probably chart the source of a river and its final merging with the sea. But if we are swimming in its midst and middle, both source and endpoint will be hidden, however much both have agency over our present.

Does the imprint of uneven commitments to Regine wash away once Kierkegaard decides to shatter the engagement and get on with his life? If we were in a blimp, perhaps we could pinpoint the source of a hurt and its final merging with wider currents down the river of time. But hurt in his soul no doubt lies out of a cartographer's view, its tendrils receding backward and reaching forward indefinitely, even though some vivid moments of hurt may erupt in a tick of time. Death, too, might leave an imprint of indeterminate duration erupting from a place that is only strangely apprehensible. The death of Kierkegaard's best friend, or of his father or his mother, enters the city clerk's records as a well-defined occurrence. But the meaning of those deaths ripples forward, back, and sideways in his life, as aftershocks that defy precise dating and tracking. This agency of death, rebounding from the deaths of others, is other than the effect of anticipating my own death, looking at my own life from beyond the grave, earnestly. In midlife, I can occupy the position of an earlier phase of life, putting myself, say, in the shoes of a child humiliated by the length of his pants, or in the shoes of an early adult scorned for his vacillation or for his refusal of love and marriage. And in midlife I can occupy the position of a later phase, or end time, of life, putting myself in the shoes of one dead looking back on life, assessing its vitality or debility. In fact, if death has agency that "gives life force as nothing else does," that occurs only insofar as temporality, like spatiality, is amorphous.

I can project myself into shoes that give a prospect on my life from beyond, so that I see I-am-alive-and-will-die. From that spot, I participate in death's retrospective transfigurations of earlier life, as a dancer embraces and moves with her partner. My dance with the thought of death is my dance in the present and with a time not of this present, as I partake of an amorphous existence. That other in whose shoes I step is myself looking back as from beyond the grave, and that self-from-beyond-the-grave is every bit as much me as the self-this-side-of-the-grave, caught up in eating, drinking, paying taxes, being with family, a solitary walker as companionable with death as with life.

A Glimmer of Light

If not a river whose source and terminus is unknown, life might be a moment of daylight before the darkness of night sets in. He suggests this image in his discourse "At a Graveside."[24] We can picture Kierkegaard's life as a luminous daytime during which he dons his trousers and wrestles his uneven commitments, and dons a way of being in Copenhagen, a person with these opportunities, these talents, these anxieties, these parents, this insufferable older brother—or perhaps it's more having a role or talent thrust upon him—throughout, dancing with the shadow of death. Here he refutes the Epicurean claim that my death and I cannot coexist.[25] For others, Kierkegaard's death is his public burial, a time his body was again exposed to praise and opprobrium. Even for outsiders, watching in a way Kierkegaard couldn't, it's natural to see the funeral as continuous with his writing, his last days in the hospital, and his earlier attacks on the church. The scandal of his life lived through and after his burial. There is the posthumous vantage he assumes preburial in surveying his writing and life, and the posthumous vantage we assume from after his burial. His life vaults over the time of his interment, just as earlier death vaults back into the flow of his scandalous and writerly life. All this wreaks havoc with a simple image of life as a glimmer of light, with darkness before and after.

Posthumous Authorship

In Christian theology God initiates transfiguration; we don't change ourselves solo. At best we perform and interpret transfiguring poetized roles that descend, as it were, from above. We cannot know but have faith alone that the taxpaying Kierkegaard is transfigured as the author of authors who speak from the pages of multiple texts. He cannot know but have faith that as author of lives he will pass transfigured into unperishing poetry. Joseph Westfall reminds us in *The Kierkegaardian Author* that "[t]he author comes to be understood by his or her readers as both author and work, *simultaneously* but *separately* the creator of the work and a created element within it." Here, God is not the sole initiator. The to-be-transfigured author "gives birth to him- or herself by writing the work in which he or she is written."[26]

Westfall develops Kierkegaard's view that writers give their work a kind of imperishable existence, a kind of immortality.[27] Death and resurrection are in play as tax-liable Kierkegaard dies, and implied author of authors Kierkegaard rises up from the grave. Accordingly, the true poet is engaged in "posthumous production," as implied in Kierkegaard's subtitle "A Posthumous Work of a Solitary Human Being." The posthumous work transfigures the life it looks back on, manifesting the agency of death to take up a life and cull out the flesh-and-blood taxpaying author, and resurrect a writer known as his papers that reveal a postburial immortal author of authors. This view raises havoc for deflationary biography that foregrounds the mortal taxpayer and flawed suitor. "The freedom of literature—its true immortality—is its absolute distance from the factual."[28] Is this the thought that death and life, love and hurt, are amorphous, anomalous, sharply etched in space and time—and equally, diaphanous, elusive, indefinite, and infinite?

The Human Mystery

The earnestness that retrospectively befalls me as I dance with the thought of death is like the earnestness that befalls me when I suddenly see things from the shoes of another and realize that I must change my ways. My friend is in pain and I just hadn't been taking its impact and importance seriously, earnestly enough (but how much is enough?). I reconfigure my sense of how it is with her. I haven't changed any fact about her life, and what I learn is elusive—I grasp, or am grasped by, the extent and intensity of things for her—which is to say that I find myself compelled where I wasn't before. Things that matter for *her* now drive *me* into recognition. The insight can be frightening, and in any case will transform my comportment toward her—become my dance with her pain, one could say.

Death is enigmatic, Kierkegaard tells us, and an enigma isn't something utterly opaque, but appears under varied aspects, something I see this moment and don't see the next, or see first as profound and then as superficial, or see first as liberating and then as constraining, first as fearful, then as wonderful. Like time and love and hurt, death is enigmatic because it is *now*—but tomorrow; it is *here*—but elsewhere. All who read these words, or read Kierkegaard's words, cannot have failed to think them partially—now *more* fully, now less so—and cannot have failed to think something like Tolstoy's syllogism: All persons die; I am a person; I will die.[29] And let the conclusion fall shallow and limp. We cannot have failed to think: Now he is dead nothing matters to him; what mattered was his life as he lived it; when I am dead nothing will matter to me; what matters is my life, this very day, as I live it. Part of the enigma of death is that I can find this flow of thought inevitable and transparent and compelling to *me*, and that I can, as if under a spell of indifference, follow this thought while utterly lacking conviction—hearing words yet not hearing them, hearing-and-not-hearing, *you will die, act now: Let the thought of death deliver earnestness that your life may be changed!*

I say to myself, "Those emaciated children in a Sudanese camp . . . put yourself in *their* shoes, or in the shoes of their *parents!* Doesn't their death matter?" Or I ask myself (but don't really ask), "Was I too brusque?—Can't I do better?" I dance and don't dance with the thought of death. Of course I may, sadly, not hear, because I find my life not to matter. Then I am other to myself: That person (who is none other than me) is afflicted by indifference, her morale and soul are emaciated—"*put yourself in her shoes*! Can't you see that she matters, that her death matters to me—*is* me?"

I can look at myself, and so can separate myself from myself, occupying two postures at once toward a soul that slips in and out of view yet is one—and doubled—and my own. Things can matter or not, and I can know and not know that my life matters, or that your life matters, or that the fall of a sparrow matters. My doubleness is requisite both to finding that my life matters and to finding that your life matters. Taking my life with earnestness (or not) is inextricably, mysteriously, tied to taking your life with earnestness (or not). The brute or subtle presence of mattering descends in resonance for and with one and all. From a discrete moment it seems to radiate in all directions, infinitely, as part of a fluid and sustained dance with death.

The strangeness of dancing with the thought of death is like the moral mystery, the human mystery, that in seeing that my life matters, I see that yours does; seeing that your life matters, I see that mine does. Death brings us there (and love might, as well). A dance with these thoughts is neither abrasive nor competitive nor vocal but nonetheless inviting and mutually satisfying. A dance with death is the consummate embrace of the other, a life with the other, with the other who is other—and the other *even to myself* that I am.

NOTES

1. Herman Melville, *Moby Dick, or The Whale,* commentary by Tom Quirk (London: Penguin, 2001), ch. 60, "The Line," p. 305f.

2. Kierkegaard is a "would-be Christian" in the sense all inhabitants of Christendom are: it's as if to be a Christian is to not yet be a Christian, and so to be a would-be Christian.

3. *Philosophical Crumbs* gives an extended treatment of the way non-Socratic learning occurs through the invasive restructuring of revelation. See *Kierkegaard's Repetition and Philosophical Crumbs,* ed. and intro. Edward F. Mooney, trans. M. L. Piety (Oxford: Oxford University Press, 2009).

4. In *Repetition,* the young man awaits transformation arriving as a thunderstorm, or as Job's whirlwind (R, 212–14/SKS 4, 79–81).

5. *Fragments,* p. x; my emphasis. I follow the Oxford World Classics title, *Philosophical Crumbs.*

6. CUP, 1:89/SKS 7, 88: Socrates is "a solo dancer to the honor of the [divine]." A proposed author for *Fear and Trembling* was "Simon Stylita Solo Dancer and Private Individual" (FT, 243).

7. This brings Socrates (and Climacus) close to Nietzsche, who wishes for a "music playing Socrates" (*Birth of Tragedy,* trans. and intro. Douglas Smith [Oxford: Oxford University Press, 2000], pp. 85, 93) and a "God who would dance" (*Thus Spoke Zarathustra,* trans. and intro. Graham Parkes [Oxford: Oxford University Press, 2005], p. 36). Socrates reports in *Phaedo* that he has often been visited by a dream that urges him to "make music and compose" (60e). It's possible to imagine that dream not as indicating a path not taken but as reminding him of what he has done: he has spent a life in composition in response to a muse, has made music through his conversations.

8. In his essay "Walking," Thoreau claims that only one or two persons of his acquaintance have learned "the art of walking," a kind of meditative pilgrimage among the things of creation (*The Essays of Henry D. Thoreau,* ed. Lewis Hyde [New York: North Point Press, 2002], pp. 147–78).

9. Cf. "To think this uncertainty [of death] once and for all, or once a year at matins on New Year's morning . . . is not to think it at all. . . . Therefore it becomes more and more important to me to think it into every moment of my life" (CUP, 1:66–67/SKS 7, 154–55). See also Patrick Stokes's discussion in *Kierkegaard's Mirrors, Interest, Self, and Moral Vision* (Hampshire: Palgrave, 2010), p. 126.

10. George Pattison, *"Poor Paris!" Kierkegaard's Critique of the Spectacular City* (Berlin: de Gruyter, 1999), p. 140.

11. Pattison, *"Poor Paris!,"* p. 140.

12. See Ludwig Wittgenstein, *Tractatus Logico-Philosophicus,* trans. C. K. Ogden (London: Routledge, 1996), p. 185, on death as an event I do not live through.

13. See the excellent discussions in Stokes, *Kierkegaard's Mirrors.*

14. See Stokes, *Kierkegaard's Mirrors,* p. 5 and elsewhere.

15. Compare Heidegger's picture in *Being and Time* of human life being a structure of care tilted toward death, and death tilted back. See Charles Guignon's contribution to this volume.

16. Thoreau finds the death of John Brown sublime and transformative; both Kant and Burke see the presence of *my* death to be an ingredient in any experience of the sublime. See my "Wonder and Affliction: Thoreau's Dionysian World," in *Thoreau as Philosopher,* ed. Rick Anthony Furtak (forthcoming); and *Lost Intimacy in American Thought: Recovering Personal Philosophy from Thoreau to Cavell* (London and New York: Continuum, 2009), pp. 53–77, 194–221.

17. It's merely churlish to insist that the proper statement is "It's *as if* I stepped into your shoes." There's nothing second best in saying "I step into your shoes" any more than saying "I see what you mean" (rather than "It's *as if* I see what you mean").

18. See the accounts of Peter's late life in the biographies of Kierkegaard by Alastair Hannay, *Kierkegaard: A Biography* (Cambridge: Cambridge University Press, 2001), p. 423; and Joakim Garff, *Søren Kierkegaard: A Biography,* trans. Bruce H. Kirmmse (Princeton, N.J.: Princeton University Press, 2005), pp. 807–10. John Thoreau dies of lockjaw in his brother Henry's arms; a few days later, Henry takes on all the death agony and symptoms of John; later still Henry writes a memorial to John, *A Week on The Concord and Merrimack Rivers.* See Robert D. Richardson Jr., *Henry Thoreau: A Life of the Mind* (Berkeley: University of California Press, 1986), pp. 113–16.

19. We might ask, in this age of heart transplants, whether the dead live on in the living—since a heart of the dead may.

20. Asking when death arrives (or is left behind) is a little like asking when love arrives or is left behind, or when birth arrives or is left behind. Birth might begin with the exchange of a glance between lovers, with a midwife's cry of delight, with the utterance of a first word, or with setting out from home. Death might begin with birth, or with the first failed love, or with a final gasp of the lungs, or with the departure from memory of all those who might have remembered one—as one was when alive.

21. Stanley Cavell, "Excerpts from Memory," *Critical Inquiry* 32, no. 4 (Summer 2006): p. 777.

22. Against the background of his writerly vocation and talent, his failing to achieve marriage might not be the lamentable fiasco some took it to be. In *Fear and Trembling,* those who fail as knights of faith (or resignation)—silentio's contemporaries—are consigned to the ridiculous status of "frogs in life's swamp" (FT, 71/SKS 4, 136). Thus (perhaps) his early hurts flower into marvelous art. See the biographical facts in Hannay, *Kierkegaard: A Biography,* and Garff, *Søren Kierkegaard: A Biography.*

23. The Hongs render *stemning* here as "mood" rather than "passion" (they render *lidenskab* as "passion"). However, "mood" sounds weak and fickle: "Watch

out, he's in one of his moods!" The passage is discussed in Pattison, *"Poor Paris!,"* p. 97. The importance of a calendar date for the writing of a note that shattered an engagement diminishes as we track its *meaning.*

24. Patrick Stokes provides this marvelous passage from Bede's *Ecclesiastical History of The English People:* "Your Majesty, when we compare the present life of man on earth with that time of which we have no knowledge, it seems to me like the swift flight of a single sparrow through the banqueting hall where you are sitting at dinner on a winter's day with your commanders and counselors. In the midst there is a comforting fire to warm the hall; outside the storms of winter rain or snow are raging. The sparrow flies swiftly in through one door of the hall, and out through another. While he is inside, he is safe from the winter storms; but after a few moments of comfort, he vanishes from sight into the wintery world from which he came. Even so, man appears on earth for a little while; but of what went before this life or of what follows, we know nothing." Bede, *Ecclesiastical History of the English People: With Bede's Letter to Egbert and Cuthbert's Letter on the Death of Bede,* trans. David Hugh Farmer and Leo Sherley-Price (London: Penguin, 1990), pp. 129–30.

25. See Patrick Stokes, "The Power of Death: Retroactivity, Narrative, and Interest," in *International Kierkegaard Commentary: Prefaces/Writing Sampler and Three Discourses on Imagined Occasions,* ed. Robert L. Perkins, pp. 387–417 (Macon, Ga.: Mercer University Press, 2006).

26. Joseph Westfall, *The Kierkegaardian Author: Authorship and Performance in Kierkegaard's Literary and Dramatic Criticism* (Berlin: de Gruyter, 2007), p. 143. Kierkegaard was polemical and cagey enough to revel in the changing shadows of a self and in the difficulties others would have in finding him. And he was moral and religious enough to exploit another possibility: only where radical openness to change is present—that is, only where a solid self *can't* be pinned down—can there be hope of transfiguration.

27. Westfall, *The Kierkegaardian Author,* p. 51.

28. Westfall, *The Kierkegaardian Author,* p. 135. Another consequence of a text's immortality is that SK can't fix the meaning of a part or the whole of the authorship with any authority exceeding that of any other reader. He can't provide an "incontrovertible last word on Kierkegaardian authorship" (p. 77).

29. Tolstoy isn't endorsing such a syllogism himself; he has Ivan Ilyich quote it second hand: "The example of a syllogism which he had learned in Kiezewetter's *Logic:* 'Caius is a man, men are mortal, therefore Caius is mortal,' had seemed to him all his life to be true as applied to Caius but certainly not as regards himself" (Leo Tolstoy, *The Death of Ivan Ilyich and Other Stories,* trans. Rosemary Edmondson [London: Penguin, 1960], p. 137).

8.

A Critical Perspective on Kierkegaard's "At a Graveside"

Gordon D. Marino

Preface

This short chapter is faceted to one text—Kierkegaard's "At a Graveside." While Kierkegaard's thoughts on death spill across his corpus, I believe that this nonpseudonymous discourse, published in 1845, is his most straightforward and sustained reflection on what might be termed Kierkegaard's account of "Being-towards-death." Drawing a comparison with Tolstoy, I submit that for all the epiphanies in these pellucid pages, there is something lacking. There are other lessons to be drawn.

Kierkegaard and his pseudonyms stress that thinkers who fail to express their words in their actions do not really understand what they are spouting. Over and over again, Kierkegaard inveighs that there are two senses of understanding—one abstract and the other an understanding in which one strives to live. It does not require a sophisticated reader to grasp that for Kierkegaard only the latter counts as a true understanding. There are implications following from the connection that Kierkegaard works between words and deeds, between understanding and action. Despite all of his attempts to distance himself from his texts, I think Kierkegaard invites us to examine the sense in which our ideas have or have not become inscribed in our lives. At the risk of sounding like a crier of inwardness, I bid the reader to bear with me for a couple of paragraphs of personal narrative on my Kierkegaard studies and the issue of death—or rather of my own death.

I came to Kierkegaard in my mid-thirties. Perhaps it was because I walked under the black sun and often felt dead inside, but at the time I was riveted by the idea of death and its meaning in life. The fact that Kierkegaard squarely confronted "the issue" of death attracted me to the lyrical Danish philosopher/theologian. Still, at that point, I had had very little truck with the reaper. I had only been to a few funerals and had not spent much time in the ICU with people giving birth to their own end. I am now at the far end of my fifties and things have changed. Many of my loved ones have found lumps and received sentences from the medical magistrates. And I have been around long enough to know all too well that Pascal was right: the fifth act is always bloody,[1] and, he could have added, degrading. I am no longer the philosophical goth that I was in the 1980s. Indeed, now I cannot help but think that when I earlier followed Kierkegaard through the *kirkegård,* I hadn't the vaguest notion of death and its vicissitudes. "At a Graveside" offers the frequent admonition that we can't learn anything from observing the death of another,[2] or at least that we can't learn anything about the subject that he is so occupied with—earnestness. I beg to differ.

A few years back, I was sitting at the deathbed of an author who was a well-known devout Christian. When the others left, I bumbled something like, "I know that everyone thinks of you as someone who would be eager to pass on to the next world, but are you afraid of dying?" She pressed my hand and said, "It isn't death itself so much that I'm afraid of, as the feeling that I am being left alone." Tearing up, she added, "I'm going to miss everyone terribly." Being an observer to that death, and one other—that of my mother, who confided the same fear—helped me to appreciate how foundational the ties that bind us to one another are. As I will soon complain, for all of his many trips to the graveyard, Kierkegaard seems dead to this dimension of departing.

Time and experience have raised the issue for me of who exactly has the authority to preach on the proper relationship to the thought of his or her own death. There was one person with whom I was very close. Profoundly and chronically melancholic, he moaned for years that he did not care to live anymore. He smoked and drank like someone who was to face the gallows at dawn. But when the tumors literally popped through his neck and the doctor told him that "it was over," he swooned in a panic and could not bear the fact that this was not a melancholic thought but the real thing. The end. This man did not think what he thought he thought about death. As Kierkegaard, in "At a Graveside," reminds us:

> With regard to something else, one can express an opinion and then if one is required to act by virtue of this opinion, that is, show that one has it, innumerable escapes are possible. But the uncertainty of death is the pupil's rigorous oral examiner, and when the pupil recites the explanation,

uncertainty says to him, "Well, now I will make an inquiry as to whether this is your opinion, because now, right now at this very moment, all is over, for you all is over; no escape is thinkable, not a letter to be added; so I will find out whether you actually meant what you said about me" (TDIO, 100/SKS 5, 467–68).

With regard to death, it is hard to know what we understand in that aforementioned second sense of understanding. I don't know what I really know about death or whose thoughts on this topic can be trusted and whose are just the lyrical effusions of feelings that have very little to do with death. That, of course, is to grant one of Kierkegaard's major points in "At a Graveside": that much of what goes for reflection on death is actually an expression of a mood. But then again, maybe these so-called moods, the grief and terror, can also be revelatory—can also be teachers.

Kierkegaard's Message

Although other contributors to this collection on Kierkegaard and death have commented on the signal points in "At a Graveside," I will briefly adumbrate what I take to be the pith of this meditation.

Kierkegaard's offering begins with a phrase that is reiterated throughout, "*Saa er det da forbi,*" "Then all is over" (TDIO, 71/SKS 5, 442)—as though to understand one's mortality amounted to grasping that it is certain that at some uncertain time, it will be up to here and no further. *Saa er det da forbi.* If you think of your life as a story, death is the last period on the last page. A moment before your story is over you will probably know that it is over, that there is nothing more, not one cubit that you can add to your life.

In *The Concept of Anxiety,* anxiety is presented as a teacher/examiner. The same is true of the thought of one's own death in "At a Graveside." On every third page, Kierkegaard reminds you that the thought of your own death is a potential teacher. But mind us all, it is not a schoolmarm who is going to trot after us if we act up in class and refuse to sit for the lessons. In this text, death is implacable and as unchanging as God.

In the first of *Three Discourses on Imagined Occasions,* a discourse on confession, Kierkegaard writes eloquently of finding the stillness to examine yourself before God. Finding this still point is of course no easy task, and the same, I think, can be said of taking instruction from death. Kierkegaard makes the astute observation that most of our thinking and imaginings about the end put death outside of ourselves.

Thinking ourselves dead, and so as unable to think, seems like a contradiction, a kind of Zen *koan*. Then again, Kierkegaard and all of his authorial creations maintain that contradictions are a task, and that in some existential as opposed to Hegelian fashion, we all have the work of uniting contradictions. As a prime example, we have an eternal and a temporal dimension (or whatever we might call eternity and time) and so we are charged with the work of uniting these poles of our lives.

The idea of my own death is a teacher. But of what? Of earnestness. Earnestness and earnestness alone is what recommends mentally walking over your own grave. Earnestness is one of the most dominant themes in Kierkegaard's authorship. Unlike other concepts such as stages and repetition, it does not have its day and vanish. But what is the view of earnestness that emerges from these pages?

Much of this discourse is devoted to clarifying the distinction between earnestness and mood. No matter how powerful, moods are like internal storms. In contrast to earnestness, moods are transitory internal events that we suffer. According to Kierkegaard there are moods that might seem to betoken earnestness. But do not get taken in by them. Even a father grieving over the death of his son—a scene that Kierkegaard gave a lot of thought to—is still just a mood, that is, a tsunami of a feeling, but a feeling that, like all feelings, is fleeting. More important than the transitory factor, though, moods do not involve the profound self-examination that Kierkegaard believes is at the core of earnestness.

Still, it is important to note that the Kierkegaard of the *Discourses* does not discount all emotion. It is evident that there are emotions connected with earnestness: emotions such as wonder, fear, and grief. In "On the Occasion of a Confession," Kierkegaard writes:

> If a person is to understand his sin essentially, he must understand it because he becomes alone, he alone, just he alone, with the Holy One, who knows everything. Only this fear and trembling is the true fear and trembling, only the grief that the recollection of God awakens in a person, only the repentance his love loves forth (TDIO, 27/SKS 5, 407).

The fear and trembling and the grief that comes from voluntarily trying to see yourself standing before God are not limned as moods. One would think that someone who stood before God without being shaken with these feelings was not really standing before his or her maker. While there is no emotion that defines earnestness, the discourse on confession makes it plain that there is a feeling component to this life-posture.

Earnestness is also presented as a kind of meta-cognition. The earnest individual is capable of recognizing that he or she is in the snares of a mood that might take them down the wrong path. Midway through the death discourse, Kierkegaard describes an earnest individual who, visited by the thought of death, is tempted to play dead, to sink into the numbness of depression. Kierkegaard writes,

> When it [the idea of death] sneaked in and beguiled your life force into romantic dreaming, when death's despondency would make your life a vanity . . . when the thought that it was all over would anesthetize you into the sleep of depression . . . you said to yourself, "My soul is in a mood, and if it continues this way, then there is in it a hostility toward me that can gain domination" (TDIO, 84/SKS 5, 454; trans. modified).

Again, the earnest individual has an observing ego and is wary of moods.

To continue with this summary, as Kierkegaard has powerfully put it, the thought of death possesses a "retroactive power" (TDIO, 99/SKS 5, 466). An awareness of death creates a time shortage and as such is capable of conferring more value on the moment than would have existed for the individual who, at some level, believed that he had an eternity to set things straight. In Kierkegaard's writings, time is often presented as the enemy, and earnest reflection can help us to dispel the illusion that we have days and weeks to waste, that we can put off getting serious about life. As Bob Dylan puts it, "The ringleaders from the county seat say you don't have all that much time."[3] Kierkegaard believes that anyone who properly understands that observation will eschew both recklessness and frivolousness.

Finally, earnestness is most clearly marked out by the activity of recollecting God. Enlisting the imagination, Kierkegaard often unpacks this process in the image of standing alone before God. While someone else might be an occasion, a trigger for the act of theological self-reflection, no one can drive you to it. We are all alone—isolated with regard to the essential task in life of pondering our individual relationship to God.

"At a Graveside" opens with remembrances of a merchant who has just been buried. Like the paragon of faith daubed in *Fear and Trembling*, there is nothing outwardly remarkable about this man. But the old shop owner is offered as the personification of earnestness, because while he was alive and time was passing he always remembered to recollect God, the eternal:

> In the grave there is no recollection, not even of God. See, the man did know this, the one of whom it must now be said that he no longer recollects anything, to whom it would now be too late to say this. But because he knew this, he acted accordingly, and therefore *he recollected God* while he was living (TDIO, 71/SKS 5, 442).

If we turn again to "On the Occasion of a Confession," it would seem that recollecting God entails appropriating more and more deeply the quintessentially Lutheran idea that you, a sinner, are nothing before God. Here, and in "At a Graveside," Kierkegaard insists that the earnest individual, standing alone as nothing before God, will make himself blind to all comparisons such as "I am less of a sinner than Jack but worse than Jill." In the early discourses, as well as *Works of Love,* the tendency to understand ourselves in comparative terms is described as part and parcel of a worldly thinking and sinfulness.

While someone else might be a trigger for the act of self-reflection that is recollecting God, no one can, as it were, drive you to it. We are all alone—isolated with regard to the essential task in life of reflecting on our God relationship.

Kierkegaard vs. Tolstoy

There are subtle hints in the coda that the author of "At a Graveside" does not in fact believe that the grave is the end. However, references to the afterlife are very muted in this text precisely because Kierkegaard is trying to compel his readers to come to terms with the "up to here, not one step further" (TDIO, 78/SKS 5, 449) in life. But then, why strive to become earnest, to recollect God? If we have so many years and then just disappear, why place such weight upon getting serious about our fleeting lives?

There is no suggestion in "At a Graveside" that the earnest individual will be happier than those who do not make any time for thinking about their death. It could be reasoned that the individual who is self-aware of his own mortality will be less likely to fritter away his hours, will make more of an effort to develop a life view and construct priorities, but Kierkegaard does not draw out this practical counsel. Death awareness can go either way; it can bring some to their senses and cause an immobilizing despair in others.

There are, however, other grounds for complaint. Perhaps the author of Ecclesiastes is on the mark when he writes that "there is a season, and a time for every matter under heaven,"[4] including a time to be young; and perhaps a part of being young is feeling that you are immortal. If there is no afterlife, why make yourself old before your time? Why becloud the brilliant sun of this stage of life with pale thoughts of the grave? Rest assured, the dark will roll in soon enough. Kierkegaard and Nietzsche are of a common mind and heart on many issues, but Nietzsche would surely have judged the prescription to remind yourself of your own death to be pure poison and a classic symptom of the disease that is the ascetic ideal.

Of course, "At a Graveside" and virtually everything Kierkegaard penned was produced with a nominally Christian audience in mind. More than that, these pages were written for fellow travelers, for people who were not insouciant about the spiritual life. As such, I do not mean to suggest that there is something amiss with the presumption of a feeling for Christian ideals and eschatology; nevertheless, the meditation does not carry the same wisdom for readers who find Christianity and the suggestion of entering the grave and then sitting at the right or left hand of the Father on a par with belief in the Greek pantheon. And there are today, and most especially in Kierkegaard's Denmark, many such readers.

But even apart from the theological presuppositions, earnestness may not be the only instruction that death has to offer. I would imagine that if the thought of death has some kind of unique impact on our lives then surely it ought to humanize us in some way. By humanize, I mean that if it strikes at our core, then a death awareness ought to have a positive impact on our relationships with other humans, making us better neighbors and more responsive to others. While Kierkegaard insists that comparisons are too much a part of this worldly life, comparing the conclusions that Kierkegaard draws from death with those of another author can be illuminating.

Leo Tolstoy was a contemporary of Kierkegaard's. He even read a smidgen of Kierkegaard in translation as the result of his having a Danish friend living in Russia.[5] There is, of course, a good deal of existential overlap between the two literary and spiritual giants, not the least of which are their views on faith and faith's relation to reason. Both Kierkegaard and Tolstoy held that believing in Christ meant taking Christ as a pattern. More to our point, both men were convinced that humanity would be best served by our individually and sincerely accepting the fact that our days are numbered.

After Tolstoy's brother suddenly died, the fifty-something world-renowned author sank into a long period of devastating depression and anxiety. Childish as it might seem, he could not brook the idea that you labor and love through this vale of tears and then the balloon pops and it's over and you're gone; or maybe it would be more apt to say "you have disappeared." Like Nicodemus, and the existentialist Miguel de Unamuno,

Tolstoy came to Christianity because it alone promised to meet his boundless hunger for life. While grappling with the funk, Tolstoy wrote his remarkable *The Death of Ivan Ilych.* It is this text that I would like to put next to "At a Graveside."[6]

The Death of Ivan Ilych is the story of an upwardly mobile bourgeois lawyer. Ilych is deep in a loveless marriage and, though he hardly seems to notice, he is estranged from his two children. The only subjects that Ilych and his wife could become passionate about are money, parties, and feathering the nest of their home. One afternoon, Ilych is stringing a curtain in his new digs when he slips, crashes into a ledge, and injures his side. Unlike common bruises, the pain from the accident does not recede. Soon he is losing weight and tiring easily. He visits various doctors. After weeks, it becomes clear that there is something terribly wrong with Ilych, and finally that he is spiraling toward death.

Tolstoy's Muse is at work while he daubs the paralyzing terror that consumes Ilych as he begins to comprehend that life and the world are about to roll on without him. Everyone in Ilych's circles, his so-called friends, his wife, even the doctors, refuse to acknowledge the knock at the door. As a result, Ilych is all alone with death and his all-consuming terror. If there is a gospel in this work, it is certainly that the widespread denial of death leads to people living at deadly distances from one another. But to follow Tolstoy's narrative, this isolation does not exist at every level of society.

Like Dostoevsky, Tolstoy believed that the Russian intelligentsia had been corrupted by effete European values and sensibilities. They had lopped themselves off from physical labor and the land; as a result, they were out of harmony with existence. Unlike the professional classes, the peasants in Tolstoy's works are able and willing to recognize that we are all heading for the falls. Ilych's manservant, Gerasim, is virtually the only person with whom he has physical contact. At night he holds Ilych's feet on his shoulder to reduce his master's pain. Tolstoy narrates:

> Gerasim alone did not lie; everything showed that he alone understood the facts of the case and did not consider it necessary to disguise them, but simply felt sorry for his emaciated and enfeebled master. Once when Ivan Ilych was sending him away he even said straight out: "We shall all of us die, so why should I grudge a little trouble?"[7]

As the book proceeds, the chapters shrink in length, mimicking the experience of falling into the chute that is our own death. The focus becomes more and more narrow. Alas, the experience of dying is imaged as a birth, a passing through a black sack. When Ilych finally comes to accept that he is done for—when he makes himself co-present with his own death, he attempts to reach out to his estranged wife. For what seems like the first time, he begins to think about the pain of others:

> "Yes, I am making them wretched," he thought. "They are sorry, but it will be better for them when I die." He wished to say this but had not the strength to utter it. "Besides, why speak? I must act," he thought. With a look at his wife he indicated his son and said: "Take him away . . . sorry for him . . . sorry for you too . . ." he tried to add, "forgive me," but said "forgo" and waved his hand, knowing that He whose understanding mattered would understand.[8]

The reborn and dying Ilych now feels sympathy for others and wants to mitigate their suffering.

Like Kierkegaard, Tolstoy does not omit the "He whose understanding mattered" from his reflections on death. God is there but in Tolstoy's masterpiece it is the relationship with others that is front and center. For Kierkegaard, in contrast, there is scarcely a word about the relationship between our death awareness and the ties that bind us. In "At a Graveside" there is no hint that putting the skull on our desks and developing earnestness might make us more open and responsive to others. Death can give our faith more life but it is never depicted as providing a boost to our ability to love others—to be open to their suffering. Of course, Kierkegaard wants to rigorously eliminate any possibility of tit-for-tat thinking. Human as it most certainly is, he found repugnant the desire for reciprocity, to get something back, alas, to be loved. Thus, he may have thought that the call to provide practical help to your neighbor would taint our works of love. Those who carry a brief for Kierkegaard will, of course, contend that for him the only legitimate way to love our neighbor is through loving God. Maybe so. But there is certainly no accent on my relationship to my fellow human beings in "At a Graveside," and on that score, for all of its brilliance, the discourse seems inhuman.

NOTES

1. Blaise Pascal, *Pensées,* trans. and ed. Roger Ariew (Indianapolis, Ind.: Hackett Publishing Company, 2005), p. 52.

2. For further discussion of this issue, see the chapter in this volume by Laura Llevadot.

3. This line is from the song "Up to Me," http://www.bobdylan.com/#/songs/up-to-me.

4. Eccles. 3.1 (*The New Oxford Annotated Bible,* 3rd ed., edited by Michael D. Coogan [Oxford: Oxford University Press, 2001]).

5. On Tolstoy and Kierkegaard, see Darya Loungina, "On the Original Reception of Kierkegaard in Russia, 1880–90's," *Søren Kierkegaard Newsletter* 48 (September 2004): pp. 20–24.

6. George Connell's contribution to this volume also recognizes the value in putting these two authors into conversation.

7. Leo Tolstoy, *The Death of Ivan Ilych and Other Stories,* trans. Aylmer Maudel (New York: Signet, 1960), p. 138.

8. Tolstoy, *The Death of Ivan Ilych,* p. 154.

9.

Life-Narrative and Death as the End of Freedom: Kierkegaard on Anticipatory Resoluteness

John J. Davenport

Introduction: New Problems for Narrative Theories

In three recent articles, John Lippitt has raised important questions about the notions that human selves have a "narrative" structure and that the natural development of our capacity for robust selves (including autonomy and ethical maturity) involves achieving "narrative unity" in the stories that we are.[1] His questions intersect with other critiques of narrative models raised in the wider and growing literature on this topic in the past decade. Lippitt forces us to reconsider claims that Anthony Rudd, I, and others made in *Kierkegaard After MacIntyre* that MacIntyre's famous account of narrative unity as part of the telos of human life[2] sheds light on Kierkegaard's conception of selfhood, and that insights from Kierkegaard can help us develop and defend such a narrative model. In particular, Lippitt questions whether narrative is a useful model for real human lives, and whether movement from the "aesthetic" to the "ethical" outlook or stage of life is illuminated by the idea of narrative unity.

Moreover, as Kathy Behrendt, Lippitt, and other contributors to the wider philosophical literature have recently argued,[3] the phenomenon of death poses special problems for narrative models. Patrick Stokes has shown that Kierkegaard recognizes such problems when he describes death as indefinable, inexplicable, and apparently contingent in relation to prior events.[4] Stokes agrees with George Pitcher that the meaning of our life-narrative can be altered profoundly by our death or by events following it;[5] but then, given Kierkegaard's point about the radical uncertainty of the time and manner of our death, "it cannot be brought into any narrative that might confer meaning on it while the subject lives."[6] Thus, although Kierkegaard shares MacIntyre's concern for the "unified coherence of the responsible self in time," the life in which this coherence is found can only be understood as a narrative "in a necessarily incomplete sense."[7] While it applies to all human lives, this point also extends Lippitt's worries to the religious stage, given the significance of mortality for religious life-views. We have to ask: Even *if* the choices that form an "ethical" self in Kierkegaard's sense involve an explicable kind of narrative continuity, can such a clarified narrative model also help us understand Kierkegaard's account of the transition to religious faith? Or are narrative metaphors for human life useful only through the ethical stage, not the religious?

This chapter will focus on Kierkegaard's proposal in his discourse "At a Graveside," which indicates how our narrative identity can include our mortality. But for the power of this solution to be clear, I must first briefly outline a new way of conceiving narrative identity that builds on Anthony Rudd's efforts to answer the main objections of Lippitt and other critics of narrative theory.[8]

Narrative Realism and Kierkegaardian Autonomy: An Outline of the New Account

The concept of "narravive." My new approach involves distinguishing different types of narrative unity that are discussed in the literature and arguing that the basic coherence of meaning-relations within a living person's story is ontologically prior to the sort of "telling" and reflection involved in making narrative artifacts. To clarify this distinction, I now refer to the structure of a person's practical identity as a "narravive" or lived story, as opposed to narratives about her identity or life that may either truthfully report or distort her narravive. This new account, which I call narrative realism, can be summarized in five basic theses:

(A) *The analogy thesis:* The truthmaker of a biographical story itself has something *like* a narrative structure, something similar to the multidimensional weave of temporally extended meaning-relations that we find in stories made by human recountings—even though much of it is not a result of any interpersonal or intrapersonal logos, accounting, or reflective act (see thesis E); the term "narravive" marks this difference from narratives as artifacts, told stories, or products of reflective explanation.

(B) *The level thesis:* This real structure of diachronic meaning-relations that is a unique practical identity includes as *constitutive conditions* at least minimal short-term and long-term memory capacities and unity of apperception (unity-o) and the teleological relations of significance necessary for planning agency, i.e., intentions that extend over long periods of time and coordinate multiple capacities (unity-1). These conditions make possible, but do not entail, higher levels of connection that are associated with personal autonomy.

(C) *MacIntyre's mimetic thesis:* The basic human capacity to make secondary narratives, including nonfictional or broadly historical accounts and fictional stories, is *derived from* our experience in living out primary narravives—both those that constitute individual practical identities and those that constitute the shared identities of interpersonal groups.

(D) *The incompleteness thesis:* Even the best literary depictions of a fictional life, or biographical portrayals of an actual life, or historical works about individuals or groups, necessarily fall short of the infinite detail of significance in actual lived experience, which involves networks of resonances between possible and actual acts and experiences in past, present, and anticipated future including teleological connections and myriad other kinds of association-relations.

(E) *The articulation thesis:* The narravive of one's practical identity includes, from an early age, conceptions of one's activities, character, personality, roles and relationships, etc., which often follow familiar scripts or social paradigms. These range from more or less tacit self-understandings to interpretations explicitly worked out in thorough meditation on oneself. Thus reflexive *logoi* of several kinds add to and reshape the weave of meanings already acquired and continually enlarged through prereflective experience. At least some reflection on self of these sorts is necessary for planning agency in general, and more is needed to achieve thematic coherence of one's goals and activities in one's narravive as a whole.

These theses outline a way of understanding practical identities in narrative terms that makes it possible to apply different kinds of "narrative unity" to aspects of identity. I attribute this sort of narrative realist view, which opposes constructivist and fictionalist versions of narrative identity, to David Carr, Paul Ricoeur, and Charles Taylor, and I regard it as a faithful extension of MacIntyre's sketch of a narrative conception in *After Virtue.*

Narrative and autonomy: four levels. This basic model can be expanded to link with an account of personal autonomy built on Harry Frankfurt's notions of "caring" and "wholeheartedness." Rudd has argued that to meet Lippitt's challenges, we must distinguish between the kind of narrative connection that we find in any "self-conscious rational being who has some narrative sense of his or her past" and a stronger kind of integration that involves "autonomy" and acceptance of responsibility for one's concrete personality and dispositions.[9] Narrative realist thesis B is meant to formalize this point: In particular, I now distinguish four different levels of narrative unity, each of which is necessary but not sufficient for the ones after it:

> 0. *Unity of apperception:* We immediately (or prereflectively) recognize ourselves as the *same subject* of consciousness that experienced earlier actions and events we remember in the recent and more distant past, and that we expect to experience new events in the future (which can be interrupted by amnesia, extreme dissociate disorder, extended automatism, or "episodic" consciousness).
>
> 1. *Unity of planning agency:* We experience most of our actions as nested in intentional chains moving out from shorter- to longer-term plans and thus as under a conscious control steered by teleological connections between past commitments and expectations about future options (a necessary condition for ordinary moral responsibility that can be interrupted by long-term recall impairment, traumatic stress disorders, psychoses that alter understanding of our history, etc.).
>
> 2. *Continuity of cares* through willed devotion to ends, persons, or ideals. Threshold levels of unity-0 and unity-1 enable planning agents to make the volitional and cognitive efforts needed to achieve further integration of ends and activities associated with *personal autonomy*; commitments involving higher-order volitions actively sustain the agent's projects and relationships over time.
>
> 3. *Wholeheartedness:* (a) The agent is fully dedicated to the goals of each of her cares and (b) has no conflicting higher-order volitions; (c) the strong evaluations that ground her different cares are not in any essential conflict, and (d) she makes a reasonable effort to balance their pursuit and reduce pragmatic conflict between them within a single life, while (e) remaining open to learning new values and accepting criticism of her existing cares.

This conception of wholeheartedness is a significant refinement of Frankfurt's weaker notion,[10] since it holds that caring depends on what agents take to be objective values, and hence that unity of purpose requires coherence among these values. It also distinguishes positive and negative conditions of wholeheartedness and holds that caring implicitly commits the agent to caring about the adequacy of her grounds for caring (which avoids the problem of fanaticism).

Even short of wholeheartedness, caring involves a type of volitional unity going well beyond both unity of apperception (unity-0) and the extended temporal awareness required for any robust kind of long-term intentional action (unity-1), which agents may enjoy when simply acting on their strongest desires. As Lippitt recognizes, this kind of psychic unity is common to several of Kierkegaard's aesthetes and to agents who enter "the ethical" stage by forming higher-order volitions concerning their own character, or moving away from wantonness toward personal autonomy. Still, agents with "ethical" life-views in Kierkegaard's sense take responsibility for their own character through caring in ways that most aesthetic agents do not, i.e., through commitments to goods taken to be worth caring about—commitments that are maintained by cultivating the requisite motives and attitudes—which constitute an enduring volitional identity. Thus autonomy conceived in terms of self-perpetuating cares implies another level of narrative unity (unity-2): the person who forms lasting cares (the strongest variety of which are "ground projects" for which she would die)[11] brings under common themes the meaning that many aspects of her life have for her. Thus she has a type of narrative unity that is lacking in wantons and in the simpler sorts of aesthetes, such as a rich Don Juan who pursues one-night stands without reflection on his character, or an artist who enjoys her natural talent for piano and lives off this skill without caring about it in the volitional sense.

The level of narrative connection involved in long-term devotion to personal projects and relationships opens up the possibility of at least two new kinds of tension. Caring agents face *instrumental* conflicts between cares that cannot be pursued simultaneously, or that compete for scarce resources (either external or psychological), given their concrete circumstances or the situation of human life in general. A person's cares may also conflict *essentially* if they are based on inconsistent strong evaluations (in Charles Taylor's sense)[12] of goals and pursuits. By expressing opposed values, each care directly undermines the other; even given ideal external circumstances for pursuing both, the internal conflict saps our motivation for either of them. A person in this state is more autonomous than a wanton in acting on either of her cares, but she is not *fully* autonomous because of what Frankfurt calls the "ambiguity" in her will.

Likewise, in his accounts of "spirit" and "sin," Kierkegaard recognizes that someone can make real commitments or will in the way that tends to illuminate the relevance of ethical ideals for character yet remain volitionally divided. I have argued that we find such "halfheartedness" in "heroic aesthetes" who are outwardly devoted to some great work or excellence in a practice; in agents who only partially repent of some error; in agents who will to remain alienated from some of their operative motives or to continue with essentially inconsistent cares; and in those who "demonically" oppose the good.[13] All these types have volitionally developed forms of narrative continuity that are lacking in simple aesthetes. For example, Haufniensis writes that the demonic agent appears to have "an extraordinary continuity" when compared to the "vapid, enervating dissolution" of the lowest aesthete who is "continually absorbed in the impression" (CA, 129–30/SKS 4, 431). Yet their continuity is still subject to sudden reversals, because they lack the coherence among their cares necessary for wholeheartedness.

Wholehearted caring is thus another distinct level of self-integration (unity-3). For Frankfurt, it consists in agreement among the higher-order volitions involved in our cares; for Kierkegaard, who (*pace* Frankfurt) sees caring as depending on strong evaluation, this also requires valuations of activities, goals, persons, relationships, and ideals worth caring about. Negatively, a wholehearted care must not be in essential conflict with any other care; positively, it requires full devotion of one's volitional energies to the care, consistent with our practical identity as a whole. Yet wholeheartedness does not require that all our cares serve a grand single purpose; it can be realized in harmony between the main themes of our life established by our existentially central cares. This point is aptly made in Rudd's responses to Lippitt: "[Unity] is characteristically achieved in and through all the particular projects I pursue, not as one more particular project on the same level as them."[14] Whether we conceive our *telos* as a flourishing life or as a meaningful life, wholeheartedness is a higher-order end regulating other projects and commitments, not to be confused with the goals constitutive of practices or other finite goods at which first-order cares appropriately aim.

Three Kierkegaardian theses. With all these distinctions in place, Kierkegaard's contribution can be summarized in three theses that extend narrative realism beyond the basic theses (A)–(E). The first concerns some of the executive conditions of autonomy (as contrasted with what we may call cognitive source conditions involving adequate education and ability to reflect on the origins of one's values, which are also important):

> (F) *The existential coherence thesis:* Autonomy, understood as the ability to govern one's core priorities and overall direction of one's life (the control-condition of responsibility for one's identity), requires both that we freely form identity-constituting cares and commitments and that we have the

capacity to make them into a *coherent narrative whole* in which integrity and wholeheartedness are possible.

Of course, as it stands, this claim faces Lippitt's objection that a focus on unity may prevent us from appreciating the importance of novelty and a sufficient diversity of ends that can be valued in a rich life.[15] It also faces more radical objections that agent-autonomy can be episodic, requiring no long-term commitments or cares in Frankfurt's sense. It is vital in considering such objections to remember that thesis (F) does not claim that *all* the conditions of personal autonomy can be derived from, or encapsulated in, the idea of narrative unity among ends, life-goals, and ground projects—narrative integration may only be part of the explanation, though it cannot be a trivial addition if the narrativist approach is on the right track. The same applies to the most distinctively Kierkegaardian thesis in this debate:

(G) *The ethical thesis:* Personal autonomy and the kind of narrative unity it involves cannot be developed without taking seriously (as personally relevant to one's life) ethical ideals and moral obligations with objective status—some sense of "the good" and "duty" that governs other values and personal affinities reflected in one's cares, and that is not simply a function of what satisfies the agent's contingent desires and preferences.

This thesis can be strengthened by requiring that the requisite conception of ethical norms be a perfectionist one,[16] or even an agapic one. Thus the strength of (G), and of the robust narrative unity-2 involved in bringing our other cares and life-projects under ethical ideals, varies according to more specific conceptions of "the ethical" (and G as a meta-ethical thesis is neutral between these).

Of course, these theses are controversial and face several objections. For example, against (G): (i) Non-moral cares, commitments, or projects are said to be sufficient for an autonomous life;[17] (ii) "the aesthete's life has all the 'meaning' that he needs," as Lippitt puts it[18]—an aesthetic life can be sufficiently rich in personal meaning without giving priority or central place to ethical norms that regulate our personal projects and relationships. Kierkegaardian responses will focus on illuminating the ways in which nonmoral cares are subject to types of practical conflict that can only be resolved by devotion to ethical ideals that trump or outweigh the values grounding nonmoral cares.[19] However, Lippitt doubts that ethical agency requires considering the unity of one's life as a whole. He notes (correctly) that it is unusual for us to consider directly the meaningfulness of our "whole life":

> But even in such moments—which are relatively rare—intelligibility is not the issue. When my wife has left me, my teenage daughter has told me she'll never speak to me again, and I have lost my job, all in the same week, I might well face despair in a more everyday sense than Kierkegaard's. But even in such circumstances, I would be able to offer a perfectly intelligible narrative about why I married this woman; why I intervened to try and discourage my daughter from dating that Neanderthal suspected drug-pusher; why I took that job despite my knowledge of its insecurity. Intelligibility is not the problem. . . . [So] the concept of intelligibility will certainly not enable us to distinguish aesthetes from ethicists.[20]

Here the value of our level-distinctions becomes apparent. Lippitt is right that intelligibility of *a familiar, basic kind* is not the issue in this poignant case; unity-1 need not be lost in such a series of unfortunate events. The problem is unity-3. Lippitt's protagonist needs a richer sort of intelligibility than would suffice for planning agency alone. Suppose he can articulate (to some extent) why he loves his wife and daughter and why he had to oppose some of their decisions for their own good. He then has to ask whether his reasons fit together as practical considerations, what is the best way to remain loyal to what was right in these cares, and how to respond to whatever new values have been disclosed—in other words, how to go on in a way that intelligibly extends the cares that have defined him. In support of (G) note that Lippitt's protagonist clearly sees his predicament in *ethical terms.*

By contrast, aesthetes or care-evasive sophisticates would not even muster unity-2. They would drop their old ties without regret, or make light of the situation, or regard the significant others in the story as fungible and seek quick replacements, or even perversely romanticize the rejections. We see such cavalier reactions as suspect because they lack ethical depth; if the protagonist had any ongoing commitment to these relationships, he would be profoundly affected by the losses. This example illustrates the third Kierkegaardian addition to basic narrative realism:

> (H) *The regulative thesis* about unity-3: Wholeheartedness is a higher-order end regulating other projects and commitments, not to be confused with the goals constitutive of practices or other finite goods at which first-order cares appropriately aim.

This position is defended by Rudd[21] and also explored in Kierkegaard's famous discussion of "Purity of Heart," which adds the even more demanding claim that wholeheartedness ultimately requires infinite resignation in devotion to a perfectionist standard, which demands that everything be done for the sake of the good (UDVS, 78/SKS 8, 184).

The aesthetic and ethical stages restated. For Kierkegaard, then, the synchronic unity among our cares involved in wholeheartedness requires an ethical frame to guide their diachronic development; cares need to be governed by a coherent view of the values that serve as grounds for actual and possible cares, which in turn helps our higher-order volitions become wholehearted. But to $care_2$ about such an encompassing evaluative view that makes wholehearted $caring_1$ possible is tantamount to $caring_2$ about "the ethical"; evaluative coherence cannot be reached without norms that trump other values, or that *obligate* in the moral sense.[22] Then the recognition of ethical norms will be tied logically and dynamically to caring wholeheartedly about other (nonmoral) ends. Agents who begin to form autonomous cares find that attentiveness to the values grounding these cares makes salient broader ethical considerations for ordering cares together. Thus Judge William's belief that a person who commits with pathos will discover his error if his choice is ethically mistaken (EO, 2:167/SKS 3, 164) may not be an irenic fantasy. Values worth caring about are fully intelligible only in terms of a larger ethical framework, which is why an agent who cares but who denies the application of ethical obligations to her practical identity is missing latent implications of her own commitments.[23]

But how do these distinctions map onto Kierkegaard's many remarks (pseudonymous and signed) about the "aesthetic" and the "ethical"? Lippitt has argued that we cannot explain the superiority of the ethical in terms of narrative "unity or coherence *per se*." He points out that Judge William acknowledges that aesthetes who pursue "wealth, glory, nobility" and the development of a special talent do find a certain coherence in their temporal goal (EO, 2:183/SKS 3, 177).[24] He also notes that the young man "A" is more sophisticated, and we might add that A has a more abstract aesthetic project—namely, to avoid boredom by seeking aesthetic values (difference, oddity, comic aspects, thrill, etc.) in everything.[25]

Here again, space only allows a brief summary of my response. I agree with Lippitt that Kierkegaard does not mean to explain the superiority of the ethical simply in terms of "narrative unity or coherence." Rather, we have a spectrum of aesthetic types who can be partly specified in terms of the different levels of continuity. An *unawakened aesthete* is a wanton acting on strongest immediate desires with no sense of the need for autonomy or responsibility for self; at the extreme, this is a kind of dreaming without spiritual self-awareness, living entirely in the immediate flow of prereflective experience prior to any anxiety about freedom. At the point of awakening, though, we find *simple egoists* who pursue immediate pleasures, entertainment, and gain while tacitly avoiding anything that stirs awareness of the need to care about final ends based on more enduring values. This includes aesthetes who, as planning agents, pursue success via talent without caring about any "practice" that values excellence in the use of this talent for social goods. These kinds of aesthetes lack unity-2.

But most of Kierkegaard's aesthetes are not mere Frankfurtian "wantons"; the young man *A* is awakened to the existential need for a deeper identity but subsists in a shadowy, negative higher-order volition not to form any concrete cares concerning any role, end, or task in the finite world.[26] *A*'s project is not an earnest artistic endeavor; it is a "holding pattern" to avoid landing anywhere in life, to avoid the primordial choice to give ethical ideals purchase on his identity. Johannes the Seducer is even more advanced in self-deception than *A*. His abstract project of cultivating "the interesting in all things"[27]—which means focusing on their oddity, originality, difference from the norm, comic aspects, dramatic tension etc., rather than caring about any potential contribution to individual or social well-being—focuses him away from the values that are the natural objects of emotions, making his emotions into mere means for his self-fancy and sentimental indulgence.[28] Both *A* and the Seducer exhibit a semblance of unity-2, but they are not really devoted to any values outside themselves as worthy of care.

There are also what I call *heroic* aesthetes who do care about ends for the sake of some kind of greatness, e.g., an agent who dedicates herself earnestly to development of a talent for the sake of excellence in an art or science. If theses G and H are correct, then such an agent cannot be entirely wholehearted. If a conflict between his cares emerges, he lacks an ethical framework through which he can develop his present cares or articulate new cares that remain faithful to what was right in the old cares, loyal to the same ultimate values. Such an aesthete can thus manifest unity-2 for protracted periods in life, but he refuses to recognize the deeper ethical frame of reference within which the particular values he cares about are situated and rooted. Ethical ideals cannot be appropriated as just one more project alongside others; to take them seriously is to recognize the responsibility to give them priority and thus to become wholehearted through willing the good.

Hence the ethical stage is distinguished from *all* subtypes of the aesthetic only by unity-3 in Kierkegaard's analysis. This is the unity illuminated in Kierkegaard's picture of the strongest conceivable form of ethical selfhood in his discourse on "Purity of Heart." Its overall point is to ask us the existential question about our lives as a whole: "*What kind of life is yours; do you will one thing, and what is this one thing?*" (UDVS, 126/SKS 8, 226). But Kierkegaard is clear that this question about unity-3 can be fully intelligible to us only if we already have ethically informed commitments, or have "chosen the ethical" in the Judge's sense:

> Before being able to answer this earnest question earnestly, a person must already have chosen in life, chosen the invisible, the internal; he must live in such a way that he has hours and periods in which he collects his mind so that his life can attain the transparency that is a condition for being able to submit the question to himself and to answer it (UDVS, 126–27/SKS 8, 227).[29]

Thus although we rarely ask this question about our "whole life," concern about the ethical status of our other cares and personal projects should push us toward this question. Kierkegaard thinks it can only be answered through wholehearted devotion to "the good," including a willingness to suffer long and even die for it (UDVS, 78–82/SKS 8, 184–88). This devotion is a temporally extended process that persists through lived time up to death.[30] This involves a kind of infinite resignation; it is our effort that matters, since success in the outcome is never assured by our trying (UDVS, 88–90/SKS 8, 191–95). And the ever-growing robust meaning that a wholehearted life has to its agent must end in her death, when only the good she willed remains (UDVS, 27/SKS 8, 141). So we have to consider that the subjective meaning of our life will acquire *ultimate* meaning—an objective significance that no longer changes, that is eternal; in that sense, one who is dead always "remains true to himself . . . onc and the same" (UDVS, 55/SKS 8, 165). This is why "a sense of shame before one who is dead" is edifying (UDVS, 54/SKS 8, 164), for it is equivalent to the "voice of conscience" that is the judgment of our life (as lived so far) in eternal perspective (UDVS, 127–28/SKS 8, 228–29).

The link to Kierkegaard's discourse "At a Graveside" is clear here: For "the certainty of death" is the *universal obstacle* to the complete realization of our intentions in time (TDIO, 95/SKS 5, 463), even when our powers are otherwise sufficient (which is rare enough). True wholehearted willing must be able to persevere in light of this recognition. This conception of wholeheartedness depends on the idea that at death, our practical identity *is* eternally what it has become, our freedom to change ends and our character is *forever fixed.* There are weak and strong versions of this idea—while the former require no specific faith in life after death, the latter are explicitly eschatological. For example, Kierkegaard suggests that the "change of eternity" following death seals our will into its final form; if we pursued something other than the highest good as our ultimate concern, then our spirit is forever divided against itself (UDVS, 29/SKS 8, 142). On the other hand, the person who is unified by a wish that "pertains essentially to [his] whole life" and who suffers for the good in "faith and hope" finds a new hope and a love that never dies on "the other side of death" (UDVS, 99–101/SKS 8, 203–5).

Thus the volitional conditions of narrative unity-3 including infinite resignation finally bring us to the special problem that death appears to pose for narrative unity in one's identity. Does this mean that the will cannot in fact be "whole," that the very conditions of wholeheartedness finally prevent the unity built up by ethical willing from being tied together in narrative completion? It might seem that the analysis up to this point even strengthens the mortality-objection to narrativist accounts of practical identity. Yet as we will see, Kierkegaard again has an answer.

Narrative Unity-3, Mortality, and Kierkegaardian Eschatological Faith

Three versions of the problem. Although it is frequently alleged that death somehow makes narrative unity of a "whole" life impossible, it is not easy to pin down precisely what the problem is. On some construals, it seems to be the impossibility of the actual end of my story being meaningful to me. In response to MacIntyre, for example, Lippitt says, "If my death is necessarily not an event in my life, I cannot grasp it as an episode in the story of my life."[31] Kierkegaard agrees: "in death's decision, all is over and . . . the transformation cannot fall in line with other events as a new event" in the agent's life (TDIO, 99/SKS 5, 467). From an immanent perspective in any case, my being-dead is not a *living event* in my narravive; once this event is actual, I'm not there to experience it.

But when put this way, the problem also seems to have a good answer developed both by Kierkegaard and Heidegger: I certainly can grasp the fact that I will die in anticipatory understanding, and thus experience my mortality (the certainty of my temporal finitude) as part of the overall meaning of my life before my death has happened. Since I may not correctly predict the circumstances and time of my death, when it comes, it will probably leave some of my projects unfinished; moreover the manner in which I face it in my last few moments or hours could also undermine the main themes and commitments of my life. But that is precisely what "anticipatory resoluteness" toward death is supposed to prevent. In infinite resignation, the meaning of my cares to me cannot depend on their completeability in time, and I will try to die with courage, even sacrificing my life for my ground projects if necessary (though of course most people do not get such a chance). Earnestness chooses "work that does not depend on whether one is granted a lifetime to complete it well or only a brief time to have begun it well" (TDIO, 96/SKS 5, 464; compare UDVS, 141/SKS 8, 239).

Still, this may be an uncharitable construal of the objection. It may say instead that, without special religious beliefs, we must assume that we cannot experience the state of *our being* dead; thus we cannot see what our finished life-story actually is. Until then, it seems that things could always unfold more than one way for us, so the future is "always a threat to whatever 'unity' I may have achieved."[32] On this view, even if my narravive is strengthened by anticipation of a death that is certain to come eventually and may come at any moment, I still experience my narravive as fragmentary and open to a final twist that reverses or negates much of what mattered to me. Thus Sartre argues that sudden death is often "absurd" while few people's ending is like the beautiful chord that culminates a long melody.[33] This indeterminacy, like freedom according to Sartre, is a source of angst. The risky openness ceases only when I have permanently ceased to experience anything, when it is too late to experience full closure (at least in this life). In short, I lack the kind of control that would be necessary for my death to be integrated into an autonomous life-meaning.

To this version of the objection, there are at least two important responses. First, as often as existential writers have made this claim, I think it is an exaggeration. People often *do* know, or have a pretty good idea, that they will probably die soon (even within some specified time period). Although absolute certainty is impossible, since wild contingencies could always postpone or hasten their demise, they have some time to prepare and decide how to act—a few months, a day, minutes, or maybe just a few precious seconds in which to make final decisions. It is highly plausible that such "final moments" are often filled with tremendous significance for the agent living them out, as many literary and film depictions have shown to great effect. Even if we can do little but suffer with courage, or make a last remark, it can bring closure. Consider in this light the great significance people often place on "last words," such as Jesus's last words on the cross, "it is finished." There seems to be a clear sense of completion, even peace, in its simplicity. Contrast Kurtz's haunting last utterance, "the horror, the horror."[34] In this, we hear a sense of failure so absolute that it assumes eschatological proportions; it is a breath of damnation.

This is a subject deserving more phenomenological study. We have often heard that in the seconds before death, the person experiences something like a terrifying or awe-inspiring rerun of their life. Sometimes people also manage in their last few minutes to act in ways that express their practical identity: Consider the Holocaust victim who became a professor at Virginia Tech, who barred the door with his body against the shooter to give his students time to escape out the window. Of course, many people die without warning. Probably Abraham Lincoln experienced nothing at Ford's Theater other than the players on stage, a loud noise, and sudden loss of consciousness. And yet, in another sense, he was *not* entirely "unprepared." He did not expect or imagine this specific death, but for years he had known and accepted that assassination was a real danger. On leaving Springfield, at the train station, he told his friends and neighbors that he feared he might never return there. Thus, although he had no chance to finish the business of Reconstruction, he may have experienced his life as unified by the purposes for which he was willing to die. This experience, gained through much effort and reflection, could have been present to him at the prereflective level even as Booth raised his gun. We do not need time to "put our affairs in order" for our will to be "in order," ready for death. Nor do we need to make a "momentous ending" (TDIO, 72/SKS 5, 443), as Kierkegaard says.

Thus if the objection is that the time or manner of my death might undo the meaning that my life has for me in its final moments, the response is that freedom only needs to make deep narrative unity possible, not to ensure it. It is up to us to choose so that either (i) our final moments faithfully express our identity rather than undoing us, or (ii) our sense of embracing meaning continues right up to our sudden end, if it happens that way. Thus Kierkegaard thinks that witnessing a "sudden death" can help us realize that "as soon as one is dead it is too late to become earnest" (TDIO, 74/SKS 5, 445). Thus the absurd loss of meaning that Sartre finds in sudden death is only on the surface, or from the external biographical point of view; inwardly, for infinite resignation, it is false that "one minute more or less may perhaps change everything."[35] We do not need to wait to see what our freedom will do, as if we are doomed to be passive spectators of a final choice that affects the meaning of all our past choices; we can become resolute now.[36]

However, there is a third way to construe the objection: Our narravive can never achieve *complete closure* because, as beings of finite powers and limited time but indefinitely extending interests and aspirations, there is always more we would do or say if death could be postponed even for a day, an hour, a minute. In that sense, the loose ends of our story can never all be tied up in time; our narravive *must* be fragmentary at its end, leaving threads that we either experience as incomplete or would so experience if we knew our death was imminent. To a biographer, these storylines will appear merely cut off in midstream. So, Sartre says, the value of our efforts becomes indeterminate;[37] even if we have been wholehearted and feel a blessed contentment on our deathbed, inevitably some things will still feel unfinished if our memory is still working.

Kierkegaard's answer. Of the three construals, this last one is as irresistible as the fact that no one who enters the ethical can finish life without any regrets, with nothing he would change. But this does not mean that our death cannot be part of our living narravive. It is precisely because they are two sides of the same "existential incompleteness" that Kierkegaard pairs regret with guilt as "two guides" that "call" to a person to change while she still can. Thus guilt can be sharp when we feel that death is near:

> [W]hether you are guilty of much or have left much undone, the guilt makes this an eleventh-hour call; the concern of inwardness, which regret sharpens, grasps that this is at the eleventh hour. In the temporal sense, old age is the eleventh hour, and the moment of death the last moment of the eleventh hour. . . . but repentance and regret belong to the eternal in a human being, and thus every time repentance comprehends the guilt it comprehends that it is in the eleventh hour (UDVS, 14–15/SKS 8, 129–30).

In this key passage, we see the core of Kierkegaard's answer: The incompleteness recognized in the objection can *itself* be made the basis for earnest reflection on the whole direction of our life. Without a contingent life-crisis or looming threat (such as a terminal diagnosis), we can always see ourselves as running out of time. Notice Kierkegaard's wording: for a brief span of time, it is *as if* the midnight hour has already struck, as if we are already dead and our story finished, absolutely unchangeable. Thus we do experience "being dead" *metaphorically* as being out of time, much as we anticipate the heart-stopping "pencils down!" command at the end of a vital test. Of course, to feel this, we have to realize that we are taking a test and care about it—just as consciousness that our life will have an eternal meaning is the condition for asking the existential question earnestly, making it "the fundamental condition for willing one thing in truth" (UDVS, 127/SKS 8, 227).

Thus Stokes is right that such an edifying "copresence with death" in imagination requires an infinite interest in the moral quality of my life.[38] In thinking of death as "your lot" in this way, "you are then doing what death is indeed unable to do—namely, that you are and death also is" (TDIO, 75/SKS 5, 446). This enigmatic phrase means that, in the earnest thought of our own death, we actually extend our narravive to *include* our death as a possibility imaginatively actualized; in the mirror of eternity, we see ourselves as though we have lost the freedom to change yet *continue* to experience meaning.[39] As a result, we briefly exist in a kind of living death; we experience what it would "be like" to be dead, or to be unable to alter our narravive, and as if we were able to experience its final meaning.[40] We think ourselves into the state in which "all is over" for us (TDIO, 79/SKS 5, 449). This paradox is the limit of the narrative unity that mortal persons can achieve by their own efforts; we feel the *narravive* significance of "being out of time" not just for one important task, but for *all* our purposes and cares. Kierkegaard calls this the "decisiveness" of death. Nothing more can be added; "the meaning" of our life "is at an end" (TDIO, 78/SKS 5, 450).[41]

This experience does two things for us. First, it makes us measure the wholeheartedness of our commitments according to whether they are still worthwhile to us when seen in this light, as stopped by the final bell. We see whether in living death, we would still affirm our cares and the ways we pursued them. If we cannot, then we are not wholehearted about those purposes to the point of infinite resignation; when our narravive is stretched forward to overlap our death, some cares appear less worthwhile. We are "halted . . . in order to renounce vain pursuits" (TDIO, 77/SKS 5, 448).[42] Second, since we can never affirm everything about our practical identity, we feel a measureless longing for more time to correct it. That is, we feel the infinite loss of being out of time with something vital as yet undone. A child who thinks of the right answer the second after the test is whisked away can barely imagine the regret we feel in this paradoxical state.

But after earnestly imagining ourselves at the midnight hour, when we regret infinitely that we are out of time, we realize that in fact we are "still living," that we are *not* actually out of time yet, though we could be soon. So it is only the eleventh hour after all, and we can still change our answer to the existential question, and thus the final meaning of our life! This experience combines both ethical urgency and the joy of unexpected reprieve, as if the test proctor had said, "Actually, I see that you have a few more minutes." Then

> the thought of death gives the earnest person the right momentum in life and the right goal . . . Then earnestness grasps the present this very day, disdains no task as too insignificant, rejects no time as too short, works with all its might even though it is willing to smile at itself if this effort is said to be merit before God (TDIO, 83/SKS 5, 453).

In other words, authenticity in the face of death strengthens the will to sustain infinite resignation in willing the good in everything we pursue; it seals unity-3 in a "love . . . strong as death,"[43] but without hubris.

Because this limit of authentic willing is reached through imaginative inclusion of our own death in our narravive, it is a paradoxical act ripe for representation in literary form, as many stories of ghosts, or recently deceased spirits, or near-death experiences suggest. None of these narratives can quite capture the paradoxical synthesis required, because to some extent they must portray the agent either as second person looking at her or his life from the outside, or as continuing to act and change in death. But the double movement—into being-out-of-time, followed by the shift back to living freedom, in which our remaining time and open future appear in a radically new light—is perhaps best portrayed in Charles Dickens's *A Christmas Carol.* In the company of the terrible "Ghost of Christmas Future," Scrooge first sees servants happy to sell their dead master's trifles, and a debtor relieved that his creditor is deceased.[44] He enters the house of his own assistant Bob Cratchit and sees the family grieve over the recent death of their son, Tiny Tim. Finally, the Ghost brings Scrooge to an unkempt graveyard, where he sees his own name on his grave and realizes that it was *his* life that no one missed.[45] In this awful revelation, he fears infinitely that he is out of time, that his story cannot be changed. But he begs for consolation, for one more chance.

Note that there is no explicit fear of divine punishment here, nor any descent into hell (as in the famous 1964 Technicolor musical film version). What appalls Scrooge is the final meaning of this narravive, the story of a man who did no good for anyone. What he cannot bear, what he rejects now with all his heart, is the life of a man who let Tiny Tim die. This turning lies within the ethical; it does not require faith in an afterlife. As if echoing Dickens, Kierkegaard cites a literary example of a youth who dreamed he was an old man looking "back over a wasted life, until he woke in anxiety New Year's morning not only to a new year but to a new life" (TDIO, 76/SKS 5, 446–47). A life whose final meaning is entirely negative is itself sufficiently damning to have an apotropaic influence on the will that takes it to heart, as Scrooge does. What he fears most is that he is "past hope" for *this* life, for his time on Earth to mean something better.[46]

So on awakening and finding himself still alive on Christmas morning, Scrooge has the kind of experience that Tolkien calls a "eucatastrophe," namely the joy of a reprieve beyond all rational hope that is felt as grace.[47] There is a strong analogy to faith here, for in his last moments with the final Ghost, Scrooge clings to one sign that what he has seen are "shadows of things that may be only," that his fate is not totally sealed.[48] Hence his infinite joy on Christmas morning that "[t]he Time before him was his own, to make amends" parallels the joy of faith justified by miracle, eschatological trust vindicated by the "absurd."[49] And indeed Scrooge's delight in every small detail shows the dramatic paradigm shift in the meaning of temporality for him:

> He went to church, and walked about the streets, and watched the people hurrying to and fro, and patted children on the head, and questioned beggars, and looked down into the kitchens of houses and up to the windows, and found that everything could yield him pleasure. He had never dreamed that any walk—that anything—could give him so much happiness.[50]

This sounds remarkably like de silentio's "knight of faith" who finds all temporality fresh and new, who sees the miracle in every moment. But something close to this can still be felt by the person who has only achieved infinite resignation, for, "supported by the earnest thought of death, the earnest person says 'All is not over'" (TDIO, 85/SKS 5, 454). She recognizes then that "time also is a good" (TDIO, 83/SKS 5, 453). The indeterminate time remaining to her now appears as precious beyond measure, a chance to make a narravive worth having lived out to the last. The open possibility of the future is now appreciated with new inwardness: Scrooge says, "I am here—the shadows of the things that would have been, may be dispelled."[51] The remainder of his narravive becomes a wholehearted will to the good in truth. As Dickens explicitly recognizes, this is an achievement of *narrative unity.* Both as he is leaving the final Ghost, and again on awakening, Scrooge vows, "I will live in the Past, the Present, and the Future. The Spirits of all three shall strive within me."[52]

At this limit, unity-3 does become more complex. In answering the existential question about what his entire narravive will mean, the person attains what Kierkegaard calls a "wish that pertains essentially to the whole of life" (UDVS, 100/SKS 8, 204). As we see with Scrooge, this unifying wish may not be clearly formed until later in life, but it reaches backwards to transform the meaning of everything that has transpired up to that point; past errors become reasons to make restitution. Yet toward the future, it works to cultivate continuity of purpose that can last and reconciles with the possibility that the work may be ended by death at any moment: "Earnestness, therefore, becomes the living of each day as if it were the last and also the first in a long life" (TDIO, 96/SKS 5, 464). The second half of this formula expresses the agent's ethical determination; the first half expresses her infinite resignation. This is the ideal result of integrating the fact of mortality into wholehearted willing.

Conclusion: from unity-3 to faith. Admittedly, a paradox remains in this solution: Authenticity in relation to our mortality completes our narrative unity precisely by making us recognize the incompleteness of our narravive and prompting us to fix whatever is out of tune, to achieve harmony while time remains, while recognizing that we will not completely succeed. Since we can never attain that perfect harmony, it always impels us forward—until it really is too late. In that sense, I grant to the skeptics about narrative identity that there is a kind of narrative unity—call it unity-4—that we never do attain in this life. We are disunified and fragmentary in relation to this ideal, though the thought of death can have power in moving us closer to unity-4.

This concession amounts to saying that there is one problem of death that narrative theories require faith to answer: there is a point beyond which an immanent conception of narrative unity cannot go. Consider a closely related problem: at death, a narravive apparently goes out of existence; only narratives about it remain.[53] In this, there seems to be an infinite loss; this whole web of experiences, acts, and feelings, with all their meaning to the agent, should not vanish "like tears in the rain," as Roy says just before his death in the film *Blade Runner.* When this is felt to be a problem, we have crossed from purely ethical into religious categories. The issue becomes the preservation of narravive meanings in some kind of hereafter, so that all one's ethical strivings (and even one's failings) are not "for nothing" in the ultimate scheme of things. This is more than ethical ideals in themselves demand; here the motive of narrative unity actually transcends the ethical in asking for an ultimate meaning to our efforts and sufferings.

If narravive meaning is to be preserved *eternally yet as* narravive, then the agent's "life" in some sense must continue eternally. But if it continues, cannot its earthly work be completed then? Cannot our unfinished work be shown to us finally in its finished form? Can we not live the full meaning of this completion, experience the infinite plenitude of its significance? As if an artist saw her unfinished masterpiece now laid out before her, in every detail, better than she could ever have hoped? This is the eschatological narrative unity we sought but could never reach as finite mortal persons. If that is right, then the narrative structure of practical identity is incomplete in the final analysis because it points toward a telos in which we can only have faith.

NOTES

1. See John Lippitt's review of John J. Davenport and Anthony Rudd, eds., *Kierkegaard After MacIntyre,* in *Faith and Philosophy* 22, no. 4 (October 2005): pp. 496–502; Lippitt, "Telling Tales: Johannes Climacus and Narrative Unity," in *Kierkegaard Studies Yearbook 2005,* ed. Niels Jørgen Cappelørn and Herman Deuser, pp. 71–89 (Berlin: de Gruyter, 2005); and Lippitt, "Getting the Story Straight: Kierkegaard, MacIntyre, and Some Problems with Narrative Unity," *Inquiry* 50, no. 1 (February 2007): pp. 34–69.

2. See Alasdair MacIntyre, *After Virtue,* 2nd ed. (Notre Dame, Ind.: University of Notre Dame Press, 1984), ch. 15.

3. Kathy Behrendt, "Reasons to be Fearful: Strawson, Death, and Narrative," in *Narrative Understanding and Persons,* ed. Daniel D. Hutto, pp. 133–54 (Cambridge: Cambridge University Press, 2007).

4. Patrick Stokes, "The Power of Death: Retroactivity, Narrative, and Interest," in *International Kierkegaard Commentary: Prefaces/Writing Sampler and Three Discourses on Imagined Occasions,* ed. Robert L. Perkins, pp. 387–417 (Macon, Ga.: Mercer University Press, 2006).

5. Stokes, "The Power of Death," p. 396, referring to George Pitcher, "The Misfortunes of the Dead," in *The Metaphysics of Death,* ed. John M. Fischer, pp. 159–68 (Stanford, Calif.: Stanford University Press, 1993).

6. Stokes, "The Power of Death," p. 403.

7. Stokes, "The Power of Death," pp. 405–6. Yet Stokes recognizes that for Kierkegaard, in the right practical attitude of interested imagination of my possible future death, I can attain a certain "copresence" with my death or even identity with my "posthumous self" (pp. 414–15).

8. Anthony Rudd, "Kierkegaard, MacIntyre, and Narrative Unity—Reply to Lippitt," *Inquiry* 50, no. 5 (October 2007): pp. 541–49; and Rudd, "In Defense of Narrative," *European Journal of Philosophy* 17, no. 1 (March 2009): pp. 60–75. Also see Rudd's forthcoming book on self and identity. My full response to Lippitt is contained in an essay titled "Narrative Identity and Autonomy: A Kierkegaardian Approach" (unpublished manuscript).

9. Anthony Rudd, "Reason in Ethics Revisited: *Either/Or,* 'Criterionless Choice,' and Narrative Unity," in *Kierkegaard Studies Yearbook 2008,* ed. Niels

Jørgen Cappelørn, Hermann Deuser, and K. Brian Söderquist, pp. 192–93 (Berlin: de Gruyter, 2008).

10. Harry G. Frankfurt, "Identification and Wholeheartedness," in *The Importance of What We Care About* (Cambridge: Cambridge University Press, 1988), p. 166; "wholeheartedness" is closely related to "decisive identification" (pp. 168–69), and to "volitional necessity" in Frankfurt's work.

11. See Bernard Williams, "Persons, Character, and Morality," in *Moral Luck* (Cambridge: Cambridge University Press, 1980), pp. 11–13.

12. See Charles Taylor, *Sources of the Self* (Cambridge, Mass.: Harvard University Press, 1989), p. 4; and Taylor, "What Is Human Agency?" in *Human Agency and Language* (Cambridge: Cambridge University Press, 1985).

13. In John J. Davenport, "Kierkegaard, Anxiety, and the Will," in *Kierkegaard Studies Yearbook 2001,* ed. Niels Jørgen Cappelørn, Hermann Deuser, and Jon Stewart, pp. 158–81 (Berlin: de Gruyter, 2001). The same claim is defended briefly in Davenport, "Towards an Existential Virtue Ethics," in *Kierkegaard After MacIntyre,* ed. John J. Davenport and Anthony Rudd, pp. 265–324 (Chicago: Open Court, 2001).

14. Rudd, "Kierkegaard, MacIntyre, and Narrative Unity," p. 545.

15. Lippitt, "Telling Tales," pp. 75–76.

16. As the pseudonymous author Johannes Climacus suggests in the "Decisive Expression" section of the *Concluding Unscientific Postscript.*

17. See Frankfurt, "The Importance of What We Care About," in *The Importance of What We Care About* (Cambridge: Cambridge University Press, 1988), pp. 80–94. In this essay, Frankfurt claims that one can care earnestly about other things without caring about morality (p. 81). This thesis is retained through his latest writings, e.g., *The Reasons of Love* (Princeton, N.J.: Princeton University Press, 2004), pp. 9, 37.

18. Lippitt, "Review of *Kierkegaard After MacIntyre,*" p. 499; he does not assert this view, but only asks what rules out this possibility.

19. This is the sort of answer I suggested in "Towards an Existential Virtue Ethics," pp. 294–301. Also see John J. Davenport, *Will as Commitment and Resolve* (New York: Fordham University Press, 2007), ch. 14.

20. Lippitt, "Getting the Story Straight," p. 38.

21. Rudd, "In Defense of Narrative," pp. 64–65. Rudd seems to have both the negative and positive aspects of wholeheartedness in mind in this description of the coordination between projects.

22. I use subscript numbers to distinguish "first-order" and "second-order" caring and volition without an awkward sentence structure.

23. This answers Lippitt's question concerning how the Judge's arguments can reach someone who does not yet accept the authority of the ethical; see "Getting the Story Straight," pp. 37–38. The persuasion depends on the type of aesthete. A person who is just careless has to awaken to the existential importance of caring; a person who is avoiding higher-order volitions and strong evaluation has to see the

emptiness of his negative project; a heroic aesthete has to discover the way that her cares depend on a larger ethical framework to be fully meaningful.

24. Lippitt, "Getting the Story Straight," p. 40.

25. As we see in "The Rotation of Crops," in *Either/Or* vol. 1. See my discussion "Kierkegaard and Frankfurt on BS, Wantonness, and Aestheticism," forthcoming in Myron Penner and Søren Landkildehus, eds., *Living Reasonably, Loving Well: Conversing with Frankfurt and Kierkegaard.*

26. See Davenport, "The Meaning of Kierkegaard's Choice between the Aesthetic and the Ethical: A Response to MacIntyre," in *Kierkegaard After MacIntyre*, ed. John J. Davenport and Anthony Rudd, p. 95 (Chicago: Open Court, 2001).

27. See "The Seducer's Diary," in *Either/Or*, vol. 1.

28. See Rick Anthony Furtak, "The Virtues of Authenticity: A Kierkegaardian Essay in Moral Psychology," *International Philosophical Quarterly* 43, no.1 (December 2003): pp. 423–38.

29. Thus the *initial* question of the discourse is whether we will the good, or (in my terms) have started on unity-2 understood as requiring personal appropriation of ethical norms. If so, "then it would be possible that he could will one thing." Then comes the *main* question concerning whether we will the good in truth or will everything for the good, or through its regulation, or within its overriding value (UDVS, 121/SKS 8, 222). This main question involves the narrative question about one's whole life (UDVS, 100/SKS 8, 204).

30. Lippitt suggests that "purity of heart" in Kierkegaard's sense is not a form of narrative unity ("Getting the Story Straight," p. 51). My response to this analyzes "On the Occasion of a Confession" to show that its typology of "doublemindedness" agrees with the distinctions among types of aesthetes in my list (for this argument, see my manuscript, "Narrative Identity and Autonomy").

31. Lippitt, "Getting the Story Straight," p. 45.

32. Lippitt, "Getting the Story Straight," p. 46 (citing Heidegger).

33. Jean-Paul Sartre, *Being and Nothingness*, trans. Hazel E. Barnes (New York: Washington Square, 1966), pp. 685–87.

34. Joseph Conrad, *Heart of Darkness* (London: Penguin Classics, 1973), p. 111.

35. Sartre, *Being and Nothingness*, p. 689.

36. Sartre, *Being and Nothingness*, p. 688.

37. Sartre, *Being and Nothingness*, p. 690.

38. Stokes, "The Power of Death," pp. 414–16.

39. This explains why Heidegger held that in resoluteness toward death, Dasein can become "a whole" or achieve narrative unity; see *Being and Time*, trans. John Macquarrie and Edward Robinson (San Francisco: Harper Collins Publishers, 1962), pp. 343–48 (H297–301). Interestingly, Charles Guignon argues in the following chapter that Heidegger's sense of wholeness cannot be understood in this way.

40. I suggest that what Heidegger means by "death" as the "impossibility of Dasein" is precisely this loss of possibilities, the absolute inability to change, the

fixity of an essence; the loss of "being" in the case of Dasein means the loss of freedom.

41. Kierkegaard also notes that in life, the contemplation of a meaning that seems entirely finished becomes "in turn part of the meaning," showing that it was not finished. This is Mulhall's point cited by Lippitt ("Getting the Story Straight," p. 45). However, it does *not* apply to the finish that death makes (TDIO, 78/SKS 5, 449). By implication, when we earnestly imagine ourselves as dead, we imagine a state in which our *experiencing* being-out-of-time does not add anything to our narravive; we fully coincide with this narravive that we experience as closed. In Sartre's terms, it is as if we experience being a narravive that is now exactly what it is. Sartre says this is impossible, but it is not impossible in the earnest thought of our death, according to Kierkegaard. If this is correct, we have isolated a deep point of disagreement. It helps explain why Sartre cannot accept that death is meaningful to us as a "closing of the account . . . which makes one finally be what one has been—irremediably" (*Being and Nothingness,* p. 689). For Sartre, this can only amount to our becoming a mere thing, an object of biographical debate and the memory of others (p. 692), while for Kierkegaard, it is our freely developed *character* that is "fixed"—an event full of significance.

42. See Sheridan Hough, "'Halting Is Movement:' The Paradoxical Pause of Confession in 'An Occasional Discourse,'" in *International Kierkegaard Commentary: Upbuilding Discourses in Various Spirits,* ed. Robert L. Perkins, pp. 37–51 (Macon, Ga.: Mercer University Press, 2005).

43. Song of Solomon 8:6 (*The New Oxford Annotated Bible,* 3rd ed., edited by Michael D. Coogan [Oxford: Oxford University Press, 2001]).

44. Charles Dickens, *A Christmas Carol,* in Dickens, *Christmas Books,* int. Eleanor Farjeon, in *Oxford Illustrated Dickens* set (Oxford: Oxford University Press, 1987), pp. 59–66.

45. Dickens, *A Christmas Carol,* pp. 67–70.

46. Dickens, *A Christmas Carol,* p. 70.

47. See J. R. R. Tolkien, "On Fairy-Stories," in *Tree and Leaf* (London: Allen and Unwin, 1964), pp. 11–79. Also see Davenport, "Happy Endings and Religious Hope: *The Lord of the Rings* as an Epic Fairy Tale," in *The Lord of the Rings and Philosophy,* ed. Gregory Bassham and Eric Bronson, pp. 204–18 (Chicago: Open Court, 2003).

48. Dickens, *A Christmas Carol,* p. 70.

49. See my trilogy on existential faith: Davenport, "Faith as Eschatological Trust in Kierkegaard's *Fear and Trembling,*" in *Ethics, Love, and Faith in Kierkegaard: A Philosophical Engagement,* ed. Edward F. Mooney, pp. 196–233 (Bloomington: Indiana University Press 2008); Davenport, "Kierkegaard's *Postscript* in Light of *Fear and Trembling,*" *Revista Portuguesa de Filosofia* 64, no. 2–4 (2008): pp. 879–908; and Davenport, "What Kierkegaardian Faith Adds to Alterity Ethics," in *Kierkegaard and Levinas: Ethics, Politics, and Religion,* ed. J. Aaron Simmons and David Wood, pp. 169–95 (Bloomington: Indiana University Press, 2008).

50. Dickens, *A Christmas Carol,* p. 74.

51. Dickens, *A Christmas Carol,* p. 71.

52. Dickens, *A Christmas Carol,* p. 70–71.

53. See Stokes's discussion of this point in relation to *The Death of Ivan Ilyich* in "The Power of Death," p. 412. This is also the problem that Unamuno found so burning and central. It is hard to assess, since many secular thinkers today seem not to find it a problem at all. See Thaddeus Metz, "Recent Work on the Meaning of Life," *Ethics* 112 (July 2002): pp. 781–814.

10.

Heidegger and Kierkegaard on Death: The Existentiell and the Existential

Charles Guignon

The jury is still out on the nature and extent of Kierkegaard's influence on the early Heidegger, including his magnum opus *Being and Time* (1927) as well as his lectures and writings prior to that work. In the "Foreword" to the 1972 edition of his "Early Writings" in German, Heidegger speaks of those "exciting years between 1910 and 1914" when, together with the work of Nietzsche and Dostoevsky, he read translations of the writings of Kierkegaard.[1] However, it is not evident how much of Kierkegaard seeped into Heidegger's thought or precisely which texts influenced his own. Theodore Kisiel suggests that "there is no archival evidence to indicate that Heidegger really studied [central works of Kierkegaard's] before he wrote [*Being and Time*]."[2] We do know that by the 1920s he had developed an aversion to what he called "Kierkegaardism," but it is also clear that his antipathy is directed not so much against Kierkegaard as against "the modishness of 'Kierkegaardism'" then current among students.[3] So there is every reason to suppose that Heidegger greatly admired and learned from Kierkegaard while trying to avoid sinking into "Kierkegaardism."

Heidegger acknowledges the value of Kierkegaard's works for any thought about the religious life and for a deep understanding of human existence (or "*Dasein,*" in Heidegger's technical use of that German word).[4] He especially praises Kierkegaard for his "most prescient insight" into the "instant" or "moment of vision" (*Augenblick* in German; the Danish word, *øjeblik,* has similar roots: "the blink of an eye").[5] He also in various contexts applauds Kierkegaard's notions of the public, averageness, the "today," the individual, moods, anxiety, repetition, and, of course, existence (*Existenz*). It is also certain that Heidegger felt the impact of Kierkegaard's thoughts about death: In a short and undeveloped note in the appendices to his 1923 lectures, *Ontology—Hermeneutics of Facticity,*

Heidegger writes, "Experience of death in any sense, death—life—Dasein (Kierkegaard)."[6] Nevertheless, as John van Buren shows, most of Heidegger's references to Kierkegaard are drawn from Karl Jaspers's groundbreaking analyses of Kierkegaard's thought in his (still untranslated) *Psychology of Worldviews* of 1919.[7]

The few references to Kierkegaard in *Being and Time* are not especially illuminating. As a rule, Heidegger's acknowledgments of the work of his predecessors are seldom representative of the extent of their influence on his thought. But the three references to Kierkegaard in the footnotes of *Being and Time* are particularly unhelpful. He acknowledges a debt to Kierkegaard's *The Concept of Dread* for his discussion of anxiety, but remarks that Kierkegaard's work was motivated solely by a "theological" interest in a "'psychological' exposition of the problem of original sin."[8] Elsewhere he remarks that Kierkegaard "explicitly seized upon the problem of existence as an existentiell problem," though he remained trapped in the ontological assumptions of ancient ontology as handed down through Hegel (*Being and Time* [hereafter BT], 494n). Finally, a note tells us that, even though Kierkegaard saw the moment of vision as an "*existentiell* phenomenon," he failed to interpret it "existentially" (BT, 497n). The implication of these and related notes is that because Kierkegaard remained entangled in the ontic inquiry of theology, he lacked the ability to consider the fundamental questions of ontology, and that, while achieving remarkable insights at the existentiell level, he failed to move to the level of existential and ontological thought Heidegger sought to uncover.

Despite Heidegger's qualified recognition of Kierkegaard in *Being and Time*, it has always seemed to me that Kierkegaard's impact on that work is discernible in a number of passages. For example, it is hard to read such passages as "man's '*substance*' is not spirit as a synthesis of soul and body; it is rather *existence*" (BT, 153), or the "formal" definition of Dasein as a "Being" that "has a relationship towards that Being" (BT, 32), without thinking of the opening words of *The Sickness unto Death:* "Man is spirit. But what is spirit? Spirit is the self. But what is the self? The self is a relation that relates itself to its own self. . . . Man is a synthesis. . . . So regarded, man is not yet a self" (SUD, 13/SKS 11, 129).[9] But regardless of the actual presence of Kierkegaard in Heidegger's text, we should take seriously Heidegger's claims that Kierkegaard's reflections were always limited to the concerns of a "regional ontology," the domain of inquiry called "theology," and that his insights pertained solely to the "existentiell" and never to the "existential." To understand these claims, we should first try to make sense of Heidegger's technical vocabulary of "ontic," "ontological," "existentiell," and "existential." Only when these terms have been clarified can we address our principal concern, the affinities between Kierkegaard's "At a Graveside" and Heidegger's account of death in *Being and Time.*

Heidegger's Ontic/Ontological and Existentiell/Existential Distinctions

At the outset of *Being and Time,* Heidegger introduces a distinction between "ontic" and "ontological" that will be crucial to all that follows in the work.[10] The basic assumption is that reality—the totality of what is—consists of various sorts of entities (*das Seiende,* a singular term perhaps best translated as "what-is"). An entity is anything of which we can say that "it is," including physical objects, numbers, fictional characters, symphonies, relationships, humans, mythical beings, spirits, and even gods (BT, 26; e.g., if we can say such things as "God is an invention of the human mind," we have said "God is").[11] The "what-is"—entities in the broadest sense of the word—are called "ontic," where that term refers to the items (in the broadest sense of that word) that are taken as constituting reality (in the broadest sense of that word). The particular regional or special sciences are concerned with studying the properties and relationships of what-is for some specific domain of entities (e.g., geometry studies space, historiography studies past events, mythology studies mythical beings, and so forth). Seen in this light, the science called "theology"—the science of the nature of God and the human relationship to this being—is one "ontic" science among others.[12]

Heidegger holds that every science has some prior understanding of the "being" (the "*what* it is" and the "*that* it is") of the domain of entities it studies. An interest in the *being* of the entities that make up some domain of what-is arises when an ontic science shifts its focus from ordinary puzzle-solving about entities and their properties to a question about the being of the entities it happens to study (for example, mathematicians can ask "What *are* numbers?" or historians can ask "What *is* the historical past?"). When anyone asks about the *being* of entities, then the questioning has shifted from the ontic to the *ontological.* Ontological questions can be asked concerning any domain of entities. But it is also possible to ask a question about the being of entities in general, and when this happens, it is called "ontology taken in the widest sense" (BT, 31). Moreover, if one asks not just about the being of entities but about the conditions of *intelligibility* of anything "that-is"—in other words, if one asks about the *meaning* of being—then that inquiry is called "fundamental ontology." Another name for fundamental ontology is, in Heidegger's understanding of it, "phenomenology." Phenomenology studies "the Being of entities, its meaning, its modifications and derivatives" (BT, 60); hence, "phenomenology is the science of the Being of entities—ontology" (BT, 61). It follows, then, that to say Kierkegaard is engaged in theology rather than phenomenology is to say that Kierkegaard's thought remains limited to the regional, ontic science called "theology" and never addresses the questions that interest Heidegger, the questions of fundamental ontology.

The distinction between ontic and ontological illuminates the distinction Heidegger makes between the existentiell and the existential. This latter pair of terms simply designates the opposition between ontic and ontological insofar as it is applicable to humans or Dasein. There are two ways of talking about humans, on this view. We can talk about concrete characteristics of people, including ourselves. Concerns with what is of central importance to this or that person, or to groups of people, would be *existentiell* matters—for example, the fact that I identify with being a philosophy teacher or that Gandhi was a charismatic personality. But it is also possible to talk about the essential structures of human existence itself (BT, 38). Such a discussion of the *being of humans* as such would be not *existentiell* but rather "*existential.*" Existential inquiry reveals what Heidegger calls "existentialia" where these are understood to be essential traits of any human whatsoever (BT, 33). So, for example, being in a world is an *existentiale* in this sense, whereas being an American or a Christian are *existentiell* characteristics. Fundamental ontology begins with an attempt to identify the essential structures or existentialia of humans insofar as they have some understanding of being. The question about the *understanding* of being is the starting point because humans are the entities for whom being is intelligible, so that understanding humans is a first step toward addressing the question of the *meaning* of being in general, that is, the question of fundamental ontology. Heidegger notes, however, that because being is always the being of entities, any such inquiry into the being of humans must begin with an examination of particular humans, namely, ourselves as we are engaged in asking the question of being. Hence, "the roots of the existential analytic [the inquiry into the being of Dasein] . . . are ultimately *existentiell,* that is, *ontical*" (BT, 34). Such an ontological inquiry therefore starts from an examination of the "possibility of the Being of each existing Dasein" (BT, 34). For this reason, "the question of Being is nothing other than the radicalization of an essential tendency-of-Being which belongs to Dasein itself," the tendency to care about, and always have some preunderstanding of, what it is to be (BT, 35).

So phenomenology begins with an examination of what it is to be human in one's own case. In order for this investigation to be fundamental and not just a recapitulation of the assumptions drawn from some regional inquiry, it is necessary to bracket or set aside the presuppositions of all regional inquiries (such as anthropology, physiology, epistemology, or theology) and to look at how a typical case of the human "proximally and for the most part" shows up in everyday circumstances. As Heidegger says, we must examine ourselves as we are in *average everydayness,* prior to the imposition of categories and assumptions drawn from the regional sciences (BT, 69). Given this terminology, Heidegger can say that because Kierkegaard is concerned with his own special project of being a Christian, he remains at the level of the *existentiell* and consequently never moves beyond that special mode of being to the position from which he can say something *existential* or *ontological* about the being of the human as such.

Kierkegaard's Aims in "At a Graveside"

Even a superficial reading of Kierkegaard's "At a Graveside" shows that the work is not a straightforward contribution to theology as traditionally understood. The discourse is mostly evocative and hortatory in its envisioning of a way of life, and the few references to God contained in the discourse appear mainly toward the end. Kierkegaard holds that we are fully alive—that we really only *exist* in the fullest sense of that word—if we are "spirited," fully engaged, and passionately concerned about our own lives. In his view, a cool, dispassionate, disengaged theoretical attitude toward matters of importance for life tends to distort our sense of what we are and what is at stake in being alive. Such a cold and bleached-out vision of life conceals more than it reveals. It is in this sense that subjective truth is higher than objective truth. What life is all about is something that comes to light only from the standpoint of committed intensity in relation to ultimate, worthy ends, not from the cool moment of reflection. Just as Heidegger claims that our emotional involvements light up reality for us in some distinctive way, Kierkegaard holds that we gain insight into things that matter to us as existing beings only through our affective involvements in the world.

In "At a Graveside," two different types of affective involvement are distinguished. One sort of emotional response to things is called "mood," where this term seems to refer to vapid attitudes of the sort that typically accompany passing interest, bemused recognition of some fact, bland acceptance, or the sorts of feelings we indulge in when we want to avoid facing something unpleasant. We can get a feel for what Kierkegaard means by "mood" if we think of the moodiness of an adolescent who tries to prove he is "cool" by never letting anything get to him. Moods are extremely weak motivators; they provide us with little inclination to do anything in particular. In their more extreme form, moods might become manifest in such "dark" states of mind as sorrow, fear, or depression.

A second type of affective response Kierkegaard envisions is what he calls "earnestness." Earnestness is a response of intense wakefulness and commitment, a way of being fully present to the gravity and seriousness of what stands before one. In earnestness, a life as a whole is lit up, and what is at issue in living becomes visible. In this affective stance, we clear-sightedly recognize what is at stake in our own lives and we give ourselves over to it. Earnestness "is the inner being and the thinking and the appropriation" that ennobles experience (TDIO, 74/SKS 5, 445). The main discourse of "At a Graveside" is devoted to suggesting that the right sort of confrontation with death can bring a genuine sort of earnestness into a life. Facing death reveals that earnestness is not a matter of what occurs in the public world; it is not a matter, for example, of attending burial services or of passing away in the company of family and friends. Instead, death, when properly thought, can show us that real earnestness lies in the "inner being" of humans and that an authentic relationship to death involves a lucid awareness of one's *own* death, not death in general. The earnest confrontation with death is a solitary experience, unsupported by familiar platitudes or comforting moods.

Kierkegaard explicates this idea of death as "one's own" by contrasting it with the idea of death in Epicurus, who famously remarked that when death is, I am not, and when I am, death is not. Kierkegaard calls this philosophical approach to ameliorating death a "jest" by which one tries to place oneself outside of death by regarding it as a turning point in which all cares and worries disappear. In contrast to this philosophical jest, Kierkegaard imagines a stance toward death in which one thinks of oneself *in* death, and thinks of it not as our shared human condition, but as something that is one's own (TDIO, 73/SKS 5, 444).[13] The difference is between thinking of death as a future event that, so to speak, closes the book on one's life, and thinking of death as the ever-present fact that runs throughout and is definitive of one's life as a finite, mortal being.

We have access to death as death, then, only in earnest engagement in the awareness of death and its consequences. When death is understood as something to be appropriated in the inwardness of life itself, it can never be seen as something "actual," something that actually occurs in the course of one's life. In this sense, of course, the philosophical jest is right: when death actually comes, there is no longer an "I" to have a relationship to death. But this apparent paradox only proves the point that death, properly understood, has to be seen as something that shapes the inner being of a person throughout that person's life. This is what Kierkegaard means when he says, "Earnestness is that you think death, and that you are thinking it as your lot, and that you are then doing what death is indeed unable to do—namely, that you are and death also is" (TDIO, 75/SKS 5, 446). Earnestness in the face of death involves a double movement that is not unlike the double movement involved in faith as described in *Fear and Trembling.*[14] Earnestness is "to be wide awake and to think death, . . . to think that all was over, that everything was lost along with life," but to do so "in order then to win everything in life" (TDIO, 76/SKS 5, 447). What is discovered in the earnest confrontation with death is not the end of one's being, but precisely what one's being *is.* As Kierkegaard suggests in a note composed at the same time as "At a Graveside," the concern with death is a concern with one's own being: "*To concern* **oneself about** *oneself*" (TDIO, 117).

The discourse at the graveside, a product of the earnestness of thinking oneself *in* death, brings to light "death's decision," the fact that death is decisive. Death has the ability to put an end to all my undertakings: with death, everything "is concluded, not a letter is added; the meaning is at an end . . . all is over" (TDIO, 78–79/SKS 5, 449). This is not to say that death is an event in time, for with death there simply is no time. But recognizing the finality of death does not produce in the earnest thinker a mood of depression or discouragement, as if the finality of death were to indicate that something valuable would be lost. On the contrary, Kierkegaard holds that the fact of death retroactively throws us back onto our lives with renewed vitality and intensity: "earnestness and death . . . teach [a person] that he had no time to waste" (TDIO, 78/SKS 5, 448).

Death is both certain and indefinite. The *certainty* of death "gives life force as nothing else does." For an earnest person, death's certainty leads neither to a single-minded *carpe diem* attitude nor to a deflated mood of hopeless fatalism. As Kierkegaard says, "the thought of death gives the earnest person the right momentum in life and the right goal toward which he directs his momentum," and it does so in "the present this very day" (TDIO, 83/SKS 5, 453). "Death in earnest gives life force as nothing else does; it makes one alert as nothing else does" (TDIO, 83/SKS 5, 453). Recognizing death as certain enables us to clarify our goals, to be decisive about what is really worth pursuing, and to pursue those goals at the right momentum. In facing death, earnestness "disdains no task as too insignificant, rejects no time as too short" and, in Kierkegaard's view, brings one into a mature relation to God (TDIO, 83/SKS 5, 453). It imparts a sense of the meaningfulness of life and motivates the individual to appreciate the scarce time allotted to him or her (TDIO, 84/SKS 5, 453).

As well as being certain, death is also *indefinable* in the sense that it has no distinctive features and it does nothing to make anyone's life outstanding or unique in any respect. It cannot even be said of death that it is "the great equalizer," because being equal is a determinate quality, and death, insofar as it is indefinite, has no defining qualities. But even though death is indefinite, there can be great differences in how individuals take a stand in their lives in relation to death. The common way of taking the idea that death is an equalizer is to suppose that all differences of status, material wealth, and achievement are obliterated by death, so that all are on the same footing vis-à-vis death. But such a comforting image of a self-extinction that irons out all differences is a mood of depression and a manifestation of envy. The person who craves death as a great equalizer is resentful about the disparities of this world and wants to eliminate them by reducing all to nothingness.

It seems, then, that treating death as a way to eliminate worldly differences offers only a poor sort of consolation. But, Kierkegaard says, there is a way to think of death as an equalizer that understands it in another way. Earnestness can understand death as a call to close the gap between ourselves and God. In bringing us this insight, "the earnest [person] discovers a difference, namely, his own distance from the goal that is set before him" (TDIO, 89/SKS 5, 458).[15] So the earnest person feels called forth to close the gap between him/herself and the goal that is assigned him or her. The thought of the distance between where one is and where one should be "impels" such a person to try to fill the gap and to become what he or she is called upon to be. The call from the future that impels a person to act in order to fill the open space comes from the recognition of the indefiniteness of death, the recognition that it could come at any moment, so that there is no time to waste. As Kierkegaard says, "every good spirit shudders before the empty space, before the equality of annihilation, and this shudder that is productive in the life of nature is impelling in the life of spirit" (TDIO, 89/SKS 5, 458). The distinctively religious intention motivating this discourse becomes apparent when Kierkegaard says that

> the earnest thought of death has taught the living person to permeate the most oppressive dissimilarity [that is, differences in worldly matters] with

> the equality before God. No comparison has that impelling power and so reliably gives the urgent person the true direction as does the comparison the living person makes between himself and the equality of death (TDIO, 89/SKS 5, 458).

The earnest thought of death is the greatest motivator for fulfilling the project of an individual life's "true direction."

The ethico-religious dimension of this discourse comes out most forcefully in its reflection on the disparities in worldly life. In the thought of the equality of death, even the greatest advantages and disadvantages of worldly life mean nothing. The earnest thought of death, Kierkegaard says, "has helped the earnest person to subordinate the most advantageous dissimilarity to the humble equality before God and has helped him to raise himself above the most oppressive dissimilarity into the humble equality before God" (TDIO, 89–90/SKS 5, 458). For this understanding of death, the impulse to achieve what one can and should achieve in life comes not from some ego-driven desire for personal success, but from the humble recognition of the equality of the task set for all of us by God.

Kierkegaard ends the discussion of the indefinable nature of death with a reflection on how one learns how to be earnest in one's relation to death. To learn "the practice of earnestness," he says, a person first "concerns himself . . . about some object with his whole soul, and in this way the certainty of death becomes an object of concern" (TDIO, 94/SKS 5, 462). In other words, it is only when one has a world-defining commitment to something that gives one's life meaning that one can be struck to the core by the gravity of life's inescapable finitude. The inevitability of total annihilation can be a matter of total concern only for someone who cares about something with an "infinite passion." Death's certainty means that our worldly cares must terminate. At the same time, the uncertainty of death—the fact that we never know when it will come—makes us aware that the defining relation is not futile, but "is possible" (TDIO, 95/SKS 5, 463). The lucid awareness of death's certainty and uncertainty gives us a way of living life in which each moment is experienced as if it were the last: "Earnestness, therefore, becomes the living of each day as if it were the last." But it is also living life as if it were open to possibilities; though each day is lived as if it were the last, it is also lived as "the first in a long life" (TDIO, 96/SKS 5, 464).

"Being-toward-death" in Heidegger

Although the style and length of the discussions of death in "At a Graveside" and in *Being and Time* are very different, there are certain striking similarities between the mode of presentation and the core assumptions in the two works. Kierkegaard often begins with an account of "the ordinary view of death" in order to set up a contrast with the view one gets from the sphere of existence of earnestness. The former is an understanding of some aspect of death as seen from the standpoint of some mood or other, whereas the "earnest thought" of that same feature gives a considerably different understanding. Kierkegaard's goal is to lead people away from the ordinary views, the ones that seem to be "common sense" in Danish society, and lead them to the earnest thought's deeper insight. For this reason, much of what Kierkegaard says can be understood as "upbuilding" in nature, designed to invite the reader to look at things in a new way. Such a change in viewpoints is needed because only the earnest thought can capture what is right about the subject matter under discussion. The discourse therefore presents different points of view while also engaging in persuasion aimed at bringing about a profound change in the way we see things.

Heidegger's chapter on death (the first chapter of the second division of the work) follows a similar strategy. The early sections of the chapter begin with a consideration of the "average, everyday" understanding of death as it is made manifest in our ordinary responses to the death of others and the prospect of our own death. So, as Heidegger notes, death is thought of as something that is always "not yet," as something that happens to others "and not to me," as the "end," as what imparts "wholeness" to a person's life by bringing it to "fruition," and so forth. The opening sections of the chapter aim at debunking various misleading ideas about death, though Heidegger thinks there is always something right about our average, everyday understanding that should be preserved in the final, "authentic" account.[16] As he says, it is because the "ordinary interpretation" of basic phenomena "point back to the primordial meaning . . . when they are understood in a way that is ontologically appropriate," that we must "show that the ordinary interpretation springs from the limitations of the way Dasein interprets itself in falling," though such an interpretation "*is by no means accidental*" (BT, 341).

Heidegger follows Kierkegaard in proceeding by way of a contrast between the ordinary and the more authentic understanding of phenomena, and he agrees with Kierkegaard in holding that the same phenomena can be seen in very different ways from different viewpoints depending upon the sphere of existence in which one lives. There is also another—less obvious but in some ways more important—similarity in their accounts of death. Both thinkers are committed to the idea that the actual termination of life is a crucial aspect of understanding death. Kierkegaard repeats again and again such formulations as "It is over," "in death's decision all is over," "Now all is over," and so on. Death, however it is interpreted, cannot be thought without recognizing that it is a finishing point. "When death comes, the word is: Up to here, not one step further; then it is concluded, not a letter is added; the meaning is at an end" (TDIO, 78/SKS 5, 449). Death is certainly not an *event in* a person's life. What we call an "event" is something that makes a difference in a life, and death can make no difference for the simple reason that, with death, there is no longer any life *in* which to make a difference. Kierkegaard says that "in death's decision all is over . . . the transformation cannot fall in line with other events as a new event—because in death it is finished" (TDIO, 99/SKS 5, 467). Yet, at the same time, both thinkers would agree that if we had no basis for the idea of death as a termination, then we might think and act as though we were immortal gods (or like lower animals, according to most views) who lack any notion whatsoever of an end. In the same way, Heidegger holds that the fact of demise is crucial to the proper understanding of death. The early sections of the chapter on death find that there is something right in the ordinary view that death is an end, the point where all is finished, and that there is an issue about what sort of lives we lead in relation to that completion—our "being-*toward*-death."

But Kierkegaard and Heidegger agree that it is not our attitude or stance in relation to some future event that is of interest in examining death. Instead, the issue is how the recognition of our finitude and mortality affects the way we live out our entire lives, "from start to finish." For Kierkegaard, the point of thinking of death as *inexplicable* is not to work harder in order to find an explanation (for there is none), but "to give the thought of death retroactive power and make it impelling in life, because with the decision of death [i.e., death's decision to come] all is over, and because the uncertainty of death [i.e., that we never know for sure when it will come] inspects every moment" (TDIO, 100/SKS 5, 468). In other words, the significance of death lies in its retroactive power to motivate life, not in "morbid" thoughts about one's demise.

Heidegger also shifts from everyday conceptions of death to a conception designed to capture our "existential" condition as beings that are mortal. As for Kierkegaard, the lived phenomenon of death is inseparable from the "it is over," the "it is finished." Heidegger says that death is to be understood as "the possibility of the absolute impossibility of Dasein" (BT, 294), the possible extinguishing of all possibilities whatsoever. To speak of Dasein as being-toward-death is to understand human existence as facing, and moving toward, the ultimate boundary of existence, as a "Being-towards-the-end" (BT, 293). As always being propelled toward the end, Dasein's "Being-a-whole" is revealed, and the totality of its life "from start to finish" is at issue. But this attempt to grasp our being-toward-the-end focuses not on the end itself, but rather on the finite, bounded "being-toward" that is definitive of our lives as mortals. As Heidegger notes, "Death is a way to be [*eine Weise zu sein*]" of Dasein and must be understood not in terms of "Being-at-an-end," for Dasein "*is* already its end too"—its ending is also always part of its being (BT, 289). Heidegger specifies that the term *dying* (*Sterben*) will be used to refer to "that *way of Being* in which Dasein *is towards* its death" (BT, 291). What is of existential interest about death, then, is not the existentiell phenomenon of *passing away* or *demise*, but rather the distinctive way of being human as being mortal.

This interpretation of death as a "happening" suffusing an entire lifetime rules out one of the most intuitively plausible ways of thinking about being-toward-death, the conception of the meaning of death as showing that life has the structure of a narrative.[17] This sort of reading is supported by Heidegger's central claim that being-toward-death will give us a way of understanding the totality of Dasein's being, its "Being-a-whole," and hence a way of getting all of Dasein's being into our purview. According to a narrativist interpretation, the idea of existence as a *being-toward* the culmination or completion of the story enables us to think of death as the fulfillment of a total life story. Seeing death in this way helps to clarify the conception of human existence as a future-directed "projection" toward realizing certain possibilities. It tells us that a life story must always involve an experience of life's going somewhere or adding up to something, even if we do not always achieve our aims. It is in this sense that the "end"—the overriding goals—should be regarded as part of the existential meaning of the concept of death.

Such a narrativist interpretation has an immense plausibility and can be used to account for many other features of Heidegger's early thought. Even the "essential structure" Heidegger ascribes to human existence called "historicity" comes from the German word for "story" (*Geschichte*), which seems to support a view of the self as "story-shaped." But such a "whole story" characterization of Heidegger's conception of being-toward-death runs into insuperable difficulties. For one thing, it is often hard to see how a person's death "sums up" or provides a meaningful "conclusion" to a person's life in every case. We can, as Nietzsche says, grow too old for our victories;[18] whatever we may have accomplished may come to appear insignificant if we live so long that new and more interesting things supplant our achievements. Or we can die too soon, in which case our ambitions and projects can come to look like pipe dreams, more a sign of overreaching than an indication of what a life means as a whole. Moreover, thinking of being-toward-death as a relationship *toward* something tends to picture death as an event we stand before all our lives (even if it is granted that it is an event *we ourselves* will never experience). In general, thinking of the completion of a lifetime as something that endows life with a meaning seems wrongheaded, because the end of life is so often a dreary or drawn-out ordeal that has no relevance for what a person has been or done.

Any account of Heidegger's conception of being-toward-death will have to take seriously his claims that death is a characteristic of Dasein—a "way to be" Dasein undertakes as soon as it exists. It will also have to show that being-toward-death properly understood can explain Dasein's "Being-a-whole" without assuming a narrativist account according to which the "whole" of a life is defined by its culmination. In a "Preliminary Sketch of the Existential-ontological Structure of Death" (BT, 293), Heidegger specifies a number of features of death, or "dying" in his technical sense of the word, as a way of being that can guide our attempts to work out a complete and "authentic" interpretation of death. According to this specification, death is (1) Dasein's *ownmost* possibility of being, the possibility that is uniquely its own to the extent that only I can die my death. As one's ownmost possibility, death is also (2) *nonrelational* in the sense that it is something that each person has to undertake on his or her own, regardless of whether that person is surrounded by solicitous others or completely isolated. So in the confrontation with death, one encounters that which is most definitive of one's own being: one's ownmost being as a nonrelational possibility. Death is also (3) something that can't be gotten around; it is insurmountable, unbeatable, *not to be outstripped* (*unüberholbar*). Because of this inevitability and unavoidability, "Dasein is essentially disclosed to itself" (BT, 294) as a forward-directed projection of possibilities that are always finite possibilities. Death is also, as in Kierkegaard, (4) *certain* and (5) *indefinite* as to when it will come.

Where Kierkegaard talks about "earnestness" as the way of life in which one faces death in the right way, Heidegger talks about *authenticity.* The word translated as "authentic," *Eigentlichkeit,* comes from a common

German word meaning "really" or "actually," but Heidegger clearly connects this word with its stem, *eigen*, which means "proper" or "own." Authenticity is therefore thought of as an owning up to and owning one's own self, a "being oneself" that comes into its own as what it really is. As such a coming-to-fulfillment of the self, authenticity reveals the "wholeness" of Dasein that Heidegger has been seeking in order to give a full and adequate account of human existence. On this basis, he can formulate his "existential" interpretation of Dasein's being—the ontological conception of the "meaning of Dasein's being" that motivates his work as a whole. It is important to see that Heidegger's ultimate motivation for developing an account of authenticity is not an existential or ethical concern, but is rather part of his overall project of fundamental ontology. Its aim is to give a full account of what it is to be human.

The final section of the first chapter of Division II presents an "existential projection of an authentic Being-towards-death" (§53). In this section, Heidegger lists some of the conclusions about authentic being-toward-death he has developed in the preceding sections. First, it is noted that being-toward-death is always a "*Being towards a possibility*" (BT, 305). This is important because it vividly reveals what possibilities are in the ontological structure of human existence. Normally, we tend to think of trying to realize possibilities as concerned with trying to *actualize* something for ourselves. For example, I strive to be a published author because that is a goal I have, and the aim in pursuing this possibility is to actualize it, that is, to become a published author. Being "out for something" as a rule is aiming to actualize some possibility. But being-toward-death, as Heidegger has described it, is one case of "being toward a possibility" in which there is no such thing as actualizing what one is "toward." There is no way I can reach death so long as I am alive, and once I am dead I cannot be "toward" anything. Moreover, since being-toward-death is my *ownmost* possibility of being, to lucidly understand that my basic possibility is one that cannot be actualized involves recognizing that what I *am* at the most basic level is a reaching forward into possibilities, not an actualizing of possibilities. I exist as a "running ahead toward" or "directedness forward to," which Heidegger calls "fore-running" or "anticipation" (*Vorlaufen*). Human existence is defined by a *futurity* or *future-directedness*, a standing out into an open space of possibilities, where actualizing specific possibilities, while generally important, is not what is crucial to our being.

The authentic stance toward death recognizes that being-toward-death is *nonrelational*, that it is a task each person must take up on his or her own, without any guarantees of validation from the public world. As a result, it is through facing death that one becomes an *individual*: "The non-relational character of death, as understood in anticipation, individualizes Dasein down to itself" (BT, 308). The authentic stance toward death also clear-sightedly recognizes the inevitability of death—that it is *not to be outstripped*—and in this lucid recognition it becomes, in Heidegger's words, "free *for* . . . death" (BT, 308). The idea here, though rather obscure in the text, is that in facing up to the inevitability of death, one can *choose* among the possibilities open to one with a heightened degree of clarity about the importance and gravity of one's choices because one sees that one is not dependent on the public understanding of possibilities. As authentic, one remains *certain* of what is revealed by being-toward-death and also remains ready for the *indefinite* threat to one's being-there, a constant threat that becomes most evident in anxiety. Heidegger concludes his characterization of human existence in its authentic stance toward death by saying that, in such a stance, "*anticipation . . . brings [Dasein] face to face with the possibility of being itself . . . in an impassioned* **freedom towards death**—*a freedom which has been released from the Illusions of the 'they', and which is factical, certain of itself, and anxious*" (BT, 311).

For Heidegger, to disclose the authentic mode of the relation to death is to reveal the possibility or potentiality (*Seinkönnen*) that underlies and provides a basis for any possible way of being of Dasein whatsoever. In other words, it is only because we are related to death and can be so related in the authentic way that we are able to exist as inauthentic average everydayness. This is what Heidegger means when he says that "inauthenticity is based on the possibility of authenticity" (BT, 303). The possibility of an authentic stance in relation to one's ownmost-potentiality-for-being makes it possible to be a "self" in the fullest sense of this word.

We might now ask: What is it about authentic being-toward-death that ensures us that we are gaining an insight into what Dasein really (*eigentlich*) is? How does authentic being-toward-death reveal the possible *wholeness* of Dasein (BT, ¶45) that is needed in order to give an ontological or existential account of Dasein as a whole? This latter question becomes especially pressing once we reject the narrativist, "whole story" account of Dasein's being-toward-death, the account that sees being-toward-death as a matter of a life story running its course—"right to its end" (BT, 353).

The question of the role of Heidegger's account of authentic anticipation as definitive of Dasein's being might be answered by seeing how this notion figures into the account of the meaning of Dasein's being as "primordial and authentic" temporality that is the upshot of the discussion of death and the later examination of conscience (BT, 375). Heidegger has already suggested that human existence is characterized by *care* and he has suggested that care has a tripartite structure made up of three essential structures: facticity, falling, and existence (where "existence" is understood as "*ex-sistere*," as being outside itself in "being toward"). According to the project of grounding being in time, these essential structures are shown to map onto three dimensions of primordial temporality: beenness, the moment of vision, and futurity. As we can now see, the dimension of future-directedness—of being "out there," underway toward possibilities in such a way that Dasein *is* "being possible"—is what was revealed by the account of anticipation at the end of the chapter on being-toward-death.

Now it would be natural to think that these three fundamental modes of temporality are themselves located in time, so that "futurity" is somehow *in* the future, beenness is *in* the past, and so on. But this would miss the whole point of the conceptualization of primordial time, according to which temporality is not *in* time, but is rather the condition for the possibility of any time whatsoever. It follows that primordial temporality has no inherent sequentiality.[19] Beenness is not "before" the present, and futurity does not come "after" the correlates of the past or the present. On the contrary, because the three essential structures that underlie Dasein's being are the structures of Dasein that make possible any form of temporality whatsoever, they themselves cannot be thought of as being "in time" in any sense. On this account of authentic and primordial temporality, Dasein's anticipatory way of being as a "coming toward" (the German word for "future" [*Zukunft*] comes from stems meaning "coming toward") is a determination of its being as, at a most basic level, always "ex-sisting," that is, as being-toward and as being-possible. This authentic futurity provides one of the bases on which our familiar, sequential lived time becomes possible.

Seen in this light, the *wholeness* of Dasein's being that is disclosed by the phenomenology of death is not a matter of reaching the last stop on the line or of coming to the terminus of a journey. It is not, as the "arrow of time" metaphor might suggest, the moment when the arrow finally hits the target and stops traveling forward once and for all. Instead, Heidegger's claim is that being-toward-death, ontologically understood, names that essential structure of human existence that consists in our always being "out there," moving *toward* something, and in general caring about where we are going. The *whole* toward which we project might never be reachable, but it is at least a regulative idea determining the movement of life, its being as *kinesis heneka tou.*[20] This movement is *toward* fulfillment not in the sense of coloring in all the spaces of a life, but in the sense of realizing a potentiality-for-being that is definitive of Dasein's being. In his early lectures, Heidegger, reflecting Greek thought, called this end (*telos*) "the good," *ta agathon.* In his lectures of 1924/25, for example, he schematizes the structure of life as follows: *arche—peras—telos—agathon.*[21] The "limit"—the *peras*—here refers not to an endpoint, but to the boundaries definitive of the potential of anything, as the oak tree is the *peras* of the acorn. We approach being "whole," on this view, by approximating "the good" as it pertains to us, and this is something that can "occur" at any time in a lifetime, not just at its termination.[22]

Conclusion

We can see why Heidegger might call Kierkegaard's reflections on death "existentiell," as he labeled some other Kierkegaardian notions, given the nature of his project of working out an "existential analytic" in *Being and Time.* If the ultimate goal of an "ontological" and "existential" investigation aims at disclosing the underlying structures that make any mode of human existence whatsoever possible, then it seems clear that Kierkegaard's thoughts about death in "At a Graveside" do not accomplish the aims of fundamental ontology. Needless to say, this is not in any sense a criticism of Kierkegaard, as if he was under an obligation to provide an existential account but failed to do so. On the contrary, not only did Kierkegaard confine himself to doing what Heidegger calls "existentiell" thinking, I suspect he would be dubious about the very idea of moving from the personal and "inner" to some sort of grand systematic account of the essential structures of human existence in general.[23]

There remains the question concerning the force of Heidegger's charge that Kierkegaard never went beyond the level of a particular regional, ontic science—namely, theology—with the consequence that his thought has no larger significance for what Heidegger calls "fundamental ontology." This question is difficult to answer, because it is not always clear how the scope of an ontological investigation is to be determined. Heidegger holds that fundamental ontology, the question of the meaning or intelligibility of being, must begin with an existentiell account of the being of a questioner. However, so far as I can see, he gives us no reason to believe that the existentiell situation of the philosopher has any privileged status in undertaking such an investigation. The fact that Kierkegaard is a religious writer and that he has religious motives for his writings does not entail that he is operating with presuppositions drawn from religious concerns. Even more important, however, there is no reason to suppose that

Kierkegaard's work should be expected to meet the requirements of an investigation called "fundamental ontology." Both the power and beauty of Kierkegaard's writings depend in part on his ability to put in question such grandiose projects and to insist on the intensely "subjective" and personal nature of the truth we are seeking about life-defining matters.

NOTES

1. *Frühe Schriften* (Frankfurt a. M.: Klostermann, 1972), p. x.

2. Theodore Kisiel, *The Genesis of Heidegger's "Being and Time"* (Berkeley: University of California Press, 1993), p. 550 n. 9.

3. Kisiel, *Genesis,* pp. 275, 541 n. 2.

4. Kisiel, *Genesis,* p. 452.

5. Kisiel, *Genesis,* p. 492.

6. *Ontology—Hermeneutics of Facticity,* trans. John van Buren (Bloomington: Indiana University Press, 1999), p. 86; *Gesamtausgabe,* vol. 63, p. 111. On the topic of Kierkegaard's influence on Heidegger's account of death, see also Michael Theunissen, "The Upbuilding in the Thought of Death: Traditional Elements, Innovative Ideas, and Unexhausted Possibilities in Kierkegaard's 'At a Graveside,'" in *International Kierkegaard Commentary: Prefaces/Writing Sampler and Three Discourses on Imagined Occasions,* ed. Robert L. Perkins, trans. George Pattison, pp. 321–58 (Macon, Ga.: Mercer University Press, 2006).

7. *Die Psychologie der Weltanschauungen,* 5th ed. (Munich: Piper, 1977). According to John van Buren, "Heidegger's initial reception of Kierkegaard came through his 1919–21 review-essay on Jaspers's book, . . . [and] he continued to rely heavily on Jaspers's detailed expositions [in his early lectures and writings] of such Kierkegaardian concepts as *Existenz* . . . 'the individual,' 'subjective truth,' 'passion,' 'anxiety,' 'death,' 'dispersion,' 'curiosity,' 'being closed off,' 'conscience,' 'guilt,' 'becoming manifest,' 'indirect communication,' 'time,' and the moment (*Augenblick*)" (John van Buren, *The Young Heidegger: Rumor of the Hidden King* [Bloomington: Indiana University Press, 1994], p. 170).

8. *Being and Time,* trans. John Macquarrie and Edward Robinson (New York: Harper & Row, 1962), p. 492 n (hereafter BT). The English edition contains the pagination to the German edition of *Sein und Zeit, Gesamtausgabe,* vol. 2, in the margins.

9. Quoted from *Fear and Trembling and The Sickness unto Death,* trans. Walter Lowrie (Princeton, N.J.: Princeton University Press, 1954), p. 146.

10. This distinction is clearly formulated by Hubert Dreyfus in his *Being-in-the-World: A Commentary on Heidegger's "Being and Time," Division I* (Cambridge, Mass.: The MIT Press, 1991), p. 20.

11. According to Heidegger's precise wording, we say "it is" of "[e]verything we talk about, everything we have in view [*meinen*], everything toward which we comport ourselves in any way" (BT, 26).

12. In 1927 Heidegger states that "etymologically regarded, theo-logy means: science of God," but "*what is given for theology (its positum) is Christianness . . . theology is the science of faith*" ("Phenomenology and Theology," in *Pathmarks,* trans. James G. Hart and John C. Maraldo, ed. William McNeill [Cambridge: Cambridge University Press, 1998], pp. 43, 45, 48).

13. Kierkegaard's response to Epicurus is discussed in great detail by Patrick Stokes in his "The Power of Death: Retroactivity, Narrative, and Interest," in *International Kierkegaard Commentary: Prefaces/Writing Sampler and Three Discourses on Imagined Occasions,* ed. Robert L. Perkins, trans. George Pattison, pp. 387–417 (Macon, Ga.: Mercer University Press, 2006).

14. In *Fear and Trembling,* the faith of both Abraham in sacrificing Isaac and of the "knight of faith" is described in terms of the double movement of (1) renunciation of this world ("infinite resignation") and (2) paradoxically getting it all back again so that one lives fully, intensely, and joyfully in this world here and now (FT, 36–41, 45–49/SKS 4, 131–36, 139–43).

15. Quoted from the first English translation of Kierkegaard's death discourse in *Thoughts on Crucial Situations in Human Life,* trans. David F. Swenson (Minneapolis: Augsburg Publishing House, 1941), p. 98.

16. Heidegger's method of "formal indication" uses commonsense formulations to gain "hints" or "clues" as to what ontological concepts mean, and then shows how such formulations are inadequate to the phenomena, while tacitly retaining the "something right" in the formulation. The first two-thirds of the death chapter does this; all talk of "end" and "coming to fruition" has something right about it, though it is never sufficient. The clues build to the final ontological formulation.

17. Such a narrativist account of Heidegger's conception of being-toward-death is worked out by Paul Ricoeur in "Narrative Time," *Critical Inquiry* 7 (1980): pp. 169–90, and in his *Time and Narrative,* vol. 1, trans. K. McLaughlin and D. Pellauer (Chicago: University of Chicago Press, 1984), pp. 52–87. I have explored such a narrativist approach in a number of places—see, for example, my "Becoming a Self: The Role of Authenticity in *Being and Time,*" in *The Existentialists: Critical Essays on Kierkegaard, Nietzsche, Heidegger, and Sartre,* ed. Charles Guignon, pp. 119–34 (Lanham, Md.: Rowman & Littlefield, 2004). My own reading of Heidegger was strongly influenced by Alasdair MacIntyre's *After Virtue,* 2nd ed. (Notre Dame, Ind.: University of Notre Dame Press, 1984), pp. 204–25, where MacIntyre offers an account of the unity of life in terms of an unfolding narrative with a beginning and an end (= death). Interesting developments of this idea are found in Norman Lillegard, "Thinking with Kierkegaard and MacIntyre about the Aesthetic, Virtue, and Narrative," and John J. Davenport, "Towards an Existential Virtue Ethics: Kierkegaard and MacIntyre," both in *Kierkegaard After MacIntyre: Essays on Freedom, Narrative, and Virtue,* ed. John J. Davenport and Anthony Rudd, pp. 211–32, 265–323 (Chicago: Open Court, 2001).

18. Friedrich Nietzsche, *Thus Spoke Zarathustra,* ed. Adrian Del Caro and Robert B. Pippin, trans. Adrian Del Caro (Cambridge: Cambridge University Press, 2006), pp. 54.

19. This point has been clearly made by William D. Blattner in his *Heidegger's Temporal Idealism* (Cambridge: Cambridge University Press, 1999), see especially chapter 2.

20. This is John van Buren's general characterization of Dasein's being as "movedness" (*Bewegtheit*) (*The Young Heidegger,* p. 331).

21. Martin Heidegger, *Plato's "Sophist,"* trans. Richard Rojcewicz and André Schuwer (Bloomington: Indiana University Press, 1997), p. 85, *Gesamtausgabe,* vol. 19, p. 123.

22. Even in his later work, Heidegger talks about this "essential unfolding" toward the *peras.* This ontological teleology is the core of Heidegger's thought from start to finish.

23. Although in Kierkegaard's pseudonymous parodies of philosophical writings, he *seems* to want to arrive at universally valid generalizations about the human as such, this is not the main thrust of the nonpseudonymous religious writings.

11.

Kierkegaard, Levinas, Derrida: The Death of the Other

Laura Llevadot

"Write!" "For whom?" "For the dead, for those whom you have loved in some past." —JOHANN GOTTFRIED VON HERDER, *ABHANDLUNGEN UND BRIEFE ÜBER SCHÖNE LITERATUR UND KUNST*

Introduction: Philosophy and Death

"A free man thinks of nothing less than of death"[1] according to proposition 47 of Spinoza's *Ethics,* in which death is portrayed as a saddening thought, one which, moreover, depletes our potential to work and to think. The refusal to think about death, and specifically its association with sadness and pain for those left behind, is a constant theme in the history of philosophy. The image of Socrates presented in *Phaedo,* happy to accept his own death, is emblematic of the philosopher who has learned how to die. Xanthippe, his wife, is expelled from this scene in which philosophy and death come together.[2] Xanthippe is not excluded just because she is a woman, but because she allowed herself to be affected by the excessively painful nature of death, and particularly the death of the Other whom we love. At one end of the spectrum stands the figure of the free man, the philosopher, who has no fear of death; at the other, in stark contrast, the figure of Xanthippe, slave to her passions, who stands as a reminder of the fragility of our relationship with death—and with life.

Very little changes when death appears on the horizon of contemporary thought in the work of Heidegger. From the ontological perspective in *Being and Time,* death is not conceived in connection with emotions—or the excesses thereof—which are experienced upon the death of the Other. Death, viewed in this way, would fall back into the ontic sphere, in which death is assumed to be a fact that concerns *human beings;* but Dasein[3] is not a human being, a substance: "We are asking about the ontological meaning of the dying of the person who dies, as a possibility-of-Being which belongs to *his* Being. We are not asking about the way in which the deceased has Dasein-with or is still-a-Dasein with those who are left behind."[4] In order to regard Dasein ontologically, it is necessary to take "one's own death" (*der eigne Tod*) into consideration, in an individual and authentic (*eigentlich*) manner. Only in this way can Dasein confront its finite nature and discover itself as "Being-towards-death." But this gesture of the anticipation (*Vorlaufen*) of death has no purpose other than to redound and authenticate life. In contrast with the ignorance of death characteristic of everyday life, Dasein consists of something *more than a particular being* when it assumes its own death. Thus, we return to the figure of the free man, the philosopher, as the controlling image of living, of a way of being, in an authentic manner. Xanthippe is once again rejected; she is merely the ontic.

It is Levinas, rather than Heidegger, who introduces the concept of the "death of the other" into the boundaries of contemporary thought, and who endeavors to construct an ethics from the starting point of this experience. But it is symptomatic of the problematic status of Levinas's ethics that Levinas has to distance himself from Kierkegaard—the only thinker who really thinks through our relationship with the dead—in order to be able to assert such a proposal. My claim is that in Kierkegaard's works, the "death of the other" constitutes the enclave of the second ethics. In spite of Levinas's criticism of the concept of religion found in *Fear and Trembling,* which implies a suspension of ethics, Derrida discovers in Kierkegaard a more constraining ethics, an ethics that suspends ethics: the ethics of the survivor. Kierkegaard implements, according to Derrida, "a nondogmatic doublet of dogma . . . that 'repeats' the possibility of religion without religion"[5] (meaning that his thought here goes beyond any particular dogma) in order to demonstrate the power of Christianity that had not yet been conceived and which avoids external criticism. By rereading Christian dogmatics, Kierkegaard, according to Derrida, thinks through the possibility and the essence of the religious that precede any particular faith.

As Kierkegaard realizes, the power of Christianity, or of the twofold nature of Christianity, resides in this second ethics, which considers responsibility in terms of the death of the Other instead of one's own death. Perhaps from this perspective, Xanthippe's feelings—enslaved, ontic, excessive—could be directed toward an ethical understanding, which shatters the emphatic metaphysical duality between life and death.

Our discussion will consider the following: (1) Levinas's criticism of Heidegger and Kierkegaard, (2) the concept of absolute ethics and its relation to the death of the Other, which Derrida demonstrates in his analysis of *Fear and Trembling*, and (3) the importance of the death of the Other in Kierkegaard's second ethics, as developed in *Fear and Trembling*, *The Sickness unto Death*, and *Works of Love*.

Dying for the Other

In his meditations on death and ethics, Levinas criticizes Heidegger's privileging of Dasein's own death. The first issue that should be considered, from Levinas's perspective, is not one's *own* death but the death of the *Other*—a recurrent theme in Levinas's work. In the first instance, death appears as a condition of possibility in the relation to the Other. Here, the angst concerning one's own death, which modulates Heidegger's phenomenological analysis, translates into "the fear of being able to kill the Other." The "self" has an infinite responsibility with regard to the Other to the extent that he discovers that he can kill him: "The will is under the judgment of God when its fear of death is inverted into fear of committing murder."[6] The face of the Other, its alterity and transcendence, resists this violent act, and the "self" enters into a relationship of responsibility with this transcendence to the extent that it recognizes this resistance in the face of the Other. In a reversal of Heidegger's famous saying, Levinas claims that it is the Other's Otherness that exposes the impossibility of our own possibilities.

In the second instance, the responsibility for the death of the Other extends itself to the human condition: "*I am responsible for the other in that he is mortal.* The death of the other: therein lies the first death."[7] The decisive factor is no longer that the "Self" discovers his responsibility for the Other to the extent that he can kill him, but instead that the framework of murder is implicit in every death. The death of the Other compels me to "survive as a guilty one."[8] We always live in place of the Other, occupying a place that does not belong to us, which the Other would possibly occupy if he were still alive, but which, through his death, he has vacated for a survivor who will always feel guilty and responsible for what he has allowed to transpire (in this respect, the experience of the survivors of Auschwitz is a good example). And so Levinas insists, against the philosophical tradition, that "[w]e should think of all the murder there is in death: every death is a murder, is premature, and there is the responsibility of the survivor."[9]

But ultimately, it is the enormity of sacrifice, of the capacity to "die for the Other," which fundamentally articulates Levinas's ethics. Heidegger rejected the concept of "dying for the Other" as the original framework of Dasein, in that an act of this type can never free the Other of his death: "death is in every case mine, in so far as it 'is' at all."[10] Levinas, on the other hand, sees a truly human side to this supplanting of death: "The fact of admitting that the death of the other is more important than mine, that it precedes mine, is the very miracle of humanity within Being: the ground of every obligation."[11] It is clear that it is not a question of establishing an ethics of sacrifice, but rather of interrogating sacrifice as a human potential that is indeed real and does indeed happen. The gratuitousness of sacrifice goes beyond a human's status as a reasonable being, and exceeds his mere condition of *conatus.* The priority of the Other over the self, even in the extreme case of death, expresses the self's humanity when he responds to the call of the Other: *'here I am'* (*me voici*).[12]

But '*here I am*' is precisely how Abraham responds to God when he is ordered to kill his son, and it is this absolute duty to respond to the absolutely Other that Kierkegaard deals with in his apology for faith in *Fear and Trembling.* And so Levinas needs to be aware of his considerable distance from Kierkegaard on this topic. In fact Levinas settles his account with Kierkegaard in 1963 in an article titled *Ethique et Existence,*[13] in which Levinas criticizes the way in which the limits of ethics are defined in *Fear and Trembling.* Kierkegaard's reading of Abraham's sacrifice demonstrates the opposition between the affirmation of subjectivity on the one hand and singularity in the face of ethics (taken as the sphere of generality and discourse) on the other. In this sense, religion would take priority, as the realm of secrets and silence, of the unspeakable truth of suffering, of entrenched subjectivity, over ethics as the realm of community and therefore of intersubjectivity. Faith in God isolates the believer from the rest of humankind, to the point of sacrificing them—as Abraham intends to do with Isaac—through obedience: "The suffering truth does not open us out to others, but to God in isolation."[14] Religion requires a suspension of the ethical order, what Kierkegaard calls "the teleological suspension of ethics," as a condition *sine qua non* for comprehending the actions of Abraham. Here Levinas reproaches Kierkegaard for the violence Levinas would not permit in his own discourse: "Kierkegaard's violence begins when existence, having moved beyond the aesthetic stage, is forced to abandon the ethical stage (or rather, what it took to be the ethical stage) in order to embark on the religious stage, the domain of belief."[15] For Levinas, ethics does not lie in the domain of the masses but, on the contrary, in meeting the Other who has priority over the self: "The Self is infinitely responsible when it stands before the Others"; "Subjectivity *exists* within this responsibility, and only an irreducible subjectivity can take on a responsibility. That is the meaning of the ethical."[16] This space in which we meet the Other, where responsibility and answers are possible, is the realm of ethics and indeed of communication. Certainly, the communicative language, which occupies this space in relation to ethics, is not the totalitarian language of ontology, but it is nevertheless the communicative *saying*[17] that condemns the silence of Abraham.

Therefore, what differentiates Levinas's ideas from Kierkegaard's are their respective dealings with the "death of the Other" and sacrifice as an enclave in which to contemplate ethics or religious ethics.[18] As has been demonstrated, Levinas articulates ethics from the viewpoint of "dying for the Other," while in Kierkegaard's interpretation of the biblical passage about Abraham, what is in question, as Derrida demonstrates, is "killing" the Other in response to a "superior" request. The concept of "dying for the Other" that Levinas defends is, in fact, contemplated by Kierkegaard himself in *Fear and Trembling* as the act of the tragic hero, but not of the father of faith. Kierkegaard/de silentio even raises this possibility in reference to Abraham himself:

> If Abraham had doubted, then he would have done something else, something great and glorious, for how could Abraham do anything else but what is great and glorious! He would have gone to Mount Moriah, he would have split the firewood, lit the fire, drawn the knife. He would have cried out to God, "Reject not this sacrifice." He would have thrust the knife into his own breast. He would have been admired in the world, and his name would never be forgotten; but it is one thing to be admired and another to become a guiding star that saves the anguished (FT, 20–21/SKS 4, 117).

If Abraham had doubted, if he had given his own life in sacrifice, if he had died instead of Isaac, he would have behaved like a tragic hero, but not like the father of faith. On the contrary, faith consists in the giving up to death of a loved one, in responding to the excessive demands of the Other: *Here I am,* just because he believes by virtue of the absurd that Isaac will not be taken away from us. This is the realm of religion as depicted in *Fear and Trembling,* the sphere of belief that necessarily implies isolation and the suspension of ethics. Abraham cannot speak, because to speak would be to lose his responsibility, to become ordinary, to break the oath of obedience. Does this mean that ethics have been lost? How could Abraham lift the knife to Isaac? Can such an atrocity be justified morally? This is where Derrida's work is extremely relevant.

Killing the Other

Derrida proposes an ethical interpretation of religion (as it is outlined in *Fear and Trembling*) to the extent that he assumes that Kierkegaard does not yield himself to dogma, but instead implements "a nondogmatic doublet of dogma . . . that 'repeats' the possibility of religion without religion." The question Derrida directs toward Kierkegaard's text, having taken on board Levinas's criticism, is this: What if the suspension of ethics undertaken by Abraham implies not the defense of irrational religion, but the appearance of a second ethics? This question, which is not made explicit by Derrida but to which he responds, finds justification within Kierkegaard's texts.[19] The second ethics, which is proposed in the introduction to *The Concept of Anxiety*, already appears in *Fear and Trembling* when he warns that the absolute duty to love God does not revoke but rather transforms ethics: "From this it does not follow that the ethical should be invalidated; rather, the ethical receives a completely different expression, a paradoxical expression" (FT, 70/SKS 4, 162). This paradoxical expression of ethics is what Derrida understands as the "ethics of absolute duty," an infinite responsibility, which takes as its model the sacrifice of Abraham exactly as Kierkegaard understands it. Derrida therefore opposes this ethics of absolute duty to the universal ethics of duties and rights—to those ethics that are based on universality, generality, and discourse. Derrida's criticism of this type of universal ethics is presented in two arguments:

> (1) In the first place, the ethics of universal rights and duties is upheld, in spite of itself, in the framework of sacrifice. Abraham's act is not extraordinary because he tries to kill his son; we all do this every day when, because of our preferential love, we look after our own and let the others die. My responsibility toward the Other always implies sacrificing everyone else, the Other whom I do not look after, whom I do not choose to love, whom I let die, often of hunger. What Derrida criticizes is the way that our good conscience tries to hide this daily sacrifice under the veil of good deeds and righteous causes: "What the knights of good conscience don't realize is that *the sacrifice of Isaac* illustrates—if that is the word in the case of such a nocturnal mystery—the most common and everyday experience of responsibility."[20] By preferring the Other, by choosing him with my love

and my kindness, I am nevertheless sacrificing my fellow men "who are dying of starvation or sickness."[21] But we can conclude something from this affirmation which becomes relevant in a reading of Kierkegaard's *Works of Love* and Derrida's *Spectres de Marx*:[22] by preferring the presence of the living, of those who are here and demand my attention, I am also betraying those who are absent, those who are no longer here and those who have not yet arrived, both the dead and the unborn. We will revisit this theme later on, in order to be fair to both Kierkegaard and Derrida.

(2) Secondly, the concept of responsibility that motivates this type of ethics dilutes the absolute responsibility conferred by discourse: "What does Abraham teach us, in his approach to sacrifice? That far from ensuring responsibility, the generality of ethics incites to irresponsibility. It impels me to speak, to reply, to account for something, and thus to dissolve my singularity in the medium of the concept."[23] Kierkegaard insists repeatedly that Abraham *cannot speak*. To speak would be to justify himself to others, to try to be understood, to look for their solidarity and their consensus, in an effort to convert himself into a tragic hero and be admired for it. But it is essential to absolute responsibility that the decision is intimate and unspeakable. Not even the communicative language that Levinas calls on would be able to realize this absolute relationship with the Other.

So what exactly would this second ethics be, this absolute ethics, which Derrida refers to in his interpretation of Kierkegaard? It would be, in the first place, an ethics that, against a good conscience, assumes its guilt for the death of the Other, and whose role model would be Abraham's relationship toward God. Because God is here "every other (one) as every (bit) other," all others are for me "the wholly other." The answer to every Other would therefore be, as Levinas proposed, the *here I am*, to behave with everybody like a knight of faith. Herein lies the extraordinary nature of Abraham's act: "At the instant of every decision and through the relation to *every other (one) as every (bit) other*, every one else asks us at every moment to behave like Knights of Faith."[24] However, it should be added that the Other is not necessarily present here and now, nor even alive. If we follow the thread of the argument in *Spectres de Marx*, we will remember the ethical call Derrida makes:

> no ethics, no politics, whether revolutionary or not, seems possible and thinkable and *just* that does not recognize in its principle the respect for those others who are no longer or for those others who are not yet there,

> *presently living,* whether they are already dead or not yet born. No justice . . . seems possible or thinkable without the principle of some *responsibility,* beyond all living present, within that which disjoins the living present, before the ghosts of those who are not yet born or who are already dead.[25]

Thus far, the absolute ethics could coincide with Levinas's notion, at least as it is developed in *Otherwise than Being or Beyond Essence,* of the point where the Other loses his phenomenality and his presence. However, the second aspect, that of silence and the impossibility of speech, clearly breaks away from Levinas's theorem. Abraham's silence implies that singularity is incompatible with actuality and discourse. He who speaks is not talking about himself; the subject of the enunciation does not coincide with the subject of the enunciated. From Kierkegaard and Derrida's perspective, singularity is a resistance to any direct reference or any integrated discourse with oneself; language cannot *say* what is purely subjective. This hidden and untranslatable depth is what Kierkegaard called inwardness, and which Derrida calls God in a bid to repeat "religion without religion":

> God is the name of the possibility I have of keeping a secret that is visible from the interior but not from the exterior. . . . Once I can have a secret relationship with myself and not tell everything, once there is secrecy and secret witnessing within me, then what I call God exists, (there is) what I call God in me. . . . God is in me, he is the absolute *me* or *self,* he is that structure of invisible interiority that is called, in Kierkegaard's sense, subjectivity.[26]

This space of untranslatable inwardness, of entrenched subjectivity, should be retained—because it is the place where the dead live, where we interact with those who are no longer here or those who have not yet arrived, and therefore where the possibility of the second ethics lies, the possibility of a relationship with the others in terms of infinite responsibility and of faith, a "religion without religion." When Derrida declares, in the footsteps of Patočka, that "perhaps Christianity has not yet thought through its own essence," it is possible to respond that such an essence had already been conceived, that this unthought essence of Christianity that resists its external critics is exactly what Kierkegaard calls the second ethics and which he develops in *Works of Love.* In this text, Kierkegaard chooses our relationship with the dead as a model of this second ethics. Here the relationship of the survivor with the death of the Other, as opposed to his own death, the relationship of dying *for* the Other, opens up the possibilities of the ethical. We will now see how this happens.

The Death of the Other in the Second Ethics

What was referred to in *Fear and Trembling* as a transformation of the ethical into the religious, by virtue of which the ethical receives a paradoxical expression, is now formulated in *The Concept of Anxiety* as the second ethics: "So the new science begins with dogmatics in the same sense that immanental science begins with metaphysics. Here ethics again finds its place as the science that has as a task for actuality the dogmatic consciousness of actuality" (CA, 20/SKS 4, 328), and: "The first ethics [*Den første Etik*] ignores sin. The second ethics [*den anden Etik*] has the actuality of sin within its scope" (CA, 23/SKS 4, 330). But what does sin mean here? How does it relate to ethics? The second ethics certainly does not *explain* sin, but rather it *presupposes* sin, as part of "the dogmatic consciousness of actuality," the reality of sin. In the "nondogmatic doublet of dogma" that Kierkegaard develops here, sin is, above all, the subject's awareness of his nontransparency to himself; it is the assumption that "[s]ubjectivity is untruth" (CUP, 1:207/SKS 7, 189), that man has lost the truth through his own fault. Sin accounts for the subject's impotence with respect to realizing the first ethics, a science that is too ideal (CA, 16/SKS 4, 323–24). The first ethics, which Derrida referred to as the ethics of duty and universal rights, presupposes the capacity of the subject to fulfill his duty and the possibility of doing so in a communal context, whereas the second ethics sets out from failure and becomes an "ethics conditioned by collapse. It originates in the fact that man fails in his ethical aspirations."[27] In its relation to death, sin implies the consciousness of what Levinas describes as "surviv[ing] as a guilty one" in the face of the death of the Other. However, the second ethics is not constructed around the framework of "dying for the Other," nor even of "killing the Other"—an inherent element of experience—but around the duty to love the dead. The second ethics revolves around our relationship with the dead, the way we live with the death of the Other.

We can find a preliminary approach to this issue in Anti-Climacus's *The Sickness unto Death,* which depicts the passage from the despair of the "man of immediacy" to the faith that implies the disproportion of sin. Interpreting this text from the perspective of *Works of Love,* what is outlined here is the journey between two forms of life distinguished by their relation to death. The first form of life is that of the immediate man who despairs over the earthly. The immediate man is "in immediate connection with 'the other'" (SUD, 51/SKS 11, 165). When something earthly is taken away from him, when he misses the Other whom he loved, this man despairs. He even desires his own death, or, equivalently, wishes not to be himself. According to Anti-Climacus this type of despair is the lowest form of all (although it must be admitted that it is also the most common), one that makes us aware of the frailty of immediacy, of the weak bond that ties us to life. Xanthippe reappears again here in the role of the immediate man. The extreme opposite of this despair is constituted by faith, which, in this context, is defined as that situation where "in relating itself to itself and in willing to be itself, the self rests transparently in the power that established it" (SUD, 14/SKS 11, 130). What is interesting to emphasize here is that this model situation cannot be reached without the assumption of sin (of impotence) and its relation to ethics. Anti-Climacus observes that "[s]peculation does not take into consideration that with respect to sin the ethical is involved" (SUD, 120/SKS 11, 231). The ethics referred to here is therefore the second ethics, which is expressed with the injunction "You shall" (SUD, 129/SKS 11, 240). The duty referred to here is that of wanting to believe, but it always involves believing in this life, as opposed to another life (after death) or a transformed life.

With regard to death, Anti-Climacus points out right from the introduction that "Christianly understood, there is infinitely much more hope in death than there is in life" (SUD, 7–8/SKS 11, 124). Does this mean that Christianity gives hope in the face of death because it promises another life beyond this one? Absolutely not. To believe this would be to contradict the Kierkegaardian understanding of Christianity, which has not been thought of yet and which escapes external criticism. It cannot be overemphasized: "Abraham had faith, and had faith *for this life.* In fact, if his faith had been only for a life to come, he certainly would have more readily discarded everything in order to rush out of a world to which he did not belong" (FT, 20/SKS 4, 116; my emphasis). The question as always, both in *Fear and Trembling* and in *The Sickness unto Death,* is: How can we believe, in this life, when death takes away what we love most? How can we believe when we ourselves are responsible for killing, when we are asked to kill, when we survive as guilty? *The Sickness unto Death* responds to this question with an inarticulate "*You shall,*" probably because this duty is fueled by the actions described in *Works of Love*—particularly in the penultimate chapter entitled "The Work of Love in Recollecting One Who Is Dead."

This chapter of *Works of Love* allows us to understand the second ethics from the point of view of our relationship to the dead. Far removed from Spinoza, in this work the contemplation of death is depicted as the appropriate place to think about life, offering the criterion for living: "In the relationship to one who is dead, you have the criterion by which you can test yourself" (WL, 358/SKS 9, 351). The deceased is the one we have loved with preferential love, the loss of whom has thrown us into despair (which is sin) up to the point of "not [willing] to be oneself." The second ethics seems to reject this preferential love, inciting the duty to love beyond the concrete object, although it is through our relationship with the dead, through the duty to love the dead—those whom we have loved concretely—that the model of the second ethics is established. Why?

Kierkegaard's argument is as follows: unlike the living loved one, one who is dead is no actual object. "One who is dead is silent and says not a word" (WL, 352/SKS 9, 346). The dead do not hurt us, do not demand anything from us, and do not seek our love. In fact, reality always works against the dead. The living encourage us to forget the dead, as if they were saying, "Come to us; we will like you" (WL, 354/SKS 9, 348). But actuality, in order to be ethical, should have some relation with the nonexistent, with the phantom, as Derrida would argue. *Because* the deceased person is not real, because he is silent, he provides an opportunity to discover the type of love that resides in the living. As in Kierkegaard in general, the silence of the dead "is only the occasion that continually discloses what resides in the one living who relates himself to him" (WL, 347/SKS 9, 341). He who follows the precept of loving the dead discovers a love that is free, disinterested, and without hope, because the dead have no expectations and cannot reward us in the way we would like and expect of the living. The duty to love the dead expresses the duty to love unconditionally and without interest. This concept of love, which is lodged in the second ethics, is, according to Kierkegaard, the unthought essence of Christianity. By virtue of this duty to love the dead, preferential love is converted into love for one's neighbor.[28] The deceased is he whom we have loved with a preferential love but who, by departing, by becoming deceased, has converted himself into the silent but demanding motive of our love. The "You shall" is expressed here as "the need to love one's neighbor" by virtue of the absurd, where our neighbor is the dead, the living, anybody at all. For this type of love the object is indifferent. Adorno is correct when he states, "Perhaps one may most accurately summarize Kierkegaard's doctrine of love by saying that he demands that love behave towards all men as if they were dead."[29]

But far from implying any sort of fetishism, to love the living as if he were dead implies being able to "not see" his responses, his complaints, his rewards—in a word, his "impotence," or what Kierkegaard calls sin. To love the Other in this way means that one is able to "not see" that the Other is a sinner. Adorno hits the mark with regard to criticism of capitalism when he recognizes that Kierkegaard implies that "[a]gainst capitalist society, the relation to the dead is characterized as one free of aims."[30] There is no need to defend Kierkegaard from Adorno's criticism in this chapter; there is no point in continuing to remind Adorno that this framework for loving is directed toward the living, and even less to resort to intersubjectivity to save something from the Kierkegaardian gamble in relation to the Other.[31] We should agree with Adorno against any effort to temper Kierkegaardian excess or the radicality of Christianity as conceived by Kierkegaard. It is precisely within this excess that the opportunity to perceive the significance of the second ethics, as opposed to any universalist ethics of rights and duties, lies.

Love for the present, the priority of the living over the dead, responsibility toward the real, expresses the submission of the first ethics (which Derrida criticizes) to the logic of interchange. On the other hand, love for one's neighbor, the duty to love the dead, and the duty to love the living as if they were dead (before consideration of any preferences), points to the possibility of a second ethics that would be characterized by the following principles:

> (1) In this ethics the subject admits the nontruth, he takes responsibility for his guilt as a survivor, he appropriates sin. He assumes the impossibility of good conscience, which the first ethics had assumed, and he positions himself with respect to others who are not preferentially loved, those who suffer or who are no longer here.
>
> (2) In this ethics responsibility is infinite, because it is not directed solely at those present who do us harm and complain to us, but also to those who have passed away and those who are still to arrive, those who are not "real objects" and who nevertheless insist, who provide motive, and haunt us—as Derrida would say—like ghosts.
>
> (3) The second ethics is not established between communicative subjects, but rather between particularities that are irreducible to language. It is in the silence of entrenched inwardness where we can establish our relationship with the dead, irreducible by any aspiration of reasoning or any demand to account for oneself or what is real. In the depths of this silence, as Adorno observes, lives the hope against all hope that the dead will wake up.[32]

We have wondered about Xanthippe's suffering with regard to Socrates's death and whether this pain could be transmitted, beyond philosophical indifference, toward an ethical relation with the Other. The second ethics I have endeavored to present here, as articulated in the works of Kierkegaard and Derrida, is not modulated either from the framework of one's own death, as in Heidegger's ontological perspective, or the framework of "dying for the Other" as presented by Levinas, which from the Kierkegaardian perspective would allow only a tragic ethics. The duty to love the dead, those who do not respond and are not present, who do not complain to us with their cries or console us with their actions, arises from the awareness that every day we "kill" the other—that we continually live in place of the Other. This is the model of love for our fellow humans that governs the second ethics, and certainly this ethics suspends ethics since it annihilates the good conscience of those who are too alive, too communicative, too satisfied with their actions and reasons, but who soon forget the dead because of their responsibility to the living. With regard to our love for our neighbor—who is nobody and everybody and from whom we do not expect anything—we can only wait in silence for the impossible, like Abraham: that one day the departed will wake up again. "We ought to treat one who is dead as we treat one who is sleeping, whom we do not have the heart to awaken because we hope that he will wake up by himself" (WL, 348/SKS 9, 341–42).[33]

NOTES

The epigraph is from Johann Gottfried von Herder, *Abhandlungen und Briefe über schöne Literatur und Kunst* II 45, in *Johann Gottfried von Herder's sämmtliche Werke zur schönen Literatur und Kunst,* I–XXX (Stuttgart: Tübingen, 1827–30), XVI, p. 114, quoted in WL, 362/SKS 9, 356.

1. Benedict de (Baruch) Spinoza, *The Ethics,* in *The Chief Works of Benedict de Spinoza,* trans. R. H. M. Elwes (New York: Dover, 1955), p. 232.

2. Plato, *Five Dialogues,* 2nd ed., trans. G. M. A. Grube, ed. John M. Cooper (Indianapolis, Ind.: Hackett Publishing Company, 2002), p. 97 (60a–b).

3. Heidegger's term for the kind of self-aware being that humans can, but do not necessarily, possess.

4. Martin Heidegger, *Being and Time,* trans. John Macquarrie and Edward Robinson (New York: Harper & Row, 1962), p. 283.

5. Jacques Derrida, *The Gift of Death,* trans. David Wills (Chicago: University of Chicago Press, 1995), p. 49.

6. Emmanuel Levinas, "La volonté est sous le jugement de Dieu lorsque sa peur de la mort, s'invertit en peur de commetre un meurtre," in *Totalité et Infini,*

Essai sur l'exteriorité (La Haya: Martinus Nijhoff, 1961), p. 222; *Totality and Infinity*, trans. Alphonso Lingis (Pittsburgh: Duquesne University Press, 1969), p. 244.

7. Emmanuel Levinas, *God, Death and Time*, trans. Bettina Bergo (Stanford, Calif.: Stanford University Press, 2000), p. 43.

8. Levinas, *God, Death and Time*, p. 39. Bernhard Waldenfels points out this tendency in Levinas's thinking, which extends from the concept of the Other as present in *Totality and Infinity* to the understanding of the Other as absent in *Otherwise than Being or Beyond Essence*, the point at which the other is no longer there, so that the notion of the "Other" loses its phenomenality. See Bernhard Waldenfels, "Levinas and the Face of the Other," in *The Cambridge Companion to Levinas*, ed. Simon Critchley and Robert Bernasconi, pp. 63–81 (Cambridge: Cambridge University Press, 2002).

9. Levinas, *God, Death and Time*, p. 72.

10. Heidegger, *Being and Time*, p. 284.

11. Emmanuel Levinas, *Racismes, l'autre et son visage* (Paris: Cerf, 1988), p. 99. [The editors thank Dario Gonzales for this translation.]

12. Emmanuel Levinas, *Otherwise than Being or Beyond Essence*, trans. Alphonso Lingis (The Hague: Martinus Nijhoff, 1981 [1974]), p. 114.

13. Emmanuel Levinas, "Éthique et Existence," in *Noms Propres* (Montpellier: Fata Morgana, 1976), pp. 99–109 (originally published in German in *Schweizer Monatshefte*, 1963); "Existence and Ethics," trans. Jonathan Rée, in *Kierkegaard: A Critical Reader*, ed. Jonathan Rée and Jane Chamberlain, pp. 26–38 (Oxford and Malden, Mass.: Blackwell, 1998).

14. Levinas, "Existence and Ethics," p. 30.

15. Levinas, "Existence and Ethics," p. 31.

16. Levinas, "Existence and Ethics," pp. 32–33.

17. "The Saying, prior to any language that combines information or content, prior to language as a Said, is exposure to that obligation for which no one can replace me, and which strips the subject right down to his passivity as a hostage" (Levinas, *God, Death and Time*, p. 161).

18. Along these lines, see also the essay "Does a Human Being Have a Right to Let Himself Be Put to Death for the Truth?" by the pseudonymous H. H., in which he claims that humans do not have such a right.

19. As early as Jacques Derrida, "Violence and Metaphysics: An Essay on the Thought of Emmanuel Levinas," in *Writing and Difference* (Chicago: University of Chicago Press, 1978), pp. 79–153 (*Revue de métaphysique et de morale*, 3 and 4, 1964), Derrida notes that Kierkegaard's criticism of the ethical order did not stop him from "reaffirming an ethic in ethics, and from reproaching Hegel for not having constituted a morality" (p. 111).

20. Jacques Derrida, "Donner la mort," in *L'Éthique du don. Jacques Derrida et la pensée du don. Colloque de Royaumont décembre 1990* (Paris: Métailié-Transition, 1992), pp. 11–108; "Whom to Give to (Knowing Not to Know)," trans. David Wills, in *Kierkegaard: A Critical Reader*, ed. Jonathan Rée and

Jane Chamberlain, pp. 151–74, quote is from p. 162 (Oxford and Malden, Mass.: Blackwell, 1998).

21. Derrida, "Whom to Give to (Knowing Not to Know)," p. 163.

22. Jacques Derrida, *Spectres de Marx L'État de la dette, le travail du deuil et la nouvelle Internationale* (Paris: Galilée, 1993); *Spectres of Marx: The State of Debt, the Work of Mourning, and the New International,* trans. Peggy Kamuf (New York and London: Routledge, 1994).

23. Derrida, "Whom to Give to (Knowing Not to Know)," p. 157.

24. Derrida, "Whom to Give to (Knowing Not to Know)," p. 170.

25. Derrida, *Spectres of Marx,* p. xix.

26. Derrida, *The Gift of Death,* p. 109.

27. Arne Grøn, "*Anden* etik," in *Studier i Stadier. Søren Kierkegaard Selskabets 50-års Jubilæum,* ed. Joakim Garff, Tonny Aagaard Olesen, and Pia Søltoft (Copenhagen: Reitzels, 1998), p. 86.

28. As emphasized by Louise Carroll Keeley: "But the *no one* of death puts one in mind of one's neighbor" ("Loving *No One,* Loving Everyone: The Work of Love in Recollecting One Dead in Kierkegaard's *Works of Love,*" in *International Kierkegaard Commentary: Works of Love,* ed. Robert L. Perkins, p. 228 [Macon, Ga.: Mercer University Press, 1999]).

29. Theodore Adorno, "On Kierkegaard's Doctrine of Love," *Studies in Philosophy and Social Sciences* 8 (1940): pp. 413–29, reprinted in Daniel W. Conway and K. E. Gover, eds., *Søren Kierkegaard: Critical Assessments of Leading Philosophers* (London and New York: Routledge, 2002), pp.7–21, quote is from p. 10.

30. Adorno, "On Kierkegaard's Doctrine of Love," p. 20.

31. The majority of work on Adorno's criticism of Kierkegaard sets out from this position and offers a defense of the Kierkegaardian doctrine of love against Adorno's accusations. See for example Pia Søltoft, "The Presence of the Absent Neighbor in *Works of Love,*" in *Kierkegaard Studies Yearbook 1998,* ed. Niels Jørgen Cappelørn and Herman Deuser, pp. 113–28 (Berlin: de Gruyter, 1998); and Keeley, "Loving *No One,* Loving Everyone."

32. "The hope that Kierkegaard puts against the *seriousness of the eternal* is nothing but the hope of the reality of redemption" (Adorno, "On Kierkegaard's Doctrine of Love," p. 21).

33. This chapter has been made possible by the financial support of the Spanish Ministry of Science and Technology, Research Project: FFI2009-08557, IP: Manuel Cruz.

12.

Derrida, Judge William, and Death

Ian Duckles

In this chapter, I attempt to take seriously Derrida's reading of Kierkegaard's *Fear and Trembling* in *The Gift of Death.*[1] In particular, I focus on Derrida's claim that all universalizing ethical systems involve an evasion of responsibility for one's actions. As Derrida sees it, this has important connections with mortality, since (following Heidegger)[2] it is through developing the correct attitude toward my own mortality—and consequently my singularity as this particular individual—that I am able to lead an authentic life. In effect, I take Derrida to be suggesting that pursuing ethical considerations is an attempt to avoid confronting one's own mortality and thus avoid the demands of an authentic existence. Having developed this reading of Derrida I then read it back into Kierkegaard's conception of the ethical, particularly as it is articulated by the Judge William pseudonym in *Either/Or* part 2 and *Stages on Life's Way.* In so doing I argue that Derrida's articulation of the ethical is an acceptable gloss on these two works. More specifically, I will suggest that this is how Kierkegaard intended the Judge William pseudonym to be interpreted. In this way, I use Derrida to aid in understanding what I take to be Kierkegaard's position and criticism of the ethical, as well as bring out issues related to human mortality that are not explicit in these texts.

Derrida's Account of the Paradox of Responsibility and Death

There are three major claims that Derrida makes in *The Gift of Death* that are relevant to the issues I want to discuss. First, Derrida claims that, contrary to our ordinary understanding of the issue, ethics and a commitment to ethical norms involves a loss of personal responsibility and autonomy. Derrida writes, "The ethical can therefore end up making us irresponsible" (*The Gift of Death* [hereafter GD], 61). The second claim, connected to the first, is that the story of Isaac and Abraham as recounted by Kierkegaard's pseudonym Johannes de silentio (the author of *Fear and Trembling*) can and should be read as a parable, the moral of which is the first claim. Quoting again from Derrida, "The account of Isaac's sacrifice can be read as a narrative development of the paradox constituting the concept of duty and absolute responsibility" (GD, 66). In effect, Derrida argues that the story of Abraham and Isaac amounts to a literary depiction of his philosophical claim about the irresponsibilization function of ethics. Lastly—and this is the third claim—the first two claims are related to issues of mortality in that it is the fact of my mortality that makes me a responsible agent in the first place, and a commitment to a universalizing ethical system is an attempt to evade this responsibility and the implications of one's mortality. I will now examine each of these claims in turn.

In our ordinary understanding of the nature of ethics we tend to say that an individual is most responsible and most in control of her actions and her self when she submits to universalizable ethical norms. This certainly appears to be the view of figures as diverse as Aristotle, Kant, Hegel, and Mill, each of whom (in very different ways) argues that the best sort of human existence—the most authentic way to live—is through a commitment to universalizable norms.[3] Connected to this is the idea that an individual is most responsible for her actions when she can give a rational justification, a reason understandable to others, for her behavior. As Derrida writes:

> For common sense, just as for philosophical reasoning, the most widely shared belief is that responsibility is tied to the public and to the nonsecret, to the possibility and even the necessity of accounting for one's words and actions in front of others, of justifying and owning up to them (GD, 60).

That is, what makes me a responsible agent who is in control of and accountable for my actions is my ability to justify my actions and behaviors to others, to give a reason for what I do.

This is the received view, but it is one that Derrida wants to call into question. In fact, Derrida argues that this received view is ultimately paradoxical. What is the nature of this paradox? As Derrida sees it, when an individual seeks to justify his actions to others, this involves the individual actually giving up control and responsibility for his actions because he no longer sees the action as emanating primarily from his own will, but instead as emanating from or dependent on a will that transcends his own. "The first effect or first destination of language therefore involves depriving me of, or delivering me from, my singularity" (GD, 60). Part of our ordinary understanding of what it means to be responsible for an action is that the action in some way stems from the will of the particular individual (in Derrida's language, from my singularity). However, Derrida suggests that in requiring that my action be justifiable to others as a condition of being responsible for my action, we lose that element of singularity that is so important in assigning the individual responsibility for her actions: "far from ensuring responsibility, the generality of ethics incites to irresponsibility. It impels me to speak, to reply, to account for something, and thus to dissolve my singularity in the medium of the concept" (GD, 61). By justifying my action to others (dissolving my singularity in the medium of the concept), that action is no longer seen as stemming from my particular will (my singularity). Thus, there are two components to our ordinary understanding of responsibility that are in conflict or in tension. On the one hand there is the idea that the action must come from choices made by a particular individual. On the other hand is the belief that those choices can and should be understandable by and justifiable to other people. However, Derrida argues, if one sees her actions as justifiable to other people, she loses the uniqueness and singularity that are essential to holding her accountable for her actions.

I think an example will be useful in elucidating this point. Let us take the case of what de silentio calls a tragic hero: Agamemnon (FT, 57ff./SKS 4, 152ff.). Agamemnon was the leader of the Greek forces during the Trojan War. Before setting out with the Greek army for Troy, Agamemnon angered the goddess Artemis, who prevented his fleet from leaving harbor. A prophet tells Agamemnon that in order to appease Artemis he must sacrifice his daughter Iphigenia. Being a good king, Agamemnon does his duty and sacrifices his daughter, and the Greek fleet is allowed to set sail for Troy. Let us examine Agamemnon's responsibility for his actions here. It is clear that as ruler of Greece it is up to Agamemnon to decide on the fate of his daughter. In this way, the action stems from his singularity as the unique and only father of Iphigenia and as the sole ruler of Greece. However, Agamemnon can justify his actions to himself and the rest of Greek society by arguing that his decision was in the best interests of Greece. But notice now, by providing a reason that is accessible to others, Agamemnon in an important sense can deny his own agency. He might reasonably be expected to say something like, "I didn't want to sacrifice my daughter, but as King of Greece I have a responsibility to my subjects that transcends my obligations as a father." However, in making this claim, the sort of claim we would expect an individual to make in justifying his actions to others, Agamemnon is actually denying his responsibility for the action. He didn't do it; he was forced to perform this action because of his ethical and moral obligations as a king. In this way, even though Agamemnon appears responsible for his actions, his justification to others for those actions involves a kind of shirking of his responsibility. In taking responsibility for his actions by justifying those actions to others, he at the same time avoids being held responsible by pushing the blame onto impersonal ethical norms that he is bound to follow. In this sense, I think we can understand Derrida's claim that ethics involves an irresponsibilization.

So, how is it that the story in Genesis 22 is a parable, the moral of which is the above claim? For Derrida, the key here (and this is also, I think, the key for Kierkegaard/de silentio) lies in Abraham's silence, in his refusal to communicate his intention to anyone (his family, servants, etc.). As Derrida sees it, by keeping silent Abraham affirms the paradox of responsibility in the sense that he is now most responsible for his action because he treats the action as incommunicable. In refusing to justify or explain his actions to others, Abraham refuses to place moral responsibility for his actions onto impersonal ethical norms (as Agamemnon does in the example discussed above). Even when Isaac asks him almost directly what he is doing, he only responds with an ironic evasion.[4] In this way, Abraham reveals the paradox and demonstrates his commitment to a conception of responsibility and duty that transcends our everyday understanding of these notions. In effect, Abraham sacrifices our commonsense notion of duty for a higher conception of absolute duty:

> Absolute duty demands that one behave in an irresponsible manner (by means of treachery or betrayal), while still recognizing, confirming, and reaffirming the very thing one sacrifices, namely, the order of human ethics and responsibility. In a word, ethics must be sacrificed in the name of duty (GD, 67–68).

Thus, Derrida suggests that in obeying God's command and remaining silent Abraham acknowledges the paradox of responsibility and in fact merely confronts what we all experience any time we attempt to satisfy a moral obligation. How then is this connected to death and mortality?

For Derrida, death is important because it is through the necessity of our death that we become responsible agents who can be held accountable for our actions in the first place. Derrida begins his meditation on death by invoking the Platonic account of death as it appears in the *Apology* and the *Phaedo.*[5] According to Derrida, on this model, "By means of the passage to death the soul attains its own freedom" (GD, 40). Derrida then goes on to suggest that this account of death is appropriated and transformed by Christianity[6] (and the Abrahamic religions generally).[7] Unlike the Platonic model, in which death is something the individual gives to himself (an idea seen most clearly in Socrates's willingness to carry out his own execution combined with his argument in the *Phaedo* that philosophy is a preparation for death),[8] in the Christian appropriation, death now becomes something bestowed upon the individual by a radically distinct other, God.

For Derrida, notions of death and responsibility are intimately tied to an individual's relation to the good as the source of meaning in one's life.[9] Thus, one can rearticulate the distinction between the Platonic and the Christian in terms of how one is related to the good. On the Platonic account, the good exists as "a transcendental objective, a relation between objective things" (GD, 50). It is this conception of the good that supports Socrates's assertion in the *Phaedo* that philosophy is a preparation for death, and that we can see in Plato's Allegory of the Cave. The basic idea here is that the philosopher devotes her life to discovering and studying the forms. When she dies, she finally gains an unmediated contact with these forms. Thus, as a philosopher, she devotes her life to attaining the condition she will be in when she dies. This contrasts with the Christian conception, where the good is understood as a *mysterium tremendum.* Derrida quotes the Czech philosopher Jan Patočka:

> a *mysterium tremendum. Tremendum* because responsibility resides henceforth not in an essence that is accessible to the human gaze, that of the Good and the One, but in the relation to a supreme, absolute and inaccessible being that holds us in check not by exterior but interior force.[10]

Under the Platonic account, I can literally see the Good if I employ the proper mental discipline. By contrast, in the Christian account, the good (God) is separate from me and, in effect, unknowable (God is infinite, I am finite).

On this new model, death now becomes the source of individual responsibility. Why is this? Under the Platonic account an individual can see and know the good. Thus the individual has a clear conception of who she is and what she should be doing in her life. Her responsibility and freedom consist in following a behavioral algorithm: "if decision-making is relegated to a knowledge that it is content to follow or to develop, then it is no more a responsible decision, it is the technical deployment of a cognitive apparatus, the simple mechanistic deployment of a theorem" (GD, 24). In effect, individuality is subsumed under the Good. As noted above in my discussion of the ethical, this is a perspective in which freedom and responsibility are lost.

To regain this freedom and responsibility, Derrida argues, we must move to the *mysterium tremendum.* Why this should be the case is not exactly clear, but the cornerstone of Derrida's analysis lies in the fact that through the hiddenness of God, through his terrible mystery, we lose the stability and assurances provided by the Platonic. We become responsible through the existential recognition that only we can decide the course of our lives, and this realization comes about through the recognition of our irreplaceability as individuals. "My irreplaceability is therefore conferred, delivered, 'given,' one can say, by death" (GD, 41). It is because I can die, and furthermore because only I can experience my own death, that I take on the status of a unique individual. In effect, my mortality and the consequent necessity of my death is what defines and distinguishes me from all others. Many of the jobs and roles I play in my daily life can be taken over by others and I can have substitutes for them, but no one can die for me. Derrida of course recognizes the possibility of sacrifice, but even if someone sacrifices her life for me, she doesn't take my death, she merely delays my death. At the end of the day, I am the only individual who can undergo my own death.

This singularity, this individuality conferred upon me by my own death (and the individuality conferred upon other individuals by their own deaths) is what in turn makes me a responsible agent. "Everyone must assume his own death, that is to say the one thing in the world that no one else can *either give or take:* therein resides freedom and responsibility" (GD, 44). Again, Derrida is not as clear here as we might like, but I take it that the essential claim is that my awareness of the necessity of my own death, and my awareness of the possibility of death at any time, makes me sensitive to and responsible for my actions. Because my actions and choices can result in my death (or the death of others), and because there will eventually be a time at which I can no longer act or choose, my actions and choices become meaningful and significant. Through a meditation on death I become aware of what is at stake when I act, and this awareness translates itself into a kind of responsibility and freedom. I am concerned about my own death and thus take care or concern about my own life and what happens to it (as well as a concern for the lives of others). In this way, according to Derrida, it is through an awareness of death that I become a free and responsible agent.[11]

On this account, then, we can view ethics as, at least in part, a strategy for avoiding a confrontation with my own mortality. For Derrida, notions of singularity, death, and responsibility or freedom are intimately connected. From a psychological perspective we can see how traditional models of ethics in their denial of singularity also amount to a strategy for avoiding a confrontation with one's own mortality. In hiding behind my duty I avoid taking responsibility for my action as this singular individual, and in so doing I avoid recognizing the very thing that confers singularity and individuality upon me, namely, my death.

The next question, of course, concerns how this discussion is related to Kierkegaard generally and, as is my focus here, the Judge William pseudonym in particular. To this I now turn.

Judge William

Judge William is one of the earliest pseudonyms employed by Kierkegaard and is the pseudonym that takes itself to be ethical and a proponent of this position. In addition to writing the bulk of volume 2 of *Either/Or*,[12] Judge William is also the author a few years later of an essay titled "Some Reflections on Marriage in Answer to Objections by a Married Man" that is included in *Stages on Life's Way* (published in 1845).[13] My goals in examining these essays are as follows: First, I intend to show that Judge William acknowledges to some degree, within his own ethical system, the paradox and irresponsibilization function of ethics as described by Derrida. Second, in the face of this realization Judge William nevertheless suggests that individuality and singularity must be suppressed in favor of ethical considerations, even though ethics depend upon the singularity of the individual. This would appear to be what characterizes Derrida's interpretation of ethics as well: namely, that traditional conceptions of ethics involve a paradox that is dealt with by suppressing individuality in favor of universality. I conclude by once again connecting these issues up with death, a move Kierkegaard/Judge William does not make, but which I hope to argue is nevertheless a plausible and illuminating one.

Before launching into my analysis, I want to argue that the categories that generate the tension in ethics articulated by Derrida are relevantly similar to the categories employed in Judge William's own analysis of ethics. Interestingly enough, if we turn to *Either/Or*, particularly the second essay, "The Balance Between the Aesthetic and the Ethical in the Development of the Personality," we can see Judge William himself articulate almost the identical problem that Derrida articulates. Judge William writes, "But there is another skepticism that applies to every duty; it is the skepticism that I cannot discharge the duty at all. The duty is the universal. What is required of me is the universal; what I am able to do is the particular" (EO, 2:263/SKS 3, 251). A little later in the text Judge William describes this as "the dialectic of duty" (EO, 2:264/SKS 3, 251). In the context of *Either/Or* Judge William does not himself see this as any kind of problem with the ethical. In fact, just the opposite is true, in that he sees this dialectic as a vindication of the ethical project insofar as ethics is able to maintain the particularity of the aesthetic while at the same time transforming, securing, and enriching it.[14] In a sense then, part of Judge William's argument in favor of the ethical as against the aesthetic is that the ethical contains everything the aesthetic does, but adds more.

Marriage is a nice illustration of the ethical and the dialectic of duty, because in marriage one is drawn to another person as a result of accidental characteristics that person possesses as well as one's own personal idiosyncrasies that find those characteristics appealing. Further, in the marriage ceremony itself one stands before the public and essentially communicates and justifies that love to the world and the public at large. The decision to marry is described by Judge William as a synthesis of immediacy and resolution: "I rejoice in thinking that marriage is precisely so constituted, which, as stated, I assume for the time being to be a synthesis of falling in love and resolution" (SLW, 109/SKS 6, 104). The immediacy of marriage is that one falls in love, that one finds oneself in a certain relation to another individual. This "falling in love" is immediate in the sense that it stems from an individual's particularity. We don't control when we fall in love, or whom we fall in love with. In this way, falling in love is immediate in that it stems from unique characteristics and idiosyncrasies of a particular individual. As Judge William puts it in *Either/Or*, "[e]thics tells him only that he should marry, it does not say whom" (EO, 2:305/SKS 3, 288). In Derrida's language, the choice of whom to marry stems from the singularity of the individual.

This "falling in love" does not, of course, a marriage make. The mere fact of falling in love only makes one a seducer, and one need only invoke aesthetic categories in explaining and understanding it. In order to have a marriage this immediate moment must be combined with a resolution. "But if [marriage] is a τελος, it is not something immediate but an act of freedom, and belonging under freedom as it does, the task is actualized only through a resolution" (SLW, 101–2/SKS 6, 97). As an act of freedom, as something the individual controls and chooses (unlike the immediacy of falling in love), this resolution requires that the agent engage in reflection, "and such exhaustive deliberation that from it a resolution results" (SLW, 102/SKS 6, 98). The resolution to marry requires "exhaustive deliberation" and examination of the reasons for marriage, and in the marriage ceremony itself one is translating the immediacy of love into a public event. Thus, marriage combines both elements that make up the dialectic of duty. There is the singularity of the individuals in love combined with the universalizing function of the marriage ceremony.

We are now in a position to see Judge William acknowledge the same paradox of responsibility articulated by Derrida. "Here, then, I pause at the crucial point: a resolution must be added to falling in love. But a resolution presupposes reflection, but reflection is immediacy's angel of death" (SLW, 157/SKS 6, 147). According to Judge William, the ethical requires two moments: immediacy and resolution or choice. This moment of resolution in turn requires reflection and "exhaustive deliberation," but this reflection, which is infinite, when carried out undercuts and destroys the immediacy of falling in love that is required for the ethical. Thus, we have come to a paradox. The ethical requires a resolution, but the reflection required for this resolution to be authentic destroys the other moment of the ethical: immediacy.

As a consequence of this, the two components of the ethical appear to be incompatible. This is another way to articulate the "dialectic of duty" discussed above, and this position is nearly identical to Derrida's claim that if one sees her actions as justifiable to other people, she loses the uniqueness and singularity that are essential to holding her accountable for her actions. As Judge William writes, "[ethics] takes away from him the vain joy of being out-of-the-ordinary in order to give him the true joy of being the ordinary" (EO, 2:304/SKS 3, 287). In ethics, one loses one's quality of being "out-of-the-ordinary" (i.e., this individual with these unique qualities and characteristics) and one becomes ordinary (i.e., an individual who acts and is motivated by the same universal ethical considerations as everyone else).

As a piece of corroboration for my analysis, we can see a very similar view attributed to A (the author of volume 1 of *Either/Or* and the major pseudonym representing the aesthetic worldview) as a reason for rejecting the ethical in favor of the aesthetic. A's position is revealed by a conversation that Judge William reports concerning A's response to an anecdote about horse racing. A says that "it was a dubious matter to run a race for three days; one took the risk of working up such momentum that one could never stop, and therefore [I] wisely refrained from all such violence" (EO, 2:198/SKS 3, 191). The point here is that A is unwilling to commit to any long-term projects or to the ethical because he sees them as a limitation on his freedom and autonomy; a limitation on his ability to pursue and act in accordance with whatever whim strikes him at any moment. This demonstrates A's commitment to freedom, but it is interesting as well insofar as it suggests a reason why A rejects the ethical: he sees it as incompatible with his freedom and autonomy; to use Derrida's language, his singularity. Thus, we can see in A an articulation of Derrida's own criticism of the ethical (in this case of course it is used to provide support for the aesthetic, a position with its own set of problems, the articulation of which is beyond the scope of this chapter).[15]

But how is this connected with issues of mortality and death? In his writings, Judge William makes only passing references to death and mortality (unlike in Kierkegaard's larger authorship where death is a more significant topic of discussion). He does, however, discuss in some detail the ways in which the ethical orients an individual toward temporality, and it is in these discussions that we can discover echoes of the points Derrida is making. Of particular concern for Judge William is the way in which ethics and a commitment to ethical duty "fills up" time for the individual.

> When a person has a calling [one of the ethical duties Judge William discusses] he generally *has a norm outside himself* which, without making him a slave, nevertheless gives him some indication of what he has to do, *maps out his time for him,* often provides him with the occasion to begin (EO, 2:294/SKS 3, 278; emphasis added).

This notion of the ethical "mapping out" or structuring the individual's relation to temporality is one that recurs throughout *Either/Or.* A cornerstone of this conception is that Judge William rejects the aesthetic because it ties the individual to finitude while the ethical connects the individual to the infinite and eternal. This aesthetic immersion in finitude is identified as despair, and this despair is, for Judge William, overcome by choosing ethical values: "And in despairing a person chooses again, and what then does he choose? He chooses himself, not in his immediacy, not as this accidental individual, but he chooses himself in his eternal validity" (EO, 2:211/SKS 3, 203).

Key here for my analysis is the way in which ethical choice is a choice that turns the individual away from his immediacy (in Derrida's language his singularity) and focuses the individual on the eternal, the abstract, and the universal. In this way the ethical is a turning away from singularity, an avoidance of those qualities that make the individual an individual (which, following Derrida, include my mortality), in favor of an abstract conception of the self that is defined by a series of ethical obligations one needs to fulfill. It is also important to note how ethical norms exist outside the individual. As with Agamemnon, the individual is not responsible for his actions; he is merely following already existing ethical norms.

Judge William goes on to assert that when an individual has chosen ethically, "Temporality vanishes for him" (EO, 2:231/SKS 3, 221). It is this vanishing of temporality, the vanishing of the individual's mortality (since what is temporality other than a recognition of the individual's embededness in time?) that most clearly connects with Derrida's assertion that a commitment to a universalizing ethics is an attempt to flee or hide from one's mortality.

An even clearer articulation of this point can be found in Judge William's own discussion of a situation in which the ethical appears to break down:

> It sometimes happens to me . . . that I sit and settle into myself. I have taken care of my work; I have no desire for any diversion, and *something melancholy in my temperament gains the upper hand over me*. . . . It seems to me as if I myself were an old man, my wife my happily married younger sister in whose house I am sitting. In such hours, *time almost begins to drag for me* (EO, 2:307/SKS 3, 290; emphasis added).[16]

A major consideration in favor of the ethical over the aesthetic is the promise of the dissolution of temporality, the freeing of the individual from the demands of his particularity and his mortality. Yet, as this quotation suggests, this particularity continues to assert its demands over the individual. It is something in his temperament, something connected to his singularity that presents a problem for Judge William. Even as one flees the demands of mortality through a commitment to ethical norms, temporality returns to "gain the upper hand" over the individual. This points to a significant problem in the ethical, in that it is a position that is unable to satisfy its own promise of a flight from temporality. In the context of *Either/Or* Judge William ignores this problem, but looked at from the broader view of Kierkegaard's authorship this suggests why the ethical is inadequate and must ultimately be subsumed under the religious conception of life; a view Kierkegaard articulates more fully in *Fear and Trembling* with the figure of Abraham.

In this way we can, following Derrida, see within Judge William's account of the ethical the same constellation of issues connecting ethics, singularity or individuality, and death. More abstractly, I think this should come as no particular surprise. If there is a kernel of truth in Derrida's interpretation of ethics in *Fear and Trembling* (and I believe there is), then it is only natural that similar issues would emerge in the writings of the pseudonym most responsible for articulating the ethical. Now certainly much of what I have said goes beyond the claims made directly by Judge William. In reading through the essays written by Judge William, one finds almost no discussion of death or mortality. However, this lack of a discussion can be used as evidence for my interpretation. Generally, of course, lack of evidence is never a good justification for a claim, but in this context I think it can be legitimate. Given Kierkegaard's general interest in and discussion of death elsewhere in the authorship, and given that, if my analysis is correct, the ethical involves an avoidance of mortality, it should not be surprising that the pseudonym responsible for articulating and promoting the ethical fails to discuss death, since he, qua ethical agent, is in the very act of fleeing from death and mortality. Given this, I hope to have shown that there is a benefit and profit to be found in reading the works of Judge William in close connection with Derrida's meditations on death and mortality.

NOTES

1. Jacques Derrida, *The Gift of Death,* trans. David Wills (Chicago: University of Chicago Press, 1995) (hereafter GD).

2. Martin Heidegger, *Being and Time,* trans. John Macquarrie and Edward Robinson (New York: Harper Collins, 1962), see in particular section I of Division II, p. 279ff.

3. Many scholars have argued that Kierkegaard's "ethical" owes a debt to earlier ethical/moral systems. Among the many philosophers who stress the Hegelian dimensions of the ethical are: Alastair Hannay, *Kierkegaard* (London: Routledge, 1982), p. 59; Anthony Rudd, *Kierkegaard and the Limits of the Ethical* (Oxford: Clarendon Press, 1993), pp. 71, 145; and Merold Westphal, *Becoming a Self* (West Lafayette, Ind.: Purdue University Press, 1996), p. 24. Those who argue that the ethical is Kantian include James Collins, *The Mind of Kierkegaard* (Princeton, N.J.: Princeton University Press, 1983); C. Stephan Evans, *Kierkegaard's "Fragments" and "Postscript": The Religious Philosophy of Johannes Climacus* (Atlantic Highlands, N.J.: Humanities, 1983); Ronald Michael Green, *Kierkegaard and Kant: The*

Hidden Debt, SUNY Series in Philosophy (Albany: State University of New York Press, 1992); and Ulrich Knappe, *Theory and Practice in Kant and Kierkegaard,* Kierkegaard Studies Monograph Series No. 9 (New York: de Gruyter, 2004).

4. The passage in question is Genesis 22:8. "And Abraham said: God himself will provide the lamb for the burnt offering, my son," which de silentio discusses in detail in FT, 115ff/SKS 4, 203ff. He describes this passage as a form of irony at FT, 118/SKS 4, 206.

5. Plato, *Five Dialogues,* trans. G. M. A. Grube and John M. Cooper (Indianapolis, Ind.: Hackett, 2002). As the editors note in their comments on an early draft of this chapter, it is not entirely clear that Plato is consistent in his two accounts of death in these respective works. Despite this, I do believe there is enough similarity between the two accounts to group them together here. If anything, Derrida's own reading of the Platonic account of death relies more on the *Phaedo* than on the *Apology.*

6. In this context, when Derrida talks about "Christianity" he has in mind an authentic version of Christianity that has thought through and acknowledged the full implications of its worldview. This authentic Christianity (which in several places Derrida suggests has yet to come into existence) must be distinguished from a kind of everyday Christianity as practiced by most people. "Something has not yet arrived, neither at Christianity nor by means of Christianity. What has not yet arrived at or happened to Christianity is Christianity" (GD, 28). This is not so different, I think, from Kierkegaard's categories of Christianity (the authentic version) and Christendom (the Christianity that is practiced by most people).

7. The Hegelian dimensions of this *Aufhebung* are likely intentional.

8. "I am afraid that other people do not realize that the one aim of those who practice philosophy in the proper manner is to practice for dying and death. Now if this is true, it would be strange indeed if they were eager for this all their lives and then resent it when what they have wanted and practiced for a long time comes upon them" (Plato, *Phaedo,* 64a).

9. I am using "good" in as generic a sense as possible here, though as we will see the good for the Platonic account is the Form of the Good.

10. Jan Patočka, "La civilisation technique est-elle une civilisation de déclin, et pourquoi?" in *Essais Hérétiques Sur La Philosophie de L'Histoire,* trans. Erika Abrams (Lagrasse: Verdier, 1981), p. 116, quoted in GD, 31.

11. I realize that there is an element of circularity in the analysis of these concepts. That is, I have used death to understand responsibility, which is then used to understand death. This circularity is, however, hermeneutic and not vicious, and it merely indicates how closely aligned these various concepts are for Derrida. "Now to have the experience of responsibility on the basis of the law that is given, that is, to have the experience of one's absolute singularity and apprehend one's own death, amounts to the same thing" (GD, 41).

12. *Either/Or* volume 2 consists of three essays. The first two are letters written by Judge William to his interlocutor A. The last essay, the "Ultimatum," is a

sermon written by a pastor from Jylland, which Judge William recommends to A as a concise summary of the ethical view of life.

13. As I have argued elsewhere ("A (Partial) Defense of MacIntyre's Reading of Kierkegaard," *Idealistic Studies* 36, no. 2 [2006]), I read the Judge William in *Stages* as having advanced in his own understanding of the position he articulated in *Either/Or.* In particular, I see Judge William in *Stages* as having become aware of a problem or tension in his ethical life-view. Though this is an important point, it is not one that is relevant to the issues I am discussing in this chapter. Consequently, for the purposes of my argument here, I treat this pseudonym as articulating a generally consistent view in all these works.

14. Again, the Hegelian dimensions of this *Aufhebung* are likely intentional.

15. There is not as much written on the problems of the aesthetic as one would imagine. Naturally, I recommend my own work (referenced in a previous note) as a starting point for these debates.

16. I am indebted to Andrew Cross, who called my attention to the significance of this passage during an independent study of Kierkegaard at the University of California, Irvine during the spring quarter of 1998.

13.

The Soft Weeping of Desire's Loss: Recognition, Phenomenality, and the One Who Is Dead in Kierkegaard's *Works of Love*

Jeremy J. Allen

> We have only a little time to please the living,
> But all eternity to love the dead.
> There I shall lie for ever. Live, if you will;
> Live, and defy the holiest laws of heaven.
>
> —SOPHOCLES, "ANTIGONE"

> Follow me, and let the dead bury their own dead.
>
> —JESUS OF NAZARETH (MATT. 8:22)

In the ninth chapter of the second set of deliberations in *Works of Love,* Kierkegaard writes the following words: "I know of no better way to describe true recollection than by this soft weeping that does not burst into sobs at one moment—and soon subsides. No, we are to recollect the dead, weep softly, but weep long" (WL, 348/SKS 9, 342). Much of the work in the chapter you now read is spent setting up the problematic that aims at establishing a relation between grieving and the lack of recognition from those now absent from our experience of the physical world. I will argue that Kierkegaard's account of "the work of love in recollecting one who is dead" (WL, 345–58/SKS 9, 339–52) can be read as an application of Hegel's description of how human self-consciousness arises through mutual recognition. The work of "recollective love" is generally thought to serve as a test of sorts in which the agent learns something about his motivation for loving others. My major claim is that this work of charity is not just a test of the agent's motivation, but also, and more importantly, a test of faith for the agent in question.

The first section is a brief introduction to Kierkegaard's test of love and a consideration of the viability of emulating this work of love. I shall argue that this particular work of love *is* indeed something to be emulated *if and only if* the right existential conditions obtain. The second section takes a closer look at the Hegelian analysis of mutual recognition and intersubjectivity.[1] After establishing that Hegel's many references to mutual recognition have a strong relation to his own analyses of love, the third section will explore the vital relation between mutual recognition and "phenomenality." Ultimately, I will claim that phenomenality is a necessary condition for acts of mutual recognition and that phenomenality is precisely what Kierkegaard abstracts in the relation to the one who is dead. In the final section, I will consider three different models of grieving and ask which of them fits best with Kierkegaard's suggestion that we have a duty to love the dead. Through this contrast, I hope to establish that the work of love in question does not function simply as a motivational test, but also as a test of faith.

Kierkegaard's Test of Love and Ferreira's Interpretive Advice

Kierkegaard's test of love places apparently charitable acts on trial in a way that illuminates an agent's reason(s) for action. Since works of charity can be improperly motivated, Kierkegaard is greatly concerned with stressing the importance of acting solely in response to the divine love commandment. He will ultimately claim that it is through such testing that we can rest assured that our loving acts are unselfish, free, and faithful (WL, 349, 351, 355/SKS 9, 343, 345, 348). The general structure of his test is captured by the following formulation:

> In order to test properly whether love is X, one can remove every possibility of Y. But Y is exactly what is removed in the relationship to one who is dead. If love still abides, then it is truly X (in the superlative).

X is a highly esteemed characteristic of the work of love, and Y is a corresponding motivation that can undermine X's purity. These variables are specified in three ways. *First, the possibility of repayment (Y_1) can undermine the unselfishness (X_1) of charity.* Such repayment can come in several forms, ranging from monetary compensation to a grateful glance from the recipient. *Secondly, the possibility of extortion (Y_2) can directly undermine charity's freedom (X_2).* As in his first example, this extortion may be literal or more widely understood. One can imagine a situation in which the material conditions of the recipient are the sole motivation for the work of love. Although such conditions are no doubt important for recognizing the neighbor, it seems conceivable that we find a neighbor who is not in a position of need. In this situation, love is still commanded of the agent. *Thirdly, the possibility of encouragement (Y_3) can infringe upon charity's faithfulness (X_3).* Once more, Kierkegaard stresses the importance of the motivation stemming from the agent and not from some external influence.

Kierkegaard's aforementioned concerns lead him to administer a motivational diagnostic of sorts. This test is remarkably similar in structure to Kant's search for the good will in the first section of the *Groundwork of the Metaphysics of Morals.*[2] Therein, Kant develops the examples of the sorrowful philanthropist and the cold, dutiful agent in order to shed light on human motivations.[3] In each of these examples, Kant stresses the importance of acting out of a sense of duty as opposed to inclination (even to the point of acting out of duty in the complete absence of sympathetic inclinations). Although Kierkegaard is concerned with locating the motivation for ethical action in the divine love commandment (instead of the law-like form of maxims as in Kant), he agrees that proper motivation should not be contingent. One of the reasons he prescribes this test is to show his reader the nature of commanded love so that she might direct this love to the living as well as to those who are dead.

Jamie Ferreira is correct in saying that Kierkegaard is not encouraging some morbid flight from concrete relationships with the living, making the relation to the dead individual into some sort of "fetish" or "obsession."[4] Nevertheless, one might doubt the accuracy of her remark that this chapter is merely instructional or heuristic.[5] My contention is that Kierkegaard's reader is well within her rights to ask whether this work of love has any practical import. According to Kierkegaard, the Christian has a duty to love both those who are visible to him and the dead. He writes, "The duty to love the people we see cannot cease because death separates them from us, because the duty is eternal; but accordingly neither can the duty to those who are dead separate the living from us in such a way that they do not become the objects of our love" (WL, 358/SKS 9, 351–52). Ferreira claims that when Kierkegaard's reader realizes this, she will also understand that Kierkegaard is not presenting the work of recollective love "as a model to be emulated."[6]

This remark can be understood in two ways: (1) Kierkegaard demands, as Theodor Adorno suggests, "that love behave toward all men as if they were dead."[7] If Adorno's reading is correct, we ought *not* emulate this work, and it seems that Ferreira agrees on this point. Although Ferreira is correct in her defense of Kierkegaard from this interpretation, a second reading should be considered. (2) If emulation merely means lovingly remembering the dead *if and only if a person actually encounters the death of another in his life*, this is not merely a model worthy of imitation but an eternal duty to the dead. There is no need to suggest that the living should be treated as if they were dead as in the first reading. Instead, the dead are to be treated as the dead, and the living as the living. The obligation to love all humans, living or dead, is one that should not be selfishly motivated. That said, let us now take a step back into the wider hermeneutical circle in which the text was written and consider Hegel's views on mutual recognition and love.

Self-consciousness, Recognition and Love in Hegel

Self-consciousness means many things in the *Phenomenology of Spirit*, but the clear distinction between animal consciousness and human consciousness is vitally important to Hegel's project. Animals and humans both stand in relation to sensuous objects. However, they relate to these objects differently in accordance with the desire characteristic of the species in question. Animals "do not just stand idly in front of sensuous things as if these possessed intrinsic being, but, despairing of their reality, and completely assured of their nothingness, they fall to without ceremony and eat them up" (*Phenomenology of Spirit* [hereafter PS], 65). Any being found in the natural order has a similar relation to objects of sense. Destruction of the other's (i.e., the sense object's) alterity is the task of animal self-consciousness. In this negation, "self-consciousness is thus certain of itself only by superseding this other that presents itself to self-consciousness as an independent life" (PS, 109).

Human desire, for Hegel, is fundamentally different from that of animals in that it can neither find satisfaction in the negation of external objects, nor certainty of itself in such "destructive," alterity-consuming acts. Instead, human "self-consciousness achieves its satisfaction only in another self-consciousness" (PS, 110). A very specific type of desire, one that is "directed toward another Desire," characterizes humans.[8] This relation is constitutive of what it means to be a human being. Human reality is the "'I' that is 'We' and 'We' that is 'I'" (PS, 110). Essentially, what we have here is a communitarian expression of what it means to be a self. A protracted discussion about Spirit in its many manifestations would take us too far afield in this chapter, especially since it is not certain whether any such discussion could be finished given Spirit's continual development. Nevertheless, it is noteworthy that the concept of recognition is introduced in tandem with the concept of Spirit.

According to Hegel, "[s]elf-consciousness exists in and for itself when, and by the fact that, it so exists for another; that is, it exists only in being acknowledged" (PS, 111). Another way of putting this is that the ultimate goal for humans is mutual recognition. Such recognition involves a "double movement" between two human beings in which "[e]ach sees the *other* do the same as it does; each does itself what it demands of the other, and therefore also does what it does only in so far as the other does the same. Action by one side only would be useless because what is to happen can only be brought about by both" (PS, 112).[9] Once more, we find a strong communitarian emphasis in Hegel's analysis; nevertheless, this relational dialectic begins with two independent self-consciousnesses. Initially, the two individuals "are for one another like ordinary objects, *independent* shapes, individuals submerged in the being [or immediacy] of *Life* . . . they have not as yet exposed themselves to each other in the form of pure being-for-self, or as self-consciousnesses" (PS, 113). The issue here is not each self-conscious individual's certainty of itself; rather, it pertains to its certainty of the other. Mutual recognition demands that "each is for the other what the other is for it" and it is only when this state of affairs obtains that each self-consciousness achieves "pure abstraction of being-for-self" (PS, 113). At this point, one might be tempted to ask: What is really at stake in this account of human intersubjectivity?

Hegel's description of mutual recognition is primarily a description of the transcendental conditions surrounding human freedom. Robert B. Pippin writes, "A *true individual* is a *free* subject and recognition relations function in a complex way as conditions for that possibility."[10] This freedom does not come easy since the agents in question undergo what Hegel refers to as a "trial by death" (PS, 114). Through this, each subject has "staked its life" and shown that it has "held it of no account" (PS, 114). Such risk transcends the merely animal drive for self-preservation. Again, the human being is quite different since:

> All human, anthropogenetic Desire—the Desire that generates Self-Consciousness, the human reality—is, finally, a function of the desire for "recognition." And the risk of life by which the human reality "comes to light" is a risk for the sake of such a Desire. Therefore, to speak of the "origin" of Self-Consciousness is necessarily to speak of a fight to the death for "recognition."[11]

But how does this discussion of mutual recognition have anything to do with love? Is there any justification for the application of this Hegelian notion to Kierkegaard's discussion of love?

One might worry that the foregoing analysis does not take political considerations into account. Such considerations have more relevance to how Hegel has been interpreted (by Marx, for instance) than to the actual context of *Phenomenology*'s development. Although such concerns are important, they are based upon a specific reading of Hegel's philosophy of recognition, one that is not particularly relevant to the present task. Merold Westphal provides an alternative understanding of recognition, one in which love is found playing a vital role in its original context and development.[12] The evidence for this view is found in fragments of Hegelian writings from the Frankfurt period that can be read in the English volume titled *Early Theological Writings*. In this early period, Hegel refers to love as "a reciprocal giving and taking" in which "the lover who takes is not thereby made richer than the other. He is enriched indeed, but only so much as the other is. So too the giver does not make himself poorer. By giving to the other he has to the same extent enhanced his own treasure."[13]

Hegel should not be understood to be suggesting an instrumentalist view in which one recognizes another in order to acquire the benefits of recognition. Instead, Hegel's work is a phenomenology, or descriptive analysis, of the conditions giving rise to human self-consciousness. Whereas one could claim that, in *Works of Love*, Kierkegaard is attempting to undermine Hegel's notion of mutual recognition through an instrumentalist reading, one could also make a good case that Kierkegaard assumes the truth of Hegel's account. Although one could argue that agape love is a repudiation of such an instrumental relation to the other, this would be incorrect because the mutuality of recognition already overcomes the immediacy of animal desire. Westphal provides a particularly helpful commentary on the movement from animal to human desire:

> The inherently destructive nature of domination for the one who dominates is already before us. In such a project the other is reduced to the object of animal desire. He has no meaning other than the satisfaction of my desires and it is I who will bring about that satisfaction. The unsatisfactory nature of this kind of satisfaction is what moves the dialectic from animal desire to the doubling of Self-Consciousness. This move requires the qualitative transcendence of desire and domination, for at this new level satisfaction is something that can be given but not taken. Even at the purely human level *eros* must give way to *agape*.[14]

If this is true, perhaps Kierkegaard is not dethroning one model of love and replacing it with another. Perhaps he, to a large extent, agrees with Hegel and merely wants to recontextualize the notion of mutual recognition within the experience of the loss of another. Just as animal desire is *aufgehoben* in human desire, human desire may be *aufgehoben* in an even greater context. In this, human desire is transfigured. Although the relation between the living and the dead is not mutual (at least in any verifiable sense of the word), it is possible to imagine the living subject looking forward to a time when conditions are such that the relation can be mutual once again. Before considering this possibility in detail, let us first examine the relation between recognition and phenomenality.

The Connection Between Recognition and Phenomenality

The important claim of this section is that phenomenality is a necessary condition for mutual recognition. Let us say it plainly: A human being cannot know that another recognizes her unless that other appears to her in some manner. In other words, this person must be present in order for the fullness of the recognition relation to be achieved. Now that we know *what* the claim is, it is fitting to show *how* we arrived at this conclusion. After an elucidation of an important implication of Kierkegaard's usage of "non-actual," two principal objections will be considered. Let us first provide our justification for the initial claim that recognition and phenomenality are intimately connected.

Kierkegaard claims on a few separate occasions that the dead person "is no actuality," a nonbeing (e.g. WL, 358/SKS 9, 351). In order to move forward in this discussion, one must make sense of what exactly Kierkegaard means when he talks this way about the dead. Is he saying that the dead person does not exist in any manner whatsoever, or is he perhaps suggesting that she or he is no longer present to us? It will be helpful to consider what is meant by "actual" or "nonbeing" first; then, we can come back and consider what is meant about the dead.

In an earlier chapter of *Works of Love,* Kierkegaard avers that the object of love is the one whom the agent sees (WL, 154–74/SKS 9, 155–74). This assertion conveys the duty to love those who are present to us in some way. Much is said in this chapter of the text, but there is a direct connection with the concept of *actuality.* Kierkegaard emphasizes the importance of "loving the actual individual person" and not substituting "*an imaginary idea of how we think or could wish that this person should be*" (WL, 164/SKS 9, 164). He stresses the importance of respecting the other's alterity and not viewing him as different from what he is in actuality. This is what Christian love does; it loves "the same person in all his changes, because it sees the same person in all the changes" (WL, 173/SKS 9, 173).

Sight, then, enables the lover to discover the object of love. Nevertheless, one might ask the following question: Is it *only* through sight that this occurs or can one become aware of the object by other means?[15] There is nothing at stake in an expansion from ocular imagery to sense experience in general. This is the claim on offer: *Kierkegaard promotes a duty to love the people who are present to us, in whatever manner they are presented.* This is (at least part of) what it means to be "actual" or to "be a being" in the intersubjective human context. As such, the duty to love the visible neighbor implies the broader duty to love the people who appear to us, i.e., the phenomenal other. This implies that any phenomenal object that humans encounter is known through the senses and immediate experience rather than through thought or intuition. From this, it can be concluded that "loving the one we see" involves loving a sensate being and not merely an object of thought. Such beings may exhaust our representational capacities (as in Emmanuel Levinas's work), but they are still phenomenally present in some manner.[16] This notion of phenomenality is closely connected to embodiment because if humans are not embodied, they are not candidates for intersubjective relations (at least intersubjective relations that are subject to some sort of verification by both parties). What would such verifiable relations between two disembodied subjects look like? Surely, such relations would involve something quite beyond what is normally meant by "intersubjective."[17]

Let us now consider what it means to be nonactual, or "no actual object" (WL, 347/SKS 9, 341). By applying this notion of phenomenality to the discussion about the dead, we may conclude that the dead are not phenomenally present to humans in the manner of the living. In other words, when this terminology is invoked it should be understood to mean something more like *a non-being within human experience,* or *not actual within human experience,* or better, *not an actual object of human experience.*[18] Justification for this claim is found in a passage in which Kierkegaard contrasts recollection with the actuality of one's environment, an environment that gives sense impressions to the individual:

> But in the relation to the dead, everything becomes clear. Here there is nothing, nothing compelling at all. On the other hand, the loving recollection of the dead has to protect itself against the actuality around one, lest

through ever-new impressions it acquire full power to wipe out the recollection (WL, 354/SKS 9, 347).

It does, in fact, seem that actuality is the origin of sense-impressions, and this is all that is needed to establish the claim that Kierkegaard's use of "actuality" implies "phenomenality." Let us grant then: (1) Phenomenality is a condition for the possibility of all acts of mutual recognition; (2) Since the dead are not embodied, they do not appear to us. Let us consider the aforementioned objections before proceeding to the final section of the chapter.

Objection 1: The dead do appear to us. The foregoing analysis assumes that there is something philosophically important about the claim that the dead are not phenomenal. Since this claim assumes that no dead individuals appear to the living, one might wish to simply claim that the dead do, in fact, appear to us. Such a view might be found among the practitioners of tribal religion—those once described by the antiquated label of "animist." In his monograph *The Dominion of the Dead,* Robert Pogue Harrison sets forth a vision of what he calls a "secular afterlife," one in which the dead inhabit "graves, homes, laws, words, images, dreams, rituals, monuments, and the archives of literature, whose voices always have a posthumous character of sorts."[19] His examination also involves a discussion of the responsibilities to the corpses of those who have died. He writes,

> Ritual disposal serves to detach the image from the corpse and thereby free the image for its repersonifications and reverbalizations in various culturally determined guises. To transform natural death into human death means in effect to give birth to the dead in their afterlife . . . For dying in the full human sense is a kind of birth, while the afterlife—understood phenomenologically and not necessarily religiously or doctrinally—is the new and altered condition the dead are born into (as souls, images, voices, masks, heroes, ancestors, founders, and the like). Eventually this afterlife will itself expire, at which point human dying gives way to the remorseless oblivion of natural death. Yet as long as the living "care" for the dead, the place of that persistence remains open.[20]

On this view, corpses are put underground, and then the dead person is imagined as being *in* various objects or people in accordance with the dominant cultural traditions. Although this is very interesting and perhaps even aesthetically pleasing, this altered condition of the dead as embodied in various objects is nothing more than some sort of imaginative projection by those who survive the dead. When these dead individuals were living they were present in a very specific manner: they were embodied *in their bodies.* Is it not easier to simply say that the dead no longer appear to us, or that they appear to us only as an absence in our consciousness that is only partially fulfilled through episodic memory or dreams? Clearly, such imaginative projection can serve a practical purpose; in fact, it might be one particular way of coping with grief. Nevertheless, such a view ignores the absence that death brings, which is perhaps one of the more central matters of this study.

Objection 2: Phenomenal humans sometimes fail to recognize others. It has been argued that if the other is not phenomenal, we are incapable of entering into mutual relations of recognition. Is it not true that there are humans who appear to others yet nevertheless fail to reciprocate recognition? Although there are several examples, one from contemporary medicine should suffice in our attempt to defend this connection between phenomenality and recognition. Pick's Disease, or what is now called Frontotemporal dementia (FTD) is the condition that, several years ago, led to the death of one of my own loved ones. *The National Institute of Neurological Disorders and Strokes,* which is a division of the *National Institutes of Health,* provides some introductory information about the disease. "FTD describes a clinical syndrome associated with shrinking of the frontal and temporal anterior lobes of the brain . . . The symptoms of FTD fall into two clinical patterns that involve either (1) changes in behavior, or (2) problems with language."[21] My relative's symptoms were primarily behavior changing, although there were also issues with language, e.g. saying "no" when she meant "yes" and "yes" when she meant "no." The most obvious symptoms of the disease involved "inappropriate social behavior; lack of social tact; lack of empathy; distractability; loss of insight into the behaviors of [herself] and others."[22] It is common for extended family members to feel alienated in such a situation, especially if they are uninformed about the condition. As this disease progresses, the sufferer is often unable to speak and does not have the capacity to regard loved ones in the regular manner. In some instances, it appears as if recognition relations break down altogether.

The objection states that such people do in fact appear to others, yet they do not reciprocate recognition. Does this example not suggest that the earlier analysis is flawed? The short answer is "no," but the long answer should help clarify this account of the relationship between phenomenality and recognition. Phenomenality is a *necessary* but *not sufficient* condition for relations of mutual recognition. In other words, if there is some sort of acknowledgment involved in the relation, one person, at the very least, must appear to another in a way in which some sort of sensory cognition is at work.[23] The model presented here does not suggest that phenomenality necessitates mutual recognition; rather, the model claims that phenomenality is a condition for its possibility. Let us now take a closer look at the work of love in recollecting the dead and ask whether it is an act of wish, resignation, or faith.

Is Recollecting the Dead an Act of Wish, Resignation, or Faith?

Since the death of a loved one is an experience common to all human beings, one does not have to look very far in one's mind for an object of remembrance.[24] Nevertheless, the question still remains: How should humans respond to the death of another? How should the dead be remembered? Does this dutiful act resemble the action of Kant's sorrowful philanthropist? Or does recollective love look forward to an event that can only be explained "by virtue of the absurd?" Perhaps we can project our desire for reciprocity of recognition into a transcendent other? Each answer to these questions has consequences for the agent engaged in remembering. In particular, the way we remember the dead is an indicator of how we respect their alterity.

Respect for the alterity of persons is one of Kierkegaard's major concerns in *Works of Love,* and this concern is also operative in his discussion of the work of love in remembering the dead. He is clear that the dead are nonentities that, as I have argued, are beyond the range of human experience. Given this, it seems that we are well positioned to look at Kierkegaard's model of dead remembrance in comparison with a more common way of remembering the dead, one that can only be called wishful thinking. In this final section, I will examine three types of grieving: wish, resignation, and faith. I shall argue that wish is a particularly weak position that falls prey to Hegel's critique of the "Unhappy Consciousness." After this, the distinction between resignation and faith from *Fear and Trembling* will be applied in order to discover the nature of Kierkegaard's work of recollective love.

The Wish Model of grieving. The Wish Model is one in which the survivor of the dead projects recognition into a transcendent object. This is a common occurrence in everyday life. One often hears remarks like the following: "I know he looks down from heaven and sees me." In such remarks, the grieving individual posits the dead as an actuality, yet one that lies outside of the scope of any recognizable experience. Even though the one dead is primarily an object of the griever's thought, he believes that the dead are capable of completing the circle of reciprocity. Although one cannot know that mutual recognition relations obtain between the two individuals, such relations are posited as a reality.

This view, although common, is problematic for many reasons. Hegel draws attention to one such difficulty—the "Unhappy Consciousness." Any model that posits the dead as a transcendent, self-subsistent entity of its own (thus falling outside of the scope of human experience and concrete recognition relations) is a manifestation of this form of consciousness. Charles Taylor understands this relationship as one in which humans "strive to unite with a transcendent reality."[25] Of course, this reality is generally understood to refer to a transcendent God, but there is warrant for an application to dead individuals. Support for this application is found in Hegel's discussion of the burial rituals of the family, particularly the "religion of the underworld" (PS, 322, 410).

> Blood-relationship supplements, then, the abstract natural process by adding to it the movement of consciousness, interrupting the work of Nature and rescuing the blood-relation from destruction; or better, because destruction is necessary, the passage of the blood-relation into mere being, it takes on itself the act of destruction. Through this it comes about that the *dead*, the universal *being*, becomes a being that has returned into itself, a being-for-self, or, the powerless, simply isolated individual has been raised to universal individuality (PS, 271).

Such rituals serve as the "last duty" in the fulfillment of the divine law and the "positive *ethical* action towards the individual" (PS, 271). Although Hegel's story is long and complicated, his reader finds that the dead "draws . . . back into the essence which is its ground" (PS, 272). This aversion to any discussion of the dead as concrete individuals stems from his issues with the notion of personal immortality. The problem with such immortality is that it "presupposes that an individual is sufficiently distinct from its social context."[26] One should remember that, according to Hegel, Spirit is the "'I' that is 'We' and 'We' that is 'I'" (PS, 110), not the 'I' that is 'I.'

Personal immortality is also incompatible with Hegel's historicism. "A person is too deeply embedded in and moulded by his historical situation to be reincarnated into a different historical situation or to persist outside history in a community of pure spirits."[27] It seems that we cannot posit any substantial relation to the dead because they are no longer actual in any meaningful sense of the word. Both Kierkegaard and Hegel, if asked, would have concerns about the Wish Model of grieving. In positing a recognition relation to a nonentity, the agent reduces the dead other to an object of his thought. This remaking of the dead may have a therapeutic effect, but it involves self-deception about the absence caused by his perishing. By positing a fully functional recognition relationship to the dead, the wishfully thinking subject refuses to grant the difference that death has introduced into the relationship. Insofar as this is the case, wishful thinking is at least partially motivated by a desire to keep oneself safe from the experience of genuine loss.

The Resignation Model of grieving. The motivation to protect oneself from pain and loss is something that is found in the Resignation Model of grieving as well. The most sustained discussion of the concept of infinite resignation is found in *Fear and Trembling.* The familiar story about the lad and his beloved princess is particularly helpful in conveying the meaning of this concept. Even though the lad's love for the princess has become the "substance of his life" (FT, 42/SKS 4, 136), he cannot have her. In light of this unfortunate reality, he cannot simply renounce this love in a manner akin to stoic renunciation of desire. Infinite resignation demands more of him. Even though "the princess is lost" (FT, 44/SKS 4, 138), his love continues as directed toward the eternal power. There are some noteworthy consequences of this movement. Although this knight has found "peace and rest" and "protection better than iron or steel" (FT, 45/SKS 4, 140), he has lost his interest in the world of earthy affairs. Unlike Abraham, the exemplar of faith, this knight has no inkling that he will ever receive the things that he desires. Ed Mooney's analysis of resignation is particularly helpful on this point:

> In renouncing the princess, the knight discovers (or generates) a new perspective. His life is no longer focused by concern for a finite individual. His standpoint is now *outside* the flux of petty, worldly things. . . . By withdrawing care, the self shields itself from injury or affliction. By renouncing the finite, one defeats its power to provoke passionate, painful reaction. But unlike the stoic who *extirpates* his love or attachment to the world, the knight of resignation *transforms* it. His "object of worship," his grounding and orienting absolute, is now "the eternal being."[28]

Is recollective love, then, an act of such renunciation of the finite world? At first glance, it may be appealing to claim that this work of love is one of resignation. In particular, such a view fits with certain readings of *Works of Love* that downplay the importance of preferential relations to the equality found in neighbor love.[29] The singular difficulty with this interpretation is that God is found as the "middle term" in the love that obtains between finite human beings (WL, 107/SKS 9, 111). A further difficulty arises when considering a concrete example of such resigned grieving.

Resignation seems to commit us to grieving for the dead individual before he is dead. In other words, infinite resignation places us in a situation in which we must treat the living as if he were dead (as Adorno suggests). If this were the case, recognition relations would be broken when they should not be. In this way, the agent protects himself from the finitude of the dying other by renouncing the finite altogether. Although the knight now has an eternal consciousness and is in a relation to the eternal being, he rises above the concrete relation in which any sort of real loving can occur. Furthermore, this renunciation of the finite involves the renunciation of other finite beings. Since the temporal world includes living beings that qualify as objects of commanded love, resignation (insofar as it abandons care for the finite world) does not properly describe this act in its true form.

The Faith Model of grieving. Although the lad gains an eternal consciousness, he has missed a very important lesson: The "knight of faith can both renounce and enjoy the finite. He sees or knows in his bones that renouncing all *claims* on the finite is not renouncing all *care* for it."[30] While the desire to renounce the finite world at a time when one is about to lose a loved one is understandable, it ultimately falls short of what remembrance of the dead requires. Since the finite world contains the neighbor, there must be a way in which care for it is maintained. Similarly, care for the finite dead should not be completely abandoned. It has been argued that the Wish Model prevents the subject from truly experiencing the other's death. The Resignation Model is similar because it shields itself from the death of the other through a shift in emphasis from the finite to the infinite. The Faith Model of grieving is the best description of recollective love because it ultimately does not shield itself from the death of the other and it explains how this work of love might be fulfilled in time.

Infinite resignation is described as "the last stage before faith" (FT, 46/SKS 4, 140). Furthermore, "anyone who has not made this movement does not have faith" (FT, 46/SKS 4, 140). If this is true, the Resignation Model of grieving may be right about something. It seems that giving up our claims upon the dying other is something that fits with a work of love.[31] But does this releasing of the loved one from our claims suggest that we no longer care for this person (both when he is still living and after he has taken his last breath)? The answer is no. Kierkegaard teaches his reader to maintain our care for this individual even after his death, to "weep softly, but weep long" (WL, 348/SKS 9, 342). He even goes so far as to say, "We ought not to disturb the dead by wailing and crying. We ought to treat one who is dead as we treat one who is sleeping, whom we do not have the heart to awaken because we hope that he will wake up by himself" (WL, 348/SKS 9, 341–42).

Wake up? How might this awakening occur? Clearly, this cannot be accomplished through human agency. The dead do not awake because they are remembered. This would make faith into a type of "magic wand" that one waves in order to acquire things outside of one's own agency. Contrary to this view, faith involves a certain attitude toward divine agency, one characterized by "trust in an eschatological promise whose fulfillment will be an *ethical eucatastrophe.*"[32] In other words, faith is trusting that all that is not within the scope of one's agency will be made right in the end by the only agent capable of such things, i.e., God. But again, this does not mean that faith is reducible to its perceived instrumental value. Mooney puts it nicely in the following passage:

> The knight of faith works to get the princess back, then, only in the sense that he guarantees that the ultimate obstacle to her return—lack of receptivity—will be absent. He does not by his *own* strength *effect* her return, but provides the required *condition:* He is ready in welcome. He does not believe that he can get around the impossible. But neither does he believe that what is impossible for him is impossible for God.[33]

I submit that the possibility of reinstating recognition relations follows this same progression. Although they are severed at the time of the other's death (when the dead one no longer appears to us), it is possible, by virtue of the absurd, for God to reinstate such relations.[34] This will involve the "waking" that Kierkegaard describes in *Works of Love,* which bears a remarkable similarity to the comments of St. Paul in 1 Corinthians 15:18. In this letter, the apostle refers to those who have "fallen asleep in Christ" during his discussion of the bodily resurrection.[35] This waking is believed to occur because of divine agency. Such an eschatological view demands that the fulfillment must occur in time and not in an amorphous eternity.[36] Since this is the case, recognition relations can be reinstated in a way that satisfies even Hegel's conditions for human intersubjectivity.

The work of love in recollecting the dead is not one in which one thinks that the dead other looks down from heaven and returns his glance. Neither is it one that refuses to look at the dying other because the agent's love has been transfigured into love for God. Instead, this work of love is one that looks forward to seeing the dead wake up by virtue of a power that is beyond all human capability. Although the consciousness of the grieving individual reaches out seeking an object, this search is unfulfilled. In light of this, the agent turns to what he can remember of the dead. Through such memorial acts, one *is* conscious of the individual *as remembered.*[37] Loving recollection of the dead plays a constant role in the life of the one grieving, and through this experience, the agent learns much about how to love the living. Nevertheless, the work of love in recollecting the dead is not simply about instruction. It also, and most importantly, involves the cultivation of the attitude of faith, faith that the dead might one day be present again in such a way that mutuality is once more possible.[38]

NOTES

The first epigraph is from Sophocles, "Antigone," in *The Theban Plays,* trans. E. F. Watling (London: Penguin Books, 1947), p. 128.

The second epigraph is from Barbara Aland, Kurt Aland, Johannes Karavidopoulos, Carlo M. Martini, and Bruce M. Metzger, eds., *The Greek New Testament* USB 4 (Stuttgart: Deutsche Bibelgesellschaft, 1998), p. 27; my translation.

1. G. W. F. Hegel, *Phenomenology of Spirit,* trans. A. V. Miller (Oxford: Oxford University Press, 1977) (hereafter PS).

2. Cf. Immanuel Kant, *Groundwork of the Metaphysics of Morals,* trans. Mary Gregor (Cambridge: Cambridge University Press, 1997). Of course, this is not to suggest that Kierkegaard and Kant are in agreement about practical rationality. In particular, Kierkegaard's reliance upon the divine command would be greatly frowned upon by Kant as heteronymous and derived from a hypothetical imperative. Nevertheless, both Kant and Kierkegaard share a similar concern about how selfishness in motivation should be avoided.

3. Kant, *Groundwork of the Metaphysics of Morals,* pp. 11–12.

4. M. Jamie Ferreira, *Love's Grateful Striving* (Oxford: Oxford University Press, 2001), p. 212.

5. Ferreira, *Love's Grateful Striving,* p. 212.

6. Ferreira, *Love's Grateful Striving,* p. 213. In other words, Kierkegaard is not presenting this particular work of love in a way that has any practical import in addition to what one can learn from it as a thought experiment. It does not have direct relevance to the realm of action.

7. Theodore W. Adorno, "On Kierkegaard's Doctrine of Love," *Studies in Philosophy and Social Science* 8 (1939–40): pp. 416–17.

8. Alexandre Kojève, *Introduction to the Reading of Hegel,* trans. James H. Nichols, Jr. (Ithaca, N.Y.: Cornell University Press, 1980), p. 4.

9. Hegel explicates this even more by saying, "Each is for the other the middle term, through which each mediates itself with itself and unites with itself; and each is for itself, and for the other, an immediate being on its own account, which at the same time is such only through this mediation. They *recognize* themselves as *mutually recognizing* one another" (PS, 112). Although, time and space constraints do not allow it, an analysis of the notion of "middle term" in Hegel's *Phenomenology of Spirit* and Kierkegaard's *Works of Love* may yield fruitful results.

10. Robert B. Pippin, "What Is the Question for which Hegel's Theory of Recognition is the Answer?" *European Journal of Philosophy* 8, no. 2 (2000): p. 156.

11. Kojève, *Introduction to the Reading of Hegel*, p. 7.

12. Cf. Merold Westphal, *History & Truth in Hegel's* Phenomenology, 3rd ed. (Bloomington: Indiana University Press, 1998), pp. 130–38.

13. G. W. F. Hegel, *Early Theological Writings*, trans. T. M. Knox, "Introduction and Fragments," trans. Richard Kroner (Chicago: University of Chicago Press, 1975), p. 307.

14. Westphal, *History & Truth in Hegel's* Phenomenology, p. 128.

15. It is easy to forgive Kierkegaard's fascination with ocular imagery, as it is something that has plagued much of the Western tradition of philosophy.

16. Cf. Emmanuel Levinas, *Totality and Infinity*, trans. Alphonso Lingis (Pittsburgh: Duquesne University Press, 1969); and *Otherwise than Being or Beyond Essence*, trans. Alphonso Lingis (Pittsburgh: Duquesne University Press, 1981).

17. One may object to this line of reasoning and say that surely the dead are still bodies. In order to address this objection, it is necessary to invoke the distinction between being a physical object and *being embodied*. The latter is what is involved in the presentation of oneself to another in the way that matters for recognition. Physicality is clearly involved in what Hegel calls animal desire, but human desire for recognition requires both a *physical and responsive subject*. This fact does not mean that, for instance, a patient in a persistent vegetative state is unlovable; rather, this patient is simply incapable of entering into concrete recognition relations.

18. If this is the case, then we need not make a further claim on the status of the dead. They may or may not be existent (in some sort of intermediary afterlife). Such a bodiless afterlife would be outside of human understanding and may look something like pure intellect and will. Of course, the doctrine of bodily resurrection may speak to this point, but this resurrection clearly does not occur when we lay our dead to rest. A traditional concern with this doctrine pertains to the need for there to be numerical identity between the body we lay to rest and the resurrected body. The fact that the bodies of our dead are either cremated or lie within their graves implies that this resurrection has not yet occurred. If it had, these bodies would be animated.

19. Robert Pogue Harrison, *The Dominion of the Dead* (Chicago: University of Chicago Press, 2003), p. x.

20. Harrison, *The Dominion of the Dead*, p. 154.

21. National Institute of Neurological Disorders and Stroke, NDS, Frontotemporal Dementia Information Page, http://www.ninds.nih.gov/disorders/picks/picks.htm.

22. National Institute of Neurological Disorders and Stroke, NDS, Frontotemporal Dementia Information Page.

23. One might argue that people recognize others every day by responding to personal correspondence or e-mails, but even these can be traced back to the one who produces such "works"; similarly, the individual receiving such inscriptions must receive them in a manner dependent upon sense experience, i.e. hearing, seeing words on a page or screen, etc. One cannot read (or hear) correspondence that does not appear to them in some manner.

24. The nature of the premortem relationship to the dead is well worth considering although it exceeds the scope of this chapter. One question we can ask pertains to what sort of people we have a duty to remember. Consistency demands that we recollect "the neighbor." This means that the griever is just as likely to recollect a random casualty on the freeway as he is his own father. Kierkegaard is ambiguous about whether the dead person (while still living) is actually an object of preferential love or "the neighbor," or perhaps both. Although this work of love can, I think, test the purity of supposed works of agape love, it is perhaps best suited for those with whom we have some preferred relation, i.e., parents, siblings, spouse, friends, etc. (who are, of course, still first and foremost the neighbor for Kierkegaard).

25. Charles Taylor, *Hegel* (Cambridge: Cambridge University Press, 1975), p. 160.

26. Michael A. Inwood, *A Hegel Dictionary* (Oxford: Blackwell Publishers, 1992), p. 74.

27. Inwood, *A Hegel Dictionary*, p. 74.

28. Edward F. Mooney, *Knights of Faith and Resignation: Reading Kierkegaard's* Fear and Trembling (Albany: State University of New York Press, 1991), p. 48. Cf. FT, 43–44/SKS 4, 135–37.

29. For one such treatment of Kierkegaard's critique of preferential love, see Paul J. Wadell, *Friendship and the Moral Life* (Notre Dame, Ind.: University of Notre Dame Press, 1989), pp. 74–84. For a developed defense of preferential love relations that are understood in light of agape love, see Ferreira's discussion of "Hidden Inwardness and Special Relations," in *Love's Grateful Striving*, pp. 89–93; and the entirety of Amy Laura Hall, *Kierkegaard and the Treachery of Love* (Cambridge: Cambridge University Press, 2002).

30. Mooney, *Knights of Faith and Resignation*, p. 54.

31. Mooney, *Knights of Faith and Resignation*, pp. 53–54.

32. John J. Davenport, "Faith as Eschatological Trust in *Fear and Trembling*," in *Ethics, Love, and Faith in Kierkegaard*, ed. Edward F. Mooney, p. 205 (Bloomington: Indiana University Press, 2008).

33. Mooney, *Knights of Faith and Resignation*, pp. 54–55.

34. Although this expression has been taken to support irrationalist readings of Kierkegaard (such as that in Bland Blanshard, "Kierkegaard on Faith," *Personalist* 49 [1968]: pp. 5–23; and *Reason and Belief* [New Haven, Conn.: Yale University Press, 1974]), it should be taken to mean nothing more and nothing less than what Johannes de silentio says of the Knight of Faith in *Fear and Trembling*: "Nevertheless I have faith that I will get her—that is, by virtue of the absurd, by virtue of the fact that for God all things are possible" (FT, 46/SKS 4, 141). The current application of this expression to the doctrine of bodily resurrection is in continuity with traditional understandings of the doctrine. One such understanding is that of St. Thomas Aquinas, who emphasizes that although the Resurrection is not a conclusion to a philosophical argument, it is certainly possible through the divine agency (*Summa Theologiae* Ia. 76. I ad. 6). For a helpful discussion of Aquinas's views on this subject, see Brian Davies, *The Thought of Thomas Aquinas* (Oxford: Oxford University Press, 1992), pp. 215–20.

35. I thank the editors for pointing out Kierkegaard's apparent distaste for the language of sleep in his discourse "At a Graveside." In particular, any time the employment of this language lightens the weight of the reality of one's death, the individual in question is in danger of evading the earnestness promoted in the dialogue. Of course, this does not mean that one misunderstands death if he understands it as a sleep. It is problematic only if he views death as a sleep to be sought as one seeks sleep to rest from the weariness of daily living (TDIO, 80/SKS 5, 451). Clearly, this criticism is warranted within the context of its expression; nevertheless, Kierkegaard claims, "admittedly death is a sleep" (TDIO, 81/SKS 5, 451). This may give us room to understand why he suggests that we treat the dead as if they are sleeping in *Works of Love*. One possible way to reconcile this difference is by understanding the claims in "At a Graveside" as primarily focused upon one's own death, whereas *Works of Love* is focused upon the death of the other.

36. John Davenport provides us with a helpful explanation for why this is necessary in "Faith as Eschatological Trust in *Fear and Trembling*," p. 203: "For the knight of resignation by himself, marrying the princess remains accessible only in the 'infinite' or atemporal senses of being logically possible and ethically necessary or ideal. Resignation stops with this *ersatz* state of affairs in the eternal realm, whereas the knight of faith embraces an *additional* kind of possibility, namely, that marrying the princess could *actually be accomplished* in future time through the unconjurable creative power of God."

37. It should be clear at this point that there is a divergent understanding of phenomenality assumed in this chapter as opposed to the following chapter of this book. In particular, my own concern for the alterity of the dead does not permit me to understand the memorial act as related to a phenomenal object. Rather, the memorial object is strictly a representation of an object that once appeared in

a manner subject to the intersubjective assessment of others. Although it contains phenomenality within its concept, as do all thoughts of human beings, this being is not actually present; rather, he is present only as an absence, the fulfillment of which would amount to his reappearance in the physical world.

38. This chapter is dedicated to my maternal grandfather in whom it originally found its inspiration: Aubrey Lee Decker (April 19, 1912–January 19, 2005).

14.

Duties to the Dead? Earnest Imagination and Remembrance

Patrick Stokes

Loving the Dead

Perhaps nothing in Kierkegaard's writings has proven quite as polarizing as *Works of Love.* The reception of this work has been characterized by perennial charges that it articulates an inhuman, acosmic, inward-looking vision of ethical life. These criticisms famously begin with Adorno, who claims that Kierkegaard's concern to avoid "preferential" love in all forms leads to an "object-less" love in which the other is reduced to a mere "stumbling block."[1] The result is an ethic whose "content is oppression: the oppression of the drive which is not to be fulfilled and the oppression of the mind which is not allowed to question."[2] "Never before," declares K. E. Løgstrup, "has the ethical so shut itself in and shut the entire world out as it has in Kierkegaard."[3]

Critics have particularly latched onto Kierkegaard's assertion, in the penultimate chapter of *Works of Love* (Second Series, chapter IX), that the work of love in recollecting one who is dead is a work of the most *unselfish, freest,* and *faithful* love, and therefore embodies a standard against which our love of the living can be judged:

> In the relationship to one who is dead, you have the criterion by which you can test yourself. The one who uses this criterion will easily be able to shorten the extensiveness of the most prolix relationship, and he will learn to loathe the whole mass of excuses that actuality usually has promptly at hand to explain that it is the other one who is selfish, the other one who is to blame for his being forgotten because he does not call attention to himself, the other one who is faithless (WL, 358/SKS 9, 351).

By positing how we love the dead as our criterion for love, Kierkegaard claims, as Paul Müller puts it, that if one wishes to judge whether he truly loves and what the implications of that love are, "he does not need his living contemporaries. To the contrary, his relationship to someone dead provides a more accurate measuring rod."[4] By offering the work of love in recollecting one who is dead as "a criterion for how love should be"[5] Kierkegaard has, according to critics like Adorno and Peter George, articulated a fundamentally *anti*-social view of human relationships, while D. Z. Phillips complains that Kierkegaard's picture of neighbor love "has little to say to those whose loved ones are lost. Kierkegaard's love of replaceable neighbors cannot inform loves that blossom."[6] Whilst Adorno finds both the best and the worst of Kierkegaard's philosophy in the claim made in chapter IX,[7] he ultimately sees it as a précis of the object-less, nonreciprocal character of the love Kierkegaard commends: "he demands that love behave towards all men as if they were dead."[8] The very longevity of such criticisms speaks to their *prima facie* plausibility: what can we make of an account of love that sees love's purest, best form as one that involves no actual persons other than the lover? By seemingly privileging a love devoid of reciprocity—indeed of any human exchange or interaction at all—as paradigmatic, Kierkegaardian love appears detached, inhuman, and ultimately solipsistic.

Defenders of *Works of Love* also tend to emphasize recollection's status as a criterion or test case for other works of love, but staunchly—and I think correctly—deny that Kierkegaard thereby endorses a love devoid of reciprocity or responsiveness in our treatment of the living. Commentators such as M. Jamie Ferreira, Pia Søltoft, and Louise Carol Keeley stress that the paradigmatic status of remembrance of the dead derives not from the absence of its object, but from the fact that the specific circumstances of loving a permanently absent other brings to salience crucial features of how we should love the *living* and *present*. These defenses, to which I can't do full justice here, seem to dispose quite effectively of the charges that Kierkegaard wants us to treat the living the same way we treat the dead and that positing recollection of the dead as an exemplary work of love rules out any sort of responsiveness and reciprocation in fully actualized human relationships. Indeed, according to Ferreira, "the claim that the dead one is not an actual being precludes any recommendation that we treat an actual living person in the same way as we treat one who is dead."[9] She follows this up with an intriguing ontological claim: "it is precisely because the dead one cannot respond that he or she is excluded from the category of 'actual' beings; this means that responsiveness is a necessary characteristic of our relationships with 'actual' human beings."[10] Despite

Kierkegaard's praise of the work of remembering the dead, *Works of Love* nonetheless clearly leaves room for reciprocity and responsiveness in our loving interactions with the living.

Yet in this exchange between critics and defenders of *Works of Love,* something significant has been lost sight of. In choosing as their battleground the implications of the criterion-status of recollection of the dead for *other* works of love, both sides have tended to efface the fact that, for Kierkegaard, the work of love in recollecting the dead is also *itself* a work of love. Kierkegaard is endorsing a concrete practice, not merely furnishing a particularly instructive thought experiment. However valuable the example of loving the dead is for calibrating our assessments of other works of love, it is nonetheless also to be valued as a work of love in *itself.* On the critical side, Adorno claims that Kierkegaard "never goes into any real, non-symbolical, non-metaphorical case of human love in order to apply his doctrine to it," and "[h]is failure to reach [actual] practice by his concepts, and the unyielding abstractness of his doctrine, are symptoms that it is not quite as substantial as it pretends to be."[11] Adorno here implicitly dismisses the possibility that recollection of the dead could, in fact, be a "real, non-symbolical, non-metaphorical" act of love. This may be in keeping with his concern to trace the concrete social implications of the text, but it closes off both important elements of Kierkegaard's discussion of this practice, and significant questions that Kierkegaard will have to answer if his claims are to be viable.

Among the defenders, Ferreira acknowledges the reality of the practice Kierkegaard is endorsing insofar as she claims Kierkegaard tries to prevent recollection of the dead from degenerating into fetishized or obsessive forms that might distract our attention from our duties to the living.[12] Yet she also claims that Kierkegaard highlights this "extreme" instance of unselfish, faithful, and free love "for instructional purposes, rather than to present it as a model to be emulated."[13] Ferreira's heuristic interpretation of this work of love stops just short of reducing loving the dead to a mere metaphor for proper love of the living, while Keeley locates the value of recollecting the dead precisely in the indirect, metaphorical character of this specific work of love—for its *real* object, she says, must be the living:

> Besides, if the one dead is "no one," who is benefitted or affected by this work of love? . . . to the degree that it is a work of love it must transform. But who is transformed? Since the "no one" of death cannot be, it must be the case that the one who performs the work is changed as are the living beneficiaries of one's practice.[14]

Pia Søltoft goes even further, declaring that between the living and the dead "there is in fact no relationship," merely the memory of a relationship that *has been*, and accordingly "Chapter IX is *not* actually concerned with the nature of a genuine *relationship* of love." "It is not actually the dead who are the objects of this duty," she tells us, "but the living."[15] Loving the deceased is *not* neighbor love, for "the dead are not one's neighbors, they are no one"; recollection of the dead is a work of love, certainly, but one with the *living* as its object and beneficiary.[16] All these claims imply that we have, to employ a distinction from Kant, duties *regarding* the dead rather than duties *to* the dead:

> Man can therefore have no duty to any beings other than men; and if he thinks he has such duties, it is because of an *amphiboly* in his *concepts of reflection*, and his supposed duty to other beings is only a duty to himself. He is led to this misunderstanding by mistaking his duty *with regard to* other beings for a duty *to* those beings.[17]

To make this move with regard to the dead is to give dead persons the same status as Kant assigns to "imperceptible persons" (i.e., angels and God) as well as animals, plants, and natural objects.[18] Just as Kant thinks we should refrain from cruelty to animals because such forbearance will make us less disposed to treat humans cruelly—and so we act kindly to animals *for the sake of promoting* morality but not out of moral duty itself—so the commentators I've mentioned hold Kierkegaard as implying we should recollect the dead for the sake of promoting correct love of the living. The dead, like animals for Kant, are only ever *indirect* objects of moral duty, the direct object of such duties always being the living.

These positions seem to flow naturally from Kierkegaard's strident and repeated insistence that the one dead is "no one." They also seem to cohere with the discussion of shame in "An Occasional Discourse" (a.k.a. "Purity of Heart"), where we are told that "it is truly most beneficial for a person to have a sense of shame before one who is dead, and if he has it before a living person, then to have it before him as before one who is dead" (UDVS, 54/SKS 8, 164). Here it seems that the dead *are* indeed being used merely as a heuristic device for calibrating our moral self-assessment; our sense of shame before ourselves and the living should correspond to what we'd feel before the dead, who cannot be coaxed into softening their judgment of us. However, in trying to understand the discussion in *Works of Love*, we must pay close attention to Kierkegaard's claim that "[w]e certainly do have duties also to the dead. If we are to love the persons we see, then also those we have seen but see no more because death took them away" (WL, 347–48/SKS 9, 341). This forthright declaration invites us to take seriously the thought that our duty to recollect the dead is a duty *to* the dead, and that the object and beneficiary of such a work of love is the *one dead herself.* It is also an invitation to ask of Kierkegaard how he thinks such a duty can be possible. By exploring how Kierkegaard thinks we can discharge a moral duty toward a "no one" we will connect the account of loving the dead in *Works of Love* with the earnest thought of death in the discourse "At a Graveside" and with an ancient problem of how death, conceived as absolute annihilation, can nonetheless be with us.

The Dead as No-One

The very notion of duties to the dead, as a subset of the larger question of how the dead can be harmed or benefited, has long proved puzzling. The question is generally asked against the background of a pretheoretical certainty that the dead *can* be harmed in some sense. Aristotle, displaying his customary deference to prevailing opinion, declares that it would be "unduly heartless" and "contrary to accepted beliefs" to deny that the dead are affected by the fortunes of their living descendants, but he can only speak of harms as "reaching" the dead in a "faint" way.[19] This intuition, as Raimond Gaita notes, underpins the treatment of the bodies of the dead in most, perhaps all, cultures.[20] While we sometimes say that funerals are "really for the living," there is a crucial sense in which this is not true; even in purely secular contexts with no presupposition of posthumous consciousness, what is done is, on some level, done *for* the deceased, "for the dead as irreducible objects of our affections, obligations, sorrows, and pity."[21] Using the theft of Charlie Chaplin's corpse as an example, Gaita stresses how "natural" it is "to say of a dead person that we feel sorry for *him* because his grave had been desecrated . . . If one asks who was harmed, who was defiled when Charlie Chaplin's body was stolen, for Charlie Chaplin is no more, then the answer must be that it is Charlie Chaplin who was harmed."[22]

The countervailing intuition—that the dead, as nonexistent, cannot experience positively unpleasant experiences and hence cannot be harmed—finds expression in Epicurus's famous dictum that it is irrational to fear death for "when we are, death is not come, and when death is come, we are not."[23] The apparent inability of the Epicurean position to overcome deeply ingrained intuitions about the deleteriousness of death has driven a significant effort in analytic philosophy over the past four decades to find rational grounds for fearing death itself and posthumous harms. Ingenious arguments have been marshaled in support of the contention that the dead can indeed be harmed despite not existing at the time of the harm event. As it is clearly the dead as they *were* (not their corpses) that suffer any posthumous harm, analytic philosophers have appealed to retroactive redescription (as where a current event makes it the case that the interests of a dead person while they were alive *were always going to be* frustrated) or atemporal predication (a world in which some interest of mine is frustrated is worse for me, all things considered, than the nearest possible world in which that interest is not frustrated—and this is true *at all times,* regardless of whether I am alive).[24]

Two years before the publication of *Works of Love,* Kierkegaard engages directly with the Epicurean position in the discourse "At a Graveside," where he dismisses Epicurus's argument as a mere "jest" (TDIO, 73/SKS 5, 444).[25] Importantly, he does not reject this argument simply by appealing to Christian teachings about posthumous existence. Rather, he seeks to present death as an existential problem *for the living,* and as such he chooses to fight Epicurus on his own turf by accepting the description of death as annihilation. The dead are no more, and with death "it is over" (TDIO, 74/SKS 5, 445). Yet in accepting this annihilationist account, Kierkegaard embraces the paradoxical character of death as a harm that entails the nonexistence of its subject at precisely the moment of the harm-event:

> Sorrow—if you wish to compare it to death and want to call sorrow an archer, as death is—sorrow does not miss its mark, because it hits the living, and when it has hit him, only then does the sorrow begin; but when death's arrow has hit, then indeed it is over. . . . when death tightens the snare it has indeed caught nothing, because then all is over (TDIO, 74/SKS 5, 445).

The one dead, then, ceases to be at precisely the moment death has "caught" him; hence Kierkegaard accentuates the paradoxical nonexistent-yet-harmable ontological status of the dead rather than dissolving it. In *Works of Love,* Kierkegaard once again is quite insistent that the dead person, the object of the work of love in remembering the dead, has been annihilated:

> But when a person relates himself to one who is dead, there is only one in this relationship, inasmuch as one who is dead is no actuality; no one, no one can make himself *no one* as well as one who is dead, because he is

> *no one*.... One who is dead is no actual object; he is only the occasion that continually discloses what resides in the one living who relates himself to him (WL, 347/SKS 9, 341).

It is this insistence that the other is "no one" that has led defenders of *Works of Love* to treat recollection of the dead as a merely metaphorical form of love, a heuristic device for learning how to love *actual* persons. Love of the dead, according to this reasoning, just isn't *real* love; our love for others ceases when they die. As a reading of *Works of Love* this seems entirely reasonable; how, after all, can love—real, self-emptying, faithful, life-structuring love—be directed at "no one"?

Yet once again, the ontological status of the dead is significantly more paradoxical than straightforward nonexistence. First, while the dead one now partakes of the "equality of the dead" (another theme common to both "At a Graveside" and *Works of Love*) conferred by the dissolution of differences between the dead (WL, 345–46/SKS 9, 339–40), we are nonetheless enjoined to love *specific* dead people. The dead are not mere featureless, interchangeable tokens; they are specific "people we see," and, as such, legitimate objects of love even if we "no longer see them." Indeed, Keeley notes that there is something disturbing in the declaration that the "one dead" is "no one":

> For most mourners, this is an exceedingly curious and even cruel observation: the one they are grieving is very decisively not "no one"; he is instead a very definite *this one and no other*. Though all have death in common, each death is a particular event, undergone by one alone. Similarly, it seems to the mourner that death strikes with particular force when *this one who is beloved* is taken. It seems this way because the dead one *is* beloved.[26]

Keeley here departs from Müller's insistence that "in relation to Kierkegaard's point the question about who the dead person is is indifferent; he is purely and simply one who is dead—and that is sufficient."[27] Rather, it seems that in the recollection of the dead we relate ourselves to a concrete, specific, irreplaceable other, who is, at the same time, *no one*. We could perhaps overcome this paradox in the same way Wittgenstein sought to dissolve the question of how the names of the dead can sensibly be used when the referent is nonexistent, but *Works of Love* suggests there is more to this paradox than confusing the bearer of the name with the *meaning* of the name.[28] In fleshing out the notion of loving the dead as loving those who can never *repay* our love, Kierkegaard draws a somewhat unexpected analogy:

> In this regard there is a similarity between lovingly recollecting one who is dead and parents' love for their children. Parents love the children almost before they come into existence and long before they become conscious beings, therefore as nonbeings. But a dead person is also a nonbeing, and the two greatest good works are these: to give a human being life and to recollect one who is dead; yet the first work of love has a repayment (WL, 349/SKS 9, 343).

This comparison between recollecting the dead and loving infant children suggests that the ontological condition of the dead is something more substantial than straightforward, total nonexistence. As noted above, Ferreira interprets Kierkegaard as claiming that the nonexistence of the dead is constituted precisely *by* their inability to reciprocate or respond to us. If this is the case, *some* sort of existence for the dead is preserved, and here that residual existence is likened to that of a child before it becomes a "conscious being" in the sense of a self-reflective, rational agent.[29] While it is true that parents love their children well before they attain such a status (and indeed, as Kierkegaard implies, even before they are born), this does not make the object of their love *no one* in the sense of a pure absence. The infant may be nearly as unresponsive and uncommunicative as the dead (though only if we adopt a disturbingly austere view of what counts as communication), yet it is nonetheless loved as a distinct, concrete, specific—and crucially, *irreplaceable*—individual.

The heuristic value of the example of loving the dead turns in large measure on the inability of the dead to "repay" our love, and the possibility of reciprocation and reward in raising children devalues parental love from this purely heuristic perspective. Kierkegaard tells us that:

> If parents had no hope whatever, no prospect at all, of ever receiving joy from their children and reward for their love—well, there would indeed be many a father and mother who still would lovingly do everything for the children—ah, but there certainly would be also be many a father and mother whose love would grow cold (WL, 349/SKS 9, 343).

Both types of parents are relatively easy to envision. Examples of parents loving their children without hope of reciprocation abound; severely intellectually disabled infants may have *no* prospect of meeting Kierkegaard's rather strident criteria of consciousness but are nonetheless loved, and loved as specific individuals. Anencephalic babies (who are born without a neocortex and are therefore permanently devoid of consciousness) are also loved, even though in this case whatever responsiveness might be apparent is merely a simulacrum. In these cases, we might want to contend that the child genuinely *is* as unresponsive as the dead and easily counts as "no one" if Ferreira is correct that Kierkegaard's criterion for nonexistence is the impossibility of responsiveness. But such love is nonetheless directed at a very specific, concrete being, and we would perhaps balk at the suggestion that this is not "real" parental love (whatever else we might want to say about the infant's moral status).

Sadly there are indeed examples of parents whose love "grows cold" for want of the possibility of reward. The conservative Scottish historian Michael Fry notes Edmund Burt's eighteenth-century account of Highlanders, beset by appallingly high infant mortality rates, treating their children with surprising indifference until they reached six or seven years old.[30] Fry's conclusion—that the Highlanders were prudently avoiding emotional attachment to their children until they reached an age at which they had a reasonable prospect of survival—is unverifiable and probably simplistic, but it provides an example of a parental "love" that implicitly treats the child as "no one," at least for a few years. However, Kierkegaard's point is not merely to decry the withdrawal of love based on the impossibility of eventual reciprocation or reward, but also love offered *on the basis* of that possibility. In this far more subtle (and harder to diagnose) case, parents would only love infants insofar as they *will be* rational beings. This would indeed be, in Adorno's terms, a merely "metaphorical" or "symbolic" love, in that parents declaring their love for an infant would *really* be declaring their love for an as-yet nonexistent reciprocating person to come. In the conception of parental love that Kierkegaard endorses, however, parents do not love the *prospect* of their future loving child as symbolically embodied in the nonreciprocating infant; rather they love *the infant itself.* That the child's total temporal extension is wider than that of its membership in the community of rational agents is no impediment to its being loved *for itself* at *all* times. But if we transpose this thought to the dead, the result is that we love the dead *themselves,* not their *memory.*[31] If the analogy between parental love and loving the dead holds, then if we love infants themselves and not merely the thought of their projected future, it would seem we must love the dead themselves and not the thought of their recollected past.

The conjunction of the prenatal and the posthumous also serves to connect the present discussion to the Epicurean problem by establishing resonances with Lucretius's symmetry argument. In *De Rerum Natura*, the Epicurean philosopher Lucretius argues that just as we are not distressed by contemplation of the time in which we did not exist before our birth, so too should we not be disturbed by the period of nonexistence following our death.[32] Kierkegaard also equates the periods of "nonexistence" before birth and after death, but unlike Lucretius, personal "nonexistence" continues for some time after birth, and these "nonexistent" persons are still *some* sort of object in that they are still loveable as distinct, specific beings. Does Kierkegaard's own "symmetry argument" commit us to saying that the dead, though "no more," are nonetheless still loveable beings in the same way as he takes the unborn and the newly born to be? And if so, how is this possible?

Imagination and Presence

At the heart of Kierkegaard's response to Epicurus is his contention that through "the earnest thought of death" we can, paradoxically, achieve *co-presence with death*:[33] "Earnestness is that you think death, and that you are thinking it as your lot, and that you are then doing what death is indeed unable to do—namely, that you are and death also is" (TDIO, 75/SKS 5, 446). In this discourse, Kierkegaard develops a nuanced taxonomy of the different ways in which we can contemplate the fact of our mortality. The central distinction between these modes of contemplation is that of earnestness (*alvor*) versus mood (*stemning*). Most of our ways of discussing death, according to Kierkegaard, are symptomatic of or productive of mood alone. Into this category fall a series of affective states such as horror, terror, sentimentality, detached objectivity, as well as modes of speaking of death that either mitigate its force with distorting images, such as the metaphorical "sleep" of death (TDIO, 81/SKS 5, 451) or trite explanations (death as "a transition, a transformation, a suffering, a punishment, the wages of sin"—TDIO, 99/SKS 5, 466). What is missing from all these states that prevent them from being more than mere mood is that each state "refuse[s] to understand that the discourse [about death] is about the acquiring of retroactive power in life through the explanation" (TDIO, 99/SKS 5, 466)—in other words, they deflect, dilute, and defer the force of the ethical urgency conferred upon me by the thought of *my* mortality.[34] Earnest contemplation of death, by contrast, involves an apprehension of my death (a necessarily imaginatively mediated experience) as conferring moral demands, in that it impels me to structure my actions, projects, and plans in light of death's "certain-uncertainty"—I *will* die, and at *any moment I may die.* The voice of death adds to all imagined scenarios a "yes, it is possible!" and if I hear this voice *correctly,* I hear it as making a demand on me here and now.

In earnest contemplation of my death, I apprehend my future death as presenting me with tasks here in the present. In this way I become co-present with *my dead self.* I attain with my dead future self what Kierkegaard elsewhere speaks of as "contemporaneity," a form of co-presence with temporally distant figures (paradigmatically, the figure of Christ) precisely insofar as I take them as speaking an ethical demand directly *and personally* to me. The obligating figure presents itself to me in the same fullness of presence as actual persons directly before me; it compels me in the same way, closes off avenues of escape and evasion in the same way as the direct presence of an actual moral patient.

This is why, according to Kierkegaard, only the thought of *my own death* can provide me with earnestness, as he claims in a journal sketch for "At a Graveside": "The earnestness is not to die but to think oneself dying, since another's dying provides only mood. The concept of earnestness is really illuminated here" (TDIO, 143). Nor will contemplating the fact of death *per se* help us here: "it is still only a jest if he merely contemplates death and not himself in death, if he thinks of it as the human condition but not as his own" (TDIO, 73/SKS 5, 444). Essential to earnestness, then, is a mode of self-reflexive cognition, in which I see what I imaginatively contemplate as conferring normative obligation directly upon *me.* In this way, I overcome the temporal gap between my death and myself, in a way that avoids the suspiciously artificial metaphysical devices of retroactive requalification and atemporal predication that analytic philosophers have been forced to utilize to achieve the same end.

Is this avenue for bridging the temporal gulf between us and the dead what is recommended to us in *Works of Love*? Kierkegaard does not use the language of co-presence or contemporaneity in chapter IX, but there are telling parallels that suggest attaining a type of co-presence with the dead, secured by certain modes of contemplation, constitutes the substance of our duty to the dead. Consider, first, that our duty to the dead is presented in precisely contemplative terms: "We ought not to disturb the dead by wailing and crying. We ought to treat one who is dead as we treat one who is sleeping, whom we do not have the heart to awaken because we hope that he will wake up by himself" (WL, 348/SKS 9, 341–42). How do we treat the sleeping? Not through interaction or discourse, but through *watching over* them, lovingly attending to—paying attention to—their presence in the world without disturbing them. Moreover, by directing us from the ways in which we mourn the dead—wailing and crying—toward an attention-based *duty,* Kierkegaard transfigures remembering the dead from an unbidden mental event characteristic of grief (understood here as a normatively neutral state of mind accompanied by specific emotions) into a morally charged exercise in recollection. Let's call this mode of recollection "remembrance." To recollect the one dead, Kierkegaard tells us, "is something different from not being able to forget him at first" (WL, 355/SKS 9, 348), and the difference consists in the former's status as a freely chosen action while the latter is essentially involuntary. This emphasis on attention as a conscious, volitional action is necessary because our emotions, however strong while we are grieving, cannot of their own accord ensure we will recollect the dead:

> It is a task, and one need not have seen much in life to have seen enough to be assured that it may very well be necessary to emphasize that it is a task, a duty, to recollect the dead. The untrustworthiness of human feelings left to their own devices perhaps never manifests itself more than in this very relationship (WL, 348/SKS 9, 342).

In this way, the dichotomy between mood and earnestness from "At a Graveside" is reintroduced into the context of our practices of remembering the dead. The initial period of remembering the dead "inordinately enough with crying and clamor" (WL, 351/SKS 9, 345) soon passes away, and the absence of the dead makes our recollection of them dependent upon the contingencies of free-floating emotion and circumstance. While the living compel us to notice them, through "daily sight and habit if nothing else" (WL, 354/SKS 9, 347), the dead cannot "extort" our love through begging and crying or "compel by means of visible misery" (WL, 352/SKS 9, 345–46). This makes the dead particularly easy to avoid and ultimately forget (WL, 352/SKS 9, 346)—a claim that may seem ridiculous and inhuman to those mourning the loss of a loved one. When we are grieving, the dead one seems to be, in a sense, *everywhere:* the world furnishes us with a seemingly endless stream of reminders of the person we've lost, and painful reminders at that. Yet our immersion in the minutiae of life will, inevitably, over time loosen the deceased's grip on our attention. It is against this brute fact of psychology, according to Kierkegaard, that we are to muster our attention through active remembrance of the dead:

> the loving recollection of the dead has to protect itself against the actuality around one, lest through ever-new impressions it acquire full power

> to wipe out the recollection, and it has to protect itself against time—in short, it has to guard its freedom in recollection against that which wants to compel one to forget (WL, 354/SKS 9, 347).

Grief, like all emotions, has a crucial epistemic function. It reveals to us how the world stands and discloses in an almost overwhelming way the value of the other who has been lost. Christopher Cordner has recently suggested that what is disclosed by grief is in fact nothing less than the value of human beings, which "could not be what it is for us were we not devastated by the loss of those near us, in ways explicable by nothing about them. . . . Our being subject to grief—which is, of course, experienced in relation to others—is a constituting condition of the value of a (any) human being, including the one I am."[35]

Yet in the absence of their object, our feelings of loss eventually dissipate, leaving the value of what actuated those feelings—the specific other who has died—seemingly unattested to. It's interesting to note in this context that the practice of defined mourning periods and their associated customs are always presented in a normative cast. From the Victorian "widow's weeds" to the now-ubiquitous minute of silence, mourning practices are always enforced through sanctions of moral disapprobation. The brightly dressed Victorian widow is decried by her neighbors—her lack of mourning speaks to her poor *character;* the person who talks during the minute's silence, even at sporting events, is censured in moral terms. Gaita sees these mourning practices as an attempt to ward off an innate tendency to return to normality. It's not simply that life goes on, but, as Gaita memorably phrases it, "life asserts itself imperiously and with no shame" in a "resurgence" that seems to sweep grief away too quickly.[36] Our initial reaction to bereavement is, as Auden put it, to "stop all the clocks,"[37] but we are quickly swept back into the river of temporality. These mourning practices are attempts to defend the insight disclosed by feelings of loss from the dissipating effects of temporal emplacement.[38] The enemy here is time—and time, according to the model of Kierkegaardian moral cognition I have attempted to sketch here and elsewhere, can only be overcome through a form of contemplation that brings us to presence with the past or future, to bring the object of our contemplation into immediate presence.

Living With the Dead

Bringing the deceased to "presence" in this way allows us to take the one dead seriously as a moral patient, and therefore as a legitimate object of love. Kierkegaard explicitly takes our duty to love the dead as an extension of our all-encompassing task of loving those we see no more (WL, 347–48/SKS 9, 341); while they lived, the dead were our neighbors and so legitimate objects of our freely given, faithful love. The extension of this love beyond death could be taken as a merely metaphorical form of love, given the absence of its object, but as we've seen, Kierkegaard deploys a deceptively complex dialectic in which the dead one is no *actual* object (WL, 355/SKS 9, 348), and yet is nonetheless a *real* object of duty. This dialectic licenses the knots of seemingly self-contradictory statements about the ontological status of the dead that Kierkegaard weaves throughout the text. The one dead can impact upon the living through his ingenuity, firmness, strength, and pride, either through inspiring fear or teaching precisely these qualities to the living (WL, 357/SKS 9, 351), and yet "he is no actuality, and he therefore does nothing, nothing at all, in order to hold on to you," but again, "he is not changed" (WL, 358/SKS 9, 351) and "is only the occasion that continuously discloses what resides in the one living" (WL, 347/SKS 9, 341). How can "nothing at all" be ingenious, firm, strong, or proud? The dead here occupy a curious ontological netherworld in which they are simultaneously fully devoid of being and quite capable of bearing predication.

Heidegger too saw the dead as bearing a sort of ontological ambiguity, as more than *merely* nonexistent, and he was alive to this as a key element in the phenomenology of remembrance; "the deceased *himself* is no longer factically 'there'" but "those who remain can still *be with him*" in the "respectful solicitude" of funeral rites and graveside commemorations.[39] Yet while Heidegger wants to claim that this capacity to "be with" the dead in commemoration goes beyond the status of dead bodies as *unalive* matter (matter that has lost its life, as opposed to *merely* lifeless matter),[40] his account doesn't seem to extend much beyond the funereal. Kierkegaard's duty of recollection, like our practices of remembrance, goes well beyond the treatment of corpses to embrace the recollection of "those we have seen," however long ago. (Interestingly, I'm told that in certain forms of Shinto practice, ancestors are worshipped as distinct persons until several decades after their deaths, at which point they are taken up into the undifferentiated "ancestors").[41] Indeed, our practices of remembrance stretch even to persons we have *never* seen and even to those for whom we can provide *no* determinate phenomenal content in our recollection. Commemorations at the tombs of unknown soldiers are a key case in point; the inscription "Known unto God" sometimes placed on such graves can be understood as a Berkeley-like attempt to insist that *someone* knew the deceased in his or her concrete specificity, thus securing them as loveable even if as devoid of phenomenal content as possible for *us*.[42]

This highlights another challenge for Kierkegaard's definition of "the neighbor" (*den næste*). The concept is taken from a biblical context in which it is deliberately construed capaciously in order to overcome a tendency to exclude others from the category. However, if we do have a duty to love the dead that extends to unknown soldiers, people in the distant past, etc., we need a concept of "neighbor" that will be capable of distinguishing between legitimate objects of love with little or no phenomenal content (long-dead persons at the very edge of living memory, figures from the distant past, and finally those whose concrete specifics are known only "unto God") while excluding other potential objects of love with similar types of phenomenality,[43] such as fictional characters. A response could probably be given in terms of some sort of reality constraint, whereby only those who *actually* partake (extended to cover those who *will* partake, as in infants, or *have* partaken but are now dead) of personhood, broadly construed, qualify as neighbors.[44] I don't propose to sketch such a response here, but it should be noted that though it would be almost antithetical to Kierkegaard's upbuilding purpose to circumscribe the concept of *den næste* in this way, a purely philosophical use of his thought here will need such a constraint.

This dialectic is further complicated by the *dependence* of the dead upon the recollection of the living. Importantly, whereas works of love directed toward the living involve seeing the other and loving them as the neighbor, which will involve putting oneself in an "infinite debt" of moral duty toward them (e.g. WL, 177/SKS 9, 177), our duty to the dead is precisely to recollect them—that is, to bring them into the presence in which they constitute moral patients. In recollecting the dead, we confer on them precisely the actuality that allows us to be morally claimed by them. We allow the dead to come back into being, and precisely thereby put ourselves in infinite debt to them. To rephrase things in a quasi-Levinasian way, in loving the dead I freely *give* the other his *face*, a face that I apprehend as a moral *demand*; I make it possible for the dead other to subsist in his otherness *even as I subject myself to it*.[45] This is, of course, thoroughly paradoxical, yet its dialectical subtlety and complexity is perfectly emblematic of Kierkegaard's phenomenology of moral perception.

Of course, none of this invalidates the sense in which the dead absolutely *are not*. Yet there are clearly multiple, dialectically related senses of existence at work here, and this is what makes it possible for us to have duties toward seemingly nonexistent others. The dead are beyond help, and nothing we can do can affect them experientially (presumably), but in recollecting the dead we simultaneously testify to the distinctive individuals that they were and in so doing *constitute* their continued being in the world. Through remembrance, the dead survive in moral space. In this way, this "actuality" achieved by the dead in our recollection, though clearly less than literal, is nonetheless more than metaphorical. We *really do* love the dead, even though the dead *really don't* exist anymore.

Nor does the foregoing deny that, as Keeley, Søltoft, and Ferreira have rightly noted (and Adorno and George too, from their critical perspective), how we love the dead holds crucial lessons for how we are to love the living. Pointing to this upbuilding dimension in the work of love in recollecting the dead is of course the central role of chapter IX:

> [R]ecollect the one who is dead and just in this way learn to love the living unselfishly, freely, faithfully. . . . Recollect the one who is dead: then in addition to the blessing that is inseparable from this work of love you will also have the best guidance for rightly understanding life: that it is our duty to love the people we do not see but also those we do see. The duty to love the people we see cannot cease because death separates them from us, because the duty is eternal; but accordingly neither can the duty to those who are dead separate the living from us in such a way that they do not become the objects of our love (WL, 358/SKS 9, 351–52).

Yet at all times, the discourse nonetheless takes it as given that we have duties to love those we do not see; remembrance's heuristic value for our love of the living in no way revokes its status as a work of love in itself. Pondering the work of love in recollecting the dead will show us what our love for the living must be: pure, unselfish, utterly freely given, and changelessly faithful, however much those we love might change. Keeley notes that recollecting the dead is a "maieutic assistant"[46] that has the salutary effect of "wean[ing] one (for a time!) from absorption in one's own present and giv[ing] significance to someone else's status as eternal," which reflexively leads us to ask about our *own* eternal validity; "reflection puts one in mind of one's *own* prospects and task."[47] Introspection achieves a certain clarity when the object of one's love is beyond reciprocation and communication, where, as Müller has it, "the individual is brought to the place where he is completely alone with himself in a maieutic situation where no self deception is possible, and where the rememberer is therefore unconditionally forced to make the necessary admissions which exclusively concern himself."[48] Yet while recollecting the dead, by its nature, provides an upbuilding example of what *all* love must be, it is also, in itself, a work of love. This is the presumption upon which Kierkegaard builds his account of this work of love as constituting a criterion for all other works.

In treating seriously Kierkegaard's assertion that we have duties to the dead, we gain a more thorough insight into the ethic being recommended to us in *Works of Love*. But I think we do more than this: we also see a means of articulating the phenomenological structures of recollection and grief that underpin our practices toward the dead, the practices of remembrance and commemoration that play such a large role in all cultures. Our "duties" to the dead lose their quotation marks and become fully fleshed, utterly serious ethical requirements. Of course, the precise content of those requirements, or what weight they carry relative to our duties to the living, is another matter.[49] But Kierkegaard at least provides grounds for dealing with skepticism about whether such duties can exist at all.[50]

NOTES

1. Theodore Adorno, "On Kierkegaard's Doctrine of Love," *Studies in Philosophy and Social Science* 8 (1940), p. 415.

2. Adorno, "On Kierkegaard's Doctrine of Love," p. 423.

3. K. E. Løgstrup, *Opgør med Kierkegaard* (Copenhagen: Gyldendal, 2005), pp. 116–17.

4. Paul Müller, *Kierkegaard's* Works of Love*: Christian Ethics and the Maieutic Ideal,* trans. C. Stephen Evans and Jan Evans (Copenhagen: C. A. Reitzel, 1992), pp. 51–52.

5. Peter George, "Something Antisocial About *Works of Love*," in *Kierkegaard: The Self in Society,* ed. George Pattison and Stephen Shakespeare, p. 79 (London: Macmillan, 1998).

6. D. Z. Phillips, "Kierkegaard and Loves that Blossom," in *Ethik der Liebe: Studien zu Kierkegaards "Taten der Liebe,"* ed. I. U. Dalferth, pp. 162–63 (Tübingen: Mohr Siebeck, 2002). I'm grateful to Rebekka Klein for drawing this to my attention.

7. Adorno, "On Kierkegaard's Doctrine of Love," p. 427.

8. Adorno, "On Kierkegaard's Doctrine of Love," pp. 416–17.

9. M. Jamie Ferreira, *Love's Grateful Striving: A Commentary on Kierkegaard's* Works of Love (Oxford: Oxford University Press, 2001), p. 211.

10. Ferreira, *Love's Grateful Striving,* p. 212.

11. Adorno, "On Kierkegaard's Doctrine of Love," pp. 418–19.

12. Ferreira, *Love's Grateful Striving,* p. 212.

13. Ferreira, *Love's Grateful Striving,* p. 213.

14. Louise Carroll Keeley, "Loving 'No One,' Loving Everyone: The Work of Love in Recollecting One Dead in *Works of Love,*" in *International Kierkegaard*

Commentary: Works of Love, ed. Robert L. Perkins, p. 241 (Macon, Ga.: Mercer University Press, 1999).

15. Pia Søltoft, "The Presence of the Absent Neighbor in *Works of Love,*" trans. M. G. Piety, in *Kierkegaard Studies Yearbook 1998,* ed. Niels Jørgen Cappelørn and Herman Deuser, p. 125 (Berlin: de Gruyter, 1998).

16. Søltoft, "The Presence of the Absent Neighbor in *Works of Love,*" p. 126.

17. Immanuel Kant, *The Metaphysics of Morals,* trans. Mary Gregor (Cambridge: Cambridge University Press, 1991), p. 237.

18. Kant, *The Metaphysics of Morals,* pp. 237–38; see also Kant, *Lectures on Ethics,* trans. Louis Infield (Indianapolis, Ind., and Cambridge: Hackett, 1963), pp. 239–41. In the *Metaphysics of Morals* Kant mentions only angels and God as examples of supernatural "imperceptible persons," and only discusses duty to God in any detail. In the *Lectures on Ethics,* however, he claims that we have only negative (indirect) duties toward supernatural spirits: our duty is to *avoid* interaction with them, which might make us superstitious and depreciate our rational powers. The dead, on the line I am taking here, would be "imperceptible persons" but they would not be supernatural; as such they are not affected by this injunction against commerce with spirits. In this connection it's interesting to note in passing Kierkegaard's silence on the proto-Spiritualist "table-turning" craze of the mid-1850s, which such eminent Copenhageners as Heiberg and Martensen apparently participated in. See Thomas Overskou, *Om Mit Liv og Min Tid 1819–1878,* ed. with a postscript Robert Neiindam (Copenhagen: Nyt Nordisk Forlag Arnold Busck, 1962), pp. 194–97; and Patrick Stokes, "The Science of the Dead: Proto-Spiritualism in Kierkegaard's Copenhagen," in *Kierkegaard and the 19th Century Crisis of Culture* (*Acta Kierkegaardiana IV*), ed. Roman Kralik, Abrahim H. Khan, Peter Sajda, Jamie Turnbull, and Andrew J. Burgess, pp. 132–49 (Šal̆a, Slovakia, and Toronto: Kierkegaard Society of Slovakia/Kierkegaard Circle, University of Toronto, 2009).

19. Aristotle, *Ethics,* trans. J. A. K. Thomson, revised Hugh Tredennick (London: Penguin, 1976), p. 85.

20. Raimond Gaita, *The Philosopher's Dog: Friendships With Animals* (New York: Random House, 2002), pp. 87–97.

21. Gaita, *The Philosopher's Dog,* p. 89.

22. Gaita, *The Philosopher's Dog,* p. 94.

23. Diogenes Laertius, *Diogenes Laertius, Lives of Eminent Philosophers,* vol. 2, trans. R. D. Hicks (Cambridge, Mass.: Harvard University Press, 1979–80), p. 650.

24. The key moments in this debate are helpfully collected in John Martin Fischer, ed., *The Metaphysics of Death* (Stanford, Calif.: Stanford University Press, 1993).

25. Though he doesn't mention Epicurus by name; he is merely referred to as "a pagan" (*en Hedning*). This is in keeping with the signed discourses' habit of using indirect locutions instead of proper names (I am grateful to Niels-Jørgen Cappelørn for this point).

26. Keeley, "Loving 'No One,' Loving Everyone," p. 226.

27. Müller, *Kierkegaard's* Works of Love, p. 52.

28. Ludwig Wittgenstein, *Philosophical Investigations,* trans. G. E. M. Anscombe (New York: Macmillan, 1958), p. 20.

29. In *Johannes Climacus,* Kierkegaard confirms that children lack consciousness in this fairly technical sense, while still being nonetheless sentient. See JC, 168.

30. Michael Fry, *Wild Scots: Four Hundred Years of Highland History* (London: John Murray, 2005), p. 154.

31. In his recent discussion of whether we have a moral responsibility to remember the dead, Jeffrey Blustein argues against the claim that when we cherish a dead person we are actually cherishing a *memory* of him, appealing to an intuition that the former is not reducible to the latter (Jeffrey Blustein, *The Moral Demands of Memory* [Cambridge: Cambridge University Press, 2008], pp. 255–56). Blustein also draws on Kierkegaard in this discussion and comes to conclusions quite similar to those I draw here about our duties to the dead, namely that remembrance is a noninstrumental duty *to* the dead that expresses our evaluation of them as they were while they lived, and not merely a consequentialist duty to the living (Blustein is, however, working with a different understanding of "love" and who it is owed to than Kierkegaard). He also challenges Kierkegaard's claim that the dead cannot repay us by asserting that "there are various ways in which a loved one can continue to be instrumentally valuable to us even after his death" (p. 254).

32. Lucretius, *The Nature of the Universe,* trans. Ronald Latham (Middlesex: Penguin, 1951), p. 121.

33. For a fuller discussion of this topic, see my "The Power of Death: Retroactivity, Narrative, and Interest," in *International Kierkegaard Commentary: Prefaces/ Writing Sampler and Three Discourses on Imagined Occasions,* ed. Robert L. Perkins, pp. 387–417 (Macon, Ga.: Mercer University Press, 2006).

34. Although as George Connell notes, this urgency may only be fully available to someone who already sees things in religious terms. George Connell, "Four Funerals: The Experience of Time by the Side of the Grave," in *International Kierkegaard Commentary: Prefaces/Writing Sampler and Three Discourses on Imagined Occasions,* ed. Robert L. Perkins, pp. 436–38 (Macon, Ga.: Mercer University Press, 2006).

35. Christopher Cordner, "Remorse and Moral Identity," in *Practical Identity and Narrative Agency,* ed. Kim Atkins and Catriona Mackenzie, p. 247 (New York: Routledge, 2008).

36. Gaita, *The Philosopher's Dog,* p. 89.

37. W. H. Auden, "Funeral Blues," in *The English Auden: Poems, Essays and Dramatic Writings 1927–1939,* ed. Edward Mendelson, p. 163 (London: Faber and Faber, 1978).

38. This is a version of what Blustein calls the "Rescue from Insignificance View" of the moral obligation to remember the dead: "We ought to remember the

dear departed because in doing so we declare that death has not eliminated what was distinctive and valuable about them" (Blustein, *The Moral Demands of Memory,* pp. 269–73, 281).

39. Martin Heidegger, *Being and Time,* trans. John Macquarrie and Edward Robinson (New York: Harper and Row, 1962), p. 282.

40. Heidegger, *Being and Time,* p. 282.

41. I'm grateful to James Giles for this datum. Giles relates themes of ancestor worship in Japanese practice to Kierkegaard in his "Introduction: Kierkegaard among the Temples of Kamakura," in *Kierkegaard and Japanese Thought,* ed. James Giles, pp. 12–18 and passim (Hampshire: Palgrave, 2008).

42. Another possibility is that in these cases we feel empathy for the unknown soldier as a "type" without positing any more distinctive characterization of him; see Peter Goldie, *The Emotions: A Philosophical Exploration* (Oxford: Oxford University Press, 2000), p. 204.

43. For a useful discussion of the phenomenality of the dead (which rejects my claim that remembrance can confer the right type of phenomenality to make the dead objects of duty), see Jeremy Allen's contribution to this volume, "The Soft Weeping of Desire's Loss: Recognition, Phenomenality, and the One Who Is Dead in Kierkegaard's *Works of Love.*" Blustein also discusses the role of this phenomenality in remembrance: "when we reminisce about the departed, we not only recall facts about the person's life or character or deeds. We insinuate ourselves back into that person's life in a way that brings the person him or herself back to life, and the person's presence is more or less vivid, and felt more or less powerfully, depending on what sort of relationship we had with that person and how intimately we knew him or her" (Blustein, *The Moral Demands of Memory,* p. 250).

44. Adam Buben points out to me some of the difficulties any such reality constraint will have to deal with; for instance, we might claim that my as-yet-unborn child is a legitimate object of love at least to a degree that a fictional character clearly is not—but what about children who have not yet been conceived? (Compare *Stages on Life's Way,* where a young man visits a brothel and is haunted ever after by the thought that he *may* have a child somewhere as a result—SLW, 276–88/SKS 6, 257–68.) There is a significant literature on the question of whether future generations can have moral claims on the living; the question of phenomenality and lovability may be an interesting input into such debates.

45. Buben again points out to me that, in keeping with the natality/mortality parallel discussed earlier, one could substitute "child" for "dead" here and have a similarly compelling account of parenthood.

46. Keeley, "Loving 'No One,' Loving Everyone," p. 224.

47. Keeley, "Loving 'No One,' Loving Everyone," p. 223.

48. Müller, *Kierkegaard's* Works of Love, pp. 52–53.

49. Kierkegaard, for one, finds it natural (*naturligt*) that the dead have "no rights in life" that might be publicly enforceable (WL, 352/SKS 9, 346).

50. Thanks to participants at the "Kierkegaard and Death" conference at St. Olaf College, December 2007, and the "Death: What It Is and Why It Matters" conference at the University of York, August 2008, and to James Stacey Taylor, for helpful comments on earlier versions of this chapter. This chapter is dedicated in loving memory to Greg Stokes (1950–2004) and Pamela Gunn (1962–2007).

15.

Kierkegaard's Understanding of the Afterlife

Tamara Monet Marks

Kierkegaard believed that he would experience a postmortem existence. Direct evidence for his belief may be found in his personal, pseudonymous, and signed writings. At the age of thirty-two, Kierkegaard wrote detailed instructions for the repair of his family's burial site. Among his plans one finds lines from a hymn Brorson penned for his own tombstone. The content of the hymn suggests, among other things, that the afterlife puts an end to struggle in this life. The lines read:

> In yet a little while
> I shall have won;
> Then the whole fight
> Will at once be done.
> Then I may rest
> In bowers of roses
> And unceasingly, unceasingly
> Speak with my Jesus.[1]

How Kierkegaard came to his conception of the afterlife, and what he means by the terms he uses to connote it—such as eternity, the eternal, eternal happiness, eternal salvation, judgment, immortality, and resurrection—is a long and complex story.[2] A complete account would involve an analysis of the influence of his Lutheran and Moravian upbringing, his philosophical and theological studies, the relationship between his signed and pseudonymous texts on the issue of the afterlife, and the impact on his thinking of the decade-long debates over the meaning of the afterlife in Germany and Denmark. All of these features have considerable bearing on the development of Kierkegaard's conception of the afterlife.[3] That said, one can usefully focus on Kierkegaard's discussions of Socrates's conception of the afterlife; these provide a window into Kierkegaard's general view. Socrates's account of immortality shapes one of the most important and enduring philosophical themes in Kierkegaard's assessment of eternal life. From Socrates, he develops the notion that subjective interest in the afterlife affects one's character in *this* life. Yet in spite of Socrates's deep influence on his philosophical development, Kierkegaard ultimately departs from his conception of the afterlife in order to hold up what he takes to be the Christian understanding. The Socratic account of immortality is insufficient for Christian faith in the resurrection and eternal salvation, and therefore, from Kierkegaard's perspective, untrue.[4] Focusing on a comparison of Kierkegaard's account of the afterlife with his understanding of Socrates's approach has the merit of sharply defining the main themes elemental to his overall conception, as well as highlighting what Kierkegaard sees as the difference between what may be called a philosophical approach to eternal life and his own, Christian approach.

The Dissertation and the Upbuilding Discourses

Although irony is the main topic in his dissertation, Kierkegaard engages his personal interest in the subject of the afterlife in its first chapter. He interrupts his comments on the relationship between the *Symposium* and the *Phaedo* with a footnote about two additional, often ignored, and what he considers "indirect" demonstrations of the immortality of the soul presented by Socrates in the *Phaedo.* Due to the constraints of the dissertation genre, Kierkegaard is unable to treat them in any depth there. However, he acknowledges that the two oft-ignored and indirect demonstrations have a potentially "upbuilding" and "personal," rather than "demonstrative" form, and for that reason he does not dismiss them without some analysis (CI, 67/SKS 1, 125–26). The little he does say about these proofs is instructive for how he develops his understanding of the afterlife in subsequent writings, beginning with his first upbuilding discourse and ending, for the purposes of the present chapter, with the *Christian Discourses.*

Kierkegaard refers to Socrates's warning against suicide (*Phaedo,* 61d–63d) as the first indirect, and potentially upbuilding, demonstration of immortality. Suicide is wrong because human beings are the possessions of the gods and the gods are their guardians; therefore, it would be unreasonable to put an untimely end to one's life if the gods have not willed it (*Phaedo* 62b–c). The "rich content" of the possibility of being the "deities' co-worker," Kierkegaard interjects, unfortunately never develops in Plato's dialogues. Neither Kierkegaard nor Socrates's interlocutors are convinced of the power of the demonstration as it is given in the *Phaedo.* Pressed by Cebes and Simmias to explain how his argument against suicide squares with his notion that the philosopher is always practicing for "dying and death," Socrates responds that he does not resent his nearing death because he plans to meet "other wise and good gods" in the afterlife (*Phaedo,* 63b).[5] According to Kierkegaard, this response only "obscures" things because it "fixes a chasmal abyss between this life and a next life and, since death always becomes a withdrawal from the power of the gods of this life, the ambiguous relation to them still remains" (CI, 67fn/SKS 1, 126). The problem facing the individual on this account is that he cannot be certain whether to remain in this life, within the gods' jurisdiction, or not. Even when Socrates uses the idea of immortality as a subjective point of departure, his weak explanation of the relation between life and death "remains at the abstract level and leads into Platonic metaphysics."[6] A more robust account of what it would mean to be the deities' co-worker, Kierkegaard claims, ought to clear up the uncertainties between this life and the next. In summing up his brief analysis of Socrates's first indirect proof for immortality, Kierkegaard indicates what a better understanding would entail:

> Not until one recognizes that it is the same god who has led one by the hand through life and in the moment of death lets go, as it were, in order to open his arms and receive in them the yearning soul, not until then is the demonstration fully developed in conceptual form (CI, 67fn/SKS 1, 126).

The second indirect demonstration of immortality in the *Phaedo* derives from Socrates's demeanor throughout the trial and in his subsequent interaction with friends and family in jail. Kierkegaard finds Socrates's character before death moving: the "gladness, the bold confidence, the dauntlessness with which [he] goes to his death, the indifference with which he practically disregards it, are very inspiring" (CI, 67fn/SKS 1, 126). In spite of the personal sense of contentment with which he meets death, Socrates, Kierkegaard reminds the reader, does not know that an immortal life actually awaits him. What is interesting here is that Kierkegaard considers Socrates's character, his personal attitude toward death and immortality, as a "demonstration" of the afterlife, and he sees its power to arouse conviction as being more influential than arguments designed to persuade with good reasons or strong hypotheses. On this point, Kierkegaard writes:

> All this is fine, but if one also bears in mind that he still does not really know what the shape of the next life will be or whether there will be a next life, if amid this poetry we hear the prosaic calculating that it can never do any harm to assume another life and other things that will be made clear at their proper place, then one sees that the persuasive power of this argument is considerably limited (CI, 68fn/SKS 1, 126).

The personal or subjective approach to immortality—where one's actions betray belief in immortality without knowledge of its truth—becomes a normative condition for a person's approach toward his or her own immortality in many of Kierkegaard's writings (both signed and pseudonymous), but not all (as I discuss in the third section). Kierkegaard uses Socrates's cheerful and contented disposition, in spite of his ignorance, as an example throughout much of his authorship for how one ought to relate to immortality (by contrast, Kierkegaard's treatment of immortality in his *Christian Discourses* highlights the requisite fear associated with judgment in the afterlife). Because Socrates also uses the idea of immortality as a "point of departure" for his actions in this life, he becomes the model for Climacus's development of the ethics of immortality in his *Concluding Unscientific Postscript.*

But Socrates's confident demeanor has a dark underside. Kierkegaard exposes what he sees as the negative metaphysics supporting Socrates's positive disposition. Julia Watkin rightly notes, "Though Socrates is positive in being against suicide on the grounds that humans are 'on duty' in this life . . . it is not the Pauline idea of man as a collaborator with God as the transcendent Lord of life and death."[7] According to Kierkegaard, "Platonism wants one to die to sensate knowing in order to be dissolved by death into the kingdom of immortality, where the in-and-for-itself equality, the in-and-for-itself beauty, etc., live in the stillness of death. This is articulated even more strongly by Socrates when he declares that a philosopher's desire is to die and *to be dead*" (CI, 77/SKS 1, 135–36). In sharp contrast, the Christian view holds that "the moment of death is the last struggle between day and night; death is . . . birth" (CI, 77/SKS 1, 135). Although Socrates expresses immortality as an eternal quality of his temporal life, Kierkegaard argues that his knowledge of the eternal as recollected truth coheres with an intellectual approach to God and Platonic metaphysics, which posits natural immortality and a negative view of death. This leads Kierkegaard to point out what he considers an obvious conceptual difference between philosophical immortality and Christian resurrection: On Christianity's account, that which dies "is understood in its positivity as sin," and that which is "born and *is to arise* is understood just as positively" (CI, 76/SKS 1, 135; emphasis added).

Despite his hopes to meet "other good gods" in the afterlife, in the end Socrates may very well perish in the grave—his ignorance adheres to this position. His attitude toward death, therefore, is ironic and leveling. According to Kierkegaard, Socratic irony "breaches the bastion that separates the waters of heaven and of earth and unites with the total irony that annihilates the individual" (CI, 78/SKS 1, 136). Readers know irony's capacity for destruction, he writes, because Socrates banters with the possibility that death might be his complete annihilation—"The thought that one might become absolutely nothing through death . . . does not horrify him at all" (CI, 79/SKS 1, 137).[8] In his final hour, therefore, Socrates can die with a jest, in spite of the fact that he does not live in thoughtlessness about his death. This is *his* victory over death. By contrast, in at least three of the upbuilding discourses, Kierkegaard illustrates the hope upon which a Christian can be said to face death. The philosophic search for eternal truths, including immortality of the soul, led Socrates to his principle of ignorance, which in turn gave him freedom over the prejudicial ideas in his culture. On this point, Kierkegaard writes:

> [Socrates's] ignorance is the nothing with which he destroys any knowledge. This is best seen in his view of death. He is ignorant of what death is and of what there is after death, whether there is anything or nothing at all; consequently he is ignorant. But he does not take his ignorance greatly to heart; on the contrary, he genuinely feels quite liberated in his ignorance. Consequently, he is not in earnest about this ignorance, and yet he is altogether earnest about being ignorant (CI, 270/SKS 1, 307).

On Kierkegaard's account, Christians are not liberated by irony or ignorance; rather, their temporal hopes are for a full comprehension of the meaning of eternal salvation after death (EUD, 29/SKS 5, 37). Irony and the absence of positive content bridging the relationship between this life and the next lead to intellectual uncertainty about the meaning of immortality. Kierkegaard ultimately rejects this negative aspect of Socratic immortality, both in his upbuilding discourses and in his *Christian Discourses.* Socrates's personal appropriation of immortality as an idea to guide his life is the indirect demonstration that Kierkegaard finds encouraging (most fully developed by Climacus in the *Concluding Unscientific Postscript*). Socrates's strength is that he shows no signs of anxiety over his nearing death; according to Kierkegaard, his personality or character should "inspire" belief in immortality. His interlocutors, however, find his calm disposition unsettling (*Phaedo,* 63a). Neither Cebes nor Simmias are convinced of his argument against suicide as entailing an afterlife, so they press him for a "defense" of his beliefs (*Phaedo,* 62d–63d). Still unconvinced by Socrates's positive demeanor or his stated hopes for an afterlife, Simmias requests yet another explanation from Socrates concerning his belief in the afterlife—"do you intend to keep this belief to yourself as you leave us, or would you share it with us? I certainly think it would be a blessing for us too, and at the same time it would be your defense if you convince us of what you say" (*Phaedo,* 63d). And so the "prosaic calculation" over the nature and meaning of immortality in the *Phaedo* commences. The powerful, personal, indirect demonstration dies with Socrates. The arguments remain. While "prosaic calculations" about the nature of immortality would detract from seeing Socrates's indirect demonstration of immortality abiding in his personality in the *Phaedo,* Kierkegaard finds it appropriate to calculate and assume certain things about the afterlife when he discusses the victory over death for which he thinks Christians ought to hope. By doing so in the upbuilding discourses, he begins to discuss the content with which his notion of the afterlife differs from that of Socrates.

Kierkegaard's first upbuilding discourse, "The Expectancy of Faith," ends with almost the exact same wording as did his critique of Socrates's "obscuring" remarks against suicide expressed in the dissertation.[9] While Socrates posits a chasm between this life and the next, Kierkegaard assumes a conceptual link between them. The link, moreover, provides the content that foretells the disparity between their notions of the afterlife. Toward the end of the discourse, and just before the shared quotation between his dissertation and first discourse, Kierkegaard reintroduces the reader to a familiar phrase, one typically heard by Christian congregants. He holds that the phrase is "pregnant with meaning" and may be used properly or erroneously. The phrase is "and then at last obtain eternal salvation" (EUD, 28/SKS 5, 36). If used correctly, in faithful expectancy and patience, the phrase liberates; used improperly, out of impatience or despondency over life, the phrase cultivates an "inner disquiet." Regardless of how one chooses to use it, Kierkegaard maintains that one only learns the phrase "from and through God" (EUD, 28/SKS 5, 36). Since persons have not invented the content of the phrase, complete understanding of it occurs only after death—when we are "carried away from the world . . . on this phrase to that place where we shall comprehend its full meaning, just as it is the same God who, after having led us by his hand through the world, draws back his hand and opens his arms to receive in them the yearning soul" (EUD, 29/SKS 5, 37; cf. CI, 67/SKS 1, 125–26).

Kierkegaard aims to guide congregants to what he sees as a proper attitude toward the future, most especially the impending future of one's "final hour" before death (EUD, 28/SKS 5, 37). Commit your mind and thoughts to your "Father in heaven," he advises, so that the meaning of "eternal salvation" is not forgotten in this life. Kierkegaard expects the content of the phrase "at last obtain eternal salvation" may guide one through life, providing comfort, hope, joy, exultation—used rightly, it admonishes and reproves, encourages and persuades (EUD, 28–29/SKS 5, 36–37). With trust in the content portrayed in scriptural passages such as Romans 8:28—that "all things must serve for good those who love God" (EUD, 19/SKS 5, 28)—and with the hope for eternal salvation that moves one through life, death cannot be faced with Socratic jest, ignorance, or philosophical indifference, for after death one is "carried away from the world" on certain expectations. Those expectations include a new birth in a "place where we shall comprehend its full meaning" (EUD, 29/SKS 5, 37).

But that is not all for which one hopes. In contrast to the eternity that occupies Anna of Luke 2:33–40, in the discourse titled "Patience in Expectancy," Kierkegaard writes:

> But you, my listener, you have not placed your expectancy in that which is deceitful even when it comes; your expectancies are not disappointed. You are expecting the resurrection of the dead, of both the righteous and the unrighteous; you are expecting a blessed reunion with those whom death took away from you and with those whom life separated from you; you are expecting that your life will become transparent and clear to you; your estate in blessed understanding with your God and with yourself. . . . But of course this expectancy is not disappointed, because the time of its fulfillment has not yet arrived. . . . How could this come too late—then it would itself have to be temporal (EUD, 216/SKS 5, 215–16).

Here Kierkegaard turns the matter of expecting the resurrection into a question for the reader. He uses a similar rhetorical strategy in his writings on resurrection in the *Christian Discourses* concerning the importance of a personal god, but there he assumes the afterlife as a fact. Part of the thrust and power of questioning whether the reader hopes for resurrection or believes in the promise of eternal happiness and salvation as given in 1 Corinthians 15, for example, is to distinguish sharply between the *conception* of the afterlife in a Christian context and other, to his way of thinking, contrary notions. If Anna, a Jew, cannot be disappointed even if her expectations for the eternal are not fulfilled (EUD, 224/SKS 5, 223), then why should Christians be disappointed when they allegedly expect a posttemporal, postmortem eternity in the resurrection?

In contrast to Kierkegaard's position that eternity transcends temporal order, recent scholarship on the nature of eternity in Kierkegaard's thought argues that by eternity he merely means some type of temporal existential experience. David Kangas, for example, correctly holds that "the expectancy of faith . . . does not flee the ambiguity of existence but preserves the open character of the future"; however, I disagree that for Kierkegaard it remains open "as such," essentially and indeterminately.[10] In our post-Freudian world, where the "wish" for immortality has been criticized as a self-centered wish to live forever and where behaving "as if" one believes in what ought to be seen as fiction is a "fresh psychological problem,"[11] Kangas's concerns address modern sensibilities; but I argue that they are not identical with Kierkegaard's.[12] In his discourse titled "The Expectancy of Eternal Salvation," Kierkegaard argues that the wish for heaven's salvation is an unnecessary concern provided one can assume that salvation is a given for all. But assuming universal salvation comes with a problematic understanding of God. It makes one "foolishly assume that God in heaven resembles a weak human being who does not have the heart to deny eternal salvation to anyone" (EUD, 256–57/SKS 5, 253). Kierkegaard turns the universalist assumption around and questions wherein lies the important difference between a person who with concern and longing wishes for God's salvation and another who never desires nor concerns himself with eternal salvation, yet allegedly receives it nonetheless. If it is the case that everyone becomes acquainted with heaven's salvation at the moment of death, Kierkegaard maintains that the unconcerned person would have to "die again of shame," and would have to "wish himself elsewhere again, since heaven's salvation and his unworthiness could not correspond" (EUD, 258/SKS 5, 254). Kierkegaard claims that despite the silliness of speaking about God forcing salvation on all people regardless of their desires, putting the matter this way is revealing. While he is aware of the problematic nature of wishing for more life after death, he nonetheless flatly rejects treating salvation as a matter of indifference or leaving its content open as such.

A Christian, to his way of thinking, would be horrified by the thought that there was nothing after death. This is not because Christians merely wish for their own prolongation. Christian faith in an afterlife does not begin from a personal desire to extend temporal life infinitely in perpetuity

(CD, 205/SKS 10, 214–15); rather, hope for a resurrection is placed within a narrative of cosmic redemption and a new, disambiguated creation. Faith in the resurrection is not built on an individual's temporal projects or self-reflection on their merits or lack thereof. It is, at bottom, an orientation toward a promise and a gift from God (EUD, 272/SKS 5, 267). Therefore, earnest concern and the wish for heaven's salvation are never misplaced or wasted from Kierkegaard's perspective. In spite of the dangers of the universalist position, "the one thing needful," he insists, is "the heart to wish for heaven's salvation" (EUD, 258/SKS 5, 255). Praying, wishing, being concerned, longing, and striving for it (even though one does not deserve salvation through merit) are not in vain. On the contrary, Kierkegaard writes that one becomes "qualified to inherit it only by vigilance in expectancy" (EUD, 259/SKS 5, 255). Salvation's employment, he adds, becomes a gain in this life, because "the expectancy of an eternal salvation is able (which otherwise seems impossible) to be in two places at the same time: it works in heaven and it works on earth" (EUD, 259/SKS 5, 255). This is why Kierkegaard maintains that the consequence of expectancy is "two-fold"—there is a temporal *and* an extratemporal aspect to eternal salvation (EUD, 259/SKS 5, 256).

How does one know whether one seeks God's kingdom first or whether one merely wishes for a prolongation of their temporal lives? According to Kierkegaard, the "more profoundly earnestness comprehends the anxiety of separation [of one being rejected or removed from eternal salvation] . . . the more genuine is the expectancy" (EUD, 259/SKS 5, 255–56). On Kierkegaard's reading, Socrates was not anxious before death, guided as he was by the idea of immortality. Socrates does not expect a resurrection or a new creation. If an immortality awaits him after death it is natural; he expects no "sudden transition" (EUD, 257/SKS 5, 254). That is why, in the context of the discourse on "The Expectancy of an Eternal Salvation," Kierkegaard does not draw on the figure, however inspiring, of Socrates's temporal appropriation of the idea of immortality for help in this life, but instead refers the reader to Paul and 2 Corinthians 4:17–18 for advice on how to "deliberate on what consequences the expectancy of an eternal salvation has for this earthly, troubled life" (EUD, 254/SKS 5, 251). Although people suffer and are afflicted with all sorts of troubles, Paul advises them not to "lose heart. . . . For this slight momentary affliction is preparing us for an eternal weight of glory beyond all measure" (2 Cor. 4:16–17).[13] The expectancy of victory over death on this account results from knowing, in this life, "that the one who raised the Lord Jesus will raise us also with Jesus" (2 Cor. 4:14). By referring to Paul's hope in the resurrection

Kierkegaard does not intend for faith's victory over death to remain conceptually and essentially open. Any open-endedness of faith for Kierkegaard rests in trusting the "Father in heaven" who carries the expectant one from this life to the next on the hopes of eternal salvation and a full disclosure of its meaning at some point after death (EUD, 28–29/SKS 5, 36–37). Due to the difficulty involved in acquiring a precise hold on the content of faith, Kierkegaard redirects the issue with a decisive question: "Do you expect victory?" (EUD, 27/SKS 5, 35). He expects the answer to make obfuscation disappear.

Although the upbuilding discourses articulate a concern for the development of a spiritually healthy temporal existence, Socrates's subjective appropriation of the idea of immortality as a guide for temporal expectancy and patience is absent from the discourses titled "The Expectancy of Faith," "Patience in Expectancy," and "The Expectancy of Eternal Salvation." However moving Socrates's character has been for Kierkegaard, at this point in his authorial career he finds it more useful to distance himself from the example of Socrates in order to explain the Christian conception of postmortem hopes. According to Kierkegaard, contentment in life's struggles, in the face of death, and toward the ultimate future beyond history ought not to be based on Socratic irony and ignorance nor Stoic resignation and indifference toward what is to come, but on faith that "all things must serve for good those who love God." Thus victory over death is in whatever will be part of the resurrection. If it comes, Kierkegaard says—from the position of faith—it does so with blessedness; if it does not, then that is best, because "the good never mocks a human being" (EUD, 216/SKS 5, 216).

Socrates in Climacus's *Concluding Unscientific Postscript*

In spite of the important conceptual differences on the issue of the afterlife seen in the dissertation and the upbuilding discourses, Kierkegaard's pseudonym, Johannes Climacus, draws on Socratic lessons as a guide in his discussion of immortality in *Postscript.* As David D. Possen correctly argues in another chapter in this volume, Socrates becomes the model for Climacus's development of subjective ethics precisely because he "is . . . ignorant . . . about what death brings, and about his own personal fate in the hereafter; but he nonetheless embraces the *possibility* of immortality as a lifelong ethical challenge." Climacus's treatment of Socrates does not radically differ from Kierkegaard's magisterial assessment of Socrates's personal "demonstration" of immortality. In *Postscript,* however, ignorance with respect to one's postmortem fate is given a more optimistic construction than appears in the dissertation, the upbuilding discourses, and *Christian Discourses.* As I will discuss in the third section, Kierkegaard returns to a prioritization of the objective over the subjective with respect to the afterlife in his *Christian Discourses.* What one learns there of Kierkegaard's conception of the afterlife (coupled with his critical comments in the dissertation and upbuilding discourses) contradicts the suggestion that he thinks the only, or best, way to articulate conceptions of the afterlife is to insist that existing persons ought to relate to the possibility of the afterlife in the modality of subjectively concerned ignorance.[14] Of course, Kierkegaard never advises against becoming subjective, but in a world into which revelation has come, certain content about the afterlife is put forward to be either rejected or believed. Therefore, Kierkegaard thinks his argument for immortality and resurrection in *Christian Discourses* may "wound" readers, and the "demonstration" he offers there makes relating to it more difficult, because whether one orients one's life toward it or not, to his way of thinking, the fact of postmortem judgment stands. If we keep in mind Watkin's claim that the manner in which Kierkegaard approaches the issue of the afterlife varies according to other points he attempts to make, readers should not be surprised if they come across what appear to be inconsistencies, or what sometimes seem like contradictions, in his writings on the topic. Therefore, one should expect the language, terms, and conditions meant to connote some type of afterlife to vary as well. Of course, if Kierkegaard's focus and strategy shift, then his treatment of Socrates's understanding of the afterlife may vary as well.

Since Climacus's treatment of Socratic subjective immortality has been well described in Possen's chapter, I focus instead on how Climacus uses Socrates as a corrective to certain types of arguments for immortality that were prevalent during his time. Once contextualized in this way, it is easier to see that though Socrates may be the "highest next to Christianity," he is not the absolute normative standard. He is, however, an excellent corrective to both spiritual lassitude and erroneous, revisionist formulations of the eternal life. Providing this picture adds another layer to how Kierkegaard (and not just his pseudonyms) develops his understanding of postmortem existence. This in turn enables readers to gain insight into Kierkegaard's broad concerns about the nature of the afterlife.

Climacus pits Socrates's subjective deployment of his idea of immortality against Hegelian-type arguments for a revisionist conception of eternity in order to expose the weaknesses and deficiencies in the latter's account.

Prior to any discussion of how Socrates subjectively relates to immortality, Climacus sets the stage for a comparison by bringing the reader up to speed on how the issue of immortality is generally treated by philosophers in his time. On this topic he writes:

> I know that some have found immortality in Hegel; others have not. I know that I have not found it in the system, since it is unreasonable to look for it there anyway, because in a fantastical sense all systematic thinking is *sub specie aeterni* . . . and to that extent immortality is there as eternity. But this immortality is not at all the one inquired about, since the question is about the immortality of a mortal, and that question is not answered by showing that the eternal is immortal, because the eternal is, after all, not the mortal, and the immortality of the eternal is a tautology and a misuse of words (CUP, 1:171/SKS 7, 158–59).[15]

For Climacus, the problem with the Hegelian-type argument for immortality is that it assumes a concept of immortality that differs from the antecedent and traditional conception; namely, it does not refer to the immortality of particular human beings, but merely to an abstract conception of eternity. Therefore, Climacus argues, it merely provides an inadequate revisionist formulation of the original concept, resulting in an empty tautology at best. Climacus here critiques the fact that conceptualizing immortality abstractly, in terms of generic eternity, begs the question at hand. In sharp contrast to this way of philosophizing on this subject, immortality, he insists, has an authentic significance for persons. Therefore, Climacus argues that the subjective understanding of immortality can have an effect on individual's lives. This aspect of immortality is ignored by many of the philosophers of his day. In fact, speaking to a philosopher about immortality, Climacus writes, is "like someone visiting a family whose members speak a private language and use the words of the mother tongue but understand something different by them" (CUP, 1:172/SKS 7, 159). On Climacus's account, it is quite easy for philosophers to churn out several proofs for immortality, because they have already dropped the question of what it means for existing persons to become immortal and turned to solving quandaries about abstract eternity. Moreover, they believe the difficulty of understanding the nature of immortality lies in the attempt to prove it by arguments and demonstrations. Ever fond of reversing questions, Climacus reorders the difficulty and claims that the real stumbling block results from a person's attempt to make the matter of immortality simple and about oneself.

Not all philosophers speak cryptically. According to Climacus, Socrates exemplifies what it means to address immortality simply. Unlike those who offer inadequate revisionist notions or endeavor to predicate their belief in immortality on objective demonstrations, Socrates allows the objective uncertainty of immortality to stand. Despite Socrates's ignorance, Climacus finds that he "ordered his whole life" with respect to its certainty (CUP, 1:201/SKS 7, 185). The point here is not so much that Socrates "proves" immortality by "demonstrating" it with his life,[16] but that Socrates thinks that the thought of it, as it relates to him, requires some action on his part so that his life "might be acceptable—*if* there is an immortality" (CUP, 1:201/SKS 7, 185). Socrates supersedes other philosophers when it comes to the question of how to relate to the meaning of the afterlife because he uses the idea of immortality as a standard to guide and test his action in life. Socrates supports Climacus's intuition in *Postscript* that the question of immortality cannot even be properly posed in objective form: "Objectively the question cannot be answered at all, because objectively the question of immortality cannot be asked, since immortality is precisely the intensification and highest development of the developed subjectivity" (CUP, 1:173/SKS 7, 160). In short, according to Climacus, it is not so much that there is nothing objective about the afterlife, but rather, methodologically there is nothing objective regarding one's grasp of one's own immortality. Climacus provides evidence for the notion that matters of subjective importance (such as immortality) do not preclude the existence of objectivity. In order to show that subjective issues include objectivity Climacus tells a story about two persons who go to pray at church (CUP, 1:201/SKS 7, 184). If one of them is factually mistaken (that is, believes in the "wrong" god) and the other is factually correct (believes in the "right" God), then, as a simple matter of logic, there is a fact of the matter. Even though Climacus indicates the historical and objective nature of Christianity—"the historicity of Christianity is true"—he insists that every effort to establish the certainty of it proves nothing beyond an "approximation" (CUP, 1:576/SKS 7, 524).

The strength of Socrates's subjective appropriation of the idea of immortality to guide his life also contains elements that point toward a difference with other conceptions. Christians and non-Christians are both capable of relating to the afterlife as something to guide and test their temporal lives, but Kierkegaard thinks that the "task" of immortality ultimately differs between them. As he sees it, Socrates relates himself to the "idea" of immortality in order to appropriate it "as a means to change [his] life"; a Christian, in contrast, relates to "something historical, the story of Jesus

Christ," in order to change his or her life (JP, 1:27/SKS 23, 51). On this point of difference Kierkegaard writes:

> But with regard to becoming a Christian there is a dialectical difference from Socrates which must be remembered. Specifically in the relationship to immortality—a person relates himself to himself and the idea—no further. But when a man chooses upon an *if* to believe in Christ—that is, chooses to wager his life upon that, then he has permission to address himself directly to Christ in prayer. Thus the historical is the occasion and still also the object of faith (JP, 1:28/SKS 23, 52).

Contrary notions of immortality remain between them because they face different points of departure in relating to the afterlife. The distinction drawn here is similar to that drawn between religiousness A and B found in *Postscript.* On this view, a Christian should also relate to the uncertainty of eternity as a way to test his or her actions, but the task differs because, unlike with Socrates, the possibility of eternal happiness is based on the historical events of the incarnation and the resurrection of Christ. Despite the conceptual differences in their accounts of the afterlife, Socrates remains an exemplary figure in *Postscript* because he illustrates that focusing on immortality as something one ought to prove detracts from seeing it as something that ought to shape one's life. Furthermore, the fact that Climacus describes the objective and historical nature of the Christian afterlife does not result, in his hands, in further proofs or demonstrations of immortality. The point of *Postscript* on the issue of the afterlife is that important religious or subjective issues require a personal response and not objective arguments, whether of the revisionist or traditional type.

Christian Discourses

Even if Kierkegaard had not written a particular discourse explicitly stating his understanding and belief in the Christian tenet of the resurrection of the dead (CD, 202–13/SKS 10, 211–21), his understanding of terms such as grace, eternal salvation, judgment, and resurrection within other discourses would still put his grasp of the Christian conception at odds with Socrates's account of immortality. This section answers three different questions, gleaned from three different discourses, which further clarify the difference between their conceptions of the afterlife. I should remark at the outset, if only because it would be redundant to repeat the point at each turn, that the three issues under review fall under a general position Kierkegaard assumes regarding conceptual content in *Christian Discourses.* "For a person to be a Christian," he writes, "it certainly is required that what he believes is a *definite* something, but then with equal certainty it is also required that it be *entirely definite* that *he* believes" (CD, 244/SKS 10, 250). The three questions analyzed in this section are: (1) Why does Kierkegaard privilege discussing immortality as a fact, rather than as a subjective relation based on ignorance, in his Christian discourse on resurrection? (2) Why does Kierkegaard use the figure of Socrates to test, tease, and question persons on whether they believe they are closer to salvation once they have become believers? (3) Why does Kierkegaard hold that Socrates cannot help Christians concerned with their eternal salvation?

The Christian discourse titled "There Will Be the Resurrection of the Dead, of the Righteous—and of the Unrighteous" articulates an understanding of the afterlife as a fact. In other words, whether human beings desire it, relate to it subjectively, or remain ignorant of it, Kierkegaard claims that persons are raised in the resurrection. "You are immortal whether you want to be or not," he insists (CD, 212/SKS 10, 221). No one remains in the grave after death because everyone must come up for judgment. In an early sketch for the third section of his *Christian Discourses,* Kierkegaard refers to his "new argument for immortality" as cause for joy. One no longer needs demonstrations of immortality, he exclaims, because the certainty of immortality is guaranteed by judgment in the resurrection (CD, 378/SKS 20, 289). Nevertheless, he proceeds to offer an argument for a particular understanding of immortality that stands without appealing to notions of subjectivity. Whereas Climacus critiques spiritual apathy with respect to eternal happiness, Kierkegaard here confronts what he sees as a direct attack on traditional doctrine. As I have argued elsewhere, without knowledge of the nature of the debates on notions like immortality, eternity, and resurrection in Kierkegaard's context, the novelty he sees in his own approach toward articulating the meaning of the afterlife in this discourse is not altogether apparent to contemporary readers.[17]

In his historical context, demonstrating immortality had become a sort of parlor game. "Immortality," he writes, "is on the way to becoming a kind of luxury to people," its meaning left up to "whatever one likes" (CD, 204–5/SKS 10, 213). Therefore, Kierkegaard gives the matter another turn and talks about the resurrection. More to the point, he binds the two concepts together in support of one fact—that there is an afterlife. Notwithstanding their important conceptual differences, Kierkegaard is here more concerned with highlighting something he thinks Christians overlook, and to their own peril. Given the confusion of the age, they are apt to think that the resurrection is as peaceful as is an immortality of the soul. Therefore, he begins his argument by addressing readers directly and "violating" their "private security" (CD, 202/SKS 10, 211) with respect to the issue of immortality. He "assaults" them with the question of whether they count themselves amongst the righteous or the unrighteous (CD, 203/SKS 10, 212). He considers it necessary to bring the concepts of immortality and the resurrection together because it enables him to insist on the necessity of postmortem judgment. Kierkegaard jars readers by assuming that persons are immortal because they are raised from the grave for judgment. More importantly, discussing judgment allows Kierkegaard to speak of God ("the eternal") administering the "test" or "task" of immortality in this life and salvation or perdition in the next. In sharp contrast to Socrates's positive demeanor toward death, Kierkegaard advocates that readers should "fear" their immortality; it should make them "tremble" because they will be judged by God (CD, 203, 205/SKS 10, 212, 214–15). According to his construal, notions of the afterlife should cause Christians to be "anxious and afraid" (CD, 204/SKS 10, 213) because they are essentially guilty (CUP, 529/SKS 7, 480–81), since each is a sinner (CD, 212/SKS 10, 220), and "only sin has the power to mark a person in such a way that . . . it perhaps is never overcome in eternity" (CD, 101/SKS 10, 113). Reinstating talk about a personal God acting as "lord and ruler" and as central to life's activities, death, and what happens beyond the grave corrects, to Kierkegaard's way of thinking, allegedly deficient demonstrations and erroneous arguments about the afterlife, but it also halts equivocation about postmortem existence. On this point he writes:

> It is this very shrewdness of the human race that has managed to get the position of immortality turned wrong. . . . It is the human race that has wanted to rebel against God; it is the human race that has wanted to abolish immortality and has managed to have it made into a problem. With immortality (and what it implies, the immortality of every *individual*), God is the lord and ruler, and the *single individual* relates himself to him. But when immortality becomes a problem, then God is abolished and the human race is God (CD, 213/SKS 10, 221).

Kierkegaard suspects that attempts to ignore the immortality of particular persons (the Hegelian-type approach toward eternity) really aim to disprove a personal God. In other words, he understands Feuerbach's thesis that "all theology is anthropology" to follow naturally upon the heels of getting the "position of immortality turned wrong."[18] In pointed contrast, Kierkegaard affirms what they deny—a personal God and a personal immortality are inseparable. Given his broader concerns to uphold God as "lord and ruler," Kierkegaard makes a division between "deciding immortality" and "demonstrating immortality." Demonstrating immortality involves letting the issue of whether anyone believes in it or not remain open (CD, 204/SKS 10, 213). Deciding on immortality entails that one believes *and* that one is clear about what one believes. Most importantly for Kierkegaard, it involves being "anxious and afraid" because it involves the risk of being counted among the unrighteous. Kierkegaard "demonstrates" this picture to readers in an effort to halt allegedly flawed accounts of the afterlife.

As I stated in the second section, Kierkegaard never advises against becoming subjective. One can only begin the task of immortality once one has "decided immortality," which includes belief in the resurrection, judgment, and a personal God. Although he does not predicate the meaning of immortality on the subjective appropriation of it (as did Climacus), once he has cleared room for what he sees as a corrective to erroneous portrayals and egregious omissions from what he thinks is entailed in the afterlife, then he can readdress a point in common with Socrates—"the question ought to be whether I am living in such a way as my immortality requires of me" (CD, 205/SKS 10, 214). Starting the task of immortality in this life, however, ought not to proceed from a position of ignorance, nor is it based on the self-posited idea of immortality Kierkegaard finds in Socrates. Paul, Kierkegaard maintains, infuriates people by proclaiming rather than demonstrating a conception of immortality or the resurrection, but he nonetheless knows what he believes (CD, 206/SKS 10, 214). By contrast, Socrates is free to engage in perpetual questioning in spite of his beliefs and hopes about the nature of immortality because he "had no doctrine" (CD, 219/SKS 10, 226).

In the discourse titled "We Are Closer to Salvation Now—Than When We Became Believers," Kierkegaard uses the figure of Socrates to question a person about the status of his beliefs about his proximity to salvation. The discourse also posits the importance of "self-activity" with respect to salvation (CD, 221/SKS 10, 228), a valuable lesson Kierkegaard admires (as does Climacus) in the figure of Socrates. Unlike *Postscript*'s example of Socratic ignorance with respect to immortality, this discourse does not claim that a person of faith ought to practice subjective appropriation of immortality (or their salvation) in ignorance, but rather focuses on the notion that they receive salvation as a gift (CD, 221/SKS 10, 229). However, a clarification of the gift is not the main point of the discourse. According to Kierkegaard, it is vital that a Christian be aware of two things: (1) one actually became a believer, and (2) one came to believe in something. Both requirements relate to another interesting and significant use of Socrates in *Christian Discourses.* In the discourse "He Was Believed in the World," Kierkegaard has "the single individual" talk about the value of Socrates and Christ regarding one's own eternal salvation. In satisfying the first condition (in becoming a believer), the single individual (henceforth I refer to the believer simply as a Christian) accepts the responsibility of having faith in particular content (the second requirement).

But perhaps a Christian never questions herself about whether she has become a believer if her status as a person of faith has been assumed through baptism and the culture of Christendom (CD, 218/SKS 10, 226). If that is the case, Kierkegaard considers it hazardous to assume proximity to salvation without knowing for oneself whether one became a person of faith. The stakes are that high. So Kierkegaard imagines Socrates interrogating a Christian on her beliefs in order to clarify the situation (CD, 218/SKS 10, 226). Socrates's "teasing" and persistent questioning could go on indefinitely unless the interrogated person affirms that an explicit beginning in the direction toward salvation through faith has been made. Kierkegaard maintains that "the way to deliverance is faith, and only when it is definitely fixed that one has become a believer can there be any mention of being closer *now*" (CD, 219/SKS 10, 227). Only a beginning halts Socratic questioning. But a beginning made in what exactly?

Prior to any discussion of being closer to salvation in this life, Kierkegaard insists that one become clear on the requirements (as he sees them) of faith. The content with which a Christian ought to become aware in faith entails that she be willing to leave everything in order to follow Christ. Subsequently, the possibility of the "pain of faithful suffering" opens up for a Christian the moment she becomes a believer (CD, 242/SKS 10, 249). Kierkegaard advises that one ought to see suffering faith in Christ as a blessing in this life and as foreshadowing blessings to come in the afterlife—as Matthew puts it: "Blessed are you when people insult and persecute you and speak every kind of evil against you for my sake and lie. Rejoice and be glad, your reward will be great in heaven" (CD, 230/SKS 10, 237). "Voluntarily to give up everything to follow Christ," Kierkegaard argues, "means to be convinced of the gloriousness of the good that Christianity promises" (CD, 179/SKS 10, 190).

A beginning therefore is a parting or a leaving behind. The comparative language of being closer to salvation now that one has become a believer becomes less "confused," and a blessing, if one holds the relationship between this life and the next firmly in view during one's struggles in this life. Christianity requires the ongoing possibility that one must give up everything one loves in this life in order to follow Christ.[19] In order to become a believer one must first become aware of the enormity of this responsibility. If one chooses to believe this requirement, then Kierkegaard maintains one must realize that temporal relationships may be jeopardized. In the discourse "He Was Believed in the World," Kierkegaard brings Socrates and Christ together to clarify how a Christian ought to think of the "pain of faithful suffering" caused by the requirement. The discussion also necessitates that a Christian ought to distance him or herself from Socratic ignorance in relating to his or her eternal salvation in the afterlife.

A Christian "confesses" that he finds Socrates's life inspiring and "closest to Christianity" (CD, 241/SKS 10, 247). If he finds himself surrounded by sagacious, yet indifferent and dispassionate, people, he longs to "listen" to Socrates and to learn from his "ignorance"; he finds his wisdom and service to the truth "moving"—that "face to face with death he spoke about himself . . . just as simply as he ever did in the marketplace" (CD, 241/SKS 10, 248). However, a Christian "would have" to say "[b]ut I have never believed in him" (CD, 241/SKS 10, 248). Once a Christian thinks about his or her eternal salvation then Socrates becomes "a very unimportant person, a sheer nonentity, a nobody" (CD, 241/SKS 10, 248). Socrates's life gives a Christian something to "admire." Christ's death gives a Christian life (CD, 242, 258/SKS 10, 248, 271). Without Christ, Kierkegaard writes, "it is a matter of indifference whether I live or die" (CD, 242/SKS 10, 248). In sharp contrast to the ignorance with which Socrates confronts death, a Christian faces death in the belief that "[Christ] is life" (CD, 242/SKS 10, 248). Orientation toward Christ and the matter of one's eternal salvation requires such belief. With respect to these issues, Kierkegaard writes, "I am not living on any 'if.' Dead set against an 'if' and troubled by this 'if,' I have ventured out (it is called taking a risk), and now I believe" (CD, 240/SKS 10, 247). The risk involved in the requirement to leave everything behind and follow Christ means that a Christian believes he may be called on to leave his family, friends, and loved ones. He comes to this difficult realization the moment he becomes a believer. Understandably, the possibility threatens to unsettle how one understands one's temporal life as filled with meaningful and loving relationships. But Kierkegaard thinks sacrificing one's eternal salvation by not being up for such a calling endangers the quality of one's afterlife. Without the willingness to risk disrupting temporal relations, Kierkegaard insists that "it is impossible to believe, because the obedience of faith must go that far" (CD, 243/SKS 10, 249). Moreover, a Christian also believes that God "blesses every relationship [he] has," and that it is God's "will that the son shall love his father, the husband his wife, the father his children, and so on" (CD, 243/SKS 10, 249–50). In spite of this belief, Kierkegaard writes:

> But if he in whom I believe, if it were possible that he could request it of me, I would relinquish this love—out of love for him in whom I believe. I take upon myself the pain of faithful suffering and the burden of responsibility; I patiently bear every judgment of condemnation upon me, even that of my loved ones, *until they sometime in eternity* will understand me—*he will see to that* (CD, 242–43/SKS 10, 249; emphasis added).

Should it come to pass that a Christian must struggle and suffer for the sake of his or her beliefs in temporal life, then at some point after death he or she will be understood. Faith in the promise from God guarantees such hope in the face of death. Holding onto a relation between this life and the next through faith anticipates a qualitatively new life after death. Assurance that one has faith necessitates that one loves others in this life, but also that one will gain final meaning about one's temporal efforts in the afterlife.

Concluding Thoughts

My analysis illustrates that Kierkegaard finds Socrates's conception of the afterlife wanting when held up to the Christian story of the resurrection. Kierkegaard's signed writings diminish the importance of Climacus's subjective account of immortality in order to uphold what he sees as the Christian conception of the resurrection, judgment, and blessedness in the afterlife. Although he rejects certain aspects of the Platonic and Socratic philosophical account of immortality, Socrates represents the highest a philosopher might reach in his or her personal relation to the idea of life after death. In the end, however, the Socratic notion of natural immortality is incompatible with a Christian's concern for eternal salvation. Kierkegaard believes ultimate rest from life's struggles and victory over death occurs in a new creation in the resurrection.

In spite of Kierkegaard's clear writings to this effect, scholars continue to either eliminate transcendent aspects of eternity from his work[20] or they align Kierkegaard's understanding too closely with that of Socrates.

For example, while I agree with Edward F. Mooney's claim that Kierkegaard led a Socratically inspired Christian existence,[21] he nonetheless parted with his mentor over doctrinal matters concerning the nature of the afterlife and the power of a transcendent, redeeming God. Mooney is concerned to show that Kierkegaard had no interest in the doctrine of the afterlife; for him Kierkegaard's modern triumph was that he balanced his own "Socratic abstention on doctrine" with a "vigorous *questioning* of cultural Christendom."[22] In sharp contrast to Mooney's position, I argue that Kierkegaard's positive use of Socrates reached its limit precisely because they had no doctrine in common.

There are a variety of thinkers who for assorted reasons excise the notion of a post-mortem existence from Christian theology and ethical reasoning. This is to be expected, as no religious tradition is monolithic. The historical tradition of Christianity is replete with changes in attitudes, practices, and beliefs about the afterlife. Indeed, the current normative commitment seems to jettison transcendent accounts of the afterlife. As far as intellectual history is concerned, however, I maintain that scholars who read their own contemporary normative commitments about the afterlife into writings of previous eras (which do not share those commitments) jeopardize our understanding of those traditions. If one understands Kierkegaard's conception of the afterlife as merely Socratic or merely temporal, then one neglects to describe the significance for his thought of the victorious new creation in which he hoped to partake after his death.

NOTES

1. Alastair Hannay, *Kierkegaard: A Biography* (Cambridge: Cambridge University Press, 2001), p. 418.

2. Kierkegaard uses different terms to signify the afterlife throughout his authorship. On this point see Julia Watkin, "Dying and Eternal Life as Paradox" (PhD diss., University of Bristol, 1979), pp. 189–90.

3. A detailed treatment of these factors would require more pages than are available to me here. For more information on the historical and conceptual influences on Kierkegaard's manner of arguing for and about the afterlife, see my "Kierkegaard's 'New Argument' for Immortality," *Journal of Religious Ethics* 38, no. 1 (March 2010): pp. 143–86.

4. Another way to put it is that Kierkegaard considers a subjective approach to immortality necessary but not sufficient in order to articulate a Christian account of the resurrection.

5. All quotations from Plato's *Phaedo* come from *Five Dialogues,* 2nd ed., trans. G. M. A. Grube, ed. John M. Cooper (Indianapolis, Ind.: Hackett Publishing Company, 2002).

6. Watkin, "Dying and Eternal Life as Paradox," p. 36.

7. Watkin, "Dying and Eternal Life as Paradox," p. 35.

8. Also see JP, 4:214/SKS 23, 425.

9. The Hongs point out the similar wording in the last footnote to their translation of the first edifying discourse (EUD, 505).

10. David Kangas and Martin Kavka, "Hearing, Patiently: Time and Salvation in Kierkegaard and Levinas," in *Kierkegaard and Levinas: Ethics, Politics, and Religion,* ed. J. Aaron Simmons and David Wood, p. 130 (Bloomington: Indiana University Press, 2008).

11. Sigmund Freud, *The Future of an Illusion,* trans. and ed. James Strachey (New York: W. W. Norton & Company, 1961), pp. 36, 38, 63, 69.

12. If Anna in the gospel of Luke has heuristic significance for Kierkegaard, it is because he has a peculiar understanding of her value as an example of patience. Questioning the reader's hopes for an eternity outside of time (in the form of a resurrection) only makes sense if he focuses on her nihilistic relationship toward history and communal life. For Kierkegaard, she remains alone in the temple; she is not concerned (as are others at the time) with the redemption of Israel. In responding to Kangas in their article, Martin Kavka underscores Kierkegaard's particular reading of Anna. Kavka writes, "What remains when the relationship to God is made sacred . . . is the relationship to the community. This is the dimension of Anna's prophecy that Kierkegaard almost entirely ignores, the one in which she speaks to others (Luke 2:38). . . . That group is bound together by their being the ones who expect (*prosdechomenoi*) redemption. This last detail suggests that [Anna's] patience too is for the sake of something. . . . Anna does amount to something as a result of that instant that she sees Jesus of Nazareth, for in seeking to verify her patience, she speaks of God to the community" (Kangas and Kavka, "Hearing, Patiently," p. 145). Kavka is right to insert Anna's social context back into the reading of Luke 2. I argue that Kierkegaard uses Anna's patience in expectancy not to clarify a patience that ought to remain infinitely open as such (i.e., expectancy without object), but as an example of a *different type* of expectation. Therefore, his question to readers about their hopes of resurrection makes sense. They ought to know that the time of (their) fulfillment has not yet come. In consequence, their answer to the question not only clarifies the nature of what they expect, but should point them toward a patience fitting the anticipation of eternity. This should lead us to the conclusion that Kierkegaard does not think that expectancy should remain open as such.

13. *The New Oxford Annotated Bible,* 3rd ed., ed. Michael D. Coogan (Oxford: Oxford University Press, 2001).

14. Therefore, I argue that Possen (in this volume) is not entirely correct to conclude that outside of Climacus's treatment of Socrates's subjective appropriation of immortality "we have *no* proofs, let alone good or better proofs, of the immortality of the soul, and the life of Socrates certainly cannot help us find such proof." Taking the last point first, as I have shown in the first section, Kierkegaard thought that Socrates's personality and character ought to have inspired belief in

immortality for *his* interlocutors. That is why he calls it an "indirect" demonstration of immortality in the dissertation. Of course, when no one can see Socrates in action any longer because he is dead then it makes sense to say that the demonstration cannot help, because it is not there. On the first point, Kierkegaard thinks that his "new argument" for immortality and resurrection in *Christian Discourses* supersedes others given in his intellectual context (see my "Kierkegaard's 'New Argument'" for analysis of this issue). In *Postscript,* moreover, Climacus alludes to better rhetorical demonstrations for the afterlife (CUP, 1:429–30/SKS 7, 390–91). Furthermore, Vigilius Haufniensis, pseudonymous author of *The Concept of Anxiety,* thinks that aspects of Poul Martin Møller's arguments for immortality are "true" (CA, 153/SKS 4, 452). Finally, Kierkegaard's purpose in referring to scripture and doctrine on the matter of eternal life in the *Christian Discourses* is to wrest from equivocators the notion that, in a world into which revelation has come, we are "profoundly ignorant" (as Possen puts it) of the "considerable" amount of Christianity that we know (CD, 245–46/SKS 10, 252). It is another matter, of course, whether anyone would want "to believe at least something" (CD, 246/SKS 10, 252) about such a thing as the resurrection, whether of Jesus or of anyone else. Therefore, Climacus may argue that certain people are "profoundly ignorant" of immortality, but Kierkegaard does not. In another essay, however, Possen argues that Kierkegaard is concerned to uphold a more traditionally Christian account of the hereafter. See David D. Possen, "On Kierkegaard's Copenhagen Pagans," in *International Kierkegaard Commentary: Christian Discourses and The Crisis and a Crisis in the Life of a Young Actress,* ed. Robert L. Perkins, pp. 35–59 (Macon, Ga.: Mercer University Press, 2007).

15. Also see CUP, 1:302/SKS 7, 275.

16. The second indirect and upbuilding demonstration of immortality in Kierkegaard's dissertation argued the contrary.

17. See my "Kierkegaard's 'New Argument.'"

18. See Ludwig Feuerbach, *The Essence of Christianity,* trans. George Eliot (New York: Harper & Brothers, 1957), p. 14. Feuerbach argues that God is nothing other than the human being, or human nature purified. He also denies the resurrection; see pp. 135–36. In an earlier work, Feuerbach argues against the notion that immortality entails life after death. On his account, only the "species" of human being is immortal or eternal. Individual human beings perish at death. See Ludwig Feuerbach, *Thoughts on Death and Immortality: From the Papers of a Thinker,* trans. James A. Massey (Berkeley: University of California Press, 1980), p. 71. For confirmation that Feuerbach interprets Hegel's work as denying individual immortality, see his personal letter written to Hegel, after attending his lectures for two years, in *Hegel: The Letters,* trans. Clark Butler and Christiane Seiler (Bloomington: Indiana University Press, 1984), pp. 546–50. For Climacus's rejection of Feuerbach's thesis that "all theology is anthropology," see CUP, 1:579/SKS 7, 526. For Anti-Climacus's rejection of the same, see SUD, 117–19/SKS 11, 228–31. Also see, BA, 303/SKS 15, forthcoming.

19. For more on this issue, see the chapters in this volume by Adam Buben and Simon Podmore.

20. Kangas and Kavka, "Hearing, Patiently." Also see my "Kierkegaard's 'New Argument.'"

21. See Edward F. Mooney, *On Søren Kierkegaard: Dialogue, Polemics, Lost Intimacy, and Time* (Hampshire, England: Ashgate Publishing Limited, 2007), pp. 54–60.

22. Mooney, *On Søren Kierkegaard,* p. 55.

Contributors

Jeremy J. Allen is a PhD candidate in philosophy at Fordham University, New York, where he has served as a senior teaching fellow. He is a former summer fellow in the Hong Kierkegaard Library, St. Olaf College, Minnesota, and is currently writing his dissertation on self-enclosure and recognition in the works of Kierkegaard and Hegel.

Adam Buben is a Kierkegaard House Foundation fellow at the Hong Kierkegaard Library, St. Olaf College, Minnesota. He has previously been a Fulbright fellow at the Søren Kierkegaard Research Centre, University of Copenhagen, and a visiting lecturer in philosophy at the University of Guam. He has articles published in *Kierkegaard and Religious Pluralism* (ed. Andrew J. Burgess), *Kierkegaard and Japanese Thought* (ed. James Giles), and in the *Kierkegaard Research: Sources, Reception and Resources* series (forthcoming).

George Connell is professor of philosophy and chair of the Arts and Humanities Division at Concordia College, Minnesota. He is the author of *To Be One Thing: Personal Unity in Kierkegaard's Thought,* editor with C. Stephen Evans of *Foundations of Kierkegaard's Vision of Community: Religion, Ethics, and Politics in Kierkegaard,* and is a contributor to *International Kierkegaard Commentary.*

John J. Davenport is associate professor of philosophy at Fordham University, New York. He is the author of *Will as Commitment and Resolve: An Existential Account of Creativity, Love, Virtue, and Happiness* and editor with Anthony Rudd of *Kierkegaard After MacIntyre: Essays on Freedom, Narrative, and Virtue.* He has published in a range of books and journals such as *Analysis, The Journal of Ethics, Journal of Religious Ethics, Faith and Philosophy,* and *Southwest Philosophy Review.*

Ian Duckles (currently unaffiliated) holds a PhD from the University of California at Irvine and has taught philosophy at Indiana University of Pennsylvania (as an assistant professor), University of San Diego, Chapman University, Mesa College, Miramar College, Grossmont College, and Cuyamaca College. His publications include articles in *Idealistic Studies* and *Southwest Philosophy Review.* Please visit his webpage for more information: www.ianduckles.com.

Charles Guignon is professor of philosophy at the University of South Florida. He is the editor of *The Cambridge Companion to Heidegger* and *Dostoevsky's "The Grand Inquisitor,"* coeditor of *Existentialism: Basic Writings,* and the author of *Heidegger and the Problem of Knowledge* as well as *On Being Authentic.* He has also published numerous articles and book chapters.

Laura Llevadot is assistant professor of contemporary philosophy at the University of Barcelona. Her publications include papers in *La Società degli individui, Kierkegaardiana, Convivium, Themata, Daimon, Logos: Anales del Seminario de Metafísica, Acta Kierkegaardiana, Kierkegaard Research: Sources, Reception and Resources,* and *Kierkegaard Studies Yearbook.*

Gordon D. Marino is professor of philosophy and director of the Hong Kierkegaard Library, St. Olaf College, Minnesota. He is the author of *Kierkegaard in the Present Age* and numerous journal articles and book chapters. He is the editor (with Alastair Hannay) of *The Cambridge Companion to Kierkegaard* and (with Poul Houe) *Kierkegaard and the Word(s).* His work regularly appears in publications including *Atlantic Monthly, New York Times Magazine,* and *The Wall Street Journal.* He is also editor of the *Søren Kierkegaard Newsletter*.

Tamara Monet Marks is a PhD candidate in religion, ethics, and philosophy at Florida State University and a former Kierkegaard House Foundation fellow at the Hong Kierkegaard Library, St. Olaf College, Minnesota. She has published in the *Journal of Religious Ethics* and has been an associate editor of the *Søren Kierkegaard Newsletter.*

Marius Timmann Mjaaland is associate professor of philosophy of religion at the University of Oslo and president of the Nordic Society for

Philosophy of Religion. He is the author of *Autopsia: Self, Death, and God after Kierkegaard and Derrida.* He is also the coeditor of *The Body Unbound* and *Kierkegaard, Ibsen og det moderne,* and has published more than thirty articles in journals and edited volumes.

Edward F. Mooney is professor of philosophy and religion at Syracuse University, New York. His books include *On Søren Kierkegaard: Dialogue, Polemics, Lost Intimacy, and Time, Selves in Discord and Resolve: Kierkegaard's Moral-Religious Psychology from "Either/Or" to "Sickness Unto Death,"* and *Knights of Faith and Resignation: Reading Kierkegaard's "Fear and Trembling."* He is the editor of *Ethics, Love, and Faith in Kierkegaard: A Philosophical Engagement* (Indiana University Press, 2008) and has published extensively in journals and edited collections.

Paul Muench is assistant professor of philosophy at the University of Montana. He has published articles in *Kierkegaard Studies Yearbook* and *Kierkegaardiana,* and in edited collections such as *Kierkegaard's "Concluding Unscientific Postscript": A Critical Guide* (ed. Rick Anthony Furtak), *A Companion to Socrates* (ed. Sara Ahbel-Rappe and Rachana Kamtekar), and *Kierkegaard and the Word(s)* (ed. Poul Houe and Gordon D. Marino).

Simon D. Podmore is Gordon Milburn junior research fellow at Trinity College and British Academy postdoctoral fellow in the Faculty of Theology, University of Oxford. He has previously been a teaching fellow in theology at the University of Edinburgh and a Kierkegaard House Foundation fellow at the Hong Kierkegaard Library, St. Olaf College, Minnesota. He is the author of *Kierkegaard and the Self Before God* (Indiana University Press, 2011) and has published in *International Kierkegaard Commentary, The Heythrop Journal, Literature and Theology, Acta Kierkegaardiana,* and the *Kierkegaard Research: Sources, Reception and Resources* series.

David D. Possen is a Class of 1937 visiting scholar in the Department of Humanities and fellow in the Whitney Humanities Center at Yale University. Several of his articles have appeared in the *International Kierkegaard Commentary* and *Kierkegaard Research: Sources, Reception and Resources* series, as well as in *Kierkegaard and the Word(s)* (ed. Poul Houe and Gordon D. Marino).

Patrick Stokes is a Marie Curie fellow in philosophy at the University of Hertfordshire, and an honorary fellow in the School of Historical and

Philosophical Studies, University of Melbourne. Starting 2012, he will be lecturer in philosophy at Deakin University. He has previously been a postdoctoral fellow at the Søren Kierkegaard Research Centre, University of Copenhagen, and a Kierkegaard House Foundation fellow at the Hong Kierkegaard Library, St. Olaf College, Minnesota. He is the author of *Kierkegaard's Mirrors: Interest, Self, and Moral Vision* and articles in various journals including *Inquiry, Continental Philosophy Review, British Journal for the History of Philosophy,* and *Journal of Consciousness Studies.*

Index

Printed and bound by CPI Group (UK) Ltd, Croydon, CR0 4YY

09/06/2025

14685935-0001